A THEORY OF CONTRACT LAW: EMPIRICAL INSIGHTS AND MORAL PSYCHOLOGY

A Theory of Contract Law: Empirical Insights and Moral Psychology

by Peter A. Alces
Rita Anne Rollins Professor of Law
THE COLLEGE OF WILLIAM & MARY SCHOOL OF LAW

OXFORD
UNIVERSITY PRESS

OXFORD
UNIVERSITY PRESS

Oxford University Press, Inc., publishes works that further Oxford University's objective of excellence in research, scholarship, and education.

Oxford New York
Auckland Cape Town Dar es Salaam Hong Kong Karachi Kuala Lumpur Madrid Melbourne
Mexico City Nairobi New Delhi Shanghai Taipei Toronto

With offices in
Argentina Austria Brazil Chile Czech Republic France Greece Guatemala Hungary Italy
Japan Poland Portugal Singapore South Korea Switzerland Thailand Turkey Ukraine
Vietnam

Published by Oxford University Press, Inc.
198 Madison Avenue, New York, New York 10016

Library of Congress Cataloging-in-Publication Data
Alces, Peter A., 1956-
A theory of contract law : empirical insights and moral psychology / Peter A. Alces.
p. cm
Includes bibliographical references and index.
ISBN 978-0-19-537160-4 (hardback)
1. Contracts. 2. Contracts–Philosophy. I. Title.
K840.A946 2011
346.0201–dc22

2 3 4 5 6 7 8 9

Printed in the United States of America on acid-free paper

Note to Readers

This publication is designed to provide accurate and authoritative information in regard to the subject matter covered. It is based upon sources believed to be accurate and reliable and is intended to be current as of the time it was written. It is sold with the understanding that the publisher is not engaged in rendering legal, accounting, or other professional services. If legal advice or other expert assistance is required, the services of a competent professional person should be sought. Also, to confirm that the information has not been affected or changed by recent developments, traditional legal research techniques should be used, including checking primary sources where appropriate.

(Based on the Declaration of Principles jointly adopted by a Committee of the American Bar Association and a Committee of Publishers and Associations.)

For Kelli,
My inspiration

Contents

PREMISES (and equivocations)

IN A FOOTNOTE to his enlightening *The End of Faith*, Sam Harris offers the deconstruction of a cooking recipe.[1] His point is that the exercise reveals more about the "deconstructor" than it does about the text deconstructed. This book reaches a similar conclusion with regard to normative theories of contract. The doctrine simply will not support the normative efforts to deconstruct it—there is perhaps less than meets the eye.

After teaching and reading and writing about contract law for nearly thirty years and looking for the principle or discreet set of principles that would bring it all together, I have grown skeptical that contract reveals such foundation. I am, of course, aware of the great intellectual power such a discovery would provide and I do not blame normative theorists for expending the effort, any more than I resent the search for cold fusion or the Holy Grail. What does make me uncomfortable, though, is the confusion of the positive with the normative: It is one thing to argue for what you think contract *should be*, it is quite another to declaim certainly what *it is*, and particularly to do so on insubstantial bases. In my more cynical moods, I even question the good faith of those who seem too easily to lose sight of the important difference between positive and normative theory.

This book, then, may seem to endeavor to prove a negative, with perhaps the predictable results. I firmly believe that contract is neither deontological nor consequentialist; nor, for that matter, is it a product of or even consistent with aretaic theory—which I see as not much, if anything, more than the uncertain merger of the deontic and the consequentialist.

---

[1] Sam Harris, The End of Faith 296–97 n. 15 (2005).

It would, though, be impossible to prove that *no* deontological or consequentialist theory could explain contract because there is no reason to believe that we have yet uncovered all of the possible phases of those two normative alternatives. So I formulate a working conception of deontology and consequentialism based on a representative sample of the theoretical literature. I do not presume or assert that my literature review is complete; it is not: Given practical limitations it could not be. I have not read and do not treat here every article and book that has in some way asserted a normative basis of contract in either deontological or consequentialist terms. But I believe the sources on which I have drawn are representative of the state of the normative art at the time of this writing—the end of the first decade of the twenty-first century.

I formulate the contract doctrine by reference to what I assert are the canonical cases. The cases *are* the law, and that is true even where the doctrine has been cast in statutory terms. That is also true with regard to some cases that we would, today, consider to have been unfortunately reasoned, even wrong. Wrongly decided cases complete the picture.

This book is reactionary, in its way. It is a reaction to the efforts to reconcile all of contract doctrine, the law that governs consensual relations, into neat normative categories developed wholly apart from contract. There seems to be a persistence to understand contract in terms of something else, to deny its domain specificity. Contract, we are told, only makes sense if it is understood as vindicating Kantian principles (a deontological trope), with all the normative incidents thereunto appertaining, or as the means to promote efficiency or some other laudable consequence. And in addition to those deontic and consequentialist perspectives, there are those who would understand contract as an elaboration of aretaic principles, the realization of Aristotelian conceptions of justice. Supporting those normative perspectives are certain heuristics that translate contract into, again, something else, as *promise*, or the basis of *reliance*, or as a *transfer* of something. The idea of such normative theorizing, apparently, is that we learn something important about contract if we can theorize it in terms of something else, a matter of leverage, it would seem.

Theory has generally been understood in normative terms. Indeed, even positive theories in an area of law such as contract attribute normative purpose. We may conclude that contract vindicates efficiency, a normative object, even if we do not agree that efficiency *should* be the object of consensual relations law. That description, a positive theory of contract, would rely upon normative bases. A purely descriptive account, *i.e.,* first contract does this, then it does that, would seem unhelpful, if not altogether vacuous. The vacuity would lie in the description's failure to provide any leverage, failure to suggest what the result should be in the next case (given certain normative premises) and why the result in the last case was wrong (given those same premises).

Rather than dividing the theoretical enterprise into a strict normative/positive dichotomy, it may be more helpful to appreciate theories as interpretive. That is, we could understand a theory as telling the story of how an area of the law should operate by reference to how it in fact does operate. Such an interpretive theory might well focus on the incidents of contract and demonstrate the connection between those incidents and some normative object, to tell the "best" story. Still, though, the sense of "best" would likely be informed by reference to some normative object.

There is an alternative to theorizing about contract in terms dependent at all on normative considerations. That is, we can understand contract as no more than a mechanism, as the means to facilitate realization of diverse normative objects without concluding that one object rather than another is most apt. That would provide a theory of contract, and it may be not only all the theory we need, it may as well be all the theory that is available to us. That is, contract may simply not resolve into the neat theoretical dichotomy described above: deontology and consequentialism. The theory of contract may be in our way of appreciating the amalgamation of normative inclinations that distinguish consensual relations among human agents.

This book shall suggest that an appreciation of evolutionary psychology will reveal the relationship, such as it is, between contract doctrine and the realization of apparently divergent normative objects. That is, human agents as constituted (the only way human agency matters to an enterprise such as contract) do not encounter contract contexts and so the contract doctrine in the neat compartments the conflict among the poles of the dichotomy would suggest: to appreciate that it will be necessary to spend some time on the incidents of the two perspectives. The benefits of developing such an appreciation are great so far as our understanding contract is concerned.

There is, indeed, much at stake in our discovering that contract is something more than we may first take it to be. If we make better sense of contract, we can too make better sense of our bodies of law that depend on contract, implicitly as well as explicitly. At the same time, if we mischaracterize contract, we frustrate our understanding and may be lured to results that undermine rather than serve the interests contract in fact vindicates. Contract "revealed," as it were, is worthwhile; contract obscured is ultimately deleterious. So this book focuses on contract and the extant deontic and consequentialist theory to discover whether the normative perspectives advanced so far do more good than harm. It is necessary at the outset to appreciate the nature of contract.

The contract law is multifaceted, with rules that point in different, often conflicting directions. In one case the rule is *caveat emptor* in the next it is *caveat venditor*. That difference, though, need not and in fact does not intimate inconsistency. So long as the contract law has a reasoned basis to draw the distinction from one context to the next, ostensibly opposing rules may be quite consistent. For example, the difference between *caveat emptor* in one context and *caveat venditor* in the next may be a matter of fitting transactor sophistication to transactional context. There may well be some normative object that is only served if contract sometimes protects buyers at the expense of sellers and sometimes protects sellers at the expense of buyers. Such fundamental reconciliation intimates the normative coherence of contract rather than the contrary.

For the most part, the problem with extant theoretical perspectives is that they do not track an empirical morality of the contract doctrine; in fact, the theories seem largely (though to varying degrees) inconsiderate of doctrine. It is not so difficult, or so helpful, to tell a story of contract that ignores the inconvenient parts of the story. It would also not be helpful to deny the congruities that do exist. An empirical morality of contract would attend to the doctrine, warts and all, and would make sense where there is sense to be made and reveal nonsense when the result the doctrine provides is nonsensical.

Chapter One offers a conception of normative theory, its form and function. That presentation is designed to provide the basis of contrast with a more mechanical conception of theory, which would take into account the "morality" of human agents. Chapter Two introduces the constituents of the contract canon, those cases that are fundamental and, I assert, indispensable to our conception of contract.

Chapters Three through Eight divide the canon and theory among issues of Formation, Performance, and Enforcement. Those three categories are certainly too simplistic for some purposes but suffice to support the organization of the book's thesis. Chapter Three treats Formation, and describes the doctrine in terms of the canonical cases. Chapter Four then reviews the deontic and consequentialist theories of the Formation law. Chapter Five, in turn, covers the Performance doctrine, followed by Chapter Six's treatment of the apposite theory. Chapter Seven surveys Enforcement doctrine and Chapter Eight covers Enforcement theory.

Finally, Chapter Nine describes an alternative means to make sense of the doctrine, and is theoretical insofar as it describes the way that doctrine accommodates a dialectic human agents engage in order to resolve contract controversies. We are, as it turns out, predisposed to confront bargain controversies in a way that encourages us to appreciate and resolve the tension between deontic and consequentialist normative theory.

Acknowledgements

I AM INDEBTED to many colleagues and student research assistants for their help and patience over the last few years as I completed this project. At the risk of unintentionally omitting someone, I am particularly grateful to Professors David Frisch, Nathan Oman, Michael Greenfield, John Owen Haley, Owen Jones, James G. Dwyer, Michael Steven Green, Jonathan Haidt, Brian Bix, Eyal Zamir, Eric Kades, and Kelli A. Alces. I am also indebted to my student research assistants at The College of William & Mary School of Law who have steered me through the straits: Troy Gwartney, Jeremy Hunt, Eric Bergeron, Jonathan Hitsous, Nicole Wagner, Matthew Forgue, Carolyn Opyd, Kenneth Shimizu, Ryan Millett, Brandon Murrill, Matthew Welch, Robert Friedman, Bradley Mainguy, Benjamin Wengerd, and, most especially, "the closers": Jason Howell, Lillian McManus, and Patrick Taylor.

Preliminary drafts of portions of the book were presented at Faculty Workshops at the College of William and Mary School of Law, Washington University (St. Louis) School of Law, Southern Illinois University School of Law, University of Missouri-Columbia School of Law, University of Florida College of Law, and Wake Forest University School of Law. I also presented ideas developed in this book at the Tenth Annual Conference of the Society for Evolutionary Analysis in Law, Nashville, Tennessee, April, 2009, and at the Darwin's Reach Conference, "A Celebration of Darwin's Legacy Across Academic Disciplines," Hofstra University, March, 2009. A brief portion of the analyses pursued in Chapter One, "The Failure of Normative Contract Theory," Chapter Four, "Theory of Contract Formation," and Chapter Six, "Theory of Contract Performance" were applied in my recent *Contract* Is *Context,* 45 Wake Forest L. Rev. 903 (2010) to software contracting issues.

1

FAILURE OF NORMATIVE CONTRACT THEORY

IT IS NOT immediately obvious that something as vast as contract theory should or even could be rationalized from one theoretical perspective, whether that perspective were positive, normative, or interpretive. It might well be possible, even desirable, for all consensual relations subject to legal regulation to proceed from a unitary theoretical foundation. You could, for instance, conclude that the object of contract is (positive), should be (normative), or, understood in its best light, could be (interpretive), informed by reference to a discrete value system. But that conclusion would not hold up when compared with the substance of contract, the doctrine. This book recognizes the importance of the theoretical challenge, and recognizes, too, that the *reason* contract theory fails is important, every bit as important as would be the discovery of a unitary theory. We only understand contract if we understand why it is not, why it cannot be amenable to a single unitary theory conceived along the parameters of the theoretical constructions proposed so far.

A. The Landscape

Because the effort here, at least in part, is to prove a negative—unitary deontic or consequentialist normative theory cannot account for contract—it is worthwhile to offer a brief formulation of those two dominant extant theoretical efforts. A catalog of such efforts is not, perhaps cannot be exhaustive: Theories proliferate and such a catalog could never establish the failure of the extant theories. The response could be that we have not yet found the right theory. The thesis of this project is that there is a necessary disjunction between the shared assumptions of the theories and the object of the inquiry. There is something essential to contract that defies rationalization in the terms of the theoretical enterprise as currently conceived. That is, we simply cannot understand the one thing, *contract*, in terms of the other, normative conceptions that deontic and consequentialist theory must assume in order to be what we recognize as theory. That necessarily entails a thoughtful treatment of the constituents of contract, exemplary deontic and consequentialist normative theory, and the nature of human agency, what H.L.A. Hart understood in another context as the "minimum content of natural law."

Although it is clearly correct that all normative theories of contract are either consequentialist or non-consequentialist (logically that must be so), it is less obvious that all such theories are *either* consequentialist *or* deontic. By *consequentialism*, I mean no more than a moral theory that judges actions and decisions by reference to the consequences of those actions and decisions.[1] Utilitarianism may be one consequentialist object, but it need not be the unique determinant. What distinguishes consequentialism, though, is a lack of concern with anything but consequences. If you decide that your object is to increase wealth or welfare (however understood), consequentialism, as used here, is the study of how best to do so. Construed in that way, consequentialism is essentially defined as the opposite of deontology, which entails a focus on conceptions of right and duty regardless of the consequences that attend the vindication of those conceptions. The work of Immanuel Kant provides the model of this normative perspective: There are certain normative imperatives that do not admit of consequentialist balancing, such as the categorical imperative: "Act only according to those maxims that can be consistently willed as a universal law."[2] It is the categorical imperative that assures our autonomy,[3] an idea crucial to deontic conceptions of promising and, by extension, contract. That deontic foundation of autonomy provides, too, the non-consequentialist basis of promise and its relation to contract. So deontic theory has had to take account of the *possible* normative coincidence of promise and contract, and infer a good deal about each in distinguishing one from the other.

There is also a literature that argues that consequentialism and deontology do not pre-empt the field: There may be normative conceptions of contract that are neither consequentialist nor deontic and yet do the work we expect theory to do. Two approaches in particular seem to share that perspective: contractarianism and aretaic theory. Contractarians find moral sanction in agreement, or hypothetical agreement. Thomas Hobbes, Kant, and more recently John Rawls and T. M. Scanlon rely on contractarian

---

[1] Brian H. Bix, A Dictionary of Legal Theory 40 (2004).

[2] Cambridge Dictionary of Philosophy 465 (Robert Audi ed., 1999).

[3] *Id.*

principles to discover morality. Insofar as those principles are based on and indeed responsive to individual concerns, they are at odds with communitarian theory, which focuses on corporate rather than individual welfare. But the essential device is the same: Infer morality from consent. Those who base their conception of contract on aretaic theory, Aristotelian virtue ethics, offer yet another normative basis for the enforcement of promises, and another basis which, while not consequentialist, may not be entirely deontic either:

> Virtue ethicists also claim that having a virtue, which is something that comes by degrees, contributes to making one's life a good one—to what Aristotle called *eudaimonia*, or flourishing. A life that exhibits the virtues is for that very reason a better life: not because the acts of the virtuous have good consequences (though they may); not because they lead to satisfaction or give pleasure to the agent (though, for Aristotle at least, learning to take pleasure in what is virtuous is one component of moral development). Virtues are intrinsically worth having. Being virtuous is part, at least, of what makes a life worthwhile.[4]

The cleavage between those two perspectives, contractarianism and virtue ethics, on the one hand, and a deontic–consequentialist dichotomy, on the other, is not stark. Indeed, it will suffice for the present purposes to appreciate the deontic–consequentialist dichotomy as, in fact, preempting the field. It would not seem to be too difficult to appreciate contractarianism and virtue ethics as relying on some relationship defined by the fit between consequentialist and deontic premises. But that is not a battle worth waging here. No traction is lost by dividing the normative universe into consequentialist and non-consequentialist spheres in order to reach conclusions about normative contract theory and its failure so far.

Now, though contract theory may fail as a normative project that does not necessarily mean that a theory in search of a different, non-normative, object would likewise fail. We can have a theory of the internal combustion engine that is not normative but that is also no less a theory. Indeed, such a non-normative or mechanical theory may well be able to do a better job of what we want or need theory to do if we abandon the normative mission. And that type of mechanical theory would be the only viable theory in an environment in which normativity construed in terms of consequentialism or deontology, or some amalgam of the two, is inaccessible or simply does not exist.

---

[4] Kwame Anthony Appiah, Experiments in Ethics 35–36 (2008).

B. Human Agency

For normative theory to gain any traction insofar as human institutions such as contract are concerned, we must discover some nexus between such normative theorizing and the human agent. Consequentialists assume rational choice theory: Human agents act rationally, ordering their pursuit of objects in a manner consistent with their more or less accurate perception of them. Mistakes may be made, but markets can in time overcome such mistakes by providing the information necessary to more accurate perceptions. Those premises have been rendered dubious in light of more recent research. Behavioral decision theory undermines rational choice theory, and compromises efforts to "trust the market," particularly if contract doctrine is involved.

But non-consequentialist perspectives, too, have failed to depict human agency authentically. Kantian maxims and a focus on autonomy may raise more questions than they answer, and, in any event, do not depict typical human agents' normative sense. As a result, contract theory that proceeds from such often-deontic premises is necessarily infirm. Though there may be an attractive logical consistency in Kantian theory, it cannot do the work of contract theory if it fails to appreciate properly the subject of its study: the human agent. So in this way, non-consequentialist theory is no worse than consequentialist theory, and no better either.

Psychology, more particularly evolutionary psychology, can fill the void that neither consequentialist nor non-consequentialist theories can fill. Evolutionary psychology, through experimental techniques that have empirical validity, has offered insights into the fit between emotions and morality that impact the development and application of human normative systems, such as contract. Indeed, we discover that if extant consequentialist and non-consequentialist theories fail to depict accurately the human agent, they can bring us no closer to an appreciation of a fundamental contract theory. It may be that the doctrine ultimately resists extant normative theory in a way that is hopelessly intractable. Evolutionary psychology, not consequentialist or non-consequentialist theory, will reveal the contours of that resistance. Evolutionary psychology may demonstrate that consequentialist and non-consequentialist premises, in some variable combination, best capture the normative sense of human agents. Though we may not reasonably hope to discover the certain algorithm that would reveal the combination, the more empirically sound approach can demonstrate the limitations of approaches that are insensitive to the dynamic.

C. Theory's Job

Before pursuing that possibility further, and particularly in the context of contract, it is worthwhile to take account of just what theory is for, after all. In so doing, it is important to remain mindful of the necessary limits of the theoretical endeavor. It would not be responsible (or fair to theorists) to suggest that before a theory can accomplish anything it must explain everything. There will, of course, be aberrational cases, cases that can be described only as products of historical or even judicial accident. Further, the limits of the common law process also may obscure the operation of normative principles, deontic or consequentialist. Judges, particularly those writing appellate opinions, may settle for a rendition of the facts that provokes a certain normative calculus without affording due deference to aspects of context that might matter to those trying to discern the normative force of the decision. The legal literature is rich with contributions that place the cases in social, transactional, and historical contexts, often contexts that the decision's contemporaries could not have appreciated.[5] So it may well be that what we understand a case to stand for may matter more for its fit with our theory than what the judge who wrote the opinion understood it to mean. Cases wrongly, or at least unfortunately, decided may, in our reaction to them, reveal more about the theoretical foundation of contract than would more correct but less notorious decisions. Although it may be that no unitary theory could explain all of the cases, we might find that a coherent theory could explain what is right about the correctly decided cases and what is wrong about those not so correctly decided. The object is not to discover the unitary theory that explains all of contract; it is to discover whether a unified theory can discover a consistency among the cases that establish the doctrine. At times, this may seem to be a fine distinction, but it is necessary if we are to sharpen the focus of the normative inquiry.

So from those premises, we may begin the search for the Holy Grail: How would we know a unitary theory if we found it?

It is a truism to observe that human actors, constituted as we are, rely on heuristics to do the cognitive heavy lifting necessary to navigate through our environments. We generally rely on much less than complete evidence to determine our reactions to recurring as well as novel stimuli. You recognize your spouse or child from a distance based, for example, on the way they wear their clothes, or their gait; and, of course, sometimes you err, and excuse yourself to the stranger whom you were sure you recognized. Such error is a necessary consequence of our acting, as we must, on less than complete information. The cost of accumulating complete information would be too great, would, in fact, paralyze us. So we rely on cues.

Theory, too, is heuristic; it provides intellectual leverage. If we can be convinced that *wherever A* follows *B* follows *C*, *then* 3 follows 2 follows 1, we will expect that connection to maintain throughout, so too, if we can anticipate that sometimes 3.1 follows 2. That is, what determines the reliability of a particular heuristic, theoretical or otherwise, is not a function of its relative acuity; we are not after perfect coincidence between stimulus

---

[5] *See, e.g.,* CONTRACTS STORIES (Douglas G. Baird ed., 2007); *see also* FEDERAL COURTS STORIES (Vicki C. Jackson & Judith Resnik eds., 2010); PROPERTY STORIES, 2D (Gerald Korngold & Andrew P. Morriss eds., 2009).

and reaction. It is sufficient that the connection works well enough, and what is enough is determined by reference to the acceptable margin of error.[6]

If a particular deontic or consequentialist account of contract reveals a deeper structure than is apparent from the doctrine, then we may rely on that account both to *predict* (in the positive sense) and *determine* (in the normative sense) both how the doctrine should be applied and the result of that application. Such an account, then, will have asserted intellectual leverage and may as well actually provide it, so long as the deep structure revealed actually explains the legal phenomena, the doctrine, it purports to explain. There is, then, a good deal at stake in deciding whether that claim of leverage is viable. If it is not, it may lead us into error or at least into inefficacious conclusions, such as the conclusion that efficient breach finds purchase in contract doctrine. We may well conclude that *if* consequentialist premises explain contract, or offer the best interpretation of the doctrine, *then* something like efficient breach would result from the operation of contract damages formulae, but that will be (merely) a normative rather than interpretive judgment if, in fact, the doctrine does not vindicate efficient breach. It is one thing to argue for what contract *could* achieve; it is quite another to come to terms with what contract *in fact* achieves. If we find some constraint on what contract *can* accomplish, perhaps given the essential characteristics of human actors, then it may be particularly (and perniciously) misleading to assert intellectual leverage on behalf of normative premises that ignore those necessary characteristics.

Normative theory implicates two not necessarily incompatible ideas. First, theory could tell us what the law in a particular area, say contract, *should* aspire to achieve. It is not difficult, for example, to imagine a normative theory premised on Kantian moral principles.[7] Alternatively, a consequentialist theory could rely upon a utilitarian normative perspective.[8] Second, a normative theory could describe what the particular theorist believes that the normative object of an area of law actually *is*. Here, the normative and positive seem to overlap: A theory may endeavor to reveal the morality of a particular area of law, whether or not the theorist believes that that, in fact, is the morality to which the doctrine should aspire. So we could, for example, conclude that the object of some aspect of doctrine *is* welfare maximization, in utilitarian terms, although we believe that the doctrine *should* vindicate individual autonomy. That would provide a normative theory of that aspect of doctrine, notwithstanding our disappointment with that object.

---

[6] *See* HOWARD MARGOLIS, PATTERNS, THINKING, AND COGNITION: A THEORY OF JUDGMENT (1987); Peter A. Alces, *Contract Reconceived*, 96 NW. U. L. REV. 39, 70 (2001); Peter A. Alces, *On Discovering Doctrine: "Justice" in Contract Agreement*, 83 WASH. U. L.Q. 471, 500–03 (2005); Peter A. Alces, Un*intelligent Design in Contract*, 2008 U. ILL. L. REV. 505, 551–54 (2008).

[7] This is, indeed, what Professor Charles Fried provides. *See* CHARLES FRIED, CONTRACT AS PROMISE: A THEORY OF CONTRACTUAL OBLIGATION (1981).

[8] *See* Alan Schwartz & Robert E. Scott, *Contract Theory and the Limits of Contract Law*, 113 YALE L.J. 541 (2003).

Commentators have noted that several theories in fact combine the normative and positive.[9] We may discover normative theorists who include in their observations suggestions that they are describing not just what the doctrine should be but what the doctrine is (at least in application). It is a potentially powerful rhetorical device to say that there is a coincidence of the normative and positive in one particular theoretical construction. That predisposition has led to an appreciation of *interpretive theories* that combine the normative and positive to interpret the story that doctrine tells.[10] The positive side of interpretive theory is served by the effort to explain "certain features of the law"[11]; the normative side is served by the effort to discover an intelligible order. It is the normative that makes an order intelligible. So it would seem that it is no longer necessary to divorce the positive from the normative. Indeed, it is clearly more important to appreciate their coincidence, and that is the object of interpretive theory.

Professor Stephen Smith maintains "that a good legal theory should explain the law in a way that shows how the law *might be thought to be* justified even if it is not justified. In other words, such a theory must show how legal actors could sincerely, but perhaps erroneously, claim that the law was morally justified."[12] So for Smith, there can be no theory without *some* normative component, the morality criterion. Indeed, Professor Michael Moore makes morality the sole criterion: "[T]heorizing about an area of law is an activity, and like any activity we need justification for it showing us why it is worth doing."[13] Moore understands that "a descriptive theory deals with timeless propositions of law...

---

[9] These are discussed in Brian Bix, *Contract Law Theory* 8 (Minnesota Legal Studies Research Paper No. 06–12, 2006), *available at* http://ssrn.com/abstract=892783:

> Theories about doctrinal areas of law—theories of property or contract or tort—are common and well-known.... Most such theories sit uneasily between description and prescription/evaluation. On one hand, they purport to fit most of the existing rules and practices; on the other hand, they re-characterize the practices to make them as coherent and/or as morally attractive as possible.

[10] This is essentially redolent of a Dworkinian idea. *Id.* Professor Stephen Smith has described the nature of an interpretive account:

> Interpretive theories aim to enhance understanding of the law by highlighting significance or meaning.... [T]his is achieved by explaining why certain features of the law are important or unimportant and by identifying connections between those features—in other words, by revealing an *intelligible order* in the law, so far as such an order exists. For example, the idea that the rules on consideration, mistake, and remedies are evidence that contractual obligations are rights-based promissory obligations, is an interpretive theory. So too is the idea that these rules are best explained on the basis that contract law's fundamental purpose is to promote economic efficiency. If either of these claims is true, it reveals an intelligible order in the law—it helps to "make sense" of the law—and thereby helps us better understand it.

Stephen A. Smith, Contract Theory 5 (2004); *see also* Richard Craswell, *In That Case, What is the Question? Economics and the Demands of Contract Theory*, 112 Yale L.J. 903, 917– 23 (2003) (discussing dominance of interpretivist perspective).

[11] Smith, *supra* note 10, at 5.

[12] *Id.* at 18.

[13] Michael S. Moore, Placing Blame: A General Theory of the Criminal Law 3 (1997).

and the logical relations that may exist between them."[14] The object of such descriptive theory is to offer a succinct yet comprehensive description of an area of law.[15] By describing what the law is in perhaps more accessible terms (at least more compact terms),[16] we provide legal actors—primarily judges—a recommendation: Continue to do what the law has done. That at least might satisfy some fairness criterion. "Deeply descriptive principles,"[17] may offer "enhanced predictability."[18] Moore concludes that such theories are not, cannot be value-free.[19] For theory to be viable it must state an intelligible value a particular area of law could vindicate. A theory must fit "rule of law virtues," specifically, "predictability and formal justice."[20] So for Moore, the question *is,* ultimately, one of fit: "The degree of logical fit is weighted by the rule of law virtues that justifies theories as having prima facie authority, but that we did fit is always balanced off against the moral goodness of the content of the theory. Only the two together determine the legal validity of [competing] theories...."[21] So far as Moore is concerned, for a normative theory to operate it must be consonant with the normative foundations of law generally.

A unitary theory might still be possible in a regime that recognizes multiple normative bases of the parties' undertaking.[22] Such a unitary theory would order the cooperation of those normative bases, describing their hierarchical relationship and even the contingent nature of that hierarchy. For example, while it could certainly be the case that normative theory *A* precedes normative theory *B*, in the sense that we satisfy the normative demands of *B* only after we have satisfied the normative demands of *A*, it could as likely be the case that sometimes *A* prevails and sometimes *B* prevails. We could, then, discover the means to predict and explain the relationship between *A* and *B*, if each prevails, if they cooperate, and perhaps even discover circumstances in which neither is apposite. That means to

---

[14] *Id.* at 9.

[15] *Id.*

[16] *Id.* at 11.

[17] *Id.*

[18] *Id.*

[19] *Id.* at 15.

[20] *Id.* at 16.

[21] *Id.*

[22] Herein of Rawls's concept of lexical ordering:

> [W]e may be able to find principles which can be put in what I shall call a serial or lexical order.... This is an order which requires us to satisfy the first principle in the ordering before we can move on to the second, the second before we consider the third, and so on. A principle does not come into play until those previous to it are either fully met or do not apply. A serial ordering avoids, then, having to balance principles at all; those earlier in the ordering have an absolute weight, so to speak, with respect to later ones, and hold without exception.

John Rawls, A Theory of Justice 37–38 (Rev. ed. 1999).

predict and explain would then be our unitary theory, and would itself satisfy the requirement that for a theory to be a theory it must provide, or discern, moral direction.[23]

But consider an alternative to the necessary normativity of theory: A theory could require no more than understanding the apposite doctrine as a system of rules designed to maximize contingent values of obligation, a means to create value (consequentialist or deontic). That conception of theory may just reveal doctrine as merely a non-normative, amoral mechanism. Discovering a viable theory of an area of law may be an intermediate rather than an ultimate enterprise. The question we may answer when we posit a theory is the question about the *mechanism* that distinguishes that area of law from the others. The label we attach to the law—say, *contract*—is, of course, normatively arbitrary; it may be the product of historical accident or it may have more significance than historical accident implies.[24] So we cannot infer too much from the label. Could we instead appreciate contract doctrine as merely the mechanism that might or might not vindicate some normative object (or some variety of normative objects)? Do normative patterns[25] *necessarily* follow from a mechanism common to distinguishable transactional settings?

David Hume, in his ruminations on "promise" in the affairs of commerce, captures well the distinction between the normative and the mechanical sense of promise, insofar as promise creates "obligation."

> I learn to do a service to another, without bearing him any real kindness; because I foresee, that he will return my service, in expectation of another of the same kind, and in order to maintain the same correspondence of good offices with me or with others. And accordingly, after I have serv'd him, and he is in possession of the advantage arising from my action, he is induc'd to perform his part, as foreseeing the consequences of his refusal.
>
> ... I may still do services to such persons as I love, and am more particularly acquainted with, without any prospect of advantage; and they may make me a

[23] *See* Jody S. Kraus, *Reconciling Autonomy and Efficiency in Contract Law: The Vertical Integration Strategy*, in 11 PHIL. ISSUES 420, 422 (2001). *But see* Peter A. Alces, *The Moral Impossibility of Contract*, 48 WM. & MARY L. REV. 1647, 1665 (2007) (suggesting that Kraus's formulation does not so much resolve deontology-consequentialism tension as shift it to determine lexical priority).

[24] *See* Nathan B. Oman, *The Failure of Economic Interpretations of the Law of Contract Damages*, 64 WASH. & LEE L. REV. 829, 875 (2007) (acknowledging view of some that "contract doctrine represents little more than the random final product of a long chain of historical accidents.")

[25] Consider Leo Katz, *What We Do When We Do What We Do and Why We Do It*, 37 SAN DIEGO L. REV. 753, 754–55 (2000):

> What philosophers of science have claimed about mathematics, and later about the sciences more generally, is that what it really comes down to, or what a good part of it comes down to anyway, is *the search for symmetry and asymmetry*. . . .
>
> . . .
>
> Simply put, the search for symmetry serves to reveal larger patterns in the law and these larger patterns allow us to understand all sorts of matters that previously seemed puzzling.

> return in the same manner, without any view but that of recompensing my past services. In order, therefore, to distinguish those two different sorts of commerce, the interested and the disinterested, there is a *certain form of words* invented for the former, by which we bind ourselves to the performance of any action. This form of words constitutes what we call a *promise*, which is the sanction of the interested commerce of mankind. When a man says *he promises any thing*, he in effect expresses a *resolution* of performing it; and along with that, by making use of this *form of words*, subjects himself to the penalty of never being trusted again in case of failure.[26]

Here Hume avers that what we accomplish when we assume an obligation is the projection of ourselves into the future. Strictly in the present, we can realize no more value than what we can do or provide presently. Once we are able to project ourselves and assume an obligation that will bind us in the future, we are able to increase present value. The way we can accomplish that projection is by the obligation mechanism: By assuming an obligation, we assure satisfaction either specifically by performance, or, at least, substitutionally, by provision of the value of the performance of that obligation.

To get the sense in which Hume's observation helps us characterize the nature of contract doctrine as a legal category, subject to the same tests for symmetry or asymmetry as to which any legal category would be subject, read his sentence this way: "This form of words constitutes what we call a *contract*." But the form of words alone does not answer the normative question: Should the law enforce the promise? Hume's mechanical description of the role of promise in commerce captures well the mechanics of contract. Hume's understanding of the transactions mechanism makes clear that it is distinct, and certainly may remain distinct, from the normative object of its operation. Once we separate the mechanical from the normative, we are better able to appreciate the incongruity of such a thing as a unitary normative theory of the doctrine. It may make no more sense to understand the mechanism in normative terms than it would to understand an automobile's carburetor or fuel injection system in normative terms. Both an ambulance and a thief's getaway car rely on fuel delivery systems, and we can certainly appreciate the moral distinctions between an ambulance and a getaway car. But it would be incongruous to attribute that moral distinction to the fuel delivery system, to the mechanism.

[26] David Hume, A Treatise of Human Nature 334–35 (David Fate Norton & Mary J. Norton eds., 2000) (1740). Hume here foreshadows "reciprocal altruism," performance of an apparently altruistic act at T1 or P1 in expectation of its being reciprocated at T2 or P2.

D. An Alternative Sense of Theory

The object of this argument is to suggest the necessary failure of any effort to attribute a unitary normative theory of all we contemplate under a particular doctrine. Moore also appreciates this when he understands "functional kinds" to distinguish between essential and structural features: "[A] functional kind . . . has a nature that each instance of the kind shares, but the nature is functional and not structural. . . . Certain areas of law look to be functional kinds in the sense that they are more or less successful attempts to realize some underlying kind of justice."[27] If the essential nature of an area of law is found in a structural feature of that area of law, rather than in some "distinctive end that such an area of law serves," then that area of law, according to Moore, is not a "functional kind," because its essence is the structure it uses rather than the normative object it instantiates.[28]

Imagine if we thought of morality in positive rather than normative terms, as a means of describing the way human actors are predisposed, perhaps by evolutionary forces or neural predispositions, to resolve moral dilemmas (what Llewellyn refers to as "trouble cases").[29] Such a conception of morality might, for example, discover in reciprocal altruism all the incentive human agents need to resolve recurring controversies, even if they then choose to describe those resolutions as moral, as proceeding from coherent normative imperatives. If morality comes not from "on high" but from more basic cognitive functions, then it may not make much sense to expect morality to be normative, in the familiar and maybe too simple sense. If a conception of theory requires such normativity and the morality that explains legal doctrine is not normative in that way, then there could be no theory of an area of law under that conception. That would be true even if we understood contract as an iteration of promise, notwithstanding the fact that, for some, promise necessarily imports normativity.[30]

---

[27] MOORE, *supra* note 13, at 20.

[28] *Id.* at 21. Professor Larry Alexander similarly, but for different reasons, concludes that there could not be a grand theory of an area of law such as tort "that is at all faithful to the very messy data, the jumble of judicial doctrines and statutory interventions, that make up the field." Larry Alexander, *Theory's a What Comes Natcherly* 37 SAN DIEGO L. REV. 777, 779 (2000). But here Alexander offers something else, an empirical observation that tort is too confused to be subject to "grand theory." This is an alternative means to undermine unitary theory, by arguing that the data the theory would explain lacks the symmetry theory requires. Of course that is not the same thing as saying tort would not be susceptible to theory in the way contract understood as mechanism is not susceptible to normative theory. Alexander's argument is the type of reaction to data that might well pertain with regard to each area of law. There is a difference between concluding that contract or tort *is* the product of a series of historical accidents and concluding that contract or tort *could only be* the necessary asymmetrical product of a series of historical accidents.

[29] *See* KARL N. LLEWELLYN & E. ADAMSON HOEBEL, THE CHEYENNE WAY: CONFLICT AND CASE LAW IN PRIMITIVE JURISPRUDENCE 293 (1941).

[30] *See, e.g.,* FRIED, *supra* note 7; Seana Valentine Shiffrin, *The Divergence of Contract and Promise*, 120 HARV. L. REV. 708 (2007).

Theories of doctrine, then, are normative efforts, or have been understood as such. An argument of this book is that by understanding theory in that way, we have assumed an unfortunate conclusion within our premises. Although theory can explain doctrine, or endeavor to explain doctrine in normative terms, as making a particular normative commitment, there is an alternative way to appreciate the contract doctrine, namely, as a means to facilitate an empirical morality. The *first* next step, then, is to begin with the doctrine, at its source.

2

CONSTITUENTS OF CANONICAL STATUS

CONTRACT IS THE sum of its doctrine and that is to be found first in the cases, the canonical cases that establish the substance of the consensual undertaking. An assertion of this book is that there are such canonical cases, many but not necessarily all of which have been subject to statutory formulation or elaboration, and virtually all of which have been incorporated into American Law Institute (ALI) projects. To support that assertion, it will be necessary to consider and offer a perhaps exhaustive selection of the canonical cases. I believe that there are no more than thirty cases that constitute the common law contract canon. Chapters Three, "Contract Formation Doctrine"; Five, "Contract Performance Doctrine"; and Seven, "Contract Enforcement Doctrine," suggest the list of cases that satisfy the criteria. Perhaps more important than the certain accuracy of any such list is the exercise: We learn more about contract when we endeavor to isolate its essence, and even when we confront the frustrations of trying to do so. The game is worth the candle, despite the elusiveness of certain resolution.

The object of identifying a contract canon would be to find the source of the contract law, so that we could then reach conclusions about the nature of its normative disposition(s). There is, of course, no reason why certain canonical cases need be the source of contract. Indeed, it might be the case that contract somehow preceded the cases and that the cases, canonical or otherwise, merely illuminate the object(s) of contract in varying contexts. So, assuming that the canon constitutes contract—even in some way—is an assertion about the relationship between common law and the cases that are its constituents. The assertion holds up, at least if the object is to appraise theories of contract, to the extent that the extant normative theories rely on the cases to support their constructions. If, for example, a promise theory relies on cases concerning the nature of the promise that contract would make legally binding, then that theory is dependent on the cases and must account for the decisions that would constitute a canon.

That is not to say that theorists must depend upon courts' self-conscious appreciation of the effect of their decisions. A case could be canonical, and central to a theory, even if the judge deciding the case were entirely inconsiderate of the relationship between her decision and the normative claim of contract generally.[1] It would be enough that later students (in the broad sense) of contract understand the decision to be crucial to a particular conception of contract. By this, we need mean no more than that a comprehensive unitary theory would have to *account* for the case in some way. That is not the same thing as saying that the case necessarily must have been "rightly" decided.

Preliminarily, we must posit certain determinants of canonical status, and that project must proceed from a particular conception of the case law as *canonical.* We are used to ratiocination concerning a literary canon, but the inquiry does not so obviously translate to the course of jurisprudential inquiry. Perhaps it should. Perhaps we can learn more about the substance of contract, what it is we mean when we refer to *contract*, if we spend some time coming to terms with the relationship between the idea contract and the litigation institution that is central to (perhaps determinative of) our legal system. Though we might conclude, ultimately, that contract is more than the cases, we may well also conclude that you cannot understand contract without an understanding of the relationship between the cases and contract. If that is not an absolute or virtual identity, then our starting from the premise that it is or should be will at least advance the inquiry in an important way even if we decide, ultimately, that the case has not been made.

A. Constitution of a Contract Canon

Although literary critics have devoted some attention to formulating and defending or decrying the content of the literature canon, legal theorists have not formulated, have perhaps discerned no reason to formulate, the canonical cases in contract, or any other area of the common law for that matter. Determining the substance of a canon of contract cases is not the same as determining the canonical status of literary works. But there are some common considerations, and the literary model could be a worthwhile place to start. What we could be looking for are the cases without which contract would not be contract, as we know it. Or, that might be too demanding a standard. It may be that canonical status could be conferred on any case that *does,* in fact, figure into our

[1] Whether explanations of the canon need line up with the explanations of legal actors to preserve transparency is disputed. *See* STEPHEN A. SMITH, CONTRACT THEORY 132–134 (2004) (objecting that efficiency theories, when compared to actual reasoning of judges, are "inappropriately 'external' to contract law").

understanding of contract, though not so indispensable (assuming, for the moment, that there may be degrees of indispensability). Would contract still be contract without *Hadley v. Baxendale*?[2] Probably, but a gap might exist that could best be filled by a case similar to *Hadley.* Alternatively, there may be any number of cases that offer the same analysis and reach the same conclusion as *Hadley*, but we could consider *Hadley* canonical because of the role it has played in educating lawyers about the particular damages issues it addresses. Were that our standard, a survey of the leading contracts casebooks would provide a test of canonical status. Still another alternative might be to start with a theory of contract and then determine the canonical status of a case by considering how it fits within that particular normative landscape. It is necessary, then, to start with a particular conception of canonical status, acknowledging that, under different criteria, our conclusions about a case's canonical status would be different as well.

B. Constituents of Canonical Status

A case is part of the contract canon if it determines (not necessarily uniquely) our understanding of the legal incidents of the consensual undertaking. That limitation is not too restrictive; a case may be canonical so long as it is, in fact, consistent with and generative of our understanding, even though we might have the same understanding of contract if that case had never been decided. Further, the case need not have been *rightly* decided by the court, so long as the way it has come to be understood as wrong is consistent with our understanding of the type of consensual undertaking the law will enforce: A wrongly decided case may illuminate, just as a shadow illuminates a silhouette.

A case's repeated inclusion in teaching materials may be one measure of canonical status. Presumably, the regular inclusion of a case in the casebooks reflects the case's importance in the judgment of the casebook editors, who are usually leading legal scholars. Regardless of the correctness of that judgment, the fact the case appears in a number of casebooks assures that a generation, and probably generations, of lawyers will have learned contract in the terms of that case. Lawyers may not remember that the *Allegheny College* case really had nothing to do with promissory estoppel,[3] but because Judge Cardozo's opinion appears in many or most of the casebooks used in American law schools, it is likely that the decision is part of the fabric of American contract law. If nothing else, the time spent reading and working through one case leaves less time to see the law from the perspective offered by another case.

---

[2] Hadley v. Baxendale, (1854) 156 Eng. Rep. 145 (Ex.).

[3] Allegheny Coll. v. Nat'l Chautauqua County Bank, 159 N.E. 173 (N.Y. 1927) (Defendant's promise to donate money to college after her death was enforceable because college gave sufficient consideration in assuming duty to name scholarship fund after decedent; suggests that promissory estoppel may be substitute for consideration.).

Another example: The law on contract modification is not a model of clarity. The decisions and pertinent legislative enactments reach and occasionally codify diverse conclusions. That might, from one perspective, cast doubt on the canonical status of the *Alaska Packers* decision.[4] But we might still conclude that *Alaska Packers* is part of the canon because it formulates the problem in terms that demonstrate the balance of normative considerations implicated in the contract modification setting. If law students and lawyers encounter a contract modification issue, they might only recognize it as a potential problem because of *Alaska Packers*, if that case were part of their first-year contracts experience. We understand Uniform Commercial Code (UCC) Section 2-209 as a *response* to the modification problem, though in fact the provision probably reverses the case result. *Alaska Packers* might not be good law in your jurisdiction. You must first understand the problem the case attempted to solve—a problem that remains for consideration doctrine in contract—before you can understand the cures. So, canonical status need not depend on currency; a case could be canonical because of its encounter with a fundamental strain on the fabric of contract.

We can go further. A case may be canonical *because* it is wrong, particularly because of the way in which it is wrong. For example, assume for the sake of argument (and a relatively safe assumption) that both *Peevyhouse v. Garland Coal & Mining Co.*[5] and *Groves v. John Wunder Co.*[6] cannot both be right. That does not matter for canonical status. What matters is that you need to know both to appreciate why one is wrong and the other is right, or the extent to which one is wrong and the other right. Because they concern an issue central to contract—the damages measure—it is important that we appreciate the contours of its resolution as those contours are revealed in the two decisions. The same could be said of other pairs of cases, such as *Hill v. Gateway 2000, Inc.*[7] and *Klocek v. Gateway, Inc.*[8] It is not always true that if two cases reach opposite conclusions, both will be canonical. Nevertheless, this may occur, which confirms that reaching a conclusion we deem correct (at least in the fullness of time) is not a necessary incident of canonical status.

Though it may be presumptuous, for present purposes, assume that the foregoing conception of canonical status is right as far as it goes. Were that the end of the inquiry,

---

[4] Alaska Packers' Ass'n v. Domenico, 117 F. 99 (9th. Cir. 1902) (Modification of a payment agreement requires additional consideration.).

[5] Peevyhouse v. Garland Coal & Mining Co., 382 P.2d 109 (Okla. 1962) (Correct measure of damages for breach is diminution of land value when cost of repair is grossly disproportionate to its value.).

[6] Groves v. John Wunder Co., 286 N.W. 235 (Minn. 1939) (Cost of repair is acceptable measure of damages even when disproportionate to increase in value, focusing on willfulness of breach.).

[7] Hill v. Gateway 2000, Inc., 105 F.3d 1147 (7th Cir. 1997) (Terms inside shipment box are binding, regardless of whether plaintiff reads them.).

[8] Klocek v. Gateway, Inc. 104 F. Supp. 2d 1332 (D. Kan. 2000) (Seller failed to demonstrate buyer's acceptance of terms mailed with product.).

we might be left with far too many cases for those who like to focus on a more manageable list. There is no reason why there could not be five hundred or even a thousand or more cases in the canon, but an argument of this book is that we can formulate the contours of the consensual undertaking that is the focus of contract with far fewer cases. Indeed, we might be able to agree on no more than thirty that are crucial. So we need to fine-tune the calculus.

C. The Literary Analogy

Apparently, just *what* constitutes the canon matters a great deal in English, American, and World literature curricula across higher education. Appreciated as a forum in which social and class struggles may be played out, the books we choose to read and require undergraduates (and, for that matter, graduate students) to read says much about our values and has, or may have, an impact on the values we endeavor to inculcate. In the zero-sum game of course syllabi and curricula, if Shakespeare's "voice" is privileged because it is included in the canon, then some other voice is marginalized or ignored altogether. To the extent that what and who we read comprises who we are, those who assign the reading have great power, particularly if they are deciding what the next generation of teachers will read.

Lawyers and law professors are no less given to hyperbole than literature professors and no less certain that the future of Western civilization (indeed, all civilization) depends on the choices that determine the regime's legal values. Does *promise* matter in the way some believe that Holmes thinks it does (perhaps justifying conceptions of efficient breach) or in the way Kant and Fried conceive it, in non-consequentialist terms? That may be crucial in deciding to what damages the non-breaching party is entitled and it may inform as well our conception of promise.[9] There could be a symbiosis between legally enforceable promises and those that are not enforceable in a court of law. So, the distinction could matter beyond our legal conceptions.

Myriad contract cases over the last four-hundred years or so have reached myriad conclusions pertinent to the question, "What does it mean to contract?" And students of contract cannot read them all. We make choices, initially in the law schools, in many instances, but in the practice as well. Sometimes a case attracts particular attention in the academy because the practicing bar first recognizes its importance. Still, however the next "big case" is discovered, we assume that it may be important in a way other cases are not because it adjusts or refines our understanding of the contract undertaking. The fact that it finds itself in the vocabulary, maybe even before it works its way into the casebooks, signals that it shares something fundamental with other cases that similarly attract our

[9] Seana Valentine Shiffrin, *The Divergence of Contract and Promise*, 120 HARV. L. REV. 708 (2007).

attention. Though the analogy may not be perfect, it may be that we can appreciate what that "something fundamental" is once we pursue the literary analogy further. (Harold Bloom helps here.[10])

D. What We Read

The easiest way to identify the canon, in fact, might just be to look to the casebooks and count the number of times that the same cases recur. The canon could be no more than our common reading. Such an approach would also support our fixing a canon of varying sizes: the twenty most included cases, the twenty-five, the thirty. We could also be sensitive to developments in the canon: Did some cases appear more often in the older casebooks and less frequently in the newer ones? Are there even cases that have enjoyed a renaissance? Have new transactional patterns (and economic and social adjustments) had an impact on cases' inclusion in the leading casebooks? Should we also take into account the significance of the casebooks in which the cases appear (measured, perhaps, by adoptions or academic affiliation of the editors)?

There are also collections of cases deemed to tell particularly important stories.[11] These are self-conscious efforts to identify the cases that matter more than others. They may treat a series of cases either discretely or weave them into a narrative to which each selected case is crucial in its way (and, again, not necessarily as a correct application of the law). Insofar as many of these collections are directed toward students (though not solely toward students), the cases considered can have a formative impact. In an important way, the collections beg the question: How does our understanding of contract change because of this case? In other words, how would our understanding be affected had this case not been decided?

So, what we read may determine the contours of the canon by pure force, as it were: The *fact* that a case has worked its way into the collective contracts consciousness may be enough to make it canonical even without evaluating the quality of that claim. That, of course, would explain why some perceive so much to be at stake in our deciding what to include. We cannot assume that everyone exposed to a case will make a critical and qualitative assessment of the case's claim to canonical status. Indeed, there are what we may consider non-qualitative reasons for a case's repeated inclusion in anthologies of casebooks and commentaries. Those reasons could range from the prosaic—the length of

---

[10] Harold Bloom, The Western Canon (1994).

[11] *See, e.g.,* Randy E. Barnett, Perspectives on Contract Law (1995); Marvin A. Chirelstein, Concepts and Case Analysis in the Law of Contracts (6th ed. 2010); Richard Craswell & Alan Schwartz, Foundations of Contract Law (1994); Contracts Stories (Douglas Baird ed., 2007); Robert A. Hillman, Principles of Contract Law (2nd ed. 2009).

the opinion—to the poetic—written by Cardozo.[12] Still, though, no matter why a case works its way into the casebooks and commentaries, we may deem it canonical just because it has done so, wholly apart from any qualitative judgment regarding its significance. There may, though, be more to canonical status than habit.

E. Why We Read

Succinctly, we read the contracts cases in order to understand the contract law; that is, we expect to find the law in the cases. Our objective may be instrumental: We represent a client whose interests would be served by cases going one way or the other, Alternatively, our object may be more broad: We seek to discern what contract is up to generally, in terms of its scope and purpose. That broader objective assumes a great deal in its premise, namely, that contract has a fixed and discernible scope and purpose. We are a species preoccupied by teleology, and perhaps able to discover a telos even if there is none.

Assuming, for the moment, that contract admits of determinate scope and purpose, we could read the cases because we believe that it is in the cases that we will discover that scope and purpose or purposes. (We need not assume that contract has a unitary purpose.) If that is our object, then we read (and decide what to read) based on judgments about significance and the recurrence of particular cases in the teaching materials might be *some* indication of contract's purpose, but it also may not. The fact that the same cases appear over the years and across an array of casebooks (as well as other teaching materials) may reveal more about their pedagogical value (*e.g.,* accessibility, familiarity to teachers, even entertainment value) than it would about their relationship to some fundamental sense of contract.

It would seem more likely, though, that familiarity of cases that have worn a path in the casebooks indicates some coincidence of pedagogical value and theoretical significance. Indeed, the fact that particular cases do appear frequently in the teaching materials—whatever the reason—would seem to reveal something about the fundamental nature of contract, even if by default. Suppose a case appears often because the opinion is well written, addresses accessible or familiar or interesting facts, or is just short. Over time, given the nature of canonical formation, that case may tell us more than other cases do about contract because it becomes so familiar, becomes a part of the contract vocabulary (think of the so-called "hairy hand"[13]). But surely familiarity alone should not be the sole criterion of canonical status.

Imagine the contract canon as an exclusive club, the entrance to which all contracts cases compete in terms of their significance. Now some judges may be self-consciously

[12] Considering the number of contracts cases, it must be remarkable that so many of the most famous cases were Cardozo decisions, right or wrong, earth-shaking or not.

[13] Hawkins v. McGee, 146 A. 641 (N.H. 1929).

striving to write opinions that will have canonical status (or at least get into the casebooks), but most would surely disclaim any such ambition. After all, many (most?) judges would maintain that they only discover[14] the law. If the literary analogy helps at all, given that opinion writing is creative after its fashion, we may agree that, for the contract canon just as for the literary canon, "[o]ne breaks in only by aesthetic strength, which is constituted primarily of an amalgam: mastery of figurative language, originality, cognitive power, knowledge, exuberance of diction."[15] The analogy from literature does not work perfectly, but it is not entirely inapt. For instance, "figurative language" or "exuberance of diction" would not seem pertinent, though there is no shortage of what we might deem canonical cases that include flights of fancy; again, think of Cardozo. Certainly, though, "originality, cognitive power, [and] knowledge" seem to fit the bill well. We expect that canonical opinions would be original, learned, and smart (even if perhaps not clever). If the opinion were not original, then it would be difficult to discern its claim to any exalted status. For a case to be canonical, it must demonstrate something about contract that was certainly part of contract though maybe latent before. It must be an elaboration of the fundamental nature of legally enforceable consensual relations that we had not had occasion to formulate before. Keep in mind, though, that consistency with that fundamental nature is not indispensable. It may be enough that the case reveals the foundation of contract, which is why two cases reaching diametrically opposed conclusions may both be canonical.[16]

Bloom opines that the fact that a text "demands rereading" is an indicator of its canonical status.[17] So, too, with the canonical cases. We do not just read the cases that define contract; we have a continuing conversation with them. Further, their meanings may morph as the circumstances to which they are applied diversify. A case that made some sense applied to the sale of a horse has a different significance applied to the sale of computer software.[18] In that way, the parameters of canonical status are dynamic; the relationship of the canon to contract can shift as our conceptions of the foundation of the consensual undertaking shifts.

---

[14] Ronald Dworkin, Law's Empire 6 (1986).

[15] Bloom, *supra* note 10, at 29.

[16] *Compare* Peevyhouse v. Garland Coal & Mining Co., 382 P.2d 109 (Okla. 1963) *with* Groves v. John Wunder Co., 286 N.W. 235 (Minn. 1939).

[17] Bloom, *supra* note 10, at 30.

[18] *Cf.* Lawrence Lessig, *The Law of the Horse: What Cyberlaw Might Teach*, 113 Harv. L. Rev. 501 (1999) (arguing possible benefit of examining relatively new field of "cyberlaw," including sale of software, as separate from general sales principles); Karl N. Llewellyn, *Across Sales on Horseback*, 52 Harv L. Rev. 725 (1939) (comparing merchant transactions to processes used by amateur actors, as in sale of a horse).

F. The Canon Sets Limits

Keep in mind that there is nothing particularly intentional about the canon. That is, the ambitions of some judges notwithstanding, it would be rare for an opinion to be written in order to gain canonical status. So, even if the paradigm shifts, the shift would need to be in relation to the canon. Although a constitution or statute can be amended, contract itself shifts only glacially. The canon always describes, perhaps from various and varying perspectives, the foundations of consensual undertaking. In that way, the canon assures that development will be deliberate, even grudging.

Bloom, writing about the Western canon, observes that it "exists precisely in order to impose limits, to set a standard of measurement that is anything but political or moral."[19] Although some cases may strain the fabric of the contract canon, no case could rend it. That remains true no matter how transactional patterns may shift. Electronic contracting may alter the way we do business, but cases arising in evolving transactional settings can only be contracts cases so long as they are fundamentally about the scope and substance of the bargain.

That explains both why it is difficult to appraise the canonical status of newer cases and also why a case may be canonical even though it reaches the wrong conclusion. A relatively recent case, say, *ProCD v. Zeidenberg, Inc.,*[20] for example, may be canonical because of the way it challenges our understanding about the nature of the consensual undertaking in an important context.[21] That would be true whether or not we conclude that the decision reaches the decision consistent with the foundations of contract. Whatever our ultimate understanding of contract, if we will need to take account of *ProCD,* then *ProCD* is canonical. That is true because the case is (very self-consciously) about the limits of consensual liability. Our theory of contract, however it is construed, would be incomplete if it did not make room for *ProCD*, and perhaps it could make room for the decision by providing the means to see the failure of Judge Easterbrook's argument. If the decision is wrong, it is wrong because the judge misunderstood contract or misapplied the empirical tools he used to reach his conclusion (or, just as likely, he both misunderstood and misapplied).

In any event, no one case (or even a group of cases) can get around the canon and still be about contract. It is in that way that the canon sets limits. There is another dimension of this, though, that is noteworthy. Consider analogy to the Ship of Theseus:

> Over a long period all of the planks composing a certain ship are replaced one by one. Eventually a ship indiscernible from the original, but composed of entirely

[19] BLOOM, *supra* note 10, at 35.

[20] ProCD, Inc. v. Zeidenberg, 86 F.3d 1447 (7th Cir., 1996).

[21] The fact that the decision was by Judge Frank Easterbrook of the United States Court of Appeals for the Seventh Circuit is pertinent, too.

different planks, results. Call that later ship Replacement. As each plank is removed from the original ship it is used to construct a ship that is constituted from all and only the planks belonging to the original ship. Call the ship composed of the same planks as the ones initially composing the original ship Reassembly.[22]

So too with contract, in an important way. Whatever essentially *is* contract, just like whatever essentially *is* the original Ship of Theseus, remains the same. That essence is revealed by the canonical cases, much as the original ship is revealed by both *Replacement* and *Reassembly*. Whatever *there* there was originally remains and endures. Contract has the same essential foundation, and, *vis-à-vis* the canonical cases, that essence is revealed; the cases that would (even could) reveal that essence are limited by the canon itself. This is very much a bootstrap arrangement.

G. Achieved Anxieties

Bloom concludes that "Canons . . . are achieved anxieties, not unified props of morality."[23] His point is that we cannot impose on the canonical; some datum is or is not part of the canon wholly regardless of the ways we want to use it. So, although *Henningsen v. Bloomfield Motors*[24] may or may not be part of the canon, it is or is not regardless of the political or social argument that it makes. Now, at some point, the political or social argument may resonate with the foundations of consensual relations, but a case presenting or capturing such an argument is or may be part of the canon because of that resonance and not because of the political or social argument.

Canonical contract cases (not unlike canonical literature) do not so much resolve our anxieties—the anxieties revealed in the persistent tensions underlying the scope and limits of the consensual undertaking. They instead describe the contours of those anxieties, exposing the pressure points that maintain the tension. That is why canonical cases are often close cases; that is why they suggest fuller stories.[25] We will find *a* resolution of tensions, but perhaps not the *only* plausible resolution. The sources of resolution will be discovered in the fit between a view of contract's foundation and as much of the transactional context as the court is willing to share with us. The anxiety may be dispatched, for the time, but the tension remains. That tension, a kind of "existential hum,"[26] is what the canonical cases are about.

---

[22] Stanford Encyclopedia of Philosophy (2009), http://plato.stanford.edu/entries/identity-time/.

[23] BLOOM, *supra* note 10, at 38.

[24] Henningsen v. Bloomfield Motors,161 A.2d 69 (N.J. 1960).

[25] *See* CONTRACTS STORIES, *supra* note 11.

[26] KURT VONNEGUT, PALM SUNDAY 185 (Delacorte 1981).

H. What We Are Looking For

There are, though, more prosaic indicia of canonical status than those suggested by the literary analogy. In addition to a case's recurrence in the teaching materials, we may consider treatment in the legal treatises, and it should come as no surprise that the cases that receive attention in most of the casebooks are also the focus of considerable attention in the treatises. Although that may reflect the importance of a particular case, it is certainly also consistent with the fact that the treatises may be written to support their use by the same students who use the casebooks. So, a case merits consideration in the treatises *because* it is included in many (or at least the leading) casebooks. Nevertheless, insofar as the treatises tell the story of contract, they may be trusted to cover the canonical cases, as well as a good many others. Some treatise coverage may be *an* indicator but not a *sufficient* indicator of canonical status.

Both the *Restatements of Contract* (the *Restatements*) as well as other products[27] of the American Law Institute pertinent to contract doctrine include comprehensive illustrations, comments, and *Reporter's Notes* that catalog the sources upon which the black letter of the *Restatements* is based. These products, more often than not, include cases that we would recognize as canonical because they represent the primary sources upon which a distinguished and learned society has based its conclusions about the contours of contract. Indeed, it might generally be difficult to consider a case canonical if it were not treated, perhaps at length and at several junctures, in some such products. Again, though, because the *Restatements* and similar projects include references to a very large number of cases, we could not conclude that the ALI treatment of a case is a sufficient determinant of canonical status. It would be no more than *a* determinant.

The fact that particular cases are the subject of statutory formulation is, too, an indicator of canonical status. Here, the references may not always be so obvious. Though some legislation is accompanied by commentary that reveals the common law sources (if any) on which the drafters relied, not all enactments so clearly and candidly acknowledge the case law they would codify or abrogate. We might, then, need to match the enactment up with a common law rule and then posit the source of that rule in a case or line of cases. If the result of that effort is the identification of a particular case as the source, and if the legislation itself has broad application, then we may discover another indicator of canonical status. That conclusion maintains even if the statute is in derogation of the common law rule. For, as noted above, the fact that a case might have reached a wrong (or just incomplete) conclusion should not necessarily impair its canonical status.

---

[27] *See* Peter A. Alces & Chris Byrne, *Is It Time for the Restatement of Contracts,* Fourth?, 11 DUQ. BUS. L.J. 195 (2009) (discussing variety of ALI products and what different designations mean).

The focus of this book is on the American common law of contract. But it matters, too, that particular cases or the rules derived from them have currency in more than one common law jurisdiction. If, for example, both New Zealand and the United States recognize as a crucial element of their contract jurisprudence a particular rule derived from a particular English contract case, that suggests that the case that is the source of the rule is canonical, and matters to the common law of consensual relations in a way other cases do not.

Succinctly, then, we may appreciate the determination of canonical status as contemplating the coincidence of three characteristics, however manifest: The canonical cases are foundational, venerable, and pervasive. And they are relatively few. Though the list can be arbitrarily limited to, say, twenty-five or thirty, insofar as the constituents of canonical status are matters of degree, the list could increase or decrease depending upon how compact you would want the list to be. We might well get different answers to the following questions: What are the thirty canonical contracts cases? What are all of the contracts cases that have, to some degree, the constituents of canonical status? So, this book makes two claims regarding the scope of canonical status. First, I assert that we *can* formulate the contours of the law governing consensual relations by reference to no more than thirty cases that are particularly fundamental, venerable, and pervasive. Second, the cases identified in the following chapters are, at the time of this writing, the most canonical. They are the cases from which we could build a contract law recognizable as the contract law we have today. They are what is left over after we cut away all that is "not David."

I. The Three Phases of Contract Doctrine

The rules of contract could be divided into several different groupings to focus on different aspects of the contract law and to distinguish the parts of the law in terms of their operative characteristics. But for present purposes, for the sake of ease and accessibility of presentation, the contract doctrine is divided into three parts: Formation, Performance, and Enforcement. That division is not part of the book's argument; it serves merely to accommodate presentation and nothing is lost if the conscientious reader would understand, for example, *damages* as distinct from *enforcement*. The division is admittedly artificial. Indeed, it may well be argued that some of the canonical cases could be placed in one of the other two categories rather than in the one in which they are placed for purposes of the book's presentation.

Formation, as used here, refers to no more than what it takes to get into and determine the scope of the contractual undertaking and relationship. Particularly, I focus on those cases that tell us how we may distinguish the bases of legally enforceable obligation from those of a merely voluntary undertaking not supported by the threat of legal sanction. Consideration, for example, draws that line in a way that is crucial to contract and the cases construing that requirement must be part of the canon, whether this element of contract makes much sense or not from a particular normative perspective.

Performance concerns the whole of the parties' reciprocal obligations, particularly the scope of those obligations. As long as we understand contract as no more than the allocation of risk concerning uncertainty (usually in terms of future value),[28] then we can focus on the parties' intent, actual and construed, in order to determine their reciprocal performance obligations. What makes their relationship contractual is the fact that those performance obligations are reciprocal.[29] There is a good deal caught up in that simple formulation of the contract law. For example, obligations must be real, not illusory. There must be mutuality of obligation, though not equivalence. We need to be able to determine the scope of the parties' relative undertakings in order to be able to measure the sufficiency of their performance. So, a good deal of contract can be included under the performance heading, and that is the scheme here.

Enforcement refers to damages but a good deal more as well. In order to know what enforcement entails, we need to ascertain what the assumption of contract liability contemplates. If you make a promise to me that the law will enforce, what interest of mine is compromised if the law is called upon to enforce it? Lon Fuller and his research assistant, William Perdue, recognize three interests that contract may vindicate and develop a taxonomy of contract damages rules along those lines.[30] Inspired by Aristotelian ethics,[31] Fuller and Perdue conclude that contract vindicates the reliance interest more consistently and reliably than it does the expectation interest, notwithstanding the ostensibly expectation-based damages calculus.[32] We understand that disappointed contracting parties should realize the benefit of the bargain, but we may not actually have a certain enough grasp of what that bargain is. In order to fix the enforcement measure, we need to know exactly of what breach denies the non-breaching party.

From the foregoing premises, we can begin to assemble a list of the canonical cases and support the list by reference to the criteria and indicia described in this chapter. The limitations of this enterprise are clear, and this is not just an effort to provide grist for

---

[28] Hal S. Scott, *The Risk Fixers*, 91 HARV. L. REV. 737 (1978).

[29] OLIVER WENDELL HOLMES, THE COMMON LAW 230 (Mark DeWolfe Howe, ed., Belknap Press of Harvard University Press 1963) (1881) ("Consideration ... is given and accepted as the motive or inducement of the promise. Conversely, the promise must be made and accepted as the conventional motive or inducement for furnishing the consideration.").

[30] Lon.L. Fuller & William R. Perdue, *The Reliance Interest in Contract Damages* (pts. 1 & 2), 46 YALE L.J. 52, 373 (1936).

[31] *Id.* at 56 ("In passing from compensation for change in position to compensation for loss of expectancy we pass, to use Aristotle's terms again, from the realm of corrective justice to that of distributive justice.").

[32] U.C.C. § 1-305(a) (2003) ("The remedies provided ... must be liberally administered to the end that the aggrieved party may be put in as good a position as if the other party had fully performed but neither consequential or special damages nor penal damages may be had except as specifically provided in [the Uniform Commercial Code] or by other rule of law.").

the mill in the faculty lounge. Because this book inquires into the relationship between contract theory and contract law, it is necessary to discover (or at least posit) the source of that law. Contract is the doctrine, and the cases, particularly the canonical cases, are the source of that doctrine.

For the most part, the treatment of the canonical cases will not be evaluative. That is, the cases are presented in terms that emphasize their canonical status according to the parameters suggested in this chapter. It is only after that catalog that the normative foundation of the canonical cases is considered in terms of the extant theories of contract. So, Chapters Three, "Contract Formation Doctrine"; Five, "Contract Performance Doctrine"; and Seven, "Contract Enforcement Doctrine," assert the canonical status of certain cases. Chapters Four, "Theory of Contract Formation"; Six, "Theory of Contract Performance"; and Eight, "Theory of Contract Enforcement," consider the fit of those cases with deontic and consequentialist normative theories.

3

CONTRACT FORMATION DOCTRINE

ANY DELINEATION OF A GROUP of contract law issues into discrete subject areas, such as formation, will, necessarily, be artificial and subject to challenge. Nevertheless, there may be some value in treating like subjects alike, even if the similarity is superficial. That is, there is no *a priori* reason that the group of issues that arise at the formation stage share any more common theoretical provenance than would a formation issue and a damages issue. At either the formation or damages stages, the parties' object (and the law's as well) may be consistent with one rather than another object, and that object may be deontic, consequentialist, or even some amalgam of the two. But so long as we respect that, we may aid our appreciation of a discrete portion of the contract law by focusing on the considerations that commonly attend the applications of doctrine. That is, although the deontic or consequentialist considerations that inform the parties' actions and understanding may not be the same, at the formation stage, they do share a common *object*: initiation of the contract relation.

This chapter reviews twelve canonical contract formation cases. But just because the cases are amenable to grouping under the heading of formation does not mean that they all concern the same formation issue or issues; indeed they do not. Yet we may infer something from the fact that the treatment of even related issues reveals common considerations; maybe there is nothing new under the sun. Further, we can discern from the transactional contexts in which the issues arise something about the flexibility, even malleability, of contract formation rules. It matters, too, that there seems to be something fundamental about formation, about what it takes for the law to conclude that the parties' promise has become enforceable.

A. *Raffles v. Wichelhaus*[1]

Raffles v. Wichelhaus is the famous *Peerless* case, in which plaintiff-seller and defendant-buyer attempted to enter into a contract for the sale and delivery of 125 bales of Surat cotton. By *Peerless*, plaintiff meant a ship sailing from Bombay in December and defendant meant a ship of the same name sailing from Bombay in October. When the December *Peerless* arrived, defendant refused to take delivery because, defendant averred, the contract contemplated the cotton on the October *Peerless*. The ship provided the description of the subject matter of the contract; so, again per defendant, a failure to agree on the ship constituted a failure to agree on the subject matter of the contract. And with no agreement, there was no contract formation.

The opinion mentions the admissibility of parol evidence, as to whether defendant would be permitted to distinguish, by parol, what he meant by *Peerless* as opposed to what plaintiff meant by the same identifier. The court finds that, insofar as the parties' communications gave rise to a latent ambiguity (Which *Peerless*?), "parol evidence may be given for the purpose of showing that the defendant meant one 'Peerless,' and plaintiff another."[2] It would be just as if by *mustang*, you meant a horse and I meant a car. In either event there would be "no *consensus ad idem*," no meeting of the minds, in the vernacular. The court ultimately finds no contract on the facts presented.

The case is part of the canon because it supports a good deal of the weight of contract. If contract is distinct because it governs *consensual* relations, then there can be no contract without consent. *Raffles* recognizes and gives effect to that fundamental consent criterion. The *Restatements of Contract* have incorporated and refined the *Raffles* rules. Section 71 of the *First Restatement* is entitled, "Undisclosed Understanding of Offeror or Offeree, When Material." The rule of *Raffles* is formulated most closely in subsection (a):

> If the manifestations of intention of either party are uncertain or ambiguous, and he has no reason to know that they may bear a different meaning to the other party from that which he himself attaches to them, his manifestations are operative in the formation of a contract only in the event that the other party attaches to them the same meaning.[3]

---

[1] Raffles v. Wichelhaus, (1864) 159 Eng. Rep. 375 (Ex.)

[2] *Id.* at 376.

[3] RESTATEMENT (FIRST) OF CONTRACTS § 71 (1932).

Because neither of the *Raffles* parties had reason to know that the other attached a different meaning to the same term, *Peerless*, there could be no contract *unless* both happened to have attached the same meaning to the term, which they did not. *Raffles* is the acknowledged source of the first Illustration to the section.[4]

The *Second Restatement* reforms the construction of the *Raffles* rule. Section 18 provides, quite succinctly, that "[m]anifestation of mutual assent to an exchange requires that each party either make a promise or begin to render a performance."[5] That section complements Section 17(1):

> (1) Except as stated in Subsection (2), the formation of a contract requires a bargain in which there is a manifestation of mutual assent to the exchange and a consideration. (2) Whether or not there is a bargain a contract may be formed under special rules applicable to formal contracts or under the rules stated in Section 82-94.[6]

Section 3, in turn, defines *agreement* and *bargain* and formulates their interrelation: "An agreement is a manifestation of mutual assent on the part of two or more persons. A bargain is an agreement to exchange promises or to exchange a promise for a performance or to exchange performances."[7] So a contract requires "agreement" that is a "manifestation of mutual assent," and a "bargain" is an "agreement." For there to be a contract, there must be a bargain *in which there is* a manifestation of mutual assent. A "bargain" is an "agreement," which is necessarily "a manifestation of mutual assent," so not all "bargains" are necessarily "a manifestation of mutual assent." The expression of that relationship, if not the logic of it, would seem to defy principles of transitivity. Nonetheless, it is safe to say we can get the general idea.

What matters most for present purposes, though, is the *Second Restatement's* conclusion that contract is premised on the *manifestation* of mutual assent rather than actual assent, whether manifested or not. Now, that formulation is quite sensible. Insofar as consensual obligation is bilateral, the requisite consent is necessarily a function of objective manifestations of assent. There is no assent without manifestation.[8] Still, though, the focus on manifestation, as opposed to an authentic "meeting of the minds," matters insofar as it intimates an objective theory potentially at odds with autonomy conceptions. Comment b to Section 20 of the *Second Restatement* makes that clear: "[I]t is enough that there is a core of common meaning sufficient to determine [the parties']

---

[4] *Id.* § 71, illus. 1.

[5] Restatement (Second) of Contracts § 18 (1981).

[6] *Id.* § 17.

[7] *Id.* § 3.

[8] *See* Randy E. Barnett, *A Consent Theory of Contract*, 86 Colum. L. Rev. 269, 302 (1986).

performances with reasonable certainty or to give a reasonably certain basis for an appropriate legal remedy."[9] The extent to which contract liability is imposed *on* rather than created *by* the parties is a function of the sufficiency of the common meaning. The less commonality that will suffice the less consensual contract is. The *Second Restatement* retains the vitality of *Raffles*. Illustrations 1 through 4 to Section 20 are based on the case.[10] So though the formulations of both *Restatements* differ, for present purposes (that of discovering a unitary theory of contract), there does not seem to be much difference. The *Second Restatement* may or may not be an improvement; it does nothing, perhaps can do nothing, to alter our conclusion about the theoretical ambiguity of the *Raffles* rule.

Professor Farnsworth treats the *Raffles* rule and the *Restatement* elaborations of it at length in his seminal treatise. He recounts Learned Hand's extreme rendition of the objective theory of contract: "[I]f both parties severally declared that their meaning had been other than the natural meaning, and each declaration was similar, it would be irrelevant, saving some mutual agreement between them to that effect."[11] Maybe the "saving some mutual agreement between them to that effect" proviso salvages just enough good sense to limit the sweep of the broader assertion. But if it does not, or if the requisite mutual agreement is not readily found, then Hand's assertion recites the type of arch objective standard that essentially eviscerates any suggestion that individual autonomy animates the contract law. Farnsworth reports that "such authority as there is supports giving effect to a common meaning shared by both parties in preference to an objective meaning."[12]

Holmes too construes the *Peerless* case, essentially concluding that the word *Peerless* as it referred to the October ship was not the same word as the word *Peerless* applied to the December sailing.[13] That may be a triumph of objective reading, but it fails to provide much guidance for the next case, and certainly lacks a normative justification.

Two cases from other common law jurisdictions illustrate the *Restatement's* elaboration of the *Raffles* rule, and its incidents. The decision of the Supreme Court of Canada in *Murray v. Jenkins*[14] concerns a failure of the parties' minds to meet; one contracting party erred, and the counterparty was aware of the mistake. The court concludes that the parties were not "*ad idem*" regarding the subject matter of the contract, and the buyer could not take advantage of the seller by holding her to a bargain the buyer knew to have

---

[9] Restatement (Second) of Contracts § 20 cmt. b (1981). The language tracks that of UCC § 2-204(3) (2002), which states "a contract for sale does not fail for indefiniteness if the parties have intended to make a contract and there is a reasonably certain basis for giving an appropriate remedy."

[10] *Id.* § 20 Reporter's Note to cmt. d.

[11] E. Allan Farnsworth, Farnsworth on Contracts § 7.9 at 276 (3rd ed. 2004) (quoting Eustis Mining Co. v. Beer, Sondheimer & Co., 239 F.976, 984–85 (S.D.N.Y. 1917)).

[12] *Id.* at 277; *see also id.* at 278 n.12 (citing cases in accord); Restatement (Second) of Contracts § 201 (1) (1981).

[13] Oliver Wendell Holmes, *The Theory of Legal Interpretation,* 12 Harv. L. Rev. 417, 418 (1899).

[14] Murray v. Jenkins, [1898] 28 S.C.R. 565 (Can.) (finding no contract where parties were mistaken as to exact identity of land sold).

been mistaken. To similar effect is *Taylor v. Johnson*,[15] a decision of the High Court of Australia. Again, the facts concern an alleged failure of the contracting parties' minds to meet. At issue is whether the culpability of one of the parties in failing to draw the misunderstanding of the other to the attention of that other estopped the non-mistaken party from enforcing the agreement. The court finds sufficient culpability to support estoppel. In the course of doing so, it formulates well what cases like *Raffles* intimate with regard to subjective versus objective theories of contract:

> The "subjective theory" . . . is that the true consent of the parties is essential to a valid contract. The contrary view, namely that described as the "objective theory," . . . is that the law is concerned, not with the real intentions of the parties, but with the outward manifestations of those intentions. . . . [A]llied with any assertion of the "subjective theory" is acceptance of one manifestation of the doctrine of estoppel which would ordinarily operate to preclude one who had so conducted himself that a reasonable man would believe that he was assenting to the terms of a proposed contract, from leading evidence as to what his real intentions were.
>
> . . .
>
> The important distinction between the two approaches is that, according to the subjective theory, the contract is void ab initio, whereas according to the objective theory, it is voidable only.
>
> . . .
>
> [T]he clear trend in decided cases and academic writings has been to leave the objective theory in command of the field.[16]

The void–voidable distinction does not seem to help us very much in the effort to discern a theoretical foundation that would rationalize all of contract. We cannot be certain that the solution contract has come up with, essentially a comparative fault standard, resonates with a particular normative theory. The theory would need to come before, would need to inform how we might choose between the two perspectives and how we might apply them.

B. *Lucy v. Zehmer*[17]

This canonical case relies on Section 71 of the *First Restatement* and implicates the same formation tensions as did *Raffles* before it. Succinctly, Lucy, as buyer, and Zehmer, as seller, entered into what Lucy alleged was a contract for the sale of Zehmer's farm after

[15] Taylor v. Johnson (1983) 151 C.L.R. 422 (Austl.) (finding contract voidable in equity when buyer and seller had conflicting understandings of purchase price, and when buyer was aware of seller's unilateral mistake).

[16] *Id.* at 428–29.

[17] Lucy v. Zehmer, 84 S.E.2d 516 (Va. 1954).

both had been drinking. The relative degrees of intoxication was subject to some dispute, but the Virginia Supreme Court finds "that Zehmer was not intoxicated to the extent of being unable to comprehend the nature and consequences of the instrument he executed, and hence that instrument is not to be invalidated on that ground."[18] But more to the contract formation point, even had Zehmer been jesting—as he maintained he had been—Lucy was not aware of the joke. Lucy considered the transaction to be a serious business deal.

At the critical juncture, the court's analysis *seems* to contradict itself. First, the court reasons, "[t]he mental assent of the parties is not requisite for the formation of a contract,"[19] taking a strict objective approach. But then, in the next paragraph, the court reverses course: "[A]n agreement or mutual assent is of course essential to a valid contract but the law imputes to a person an intention corresponding to the reasonable meaning of his words and acts."[20] There really is no contradiction, in fact. Mental assent is requisite; it is just that the best evidence of that assent is objective indicia. So *Lucy v. Zehmer* relies on the *Restatement* provision built on *Raffles*[21] to capture all that can be captured concerning the requisite states of mind of the parties to a contract.

In terms resonant of *Lucy v. Zehmer*, Section 2 of the *Second Restatement* makes clear the difference between manifest intent and unrevealed reservation: "A promise is a manifestation of intention to act or refrain from acting in a specified way, so made as to justify a promisee in understanding that a commitment has been made."[22] The comment explains that "[t]he phrase 'manifestation of intention' adopts an external or objective standard for interpreting conduct; it means the external expression of intention as distinguished from undisclosed intention."[23] *Lucy v. Zehmer* is also credited as a source of Section 16, "Intoxicated Persons," of the *Second Restatement*, though it is not so clear that the case has anything at all to say about the contracts of intoxicated persons. After all, so far as the Virginia Supreme Court was concerned, neither Lucy nor Zehmer was intoxicated.[24]

The *Lucy v. Zehmer* rule was anticipated in an English case, *Smith v. Hughes.*[25] Plaintiff-seller of oats and defendant-buyer, a trainer of a racehorse, entered into a sales contract. Plaintiff delivered a sample of the oats to defendant, who, after holding them for two days, agreed to buy a quantity of oats from which the sample was taken.[26] The oats were *new* oats and, after the delivery of the shipment, defendant realized that and resisted

[18] *Id.* at 520.

[19] *Id.* at 522.

[20] *Id.*

[21] Restatement (First) of Contracts § 71 (1932).

[22] Restatement (Second) of Contracts § 2 (1981).

[23] *Id.* § 2 cmt. b.

[24] *See id.* § 2 illus. 3; *see also id.* § 2 Reporter's Note to cmts. a and b.

[25] Smith v. Hughes, (1871) 6 L.R.Q.B. 597.

[26] *Id.* at 603.

paying for them. Defendant maintained that he sought *old* oats and would not have entered into the contract if he had realized that plaintiff was offering new oats for sale. Apparently, the age of the oats matters to horse trainers because the age matters to the horses they train.

At one level, the case may well present the familiar question from *Raffles*: "[I]f two persons enter into an apparent contract concerning a particular person or ship, and it turns out that each of them, misled by a similarity of name, had a different person or ship in his mind, no contract would exist between them [citing *Raffles*]."[27] And if that captured the case between the oats seller and the trainer, if the difference between new oats and old oats is the same as that between October *Peerless* and December *Peerless*, then there would be no contract between the parties in *Smith v. Hughes* and in myriad similar cases. The opinion continues, in terms that resonate with *Lucy v. Zehmer*: "But one of the parties to an apparent contract may, by his own fault, be precluded from setting up that he had entered into it in a different sense to that in which it was understood by the other party."[28] That, of course, is just where *Zehmer* found himself: *By his own fault*, his jest, he had entered into the contract (when he meant *not* to enter into it) "in a different sense to that in which it was understood by the other party."[29] The analysis is much the same whether the disagreement is about a term of the contract or the very existence of the intent to contract.

The opinion's analysis, at this point, claims a moral basis:

> The rule of law applicable to such a case is a corollary from the rule of morality which Mr. Pollock cited from Paley, that a promise is to be performed "in that sense in which the promiser apprehended at the time the promisee received it," and may be thus expressed: "The promiser is not bound to fulfill a promise in a sense in which the promisee knew at the time the promiser did not intend it."[30]

So defendant would only prevail if defendant could show that plaintiff believed that defendant believed that plaintiff had contracted to sell defendant old oats.

The case, and particularly the opinion of Blackburn, has a great deal to say about the intent to contract requisite and, as well, the relation of that requisite to a good deal of the contract law. Today, in the United States, the case would be decided under Article 2 of the Uniform Commercial Code (UCC or the Code), and Section 2-316(3)(b) would be apposite. That section provides that if a buyer, such as the trainer in *Smith v. Hughes*, examines a sample of the goods as the trainer had done, "there is no implied warranty

---

[27] *Id.* at 609 (citing Raffles v. Wichelhaus, (1864) 159 Eng. Rep. 375 (Ex.)).

[28] *Id.*

[29] *Id.*

[30] *Id.* at 610 (citing William Paley, Moral and Political Philosophy, Book III, ch. 5 (1824)).

with regard to defects which an examination ought in the circumstances to have revealed to him."[31] The only warranty in the case regarding the age of the oats that could have arisen in *Smith v. Hughes* would have been an implied warranty, insofar as the court found that the seller had never used the term *old* in relation to the oats and the buyer had not specifically inquired of their age.

Indeed, Cockburn draws a direct parallel between the *ad idem* calculus and the warranty law:

> [T]he two minds were not ad idem as to the age of the oats; they certainly were ad idem as to the sale and purchase of them. Suppose a person to buy a horse without a warranty, believing him to be sound, and the horse turns out unsound, could it be contended that it would be open to him to say that, as he had intended to buy a sound horse, and the seller to sell an unsound one, the contract was void, because the seller must have known from the price the buyer was willing to give, or from his general habits as a buyer of horses, that he thought the horse was sound? The cases are exactly parallel.[32]

Whether the cases are "exactly parallel," Cockburn's observation makes clear that the *ad idem* question, the contour of consent, resonates throughout the contract law and, if a unitary theory is to be of much help, will have to explain formation and warranty issues consistently.

A decision of the Alberta Court of Appeal, in *Ghitter Property Consultants v. Beaver Lumber Co.*,[33] demonstrates the subjective—objective tension well. The case concerned a real property sublease. The court formulates the issue as whether the agreement was sufficiently clear with regard to which of the parties, as between the sublessor and sublessee, was responsible for discharging the lease obligations to the original lessor. The court relies on a wholly objective sense of *consensus ad idem*: "Regardless of the theories underlying the enforcement of contracts, mutuality of agreement lies at the root of any legally enforceable contract. The required degree of mutuality mandates that the parties reach a *consensus ad idem* on essential terms."[34] The test is whether an "objective reasonable bystander, in light of all the material facts, [would conclude] that the parties intended to contract and the essential terms of that contract can be determined with a reasonable degree of certainty."[35] The focus is on what a "sensible third party" would infer.[36]

---

[31] UCC § 2-316(3)(b) (2002).

[32] Smith v. Hughes, (1871) 6 L.R.Q.B. at 606.

[33] Ron Ghitter Prop. Consultants v. Beaver Lumber Co., [2003] 330 A.R. 353 (Can.).

[34] *Id.* at 5.

[35] *Id.*

[36] *Id.* at 6.

That focus on an entirely objective determinant of agreement is, arguably, at odds with the UCC rule, Section 2-204, which refers only to the parties' "inten[t] to make a contract and . . . a reasonably certain basis for giving an appropriate remedy."[37] The more objective iteration of the *ad idem* requirement conflates the intent to be bound *with* the existence of a reasonably certain basis to grant relief. That is, according to opinions such as *Beaver Lumber*, the fact that there *is* a reasonably certain basis to grant relief, clarity with regard to the division of obligations between the parties, satisfies the *ad idem* requirement. An objective observer would infer from the ambiguity regarding the allocation of obligations that the parties were not *ad idem*. The following case discusses the failure of the "meeting of the minds" requirement in an instance of mutual mistake.

C. *Sherwood v. Walker*[38]

Sherwood v. Walker concerned a cow, specifically, a cow the parties understood to be sterile which was, in fact, with calf. Plaintiff-buyer of the cow brought a replevin action when it became clear that the cow was not, as both seller, Walker, and buyer had assumed, sterile. In fact, defendant had entered into a contract to purchase more than he thought he was purchasing and seller had contracted to sell more than he thought he was selling. After contracting but before delivery of the cow, it became clear that the animal, Rose 2d of Aberlone, was not sterile. Defendant argued that both buyer and seller were mistaken about a crucial quality of the contract subject matter, and that the price agreed upon based on that mistake was $80, but the price for a cow that was not barren would be between $750 and $1,000. The court finds that "[i]t appears from the record that both parties supposed this cow was barren and would not breed, and she was sold by the pound for an insignificant sum as compared with her real value if a breeder."[39]

The lower court thought that the fact that both parties were mistaken as to a crucial characteristic of the contract subject matter was not a sufficient basis upon which to void the contract. The appellate court disagrees in terms that are now canonical:

> [I]t must be considered as well settled that a party who has given an *apparent* consent to a contract of sale may refuse to execute it, or he may avoid it after it has been completed, if the assent was founded, or the contract made, upon the mistake of a material fact, such as the subject matter of the sale, the price, or some collateral fact materially inducing the agreement; and this can be done when the mistake is mutual.[40]

---

[37] UCC § 2-204(3) (2002).

[38] Sherwood v. Walker, 33 N.W. 919 (Mich. 1887).

[39] *Id.* at 923.

[40] *Id.* (emphasis added).

The focus, once again, is on intent, or rather the court's *post hoc* inference of intent, informed, as it may well be, by the facts that become salient in the course of events. The requirement that the mistake be mutual polices unconscientious behavior. If only one party were mistaken, the other may be able to enforce the bargain, else we would not incentivize care in contracting.

On the facts of *Sherwood*, in the court's estimation, there was no more a meeting of the minds than there would have been had one party had in mind a bull and the other a steer, so long as there was no basis to infer lack of care on the part of either party. If I offer to sell you my Mustang, the car, and you agree to buy my mustang, the horse, we have no contract and either of us can walk away so long as neither of us is chargeable with less than due care. But that is an easier case than *Sherwood*, where the misapprehension was with regard to a quality of the contract subject matter rather than with regard to the identity of the subject matter. The court is sensitive to this, and relies on English authority to draw the crucial distinction:

> If there is a difference or misapprehension as to the substance of the thing bargained for, if the thing actually delivered or received is different in substance from the thing bargained for, and *intended* to be sold, then there is no contract; but if it be only a difference in some quality or accident, even though the mistake may have been the actuating motive to the purchaser or seller, or both of them, yet the contract remains binding.[41]

So, whether there is sufficient coincidence of intent to find a contract is a matter of degree. Because the difference *in value* between a sterile and a breeder cow was *at least* \$670, in 1887 dollars, the difference in value was a difference in kind sufficient to find mutual mistake. The parties, of course, could have contracted around the result reached by the court. They could have agreed that the animal's fecundity was unknown, or that they were indifferent on the issue. Alternatively, the court could have focused on relative fault: Which party was in the better position to determine the cow's reproductive potential? We must assume that the court, at least implicitly, made some such judgment when it found that the cow the parties thought they had contracted for and the cow actually sold were just not the same thing. The difference was not one of degree, but of "the very nature of the thing."[42]

That analysis is certainly not convincing. If the difference in market price were \$5 rather than \$670, we must assume that the difference would not be so fundamental. What the court must mean, then, is that *at some point* a difference in value becomes so great that it is essential. Nonetheless, the result in the case is not so troubling; it seems

[41] *Id.* (emphasis added).

[42] *Id.*

just as likely that the buyer was trying to realize an unearned windfall as it would be that the seller was trying to avoid the consequences of its own inattention.

Wood v. Boynton[43] is a case that may be (and has been)[44] set off against *Sherwood*, and might be offered to impair *Sherwood*'s canonical status. In fact, though, it confirms it. *Boynton* was decided two years before *Sherwood*, by the high court of Wisconsin. In *Boynton*, plaintiff, Ms. Wood, sold to defendant-jeweler, Mr. Boynton, a gem that turned out to be much more valuable than either plaintiff or defendant realized. Plaintiff took the gem to defendant's shop and asked defendant to tell her what it was. Wood told Boynton that someone had told her the gem was a topaz, to which defendant remarked that it might be, and offered to buy it from her. She asked him what the stone might be worth and he responded that it might be worth a dollar; he said that he would buy it to retain as a "specimen."[45] Wood then declined to sell it. Sometime later, when she was in financial straits, Wood returned to Boynton and asked him again what he would pay for the stone and he repeated his initial offer, one dollar. This time she accepted the dollar and left defendant's premises.

It turns out that the stone was in fact a rough diamond, not a topaz, and worth around $700, so 700 times what defendant paid for it. Certainly, as between plaintiff and defendant, defendant had considerably greater expertise with regard to the valuation of gems. Defendant testified, and apparently the trier of fact believed, that defendant had never seen a rough cut diamond before and had no idea of the value of the stone when he purchased it from Wood. The Supreme Court of Wisconsin is able to dispense quickly with plaintiff's fraud allegation, finding no basis to support that theory, and turns its attention to the mistake calculus.

> Both [plaintiff and defendant] were entirely ignorant at the time of the character of the stone and of its intrinsic value. . . . The [plaintiff] had the stone in her possession for a long time, and it appears from her own statement that she had made some inquiry as to its nature and qualities. If she chose to sell it without further investigation as to its intrinsic value to a person who was guilty of no fraud or unfairness which induced her to sell it for a small sum, she cannot repudiate the sale because it is afterwards ascertained that she made a bad bargain.[46]

[43] Wood v. Boynton, 25 N.W. 42 (Wisc. 1885).

[44] *See, e.g.*, Randy E. Barnett, Contracts: Cases and Doctrine 1051, 1062 (4th ed. 2008); Brian A. Blum & Amy C. Bushaw, Contracts: Cases, Discussion, and Problems 618–19 (2d ed. 2008); Thomas D. Crandall & Douglas J. Whaley, Cases, Problems, and Materials on Contracts 515–25 (5th ed. 2008).

[45] *Boynton*, 25 N.W. at 43.

[46] *Id.* at 44.

There was no basis to find mistake. The buyer and seller realized full well the substance of their transaction; each received what each sought, a certain chance that his or her own assessment of the value (or potential value) of the contract subject matter might be greater than what each exchanged in return. It may well have been the case that the gem was worth $2, and then the deal would have seemed more balanced. But understood in terms of what the parties bargained for, *Boynton* and *Sherwood* are entirely consistent. In both cases, the court considers the transactional context, as the doctrine invites courts to do, and finds sufficient bargain, and that is all that matters. *Bargain* is just the type of supple conception that accommodates such contextual analysis.

The common law sources from other jurisdictions are not inconsistent with *Sherwood*:[47] They make clear the difference between mutual mistake (in which the parties fundamentally misunderstand the contract subject matter) and a bargain of indeterminate value. What obscures the analysis is reference to whether the difference turns on disparity of value. *Sherwood* was a mutual mistake case *not* because a sterile cow was worth about a tenth of what a fertile cow was worth; *Sherwood* concerned mutual mistake because the parties had not been aware of any uncertainty. In *Boynton*, there was uncertainty; the parties were aware of it (or should have been) and intended to bargain in the shadow of that uncertainty. So they were not both mistaken, even if one was ultimately disappointed.

The *Second Restatement*, in Section 152(1), formulates the mutual mistake rule of *Sherwood*, in familiar terms:

> Where a mistake of both parties at the time a contract was made as to a basic assumption on which the contract was made has a material effect on the agreed exchange of performances, the contract is voidable by the adversely affected party unless he bears the risk of the mistake. . . .[48]

Section 154 explains when a party bears the risk of mistake:

> A party bears the risk of a mistake when
>
> (a) the risk is allocated to him by agreement of the parties, or
> (b) he is aware, at the time the contract is made, that he has only limited knowledge with respect to the facts to which the mistake relates but treats his limited knowledge as sufficient, or

---

[47] *See* Ford Motor Co. v. City of Woodhaven, 716 N.W.2d 247 (Mich. 2003) (Ford and tax assessor made mutual mistakes of fact in determining that personal property statements were accurate; thus, Ford could be entitled to refund based on excess taxes billed.); Topgro Greenhouses v. Houweling, [2008] 2008 B.C.J. No. 1961 (Can.) (Mutual mistake underlying basic assumption of contract—that shares were owned by particular person—undermined parties' original intentions as to contract and thus contract was invalid.).

[48] Restatement (Second) of Contracts § 152(1) (1981).

(c) the risk is allocated to him by the court on the ground that it is reasonable in the circumstances to do so.[49]

Sherwood is cited in support of Section 152[50] and *Boynton* is cited in support of Section 154.[51] The two are, obviously, complementary. Note particularly Section 154(c), which relies on conceptions of reasonableness to determine allocation of risk in a contract. That marks a merger of the consensual and nonconsensual, not unique to the mistake context, but certainly revelatory of something fundamental about the doctrinal foundation of contract.

The formation issues in this area of the law tie into the impracticability doctrine considered in Chapter Five, "Contract Performance Doctrine."[52] That is confirmed by the language of Section 152: "a basic assumption on which the contract was made."[53] *Impracticability* excuses performance if the basis of impracticability arises after formation of the contract. *Mutual mistake* intervenes earlier: The contract is avoided because of a "misunderstanding" at the time of formation.

Just as mutual mistake polices the bargain requirement by focusing on the existence in fact of the type of bargain contract will enforce, the following canonical case concerns the *quid pro quo* that must be the parties' focus in order to find an (enforceable) bargain. Though bargain is necessary to contract, the canon makes clear that it is not sufficient.

D. *Hawkins v. McGee*[54]

Thanks to the popular culture,[55] there may be no more famous canonical case than *Hawkins v. McGee*, Kingsfield's infamous "hairy hand" case. *Hawkins* is a medical malpractice decision, and as such may tell us more about the intersection of tort and contact than it does about contract alone, but ultimately it does tell us a great deal about the limits of bargain. Plaintiff had scar tissue on the palm of his hand and defendant doctor grafted skin taken from plaintiff's chest to the hand after removing the scar tissue. In the course of the conversation leading up to the procedure, what would pass as the bargain, plaintiff's father asked the doctor "How long will the boy be in the hospital?" The doctor responded, "Three or four days, not over four; then the boy can go home and it will be just a few days when he will go back to work with a good hand." Further, the doctor

---

[49] *Id.* § 154.

[50] *Id.* § 152 cmt. b, illus. 5.

[51] *Id.* § 154 cmt. d, illus. 3.

[52] *See, e.g.,* Taylor v. Caldwell, (1863) 122 Eng. Rep. 309 (K.B.).

[53] RESTATEMENT (SECOND) OF CONTRACTS § 152(1) (1981).

[54] Hawkins v. McGee, 146 A. 641 (N.H. 1929).

[55] *See, e.g.,* THE PAPER CHASE (Thompson Films 1973).

stated, "I will guarantee to make the hand a hundred per cent perfect hand or a hundred per cent good hand."[56] There was also evidence that defendant doctor had in fact solicited, repeatedly, the opportunity to perform the surgery on plaintiff. Apparently, the doctor was interested in experimenting with certain skin grafting techniques.

In issue was whether plaintiff, through his father, had bargained for the assurance the doctor provided, and whether there was what would be, in the contemplation of contract, a warranty, at least of sorts. Under all of the circumstances—the words spoken by defendant as well as the transactional context—there was, the court finds, sufficient evidence of a bargain to go to the jury, which found for plaintiff. The New Hampshire Supreme Court's decision concerns damages for breach of the express warranty.[57] But the case also tells us something about context and bargain.

Recall that the case concerned a context generally within the scope of the medical malpractice law, a phase of tort. Doctors, given the nature of the healing *arts*, do not make warranties and so their patients should not understand them to do so; there is no bargain, as such, when a doctor describes an expected result. And there is no bargain because of the nature of the doctor's undertaking. For the same reason that the seller of the precious gem in *Boynton* could not rely on mutual mistake to recover the property she sold to the jeweler, in the ordinary course, a disappointed patient cannot recover damages from a doctor whose best hopes for a medical procedure are not realized. There is a line to be drawn, again a line between the nature of consensual and nonconsensual relations law, and contract, in the ordinary course, defers to tort in the medical malpractice setting for the same reasons that the scope of mutual mistake may be circumscribed: the limits of bargain.

E. *Carlill v. Carbolic Smoke Ball Co.*[58]

The offeror, by making the offer, confers power on the offeree to bind the offeror to contract. Once the offeror has made the offer (and before the offeror exercises any available right to terminate it), the offeror is very much exposed: The offeree has the unilateral power to impose an obligation on the offeror and the offeror has not yet any similar power to bind the offeree. So any change in circumstances between the time the offer is made and accepted may expose the offeror to risk; the offeree has a limited ability to play

[56] *Hawkins*, 146 A. at 642–43.

[57] The New Hampshire Supreme Court analogizes the warranty the surgeon made before the operation to the warranty attached to a piece of machinery designed to complete a specific task. The court concludes, "the true measure of the plaintiff's damage in the present case is the difference between the value to him of a perfect hand or a good hand, such as the jury found the defendant promised him, and the value of his hand in its present condition." *Id.* at 643–44.

[58] Carlill v. Carbolic Smoke Ball Co., [1893] 1 Q.B. 256 (U.K.).

the market, assume benefits disproportionate to the risks to which the offeror has exposed herself, including the risk of market shift.

There is, then, good reason to recognize the offeror's prerogative to control both the terms of the offer, including the means by which the offeree may accept the offer. Providing offerors that power is also in the best interests of offerees: The more discretion the offeror maintains the more likely the offeror will be to make offers and the more offers offerees may have available to them. Efforts to circumscribe offeror's rights might well disserve offerees. To the extent that you think contracting is a good thing, the law should accommodate offerors' making more offers so that offerees will have more offers to accept.

Carlill v. Carbolic Smoke Ball Co. involved the famous Carbolic Smoke Ball advertisement which read: "100£ reward will be paid by the Carbolic Smoke Ball Company to any person who contracts the increasing epidemic influenza, colds, or any disease caused by taking cold, after having used the ball three times daily for two weeks according to the printed directions supplied with each ball."[59] Plaintiff purchased the smoke ball, used it according to the directions, and nevertheless contracted influenza. So she sought 100£ from defendant who resisted payment, arguing that the advertisement did not amount to an actionable promise; "there was no more consideration in using the ball than in contracting the influenza."[60]

The court finds all the promise necessary to provide the basis to support plaintiff's action. Defendant's advertisement constituted an offer that was accepted by plaintiff's using the ball as prescribed. Plaintiff's notifying defendant of her claim to the reward was sufficient notice of acceptance of the offer. The context in which the offer was made demonstrated that defendant did not expect that each purchaser of the ball would separately notify it of the purchaser's acceptance of the offer. Here the offer could only be accepted by performance of the requested act: use of the smoke ball. Defendant had not bargained for any promise from plaintiff. So the case is quite simple really. Although an offeror may fix the form of acceptance and require an act rather than a promise, the offeree performing that act need not have notified the offeror of its intention to do so; the act is the acceptance because that is what the offeror bargained for. The case illustrates well the role of bargain in contract and also holds up well enough to be canonical.

Section 54(1) of the *Second Restatement* captures the *Carbolic Smoke Ball* rule: "Where an offer invites an offeree to accept by rendering a performance, no notification is necessary to make such an acceptance effective unless the offer requests such notification."[61] Illustration 2, to comment c, is based on *Carbolic Smoke Ball* and makes clear that "[n]o notification . . . is required until after [buyer] has contracted the disease."[62]

---

[59] *Id.* at 257.

[60] *Id.* at 260.

[61] Restatement (Second) of Contracts § 54(1) (1981).

[62] *Id.* § 54(1) cmt. b, illus. 2.

The rule of the case has also been recognized in other common law jurisdictions.[63] *Carbolic Smoke Ball* is canonical *because* it captures an important part of the offeror–offeree dynamic. The case makes sense of the dance that is the offer and acceptance, a dance in which contract builds from each party's surrender of autonomy. The offeror is at first exposed, but only enough to entice the offeree into the bargain. The offeree can bind the offeror, but to no greater extent than the offeror contemplated and subject to whatever reasonable limitations the offeror has imposed.[64] But the offeror cannot insist upon an empty formality, such as a notification the offeror could not reasonably need or want prior to the offeree's performance.

F. *ProCD, Inc. v. Zeidenberg*[65]

Contemporary contract formation conceptions are the product of common law antecedents such as *Raffles v. Wichelhaus* and *Lucy v. Zehmer*. So long as we understand that the normative bases of contract formation doctrine were established in those two earlier cases and their progeny, then we are constrained, if we want to believe in a unitary theory, to understand contemporary cases as consistent with those normative premises. That is, our theory may find its elaboration in contemporary cases, but it should not be contradicted by them. Contract can of course evolve, but our best interpretation of the fundamental theory's evolution could not account for a shift wholly inconsistent with inviolable premises. So if contemporary cases cannot be reconciled with their theoretical antecedents, then the case for a unitary normative theory is undermined. Cases that seem to represent a sea change must be accounted for. *ProCD* is one such case. The decision has been described as "one of the most important contract cases of the past generation."[66] Two companion cases, or at least two other cases that have a certain resonance with *ProCD,* are treated along with it in this exposition of the canon.

A challenge for courts confronted with the contract formation questions is to determine how to construe the agreement requirement. Is it necessary that the parties actually

---

[63] *See* Ayerswood Development Corp. v. Hydro One Networks, Inc., 39 C.L.R. (3d) 288 (Ontario Superior Court) (Program guide stating that financial incentive would be given to any new construction of qualifying buildings constituted offer that was open to anyone who complied with its terms and formed unilateral contract.); Soulsbury v. Soulsbury, [2008] 2 W.L.R. 834 (Court of Appeal) (U.K.) (Ex-husband's agreement to leave ex-wife certain sum in his will provided she did not pursue maintenance while he was still alive was contract when ex-wife accepted by performance according to their agreement.).

[64] *Cf.* Peter Benson, *Contract as a Transfer of Ownership*, 48 WM &. MARY L. REV. 1673, 1709–10 (2006) (Contract formation depends upon reasonable interpretation of offeree as to whether offeror committed to be bound by certain terms in offer.).

[65] ProCD, Inc. v. Zeidenberg, 86 F.3d 1447 (7th Cir. 1996).

[66] Richard A. Epstein, ProCD, Inc. v. Zeidenberg*: Do Doctrine and Function Mix, in* CONTRACTS STORIES 94 (Douglas G. Baird ed., 2007).

be *aware of and understand* the legal consequences of their communications (and even such awareness may be a matter of degree), or may the law infer *sufficient* agreement to support the imposition of liability? Courts that take seriously awareness and understanding can better explain their conclusions by reference to deontic precepts: For example, we vindicate individual autonomy by respecting the actor's choice to assume a legal duty. Courts concerned with finding only sufficient agreement may be more concerned with the utility of imposing the legal duty than with any particular transactor's appreciation of the legal obligation that follows therefrom. That divide is illustrated and represented well by three cases that reach opposed conclusions—two going one way, one the other—on essentially similar facts. The two cases decided by Judge Frank Easterbrook, of the United States Court of Appeals for the Seventh Circuit—*ProCD, Inc. v. Zeidenberg* and *Hill v. Gateway 2000, Inc.*[67]—and a decision of Judge Kathryn Vratil of the United States District Court for the District of Kansas—*Klocek v. Gateway, Inc.*[68]—each construe agreement in the same important contemporary context: so-called "form contracting." The courts' divergent conclusions may be manifestations of divergent understandings of the normative claims made by the contract doctrine. Apposite provisions of the UCC inform the courts' analyses.

Though there are ten sections in Part 2 of Article 2 of the UCC, entitled "Form, Formation and Readjustment of Contract," two provisions are particularly (or potentially) pertinent to aspects of the agreement calculus treated in the three cases considered here: Sections 2-204, "Formation in General," and 2-207, "Additional Terms in Acceptance or Confirmation," the so-called *battle of the forms* provision. The object of both sections is to facilitate sales contract formation, to give effect to the parties' intentions.[69] The sections should cooperate to avoid the law's frustration of the parties' plans, as well as to preclude one contracting party's taking advantage of formal contract formation rules to impose unfair surprise on the other.[70] A commercial reading of both provisions confirms that conclusion.

Section 2-204(1) provides that "[a] contract for sale of goods may be made in any manner sufficient to show *agreement*."[71] And "agreement," recall, is "the bargain of the parties in fact."[72] Subsection 2-204(3) elaborates on the nature of the requisite bargain: "Even though one or more terms are left open a contract for sale does not fail for indefiniteness if the parties have intended to make a contract and there is a reasonably certain

---

[67] Hill v. Gateway 2000, Inc., 105 F.3d 1147 (7th Cir. 1997).

[68] Klocek v. Gateway, Inc., 104 F. Supp. 2d 1332 (D. Kan. 2000).

[69] UCC § 2-204 cmt. 3 (2002).

[70] Note also that UCC § 2-201(2) operates similarly and evidences the Code's sustained effort to preclude such strategic behavior.

[71] UCC § 2-204(1) (2002) (emphasis added).

[72] *Id.* § 1-201(b)(3).

basis for giving an appropriate remedy."[73] That certainly relaxes common law requirements of agreement premised on the likes of an ostensibly subjective "meeting of the minds." The object of the UCC formulation is to facilitate the parties' attributing legal significance, enforceability, to communications lacking the formality that could frustrate rather than vindicate important contract principles, such as the wealth creation or individual autonomy realized. There may be a fine line, however, between facilitating commerce and undermining the parties' expectations. Section 2-204 endeavors to tread that line, and to afford courts the means to draw distinctions based on transactional realities rather than form.

UCC Section 2-207 offers an elaboration of that same idea if the parties exchange nonresponsive communications, or at least communications that would preclude agreement under the older common law forms. The provision has been subject to extensive, perhaps, overwhelming, critical appraisal since its promulgation over half a century ago.[74] The pith of the law of Section 2-207 as currently construed[75] and as the proposed amendments to Article 2 would provide[76] circumvents much of, indeed virtually all of, the formal common law rules that would accommodate uncommercial strategic behavior: either or both parties' efforts to gain technically what they could not gain as part of "the bargain in fact." If one party tries to impose a provision on the other party that is not the product of agreement, the court should instead impose the deal that is the product of the parties' actual intent, common law contract formalities notwithstanding.[77]

So Sections 2-204 and 2-207 approach the agreement calculus from two different directions. Section 2-204, on the one hand, effectively sifts through the parties' communications, considers those communications in context, and at some point supports the conclusion that the parties have formed an agreement: just when the communications reveal an intent to be bound and a reasonably certain basis to grant relief, no sooner and no later. For Section 2-204, the agreement question is answered when there is *enough*, and the court will decide when there is *enough* regardless of the parties'

---

[73] *Id.* § 2-204(3).

[74] For a recent and comprehensive survey of the literature, see Corneill A. Stephens, *Escape From the Battle of the Forms: Keep It Simple, Stupid*, 11 LEWIS & CLARK L. REV. 233 (2007).

[75] *See, e.g.,* Aceros Prefabricados, S.A. v. TradeArbed, Inc., 282 F.3d 92, 98 (2d Cir. 2002) (analyzing expressions of acceptance that form contract); CECG, Inc. v. Magic Software Enterprises, Inc., 51 F. App'x 359, 364 (3d Cir. 2002) (describing analysis of conflicting writings under UCC § 2-207); Bayway Ref. Co. v. Oxygenated Mktg. & Trading A.G., 215 F.3d 219, 223 (2d Cir. 2000) (finding fax effective as acceptance even though it stated or referenced additional terms); J.J.'s Mae, Inc. v. H. Warshow & Sons, Inc., 717 N.Y.S.2d 37, 38 (N.Y. App. Div. 2000) (examining whether "clause in a confirmation invoice constitutes a material alteration of an existing contract between merchants within the meaning of UCC 2-207").

[76] *See* AMERICAN LAW INSTITUTE, UNIFORM COMMERCIAL CODE: PROPOSED AMENDMENTS TO ARTICLES 2, 2A, AND 7 (Proposed Final Draft, April 18, 2003).

[77] For the seminal presentation of the provision's operation see JAMES J. WHITE & ROBERT S. SUMMERS, UNIFORM COMMERCIAL CODE § 2-3 (6th ed. 2010).

post hoc protestations.[78] Section 2-207, on the other hand, cuts through, or at least provides the means to cut through the detritus that the parties' exchange of written communications has generated in order to find the kernel of their agreement. So Section 2-204 builds up to agreement while Section 2-207 cuts down to agreement. The provisions are complementary; we should not have occasion to resolve tension between them. There should be no tension so long as we appreciate that the object of both provisions is to discern agreement, in the best commercial sense.

ProCD may not be, strictly speaking, an Article 2 case,[79] but Judge Easterbrook uses Article 2 provisions to support his conclusions. (Though it is at least arguable that his construction of those provisions is problematic.)[80] The issue is whether buyers of consumer software are bound by the terms of shrink-wrap licenses. Zeidenberg had acquired the software distributed by ProCD and then used it in a manner inconsistent with the terms of the ProCD license. While ProCD sought, by the terms of the license agreement, to limit Zeidenberg's use of the software, Zeidenberg argued that he was not bound by the terms of the license agreement because those terms were only presented to him after he had paid for the software and left the retail seller's premises.[81]

Easterbrook has no trouble finding a good commercial (and consequentialist) reason for ProCD's incorporation of the license provision limiting Zeidenberg's use of the software. The provision had enabled ProCD to discriminate between consumer and commercial buyers, or licensees, of the software in a way that would ultimately serve the interests of all licensees. The license provision would effectively police the less-than-conscientious behavior in which Zeidenberg sought to engage: license of the software at a consumer price, but exploitation of the product for commercial purposes. To effect price discrimination, ProCD relied on a limitation of use provision included within the box containing the software at the time Zeidenberg obtained it.

Easterbrook proceeds from the observation that "[t]ransactions in which the exchange of money precedes the communication of detailed terms are common."[82] He catalogs several recurring transactional contexts in which just that practice is followed.[83] The judge

[78] Note that if Section 2-204 is in issue, one of the parties is resisting the characterization of their communication urged by the other party.

[79] The UCC Article 2 scope issue, so far as computer software is concerned, has attracted a good deal of attention. *See generally* Peter A. Alces & Harold F. See, The Commercial Law of Intellectual Property Ch. 8 (1994) (surveying cases and commentary).

[80] *See* Peter A. Alces, Un*intelligent Design in Contract*, 2008 U. Ill. L. Rev. 505, 523 n.111 (2008).

[81] ProCD, Inc. v. Zeidenberg, 86 F.3d 1447, 1452 (7th Cir. 1996). The terms appeared in the box and appeared on the monitor screen when the software opened. Also, the program would not let the user proceed without indicating acceptance.

[82] *Id.* at 1451.

[83] His examples include the purchase of insurance, the purchase of an airline ticket, the purchase of a concert ticket, the purchase of a product packaged with its warranty, and the purchase of software over the phone or on the internet. *See id.* at 1451–52.

also offers a striking suggestion: "Drugs come with a list of ingredients on the outside and elaborate package insert on the inside. The package insert describes drug interactions, contraindications, and other vital information[,] but, if Zeidenberg is right, the purchaser need not read the package insert, because it is not part of the contract."[84] Actually, it is as difficult to imagine a consumer perusing such an insert as it is to imagine a drug manufacturer relying on the insert's boilerplate to insulate itself from liability arising from drug interactions or contraindications. It is unlikely that such an effort to inform patients of a drug's propensities or risks would certainly constitute a sufficient warning to preclude the imposition of liability, if that is what Easterbrook has in mind.[85]

Easterbrook relies particularly on Section 2-204(1): "A contract for sale of goods may be made in any manner sufficient to show agreement, including conduct by both parties which recognizes the existence of such a contract." Then he explains that the vendor, such as ProCD, is the "master of the offer, [and] may invite acceptance by conduct, and may propose limitations on the kind of conduct that constitutes acceptance."[86] He concludes, erroneously, that Section 2-207 is irrelevant because there was only one form in issue and he understands Section 2-207 to be a battle of the forms provision. The opinion includes a particularly curious, albeit brief, passage: "[O]urs is not a case in which a consumer opens a package to find an insert saying 'you owe us an extra $10,000' and the seller files suit to collect."[87] The passage is curious because it is not clear how the formal contract agreement rules, the doctrine, would be affected by the significance of the hidden term. Certainly Section 2-204 draws no distinction based on the dollar consequences of the term's operation. So it is not clear exactly why, as a matter of doctrine, a "you-owe-us-$10,000" term would necessarily be any less enforceable than the ProCD limitation of use provision. Easterbrook offers no additional authority to support that distinction. That is not to say that the law could not recognize the distinction; it is only to suggest that Easterbrook did not locate the source of the distinction in Section 2-204, the governing doctrine. You get the sense that there might be degrees of agreement to which the doctrine would be sensitive.[88]

In *Hill v. Gateway 2000, Inc.*,[89] Easterbrook relies on *ProCD*. The Hills called the Gateway phone sales department and ordered a Gateway computer. In the course of the telephone conversation, the Hills certainly agreed to matters such as computer model, price, and time of delivery, but never, in fact, agreed to submit any dispute with Gateway to arbitration. When the computer arrived at the Hills' residence, the shipping box

---

[84] *Id. at* 1451.

[85] *See* RESTATEMENT (THIRD) OF TORTS (PRODUCTS LIABILITY) §§ 2 (c), 6(b)(3), 10 (1998).

[86] *ProCD*, 86 F.3d at 1452.

[87] *Id.*

[88] *See generally* Peter A. Alces, *Contract Reconceived*, 96 NW. L. REV. 39 (2001).

[89] Hill v. Gateway 2000, Inc., 105 F.3d 1147 (7th Cir. 1997).

enclosed terms in addition to those discussed on the phone. Among those additional terms was a requirement that the Hills return the computer to Gateway within thirty days if they did not agree to any of the additional terms and also a requirement that the Hills submit any dispute with Gateway to arbitration.

In *Hill*, Easterbrook abjures reliance on the UCC, though the case was certainly within the scope of Article 2: The sale of the computer to the Hills was the sale of a good. Easterbrook relies on *ProCD* to provide the basis for his conclusion in *Hill*: "Plaintiffs ask us to limit *ProCD* to software, but where's the sense in that? *ProCD* is about the law of contract, not the law of software."[90] So whatever Sections 2-204 and 2-207 might have to say about agreement in sales transactions, Easterbrook finds that they have nothing to say about the terms governing the sale of the computer in *Hill*.[91]

In finding that the terms provided by Gateway were enforceable against the Hills, Easterbrook concludes summarily that "[a] contract need not be read to be effective; people who accept take the risk that the unread terms may in retrospect prove unwelcome. . . . If [the terms inside the Gateway box] constitute the parties' contract because the Hills had an opportunity to return the computer after reading them, then all must be enforced."[92] Of course, if the Hills understood the apposite contract doctrine as precluding unilateral adjustment of terms by one of the contracting parties *after* contract formation, then they would have had no reason to read terms proffered by Gateway after the fact. So Easterbrook's conclusion, that the Hills were bound to the later supplied terms, assumes its premise, that later supplied terms could become part of the agreement after the fact. Though there is a way for that to happen under Article 2, as a Section 2-209 modification, Easterbrook offers no argument along those lines, and it is unlikely that he would have been able to identify the agreement necessary to support that conclusion in any event.

Essentially the same facts—the sale of a computer over the phone with terms to follow—were in issue in a case decided by Judge Vratil, at the district court level, *Klocek v. Gateway, Inc.*[93] In her *Klocek* opinion, Vratil disagrees with Easterbrook's conclusion that Gateway as vendor was "master of the offer": "[T]he Seventh Circuit provided no explanation for its conclusion that 'the vendor is the master of the offer.' In typical consumer transactions, the purchaser is the offeror, and the vendor is the offeree."[94] It was the Hills, after all, who called Gateway to place the order, and even if that call were in response to a Gateway advertisement, we have come to understand that

---

[90] *Id.* at 1149.

[91] UCC § 2-207 cmt. 5 to amended section 2-207 acknowledges that "[t]he section omits any specific treatment of terms on or in the container in which the goods are delivered." The comment cites *Hill*. *See* American Law Institute, *supra* note 76, at 34.

[92] *Hill*, 105 F.3d at 1148 (citations omitted).

[93] Klocek v. Gateway, Inc., 104 F.Supp.2d 1332 (D.Kan. 2000).

[94] *Id.* at 1340.

advertisements are not offers, but, instead, are solicitations of offers.[95] So as a matter of basic contract formation understanding, Vratil probably has it right. Because the Klocek–Gateway transaction was not one between merchants, subsection 2-207(2) was inapposite and could have no impact on the terms of the parties' agreement. Vratil makes clear that under subsection 2-207(1), Gateway's "expression of acceptance," in response to the Klocek offer, could not constitute a counteroffer (and thereby make Gateway the offeror) because Gateway had not "made its acceptance conditional on plaintiff's assent to the additional or different terms . . . . [T]he mere fact that Gateway shipped the goods with the terms attached did not communicate to plaintiff any unwillingness to proceed without plaintiff's agreement to the Standard Terms."[96] What was lacking was any demonstration that Klocek had actually agreed to Gateway's arbitration provision; plaintiff's retention of the computer for five days after receiving it could not constitute such agreement.[97]

The *ProCD, Hill,* and *Klocek* decisions confirm that the Article 2 formation rules complement the common law structure: It is certainly no more difficult to form a sales contract within the scope of Article 2 than it is to form any common law contract, and perhaps even easier. What remains is to understand the divergent normative bases of agreement that inform the different conclusions of Easterbrook and Vratil. On the one hand, Easterbrook's conclusion maps nicely onto the consequentialist perspective: We may (indeed, should) infer agreement when to do so would further instrumentalist goals. Because form contracts maximize utility, we should find that their use supports sufficient agreement so long as finding such agreement is consistent with instrumentalist ends. Therefore, any conception of agreement that would undermine such use of standard forms would be inefficient. *Agreement,* then, means no more than it can mean in order to reduce transactions costs. Any conception of agreement that would increase transactions costs would burden transactions, and so is disfavored.

Vratil's analysis, on the other hand, finds a basis of agreement that operates independent of consequentialist considerations. For her, agreement must come closer to real understanding. That is not to say that agreement may not provide a means to an end rather than an end in itself, but it is to acknowledge that an inference of agreement based on silence or mere failure to object will not do. Vratil's focus on the buyer as the master of the offer is redolent of autonomy considerations. Gateway could not impose terms on Klocek that were outside the scope of his offer. The effort to do so would violate the

---

[95] The prevailing wisdom is that advertisements are solicitations of offers, not offers themselves. *See* FARNSWORTH, *supra* note 11, at § 3.10. *But see* Jay M. Feinman & Stephen R. Brill, *Is an Advertisement an Offer? Why it is and Why it Matters*, 58 HASTINGS L.J. 61 (2006) (arguing against that prevailing wisdom).

[96] *Klocek*, 104 F.Supp.2d at 1340–41 (citations omitted).

[97] *Id.* at 1341.

buyer's autonomy by undermining the object of his promise. That, of course, is the point of recognizing that the offeror is master of the offer.

Vratil's reliance on offer doctrine notwithstanding, there is something almost intuitively obvious about the interest in relaxing contracting formalities in order to facilitate transactions. Why should we care about the formalities if doing so costs more than ignoring them or if relaxing them benefits transactors? That is, there is a question Easterbrook implicitly puts to which neither Vratil nor doctrine responds. It is worthwhile to consider more carefully the cost–benefit analysis and its relation to the doctrinal tension revealed by *ProCD/Hill* and *Klocek*.

ProCD sits somewhat uneasily among the canonical cases. Does the decision, along with *Hill* and *Klocek*, confirm our understanding of the essence of contract formation or does this line of cases[98] redirect contract formation? One reading of the decision supports the conclusion that *ProCD* is just the necessary elaboration of contracting formalities required by transactional technological developments foreshadowed by Section 211 of the *Second Restatement*. That provision would determine the enforceability of form terms by reference to the expectations of the party who drafted the standard form agreement:

> (1) Except as stated in Subsection (3), where a party to an agreement signs or otherwise manifests assent to a writing and has reason to believe that like writings are regularly used to embody terms of agreements of the same type, he adopts the writing as an integrated agreement with respect to the terms included in the writing.[[99]]
> (2) Such a writing is interpreted wherever reasonable as treating alike all those similarly situated, without regard to their knowledge or understanding of the standard terms of the writing.
> (3) Where the other party has reason to believe that the party manifesting such assent would not do so if he knew that the writing contained a particular term, the term is not part of the agreement.[100]

[98] Other common law jurisdictions have also addressed this issue. In Australia, see Ford v. La Forrest, [2001] QSC 261, ¶ 18 (Queensl.) (Email correspondence constituted acceptance.) In Canada, see Rudder v. Microsoft Corp., (1999), 2 C.P.R.(4th) 474, [1999] O.J. No. 3778 (Ont. S.C.J.) ("Click-wrap" agreements in general should be "afforded the sanctity that must be given to any agreement in writing."). In the United Kingdom, see Microsoft Corp. v. Ling, [2006] EWHC (Ch.) 1619 (User must click to agree to that EULA, and if he does not he may return computer for refund.); Beta Computers (Eur.) v. Adobe Sys. (Eur.), (1995) 1996 S.L.T. 604 (Sess. Outer House) (Scot.) (No contract existed where unopened software is returned in compliance with license agreement found on box.).

[99] This follows the lead of Section 70 of the *First Restatement*: "One who makes a written offer which is accepted, or who manifests acceptance of the terms of a writing which he could reasonably understand to be an offer or proposed contract, is bound by the contract, though ignorant of the terms of the writing or its proper interpretation." RESTATEMENT (FIRST) OF CONTRACTS § 70 (1932).

[100] RESTATEMENT (SECOND) OF CONTRACTS § 211 (1981).

Of course, it could be argued that *ProCD* does not follow the sense of Section 211 because the Easterbrook opinion does not limit enforcement to those terms that the party who drafted the standard agreement believed would pass without objection by the subordinate party. But recall that Easterbrook makes the point in *ProCD* that

> [O]urs is not a case in which a consumer opens a package to find an insert saying "you owe us an extra $10,000" and the seller files suit to collect. Any buyer finding such a demand can prevent formation of the contract by returning the package, as can any consumer who concludes that the terms of the license make the software worth less than the purchase price. Nothing in the UCC requires a seller to maximize the buyer's net gains.[101]

The terms of that observation are ambiguous. It seems as though Easterbrook is saying that *the only way* the consumer can avoid the operation of a "you-owe-us-$10,000" clause is by returning the package. Surely that would go beyond *Second Restatement* Section 211, which clearly seems to make such a term unenforceable *ab initio*.

So it may well be that *ProCD* oversteps the authority that preceded it and *refines* the contract formation machinery in such a way as to accommodate the parties' ostensible intent. In that event, the gauntlet may have been thrown down and we may appreciate cases such as *Klocek* as a defense of the pre-*ProCD* status quo. Similarly, then, we may read legislative and quasi-legislative responses to *ProCD* as efforts to better strike the balance between efficiency and equity, or, rather, to find the accommodation of formation principles that would serve both equity and efficiency simultaneously.

One way to rest more easily with *ProCD* is to recognize it as an innovation (to the extent it may be an innovation) responsive to the new challenges presented by electronic contracting: We need new rules, or a new understanding of old rules, in order to realize the benefits we may realize from electronic commerce. That seems to be the tack pursued, for example, in *The Australian Guidelines for Electronic Commerce* (*Guidelines*). The *Guidelines* recognize the unique opportunities presented by electronic commerce and that increasing consumer confidence in electronic contracting practices facilitates growth of the transactional form: "[C]onsumers' growing confidence in this means of doing business has been fundamental to the growth of electronic commerce and the resultant benefits to consumers and businesses."[102] The *Guidelines* contemplate that businesses will provide "enough information about the terms, conditions and costs of a transaction to

---

[101] ProCD, Inc. v. Zeidenberg, 86 F.3d 1447, 1452 (7th Cir. 1996).

[102] The Treasury of Australia, The Australian Guidelines for Electronic Commerce v (2006) *available at* http://www.treasury.gov.au/documents/1083/PDF/australian_guidelines_for_electronic_commerce.pdf; *see also* The Electronic Commerce and Information Act, R.S.M. ch. E 55 (2000) (Manitoba statute addressing electronic commerce).

enable consumers to make informed decisions."[103] Of course, "enough information about terms" seems to be something less than full disclosure of all terms and to that extent the Australian *Guidelines* would seem to depart from strict contract formation formalities. But the *Guidelines* do not say that all terms need not be disclosed and, after all, are not the apposite law. There is nothing in them that displaces contract principles.

In May 2009, the American Law Institute promulgated the *Principles of the Law of Software Contracting* (*Principles*).[104] The *Principles* endeavor to refine or, at least, adapt contracting principles to evolving transactional and technological settings, specifically transactions involving the transfer of computer software. It may be that software presents unique challenges to contract that require reconsideration of familiar contracting principles.[105] Alternatively, it may be the case that the drafters of the *Principles* discerned the need to modernize contract and found that software contracting provided the opportunity (or excuse) to do just that. The *Principles* "assume [correctly[106]] that market pressure is insufficient in software retail markets to assure the production of reasonable standard terms, both in presentation and substantive content."[107]

Ultimately, the *Principles* adopt the inclination (if not the very same analysis and conclusion) as *ProCD*.[108] The drafters overcome concerns about retail buyers' actually reading standard terms and instead "opt for creating additional incentives and opportunities for transferees to read terms."[109] Section 2.02, "Standard-Form Transfers of Generally Available Software; Enforcement of the Standard Form," is the American Law Institute's latest statement on the issue:

> (a) This Section applies to standard-form transfers of generally available software . . .
> (b) A transferee adopts a standard form as a contract when a reasonable transferor would believe the transferee intends to be bound to the form.
> (c) A transferee will be deemed to have adopted a standard form as a contract if
>
> > (1) the standard form is reasonably accessible electronically prior to initiation of the transfer at issue;

---

[103] THE TREASURY OF AUSTRALIA, *supra* note 102 at 8.

[104] As to the difference between *Principles* and *Restatements* see Peter A. Alces & Chris Byrne, *Is It Time for the Restatement of Contracts,* Fourth?, 11 DUQ. BUS. L.J. 195, 198–200 (2009).

[105] Robert A. Hillman & Jeffrey J. Rachlinski, *Standard-Form Contracting in the Electronic Age*, 77 N.Y.U. L. REV. 429, 430–31 (2002).

[106] *See* Peter A. Alces, *Guerilla Terms*, 56 EMORY L. J. 1511 (2007); Xavier Gabaix & David Laibson, *Shrouded Attributes, Consumer Myopia, and Information Suppression in Competitive Markets*, 121(2) Q. J. OF ECON. 505 (2006).

[107] AMERICAN LAW INSTITUTE, PRINCIPLES OF THE LAW OF SOFTWARE CONTRACTS 2.02 Overview (P.F.D., 2009).

[108] *Id.* n.30 and accompanying text (citing *ProCD*).

[109] *Id.*

(2) upon initiating the transfer, the transferee has reasonable notice of and access to the standard form before payment or, if there is no payment, before completion of the transfer;

(3) in the case of an electronic transfer of software, the transferee signifies agreement at the end of or adjacent to the electronic standard form, or in the case of a standard form printed on or attached to packaged software or separately wrapped from the software, the transferee does not exercise the opportunity to return the software unopened for a full refund within a reasonable time after the transfer; and

(4) the transferee can store and reproduce the standard form if presented electronically.

(d) Subject to § 1.10 (public policy), § 1.11 (unconscionability), and other invalidating defenses supplied by these Principles or outside law, a standard term is enforceable if reasonably comprehensible.

(e) If a transferee asserts that it did not adopt a standard form as a contract under subsection (b) or asserts a failure of the transferor to comply with subsection (c) or (d), the transferor has the burden of production and persuasion on the issue of compliance with the subsections.[110]

The *Principles* make clear that the provision is evolutionary not revolutionary: "Section 2.02(b) adopts the flexible contract-law approach to contract formation that bases formation on the objective test of whether a reasonable transferor would believe the transferee intends to be bound."[111]

The ALI *Principles* seem to have endorsed the *ProCD* construction of common law contract formation rules. Though the *Principles* attempt to build in more safeguards, or more reliable bases to infer real agreement, the fact remains that forms are, just about by definition, writings that it is irrational to read. So whether the *Principles* or *ProCD* or the other cases on this issue have provided a convincing accommodation of the competing pressure and interests, we can confirm that *ProCD*, by just about every reliable measure, is part of the canon.

"Agreement," formal and substantive, is not the only contract formation requisite. The contract law, for reasons that have often evaded thoughtful commentators,[112] requires that in order for a promise to be enforceable, it must be supported by some *quid pro quo*, consideration. The next set of canonical cases concern the contours of that requirement.

---

[110] *Id.* § 2.02.

[111] *Id.*

[112] *See, e.g.,* CHARLES FRIED, CONTRACT AS PROMISE: A THEORY OF CONTRACTUAL OBLIGATION 28–39 (1981); PATRICK S. ATIYAH, CONSIDERATION IN CONTRACTS (1971).

G. *Mills v. Wyman*[113]

The morality of promising may tell us if we are bound by a promise we make, but it does not tell us if the law determines that we are bound by the promises we make. Whether contract *law* and the morality of promising need to be co-extensive[114] is, of course, a wholly separate question from whether the two are in fact normatively distinct. If they are not co-extensive, it would be interesting, and perhaps worthwhile, to consider why they need not or should not be. But that is a question for another day; right now, for purposes of appreciating contract doctrine through the canon, it is only necessary to consider the source of the revealed dichotomy, normatively tenable or not.

The contract law distinguishes the enforceable promise from the unenforceable promise by reference to the bargain criterion: A promise that is not the product of bargain is not the type of promise the contract law will enforce. So a promise motivated and in fact given wholly and solely in response to moral concerns will not be the product of bargain and so will not be vindicated by the contract law. That is a potentially troubling conclusion, but it is entirely consistent with our conception of bargain and bargain's relationship to the consideration doctrine. *Mills v. Wyman* makes that clear.

Levi Wyman, aged twenty-five, became ill in Hartford, Connecticut. "Poor and in distress,"[115] he was cared for by plaintiff, Daniel Mills. A few days after plaintiff completed providing services to Levi (when Levi died), Seth Wyman, Levi's father, wrote a letter to Mills promising to reimburse him for all expenses incurred on Levi's behalf. Seth in fact did not pay, and Mills brought an action on Seth's promise. Because Levi had reached the age of majority, Seth had no legal obligation to care for him or pay anyone else for doing so. Further, and crucially, Seth made the promise to Mills after the expenses had already been incurred by Mills. So Seth's promise was not supported by consideration, notwithstanding the existence of a potential moral obligation. The moral obligation could have proceeded either from the father–son relationship or from the fact that Seth made a promise to Mills.

The Supreme Judicial Court of Massachusetts has no trouble distinguishing the legal inquiry from the moral calculus:

> General rules of law established for the protection and security of honest and fair-minded men, who may inconsiderately make promises without any equivalent, will sometimes screen men of a different character from engagements which they

[113] Mills v. Wyman, 20 Mass. (3 Pick.) 207 (1825).

[114] *Compare* Seana Valentine Shiffrin, *The Divergence of Contract and Promise*, 120 HARV. L. REV. 708 (2007) *with* Charles Fried, *The Convergence of Contract and Promise*, 120 HARV. L. REV. F. 1 (2007). Professor Shiffrin decries the divergence between the morality of promise and contract doctrine, and Professor Fried wrote his article in response to, and to disagree with, Professor Shiffrin.

[115] *Mills*, 20 Mass. (3 Pick.) at 207.

> are bound in *foro conscientae* to perform. This is a defect inherent in all human systems of legislation. The rule that a mere verbal promise, without any consideration, cannot be enforced by action, is universal in its application, and cannot be departed from to suit particular cases in which a refusal to perform such a promise may be disgraceful.[116]

Wyman, the court concludes, was "willing to have his case appear on record as a strong example of particular injustice sometimes necessarily resulting from the operation of general rules."[117] So whatever the contract bargain rule may otherwise vouchsafe, it does not preclude perpetration of injustice.

The court is able to distinguish cases in which a legal obligation, once having arisen, had been extinguished by operation of law and then revived by the promise of the obligor. So debts barred by statutes of limitations, infancy, and bankruptcy could arise and become enforceable upon the excused obligor's acknowledging them. The reason for that distinction seems to rest more in formality than substance: "[T]here was originally a *quid pro quo*."[118] That is a distinction, but, from a normative perspective, it does not seem to be a distinction that makes a difference. Indeed, we could well imagine that the moral obligation of Seth Wyman might be greater than that of the bankrupt who reaffirms her debt. But the distinction does matter to the contract law, and so the court is constrained to follow the bargain conception down that curious path and absolve Seth of his undertaking. The result and rule is embedded in contract.

Section 86 of the *Second Restatement* preserves that *Mills v. Wyman* result: "A promise made in recognition of a benefit previously received by the promisor from the promisee is binding to the extent necessary to prevent injustice."[119] Illustration 1 to comment a reads, "A gives emergency care to B's adult son while the son is sick and without funds far from home. B subsequently promises to reimburse A for his expenses. The promise is not binding under this Section."[120]

Comment a, construing the black letter, explains that "moral obligations based solely on gratitude or sentiment [are not] sufficient of themselves to support a subsequent promise."[121] It is not immediately obvious that that last sentence of the comment, or the accompanying illustration based on *Mills*, is certainly consistent with the black letter. That is, given the formulation of subsection (1), we would not be surprised had the conclusion of the first illustration been that the promisee could recover. After all, the

---

[116] *Id.* at 209.

[117] *Id.*

[118] *Id.*

[119] Restatement (Second) of Contracts § 86(1) (1981).

[120] *Id.* at cmt. a, illus. 1.

[121] *Id.* at cmt. a.

promisor did make the promise on account "of a benefit previously received" and you might well conclude that had the promisor been present and able to he would have cared for his own son, so the promisee's doing so did confer a benefit on the promisor, at least to the extent of expenditures made on the son's behalf. Would it not then be unjust to let the father-promisor retain the benefit (the comfort and care provided his son during the last days of his son's life) without requiring him to pay the amount he promised to pay? You can, of course, rely on the familiar consideration fiction to deny the promisee recovery—the want of a bargain—but Section 86 is not concerned with bargain; it is concerned with promise, benefit, and justice. The problem, to the extent that there is one, is in subsection 1's inability to capture the calculus the comment asserts it has captured. The other two comments to that subsection similarly find that the promises in issue are not binding. Comment b reads:

> *Rationale.* Although in general a person who has been unjustly enriched at the expense of another is required to make restitution, restitution is denied in many cases in order to protect persons who have had benefits thrust upon them. See Restatement of Restitution §§ 1, 2, 112. In other cases restitution is denied by virtue of rules designed to guard against false claims, stale claims, claims already litigated, and the like. In many such cases a subsequent promise to make restitution removes the reason for the denial of relief, and the policy against unjust enrichment then prevails. Compare Restatement, Second, Agency § 462 on ratification of the acts of a person who officiously purports to act as an agent. Enforcement of the subsequent promise sometimes makes it unnecessary to decide a difficult question as to the limits on quasi-contractual relief.
>
> Many of the cases governed by the rules stated in §§ 82-85 are within the broader principle stated in this Section. But the broader principle is not so firmly established as those rules, and it may not be applied if there is doubt whether the objections to restitution are fully met by the subsequent promise. Facts such as the definite and substantial character of the benefit received, formality in the making of the promise, part performance of the promise, reliance on the promise or the probability of such reliance may be relevant to show that no imposition results from enforcement.[122]

Comment c reads:

> *Promise to correct a mistake.* One who makes a mistake in the conferring of a benefit is commonly entitled to restitution regardless of any promise. But restitution is often denied to avoid prejudice to the recipient of the benefit. Thus restitution of

[122] RESTATEMENT (SECOND) OF CONTRACTS § 86 cmt. b (1981).

> the value of services or of improvements to land or chattels may require a payment which the recipient cannot afford. See Restatement of Restitution §§ 41, 42. Where a subsequent promise shows that the usual protection is not needed in the particular case, restitution is granted to the extent promised.

The line between recovery and no recovery on the subsequent promise is a difficult one to draw, but comment d to Section 86 attempts to draw it along the lines suggested by *Webb v. McGowin*,[123] a case that is often reproduced or noted in the casebooks alongside *Mills*.[124] Illustration 7 formulates the aspect of *Webb* that distinguishes it, or that the commentary asserts distinguishes it, from *Mills*: "A saves B's life in an emergency and is totally and permanently disabled in so doing. One month later B promises to pay A $15 every two weeks for the rest of A's life, and B makes the payments for 8 years until he dies. The promise is binding."[125] Just why is that so?

Insofar as the application of the black letter of subsection 86(1) is concerned: Certainly it would not matter that B's life was saved while the life of the promisor's son in illustration 1 was not saved. And it is not clear why the fact that A was permanently disabled in the course of saving B's life would be determinative. Though the illustration mentions it specifically, it is not immediately clear why it would make a difference that B made the payments for eight years until he died. The language of subsection (1) does not provide us the means to draw the distinction drawn by contrasting illustration 1 and 7. Comment d, which introduces illustration 7, explains that if a benefit is conferred, "[a] subsequent promise . . . may remove doubt as to the reality of the benefit and as to its value, and may negate any danger of imposition or false claim."[126] But was there any doubt as to the reality of the benefit realized by Wyman—care for his dying child—or any danger of imposition or false claim? The *Mills* court does not suggest such doubt or danger and illustration 1 does not introduce any either. Though it might well make sense to require some surrogate for consideration to provide the evidentiary, precautionary, and channeling function of that device if bargain is not in evidence,[127] and though the commentary suggests that

---

[123] *Id.* § 86 comment d states:

> *Emergency services and necessaries.* The law of restitution in the absence of promise severely limits recovery for necessaries furnished to a person under disability and for emergency services. See Restatement of Restitution §§ 113-17, 139. A subsequent promise in such a case may remove doubt as to the reality of the benefit and as to its value, and may negate any danger of imposition or false claim. A positive showing that payment was expected is not then required; an intention to make a gift must be shown to defeat restitution.

[124] *See, e.g.,* Steven J. Burton, Principles of Contract Law 190, 193 (3d ed. 2006); John P. Dawson et al., Contracts: Cases and Comment 211, 216 (9th ed. 2008); Robert W. Hamilton, Alan Scott Rau & Russell J. Weintraub, Cases and Materials on Contracts 314, 320 (2d ed. 1992).

[125] *Id.* § 86 cmt. d, illus. 7.

[126] *Id.* § 86 cmt. d.

[127] Lon L. Fuller, *Consideration and Form*, 41 Colum. L. Rev. 799, 805–06 (1941).

material benefit followed by a promise may provide such protections, the black letter of Section 86, subsection (1) particularly, does not get us there, and, consequently, leaves the doctrine at least malleable if not uncertain.

The commentary does rely on the law of restitution to support the distinction between illustrations 1 and 7. Though restitution is available for benefits conferred it is not available if the benefit was intended to be a gift. But comment d's elaboration does not sufficiently clarify: "A positive showing that payment was expected is not then [when there is a subsequent promise] required; an intention to make a gift must be shown to defeat restitution."[128] We have no reason to believe that Mills, or A in illustration 1, expected payment from Seth Wyman, at least not until the promise was made. But the court also does not consider Mills's intent to make a gift to Wyman. So we could not say that an intention to make a gift was "shown." In any event, that intent would only be pertinent to counter a restitution claim, a claim not based on promise. Mills's action was based on Wyman's promise to him and if that promise would be sufficient to remove doubt in a restitution case, it is not clear why it would not be sufficient to provide the same protection bargain would provide.

The *Restatement* formulation of the *Mills* rule, designed to accommodate the *Webb* and *Webb*-like permutations, demonstrates the lithe nature of the doctrine in (at least) this area of the contract law. It is very easy to state the doctrine in absolute form: "Past consideration is not consideration" or "moral obligation cannot support a promise." But it is more difficult to cast the exceptions, such as "moral obligation with material benefit may support a promise," in doctrinal form without obscuring the bases of distinction on particular facts. Of course, it may be that the distinction is difficult to draw because it is untenable: The consideration doctrine is an historical accident that has lost whatever currency it may ever have had. The problem may be even more fundamental than that, and a theory of contract would need to come to terms with it.

Mills has received a good deal of attention in the secondary literature. Several law review articles have considered the problem of moral obligation's conflict with the consideration requirement.[129] And the case is a staple of the casebooks, which probably attests to the pedagogical challenge of depicting for students the uneasy fit between promise and contract. It may not be an intuitive distinction and so it may be one that, very essentially, reveals a good deal about the normative foundations of contract, whether they be unitary or not.

---

[128] RESTATEMENT (SECOND) OF CONTRACTS § 86 cmt. d (1981).

[129] *See, e.g.,* Jean Fleming Powers, *Rethinking Moral Obligation as a Basis for Contract Recovery,* 54 ME. L. REV. 1 (2002); Kevin Teeven, *A Legal History of Binding Gratuitous Promises at Common Law: Justifiable Reliance and Moral Obligation,* 43 DUQ. L. REV. 11 (2004); Kevin Teeven, *Origins and Scope of the American Moral Obligation Principle,* 46 CLEV. ST. L. REV. 585 (1998); Steve Thel & Edward Yorio, *The Promissory Basis of Past Consideration,* 78 VA. L. REV. 1045 (1992); Geoffrey Watson, *In the Tribunal of Conscience:* Mills v. Wyman *Reconsidered,* 71. TUL. L. REV. 1749 (1997).

H. *Hamer v. Sidway*[130]

Hamer v. Sidway provides the classic statement of the consideration doctrine, and it is, in a very real sense, the statement of consideration to which Cardozo responds in *Allegheny College v. National Chautauqua County Bank*,[131] the canonical case we will consider after *Hamer*. In *Hamer*, an uncle promised his nephew that he would pay the nephew $5,000 if the nephew refrained from drinking, using tobacco, swearing, and playing cards and billiards for money until he turned twenty-one years of age. The nephew did, in fact, refrain from those activities and the uncle acknowledged his indebtedness to the nephew when the nephew turned twenty-one. Rather than turn the money over to the nephew immediately, the uncle held the money, effectively in trust,[132] until the nephew would be "capable of taking care of it."[133] When the uncle died without having disbursed the funds to the nephew, the executor rejected the nephew's claim against the estate for the $5,000. The executor argued that the nephew had given no consideration to support the uncle's promise and so neither the uncle nor his estate was obligated to turn over the money to the nephew. Plaintiff-nephew, it was argued, had suffered no detriment and so given no consideration for the promise. In fact, quite the contrary, the nephew had realized a real benefit from his actions consistent with the promise he made to his uncle. Further, on the other side of the detriment–benefit ledger, the uncle had realized no benefit from the nephew's performance of the promise.

The court dismisses the executor's defense summarily, relying on Exchequer Chamber's 1875 definition of consideration:

> "A valuable consideration in the sense of the law may consist either in some right, interest, profit or benefit accruing to the one party, or some forbearance, detriment, loss or responsibility given, suffered or undertaken by the other." Courts "will not ask whether the thing which forms the consideration does in fact benefit the promisee or a third party, or is of any substantial value to anyone. It is enough that something is promised, done, forborne or suffered by the party to whom the promise is made as consideration for the promise made to him."[134]

---

[130] Hamer v. Sidway, 27 N.E. 256 (N.Y. 1891).

[131] Christopher Eisgruber, *Great Contracts Cases: Teaching Law Through Contracts and Cardozo*, 44 St. Louis L.J. 1511, 1518 (2000).

[132] *Hamer*, 27 N.E. at 258–59 (determining that trust had been formed when Willie allowed his uncle to retain $5,000 on interest, rather than mere debt, which would have been barred by statute of limitations for time elapsed).

[133] *Id.* at 259.

[134] *Id.* at 257.

Because the nephew stopped doing things that he had the legal right to do (and we must assume New York law presented no impediment to the nephew's drinking, using tobacco, swearing, and playing cards and billiards for money until he turned twenty-one years of age), the nephew had given consideration sufficient (by which we *do not* mean "adequate") to support the uncle's promise. Benefit to the promisor just is not part of the consideration calculus. That, of course, makes very good sense: first, because we may presume that the promisor found sufficient benefit to support his own undertaking and, second, because courts would not want to be in the business of assessing benefit. In any event, the court also observes that there seemed to be benefit to the promisor presented by the facts of the case.

Defendant cited cases that had found that natural love and affection and moral obligation were not sufficient as consideration. The court summarily dismisses that argument as inapposite without elaboration. It may be that natural love and affection and moral obligation present valuation issues that a court would be disinclined to pursue, and so such bases could not support a finding of sufficient consideration. But the undertaking of the nephew in *Hamer* and the promise of the uncle were not just a matter of love and affection or the stuff of moral obligation. There was the real surrender of a legal right. So although the parties' undertaking may have been motivated, in whole or part, by love, affection, or moral obligation, the substance of the consideration was the forbearance of the exercise of a legal right, and that may constitute consideration, whatever the motive.

Insofar as promised forbearance or forbearance in fact is recognized in the *Restatements* as consideration,[135] we can find that *Hamer*'s canonical status is supported by those ALI projects. The case has been described as presenting the detriment theory of consideration[136] and that seems true enough to the terms of the opinion. From the vantage of hindsight, we might find as well some intimation of an even more sophisticated conception of consideration in *Hamer*. In its deference to the parties' judgment as to what will be sufficient to bind their bargain, *Hamer* foreshadows later cases that seem more willing to assume than to question bargain. Professor Douglas Baird makes the point that, notwithstanding language of detriment and benefit, *Hamer* was about bargain:

> *Hamer v. Sidway* ... entered the canon to illustrate the idea that a bargained-for promise was enforceable, regardless of what was being promised. It was enough that the bargained-for consideration involved giving up a legal right. That the facts were extreme and unusual did not matter at all. Indeed, it underscored the idea

---

[135] RESTATEMENT (SECOND) OF CONTRACTS §§ 32 illus. 4, 75, 90 cmt. a (1981); RESTATEMENT (FIRST) OF CONTRACTS §§ 75-77, 90 (1932).

[136] Stewart Sterk, *The New York Court of Appeals: 150 Years of Leading Opinions*, 48 SYRACUSE L. REV. 1391, 1396–97 (1998).

> that a principle was at work that lived apart from the particular facts of a case. It emphasized that any bargain, even over such a matter as teenage smoking and drinking, was enforceable so long as there was in fact a bargain.[137]

Another New York decision, also certainly part of the canon, captures the evolution well.

I. *Allegheny College v. National Chautauqua County Bank*[138]

Certainly one of the more famous contract opinions is that of New York State Court of Appeals Judge Benjamin Cardozo in *Allegheny College v. National Chautauqua County Bank*, a decision that says less about consideration and promissory estoppel specifically than it does about the nature of the enforceable obligation more generally. The facts are sufficiently supple to afford the judge every opportunity to emphasize what he would and to discover an obligation where lesser jurists would not have been able to do so. Cardozo finds a deal he wants to enforce and would not let a little thing like the absence of consideration stand in the way. Even though the promissory estoppel surrogate for consideration was not available on the facts, that would not preclude creative reference to promissory estoppel to find sufficient consideration, or something like it.

Defendant bank was the executor of the estate of Mary Yates Johnston, who had pledged a charitable contribution to Allegheny College in the amount of $5,000, "[i]n consideration of my interest in Christian education, and in consideration of others subscribing."[139] On the reverse side of that writing was a memorandum to the effect that the gift would "be known as the Mary Yates Johnston memorial fund."[140] The original pledge was executed in 1921 and a first payment in the amount of $1,000 was made during the life of the donor. Then, in 1923, the donor repudiated the gift. After her death, the college brought an action against the executor of the donor's estate.

At the outset, Judge Cardozo notes that charitable subscriptions are as enforceable as, but no more enforceable than, noncharitable promises. He also observes that the New York courts had been able to find consideration in charitable subscription cases even if, in noncharitable cases, the same asserted consideration would not have passed muster.[141] So at the very beginning of his analysis, we are not sure whether Cardozo will

---

[137] Douglas G. Baird, *Reconstructing Contracts:* Hamer v. Sidway, *in* CONTRACTS STORIES 160, 165 (Douglas G. Baird ed., 2007).

[138] Allegheny Coll. v. Nat'l Chautauqua County Bank, 159 N.E. 173 (N.Y. 1927).

[139] *Id.* at 174.

[140] *Id.*

[141] Judge Kellogg disagreed with that reading of precedent in his dissent. *Id.* at 177 (Kellogg, J., dissenting).

be construing the special New York rule for charitable subscriptions or saying something more generally about the consideration requirement.

The opinion notes a then-recent adjustment of the certain consideration rule: promissory estoppel. Although Judge Cardozo is not prepared to say that promissory estoppel has been adopted by the New York courts for contract generally, he does conclude that the doctrine had certainly become part of the law governing charitable subscriptions. From that premise, then, the particular promise in *Allegheny College* would be enforceable if there were consideration supporting it and that consideration could be found "as qualified by the doctrine of promissory estoppel."[142] From there, it is not far to a conception of the consideration requisite in terms of public policy:

> Judges have been affected by the thought that "defenses of that character" [want of consideration] are "breaches of faith towards the public, and especially towards those engaged in the same enterprise, and an unwarrantable disappointment of the reasonable expectations of those interested." . . . Decisions which have stood so long, and which are supported by so many considerations of public policy and reason, will not be overruled to save the symmetry of a concept which itself came into our law, not so much from any reasoned conviction of its justice, as from historical accidents of practice and procedure.[143]

Because there was a *quid pro quo* for the decedent's promise, the college's engagement to denominate the scholarship as she wished, that promise was supported by consideration and so enforceable.

The dissent sees the facts differently and perhaps even affords them a more plausible construction. Though the testator may have bargained for a particular denomination of the scholarship, if she did so, she was bargaining for a unilateral contract that could only have become enforceable, incongruously, upon her death. Because her death would terminate her offer, the contract could not have been formed in the way Cardozo conceived it. But we get the sense that the dissenting judges'[144] reservations were not of substantial concern for Cardozo.

What matters for Cardozo, if we may presume, is finding just enough obligation to support the testator's promise. That just enough may have been really no obligation at all. The hint is in the judge's reference to decisions upholding charitable subscriptions that "will not be overruled to save the symmetry of a concept which itself came into our law, not so much from any reasoned conviction of its justice, as from historical accidents of practice and procedure." Consideration is an "historical accident," and Cardozo's opinion

---

[142] *Id.* at 175.

[143] *Id.*

[144] *Id.* at 179 (Kellogg, J., dissenting).

in *Allegheny* is canonical because it captures the evanescent nature of consideration, which emerges from *Allegheny* as more a state of mind than anything else. It is difficult to conclude that Judges Kellogg and Andrews do not have law and logic on their side; and it is just as irrefutable that Cardozo has good sense on his.

Insofar as *Allegheny* says something about the nature of contractual obligation generally, and does so in a case in which both consideration and promissory estoppel issues were raised, the decision is crucial to our understanding of contract. That is not to say other decisions over the years have failed to come to the same conclusion, but it is to recognize the unique statement Judge Cardozo makes in *Allegheny* and the significance of that statement to the contract law. Just as there are good reasons to find the charitable obligation enforceable, there are equally good reasons to find all other serious undertakings enforceable. Consideration, and promissory estoppel for that matter, can help us determine what obligations the law should enforce, but those doctrines should not get in the way of enforcement when enforcement is appropriate. *Allegheny* is canonical because it tests our understanding of promise enforceability: Why do we enforce some promises and not others? What is the significance of a *quid pro quo*? What are the limits of a consideration or promissory estoppel doctrine?

Further confirmation of *Allegheny*'s canonical status is found in the case's treatment in Allan Farnsworth's leading treatise.[145] Professor Farnsworth notes that *Allegheny* was, at least in part, responsible for our appreciating that, in the context of charitable subscriptions, promissory estoppel and consideration are equivalent. The basis of enforcement, in fact, is public policy, and *Allegheny* just provides a gloss on consideration and promissory estoppel in light of public policy.[146] So Cardozo's extension of his reasoning in dictum beyond charitable subscriptions to public policy generally reveals more about the fabric of consideration and promissory estoppel than reference to charitable subscriptions alone would have. If *Allegheny* were only about charitable subscriptions, it would not have been canonical. It is part of the canon because of the challenge it presents to the consideration and promissory estoppel bases of enforcement generally. The case tells us more about why we enforce promises (and sometimes refuse to enforce them) when we rely on consideration and promissory estoppel than do most of the cases that concern more familiar bargains.

Although the opinion may be more criticized than lauded, it is clear that Cardozo's analysis has hit a nerve; some have misunderstood him[147] and others have just agreed with

[145] *See* FARNSWORTH, *supra* note 11, at § 2.19.

[146] *See* Alfred S. Konefsky, *How to Read, or at Least Not Misread, Cardozo in the* Allegheny College *Case*, 36 BUFF. L. REV. 645 (1988); Mike Townsend, *Cardozo's* Allegheny College *Opinion: A Case Study of Law as Art*, 33 HOUS. L. REV. 1103 (1996).

[147] Corbin takes a different view of *Allegheny* by contending the decision was one furthering the doctrine of promissory estoppel. Corbin asserts that Cardozo's decision "positively advanced the stature of promissory estoppel in American law but theoretically limited it as a 'substitute for consideration' and 'an

Kellogg and Andrews instead.[148] Most importantly, though, the case has not been ignored, and continues to claim a position among those decisions that have molded our understanding of contract, and that is enough to confirm canonical status. Another Cardozo opinion that has also achieved canonical status continues the evolution.

J. *Wood v. Lucy, Lady Duff Gordon*[149]

Because the consideration requirement entails a *quid pro quo* there must be some exchange contemplated by the parties' agreement. The promise alone to do or not do something will not suffice. Indeed, it is that exchange requirement that distinguishes contract from promise. A promise only becomes legally enforceable as a contract if the promise is of exchange. At least arguably, the law should be concerned with all promises that are serious, all promises to which the parties attach significance. One of the mysteries of the consideration doctrine, though, is that it does not distinguish the enforceable from the unenforceable promise by direct reference to the promise's significance to the promisor and promisee; instead, the consideration basis to distinguish enforceable from unenforceable promises focuses on the exchange requisite. My gratuitous promise to deliver a life-saving drug to you tomorrow morning is not enforceable, for want of consideration; but my promise to deliver a package of mints in exchange for 25 cents is enforceable. So the significance of promise is not determinative; the exchange is. What then to make of the significant promise that is not the subject of an exchange? Promissory estoppel has supplied one response,[150] but within the contract doctrine itself there are means to enforce the serious promise even if exchange is not manifest: The inference of exchange will do.

At least the inference of exchange will do if the jurist drawing the inference is Benjamin Cardozo. His opinion in *Wood v. Lucy, Lady Duff Gordon*[151] is a (perhaps too) rare triumph of substance over form and is certainly of canonical stature. The opinion is brief. Defendant, Lucy, granted plaintiff the exclusive right, subject to defendant's approval, to endorse the designs of others, much as a hip hop star or athlete would lend his or her

---

equivalent of consideration.'" Eric Mills Holmes, Corbin on Contracts § 8-12 (Joseph M. Perillo ed., 3d ed. 1996).

[148] *See* Curtis Bridgeman, Alleghany College *Revisited: Cardozo, Consideration, and Formalism in Context*, 39 U.C. Davis L. Rev. 149, 174–75 (2005) (noting Justice Kellogg's disagreement with Cardozo's perceived attempt to turn gift into trade, and Kellogg's view that exchange would have required acceptance through performance, not return promise).

[149] Wood v. Lucy, Lady Duff Gordon, 118 N.E. 214 (N.Y. 1917).

[150] Daniel A. Farber & John H. Matheson, *Beyond Promissory Estoppel: Contract Law and the "Invisible Handshake,"* 52 U. Chi. L. Rev. 903 (1985); Robert E. Scott, Hoffman v. Red Owl Stores *and the Myth of Precontractual Reliance*, 68 Ohio St. L.J. 71 (2007); Edward Yorio & Steve Thel, *The Promissory Basis of Section 90*, 101 Yale L.J. 111 (1991).

[151] *Wood*, 118 N.E. 214.

name to a product to increase its marketability. Though the right granted to Wood had been exclusive, Lucy endorsed products other than those identified by Wood and did not pay to him any portion of the fee she received. Lucy did not deny having made the exclusive promise to Wood, but she maintained that the promise was unenforceable because Wood had given no *quid pro quo*, had made no promise to her in exchange.

Cardozo recognizes the business context of the agreement and takes note as well of the exclusive nature of the arrangement: "The defendant gave an exclusive privilege. She was to have no right for at least a year to place her own indorsements or market her own designs except through the agency of the plaintiff. The acceptance of the exclusive agency was an assumption of its duties."[152] In Cardozo's estimation, common sense compels the conclusion that plaintiff had indeed given something in exchange for defendant's promise. So though it may have been true that plaintiff's promise was not express, it was certainly implicit. An implied promise would suffice. Once the existence of the implied promise was confirmed, the terms of the promise were clear: "His promise to pay the defendant one-half of the profits and revenues resulting from the exclusive agency and to render accounts monthly was a promise to use reasonable efforts to bring profits and revenues into existence."[153]

It may be that the *Wood* opinion is most famous for a turn of phrase that Cardozo borrowed from another jurist: "A promise may be lacking, and yet the whole writing may be 'instinct with an obligation,' imperfectly expressed .... If that is so, there is a contract."[154] So the consideration requirement, then, is no more than a requirement that the parties share reciprocal obligations and courts may infer such obligations notwithstanding the parties' failure to specify them sufficiently.

The good sense of *Wood* is incorporated quite directly in both *Restatements*. Section 84(f) of the *First Restatement* provides that:

> Consideration is not insufficient because of the fact
>
> ....
>
> (f) that it is a promise, performance of which is conditional on either a future or past event, if when the promise is made there is any possibility, or there would seem to a reasonable man in the position of the promisor to be any possibility, that the promise can be performed only by some act or forbearance which would be sufficient consideration.[155]

---

[152] *Id.* at 214.

[153] *Id.* at 215.

[154] *Id.* at 214 (citing McCall Co. v. Wright, 117 N.Y.S. 775, 779 (N.Y. App. Div. 1909) (Scott, J.)); *see* Robert A. Hillman, *Instinct with an Obligation and the Normative Ambiguity of Rhetorical Power*, 56 OHIO ST. L. J. 755 (1995).

[155] RESTATEMENT (FIRST) OF CONTRACTS § 84(f) (1932).

Because Wood could only have performed his promise to Lucy—"his promise to account for profits [and] take out copyrights"[156]—by first marketing her designs and affixing her endorsement, that "promise [could] be performed only by some act . . . which would be sufficient consideration." But the language of the *First Restatement* provision is not as accessible as it might be, and the *Second Restatement* is not much less obscure. Section 77 of the *Second Restatement* indirectly invokes *Wood* in the most commercially significant context, exclusive dealing contracts within the scope of UCC Article 2.

Section 2-306 of the Code, in two subsections, concerns the consideration calculus treated in *Wood*.[157] The provision governs requirements contracts, output contracts, and exclusive dealing. In the case of output and requirements arrangements, the Code rule infers a sufficient reciprocal undertaking from the statutory requirement that the contracting parties act in "good faith."[158] So a contract that measures the subject matter quantity in terms of the buyer's requirements or the seller's needs is sufficiently definite, *i.e.,* the counterparty's undertaking determinable, because the Code measures the output or requirement quantity "as may occur in good faith."[159] Output and requirements contracts are treated in the first subsection of Section 2-306 and follow the *Wood* rule.

Subsection 2-306(2) concerns specifically "exclusive dealing" arrangements and more directly invokes the *Wood* analysis. That subsection establishes the *quid pro quo* basis to enforce from the statutory prescription that exclusive dealing necessarily contemplates that the "seller [will] use best efforts to supply the goods and . . . the buyer [will] use best efforts to promote their sale."[160] The exclusive dealing arrangement contemplated is a retailer's resale of goods acquired from a seller with whom the buyer has an exclusive dealing arrangement. It is the "best efforts" proviso of subsection 2-306(2) that does the work of "good faith" in subsection 2-306(1) requirements and output contracts. Of course, most such open quantity contracts will fall within the scope of both subsections. It is not immediately clear what would distinguish the "best efforts" and "good faith" requisites. For all intents and purposes, they seem to be two iterations of the same idea.

It is Section 2-306 of the Code, then, that gives substance to the *Second Restatement*'s invocation of the *Wood* rule. Comment d to *Second Restatement* Section 77, "[i]mplied limitations on promisor's choice," explains that a limitation on the promisor's freedom sufficient to satisfy the consideration requirement may be found either implicitly in the

---

[156] *Wood,* 118 N.E. at 215.

[157] Subsection 2 of § 2-306 deals most directly with the exclusive dealing contract central to *Wood,* providing that "[a] lawful agreement by either the seller or the buyer for exclusive dealing in the kind of goods concerned imposes unless otherwise agreed an obligation by the seller to use best efforts to supply the goods and by the buyer to use best efforts to promote their sale." U.C.C. § 2-306(2) (2002).

[158] *Id.* § 2-306(1). Good faith is defined as "honesty in fact and the observance of reasonable commercial standards of fair dealing." *Id.* § 2-103(j).

[159] *Id.* § 2-306(1).

[160] *Id.* § 2-306(2).

terms of the promise or by operation of the governing law.[161] Recall that a promise the promisor may avoid at whim is not the promise that can constitute consideration; the promise must circumscribe the promisor's options.[162] Insofar as Section 2-306 requires that a buyer or seller in an output or requirements contract act in good faith, or in an exclusive dealing arrangement use best efforts, the promise to buy or sell is so circumscribed. The court has an objective and external measure to appraise the buyer's or seller's performance. The buyer or seller could not walk away from the deal without also, perhaps, having broken the promise.

In *Wood*, Judge Cardozo finds the limitation on the promisor's options implicit in the terms of the promise itself, not from the operation of any apposite statutory law. So the Cardozo decision alone would support the result that UCC Section 2-306 now mandates in all exclusive dealing arrangements. In the course of making sense of the parties' commercial undertaking in *Wood*, Cardozo makes more sense of the nature of the consideration requirement.

Wood has been confirmed in the secondary literature[163] as well as in cases from other common law jurisdictions.[164] The rule is not subject to question, and all that would seem to be in issue on particular facts would be the court's ability to find an objective basis to measure the putative promisor's undertaking. A 1937 decision of a Manitoba court illustrates just the type of exclusive dealing arrangement that will not pass muster, *Wood* notwithstanding. In *Tobias v. Dick & T. Eaton Co.*, the agreement purported to grant Tobias "an exclusive selling agency."[165] Though the parties had proceeded through the litigation on the assumption that they were party to a contract, the court finds that there was in fact no contract at all.[166] Dick granted Tobias the exclusive right to sell Dick's machines, but Tobias had never undertaken to sell any of them or even to use his best

---

[161] RESTATEMENT (SECOND) OF CONTRACTS § 77 cmt. d (1981).

[162] *Id.* § 77.

[163] *See, e.g.*, 2-5 JOHN EDWARD MURRAY, CORBIN ON CONTRACTS § 5-27 (2009); 2–6 JOHN EDWARD MURRAY, CORBIN ON CONTRACTS § 6.5 (2009); 1–3 JOHN EDWARD MURRAY, MURRAY ON CONTRACTS § 58 (2001); JOSEPH M. PERILLO & JOHN D. CALAMARI, CALAMARI AND PERILLO ON CONTRACTS § 4.12 (6th ed. 2009); 1 SAMUEL WILLISTON & RICHARD A. LORD, A TREATISE ON THE LAW OF CONTRACTS § 48.3 (4th ed. 2009); Monroe Freedman, *Cardozo's Opinion in Lady Lucy's Case: "Formative Unconscionability," Impracticality, and Judicial Abuse*, 28 PACE L. REV. 395 (2008); Victor Goldberg, *Desperately Seeking Consideration: The Unfortunate Impact of U.C.C. Section 2-306 on Contract Interpretation*, 68 OHIO ST. L. J. 103 (2007); Hillman, *supra* note 154.

[164] Meehan v. Jones (1982) 149 C.L.R. 571 (Austl.) (In contract for sale of land with "subject to finance" clause, purchaser must make reasonable efforts to find financing and must act honestly in deciding whether or not financing on offer is satisfactory.); Tobias v. Dick & T. Eaton Co., [1937] 4 D.L.R. 546 (Man. K.B.) (Agreement which conferred on buyer exclusive right to sell was not binding on seller when buyer had not undertaken any obligation to sell buyer's goods; reaches opposite result on facts but *Wood* principle applied).

[165] Tobias v. Dick & T. Eaton Co., [1937] 4 D.L.R. 546 (Man. K.B.).

[166] *Id.* at 547.

efforts to try to effect sales.[167] Insofar as Dick surrendered all control over the machines upon their sale to Tobias, no agency relationship was created between them.[168] What *Wood* supplied that is lacking from *Tobias* is any ancillary undertaking (*i.e.,* to account) upon which the court could infer Tobias's promise to sell the machines on Dick's behalf. Now whether a Cardozo could have found such an ancillary undertaking on the *Tobias* facts may be subject to some speculation, but it is clear that if the court finds the factual foundation for such an undertaking lacking, there is no consideration and so no contract. Whatever distinction we might draw between *Wood* and *Tobias*, then, reveals something about the tension the consideration requirement would resolve in contract.

The next canonical case is treated at two junctures in this book. First, we consider its fit with the *quid pro quo* requirement; we return to the case again in Chapter Seven, to appreciate its significance with regard to enforcement issues.

K. *Hoffman v. Red Owl Stores, Inc.*[169]

Joseph Hoffman and his wife brought an action against Red Owl stores alleging that an agent of Red Owl, one Lukowitz, "represented to and agreed with plaintiffs that Red Owl would build a store in Clinton and stock it with merchandise for Hoffman to operate," in return for plaintiffs' investment of $18,000. Red Owl responded that there was no promise made to plaintiffs. The court clearly believes that the facts present a question of promissory estoppel, a doctrine not yet recognized in Wisconsin at the time of the litigation, and begins its analysis by reproducing the *First Restatement*'s Section 90 iteration of the doctrine: "A promise which the promisor should reasonably expect to induce action or forbearance of a definite and substantial character on the part of the promisee and which does induce such action or forbearance is binding if injustice can be avoided only by enforcement of the promise."[170]

The court concludes (or at least *assumes* for purposes of analysis) that Red Owl had made a promise that Red Owl should have reasonably expected would induce reliance of a definite and substantial character on the part of Hoffman and that Hoffman had in fact so relied: "The record here discloses a number of promises and assurances given to Hoffman by [Red Owl's agent] upon which plaintiffs relied and acted upon to their

---

[167] *Id.*

[168] *Id.*

[169] Hoffman v. Red Owl Stores, Inc., 133 N.W.2d 267 (Wis. 1965).

[170] RESTATEMENT (FIRST) OF CONTRACTS § 90 (1932).

detriment."[171] The court believes it is confronting the promissory estoppel doctrine head on,[172] and cites cases that had done so before it.[173]

The decision, then, is not the source of the doctrine, but it is *a* (not *the sole*) canonical statement of it. The court is aware that the promise made by Red Owl was not dispositive of the full range of issues that might need to be resolved were the parties to negotiate a fully integrated agreement:

> If promissory estoppel were to be limited to only those situations where the promise giving rise to the cause of action must be so definite with respect to all details that a contract would result were the promise supported by consideration, then the defendants' instant promises to Hoffman would not meet this test.[174]

The promissory estoppel doctrine, as the court understands and applies it, does not provide all of the terms of the parties' agreement; it just provides for enforcement "if injustice can only be avoided by enforcement." Interestingly, the court does not construe promissory estoppel as a substitute for consideration: "We deem it a mistake to regard an action grounded on promissory estoppel as the equivalent of a breach of contract action."[175]

Left unresolved after *Hoffman* was whether recovery based on promissory estoppel is contract recovery. Referring specifically to the promissory estoppel doctrine as applied in *Hoffman*, Professors Calamari and Perillo very clearly conclude that it was not even a species of contract: "The doctrine is the basis of a cause of action that is not contract, tort, or quasi-contract."[176] Now that academic conclusion may seem to be of no more than, well, academic interest, but insofar as it makes an assertion about the nature of doctrine, perhaps contract doctrine, it does have some resonance with the focus of this book's inquiry. If we decide that promissory estoppel is not contract, it must not be contract for some reason that is fundamental to contract. As review of *Hoffman* reveals, the promissory estoppel doctrine framed in that case may be satisfied with a less certain promise than contract would require to satisfy the consideration requirement. The Hoffmans were able to enforce a promise that would not, or so it would seem, be sufficiently certain to support contract. The court recognizes that and confronts the discontinuity:

> This poses the question of whether the promise necessary to sustain a cause of action for promissory estoppel must embrace all essential details of a proposed

[171] *Hoffman*, 133 N.W.2d at 274.

[172] *Id.* at 273.

[173] *Id.* at 274 (citing, among other cases, Drennan v. Star Paving Co., 333 P.2d 757 (Cal. 1958), Chrysler Corp. v. Quimby, 144 A.2d 123 (Del. 1958), and Northwestern Engineering Co. v. Ellerman, 10 N.W.2d 879 (S.D. 1948)).

[174] *Id.* at 275.

[175] *Id.* at 275.

[176] Perillo & Calamari, *supra* note 163, at 232 n.42 (6th ed. 2009).

> transaction between promisor and promisee so as to be the equivalent of an offer that would result in a binding contract between the parties if the promisee were to accept the same. . . . If promissory estoppel were to be limited to only those situations where the promise giving rise to the cause of action must be so definite with respect to all details that a contract would result were the promise supported by consideration, then the defendants' instant promises would not meet this test.[177]

The court concludes that the promissory estoppel action would not be "the equivalent of a breach of contract action."[178] The focus of Section 90, the court reasons, was the avoidance of injustice, and constructions of the promise requisite must give way to conceptions of "justice."

Hoffman has been read as a case more about the enforceability of promises made in the course of preliminary negotiations than a case about the contours of the promissory estoppel doctrine.[179] It clearly does present, if not so thoroughly illuminate, the questions surrounding liability arising in the course of preliminary negotiations. There has also been a relatively recent and rich literature concerning the substance of the doctrine. Is reliance necessary at all?[180] Or is a "serious promise"[181] enough? Does the doctrine matter all that much at all?[182] This is not the place to recount the contours of that dialog or to offer empirical conclusions about the doctrine's viability in the courts. For present purposes, identifying the contract canon, it suffices to note the vibrancy of the debate as evidence of the doctrine's vitality.

Promissory estoppel is clearly doctrine contract theorists need to explain. The idea that a promise may be enforced with or without some modicum of reliance and certainly *without* consideration helps us make sense of, or at least supports our positing, a normative basis of contract. Promissory estoppel, as an enforcement mechanism operating without the consideration formality, presents starkly the normative challenge: *Why* do we enforce some promises but not others? The empirical conclusions of those who have

---

[177] *Hoffman*, 133 N.W.2d at 275.

[178] *Id.*

[179] *See* Joel M. Ngugi, *Promissory Estoppel: The Life History of An Ideal Legal Transplant*, 41 U. RICH. L. REV. 425 (2007); Jean Fleming Powers, *Promissory Estoppel and Wagging the Dog*, 59 ARK. L. REV. 841 (2007); Kevin M. Teeven, *A History of Promissory Estoppel: Growth in the Face of Doctrinal Resistance*, 72 TENN. L. REV. 1111 (2005).

[180] Juliet P. Kostritsky, *The Rise and Fall of Promissory Estoppel Or Is Promissory Estoppel Really as Unsuccessful As Scholars Say It Is: A New Look at the Data*, 37 WAKE FOREST L. REV. 531, 537 n.32 (2002).

[181] Farber & Matheson, *supra* note 150.

[182] Juliet P. Kostritsky, *Uncertainty, Reliance, Preliminary Negotiations and the Holdup Problem*, 61 SMU L. REV. 1377 (2008); Hillman, *supra* note 154.

tracked the cases, though, certainly matter.[183] But it may be at least premature to conclude that the doctrine does not matter, or matters less because the cases do not take sufficient advantage of it.[184] Insofar as the doctrine takes up so much space in the *Restatements* and the casebooks (and time in most first-year contracts courses), we can easily conclude that promissory estoppel, as described if not strictly applied in cases such as *Hoffman*, informs our understanding of what contract would be without it. There must be a gap to which the doctrine responds; promissory estoppel must accomplish something that contract could not accomplish without it. Promissory estoppel completes, or at least complements, contract.

L. *Dickinson v. Dodds*[185]

In the ballet that is contract formation, there needs to be a certain coincidence of communication and meaning that provides the basis to discern an intent to be bound. *Dickinson v. Dodds* is in important ways opaque and makes more sense in terms of what we have decided that it says than in the actual terms of the court's opinion. The case is canonical because it demonstrates well the significance of the coincidence between offer and acceptance, and makes clear that a promise to keep an offer open may be a contract in its own right, indeed, *must* be a contract in its own right if it is to be enforceable.

On June 10, Dodds signed and delivered to Dickinson a signed writing pursuant to which Dodds offered to sell to Dickinson certain real property described, the "offer to be left over" until 9:00 a.m. two days later, June 12.[186] Though Dickinson apparently formed the intention to accept the offer sometime during the day of the tenth of June, he did not actually take a written acceptance to Dodds until later that day, after he learned "that Dodds had been offering or agreeing to sell the property to"[187] a third party. As it turned out, Dickinson had left the acceptance with Dodds's mother-in-law, who neglected to give it to Dodds.[188] Dickinson's agent also found Dodds at the railway station at 7:00 a.m. Friday, June 12, and gave Dodds a copy of the acceptance.[189] Dodds told the agent that the

---

[183] *See* Sidney W. DeLong, *The New Requirement of Enforcement Reliance in Commercial Promissory Estoppel: Section 90 as Catch-22*, 1997 WIS. L. REV. 943 (1997); Robert A. Hillman, *Questioning the "New Consensus" on Promissory Estoppel: An Empirical and Theoretical Study*, 98 COLUM. L. REV. 580 (1998); Kostritsky, *supra* note 182.

[184] *See* DeLong, *supra* note 183; Hillman, *supra* note 183; Kostritsky, *supra* note 182.

[185] Dickinson v. Dodds, [1876] 2 Ch.D. 463 (U.K.).

[186] *Id.*

[187] *Id.* at 464.

[188] *Id.*

[189] *Id.*

acceptance was tendered too late; Dodds had already accepted another offer to buy the property.[190]

Was the offer still open at the time Dickinson tried to accept it? There are two ways that it might remain open, notwithstanding Dodds's acceptance of the third party's offer: First, by representing that the offer to Dickinson would remain open until June 12, Dodds may have been precluded from terminating the offer any time before then. Alternatively, the offer might be deemed open to Dickinson, notwithstanding Dodds's commitment to the third party because Dodds had not actually terminated the offer to Dickinson. That is, the fact that Dickinson heard that Dodds was entertaining other prospects would not foreclose Dickinson's right to accept (or Dodds's obligation to honor an acceptance received before the offer was clearly and explicitly terminated, assuming that Dodds retained the right to terminate the offer after representing that it would be held open until June 12).

So long as we recognize that contract resides in the world of objective indicia, it would seem that Dodds's having formed the intent to sell to someone other than Dickinson could not alone terminate the offer and Dickinson's power to accept it. That, and a sense of equity, informs the decision of Judge Bacon to conclude that Dickinson should prevail.[191] But the other two judges, James and Mellish, focus on what we have come to understand as the option contract: the contract to keep an offer open, which, as any contract, must be supported by consideration in order to be enforceable.[192] Because there was no consideration supporting Dodds's undertaking to leave the offer open until June 12, that undertaking was not enforceable.[193] Further, when Dickinson "heard" that Dodds had made plans to sell the property to a third party, that knowledge effectively terminated the offer and with it Dickinson's power to accept and impose contract liability on Dodds.[194] Once Dickinson had reason to know that Dodds no longer considered the offer open, Dickinson could not be of one mind with Dodds; there could be no meeting of the minds that would support contract.

So *Dickinson v. Dodds* is an important case, a canonical case. It reinforces what we know about the coincidence of intent requisite to formation of a contract, and it makes clear that a promise to keep an offer open, just like any other promise, must be supported by consideration in order to be enforceable. But it may also be canonical because it challenges the limits of contract: How perfect must the offer–acceptance symmetry be? Is a promise to hold an offer open indistinguishable from other promises reliant on

---

[190] *Id.*

[191] *Id.* at 468–69.

[192] *Id.* at 471–76.

[193] *Id.* at 474.

[194] *Id.*

consideration in order to be enforceable? The *Restatement* gloss on *Dickinson* demonstrates the flexibility of the opinion that ensures its canonical status.

The *First Restatement*, in somewhat curious terms, provides that:

> [W]here an offer is for the sale of an interest in land or in other things, if the offeror, after making the offer, sells or contracts to sell the interest to another person, and the offeree acquires reliable information of that fact, before he has exercised his power of creating a contract by acceptance of the offer, the offer is revoked.[195]

Although it is not clear why the prefatory language is necessary ("for the sale of an interest in land or in other things"), the sense of the provision is not difficult to grasp: An offer is terminated when revoked, and the offeree can learn that it has been revoked other than by a direct communication from the offeror. Sections 42 and 43 of the *Second Restatement* reiterate that.[196]

It is the other part of *Dickinson*, the part about so-called option contracts, that has met more resistance as contract has evolved. Given the curious nature of the consideration requirement—it seems to divorce the enforceability of promising from the morality of promising—there is good reason to expect that the requirement would be subject to evaluation as it operates in different contexts throughout contract. That is, there seems to be a pervasive and persistent sense that if we could only understand the *why* of consideration we could better make sense of *how* it works, or should work. Well-worn legal realistic tendencies militate in favor of the doctrine's reach not exceeding its grasp. So though we may acknowledge, as a general matter, that the primary contract needs to be supported by consideration, there may be less reason to insist that the requirement be satisfied if the promise is subordinate, such as the promise to keep an offer open.

There is no question that had Dickinson provided some consideration supporting Dodds's undertaking to hold the offer open until June 12 at 9:00 a.m. Dickinson's acceptance would have been timely and would have bound Dodds to the deal. Just as clearly, had Dodds merely made the offer to Dickinson and said nothing about its duration, Dodds would have been free to terminate the offer at-will and make a deal with any third party, or make no deal at all. An offer may be accepted until the offer terminates, and the offeror is the master of the offer and its termination, unless the offer is supported by consideration.

If Dodds meant to maintain control of the offer, and the power to terminate it at-will, what was the point of representing to Dickinson that it would be held open until 9:00 a.m. on June 12? Certainly the only reason Dickinson would have bargained for such a

---

[195] Restatement (First) of Contracts § 42 (1932).

[196] Restatement (Second) of Contracts §§ 42, 43 (1981).

representation was because he wanted Dodds's assurance that the offer would be held open. It would seem to elevate form over substance to recognize the offeree's interest in the offer's being held open and then to rely on the consideration doctrine to undermine that very expectation, an expectation reinforced by the form of the offer (remembering that the offeror is the master of the offer).

Section 42 of the *Second Restatement* confirms that the general rule, or predisposition, has not changed since *Dickinson v. Dodds*, and the apposite comment explains:

> [T]he ordinary offer is revocable even though it expressly states the contrary, because of the doctrine that an informal agreement is binding as a bargain only if supported by consideration. *Inroads have been made on that doctrine by statute and by rules giving effect to nominal consideration and to action in reliance on a promise.*[197]

The type of statute to which the comment refers is Section 2-205 of the UCC, which provides that an offer made by a merchant buyer or seller of goods is "not revocable, for lack of consideration,"[198] for the time stated or a reasonable time. The offer must contain a sufficient assurance that it will be held open and must be in a signed writing.

Similarly, even though the general rule is that nominal consideration is not consideration,[199] Section 87 of the *Second Restatement*, "Option Contracts," provides an exception to that general rule in the case of irrevocable offers:

> A nominal consideration is regularly held sufficient to support a short-time option proposing an exchange on fair terms. The fact that the option is an appropriate preliminary step in the conclusion of a socially useful transaction provides a sufficient substantive basis for enforcement, and a signed writing taking a form appropriate to a bargain satisfies the desiderata of form.[200]

So though nominal consideration will not support a contract, it can support a promise to keep an offer open, so long as the form of bargain is respected. Indeed, it is enough that the nominal consideration be recited; it need not actually be exchanged: "the option agreement is not invalidated by proof that the recited consideration was not in fact given."[201]

---

[197] *Id.* § 42 cmt. a (emphasis added).

[198] UCC § 2-205 (2002).

[199] Restatement (Second) of Contracts § 71 cmt. b (1981).

[200] *Id.* § 87 cmt. b.

[201] *Id.* § 87 cmt. c.

Because the law of offer and acceptance is so fundamental to the law of contract, it is not surprising that the incidents of the doctrine in this area have been fixed for some time. *Dickinson v. Dodds* is venerable English authority that has resonated through the contract law of other common law countries.[202]

[202] *See* Davison v. Vickery's Motors (1925) 37 C.L.R. 1 (Austl.) (revocation effective when offeror "cancel[led]" offer rather than "withdr[e]w" because offeree had clear understanding to not continue contract); Davidson v. Norstrant, [1921] 61 S.C.R. 493 (Can.) (no implied revocation when offeror sold portion of land of which he had offered one-half for sale to offeree); Cravide v. Nielsen, [1998] 55 O.T.C. 74 (Ont. Trial Ct.) (no constructive revocation on facts similar to *Dickinson* with exception that offeree was not aware that property had already been sold at time of acceptance).

4

THEORY OF CONTRACT FORMATION

CONTRACT PROVIDES THE means for an individual to assume obligation, to project himself into the future and thereby increase his present value. So long as you may rely on the enforceability of my undertaking with regard to the future, I may capture some of the value created by the obligation. So I want to be able to obligate myself; only then will I realize greater value than the value of what I can deliver this instant. It is that obligation that turns promise into contract. Now there might be reason to conclude that the normative reach of promise should be co-extensive with the normative reach of contract.[1] Alternatively, you could conclude that it is important to keep the two distinct and that it would make good sense to multiply the bases of duty, to distinguish the duties imposed by a promise from those imposed by a contract. The distinct devices could then serve or accommodate different interpersonal and transactional goals. We would have more tools at our disposal, to serve either deontic or consequentialist objects.[2]

Our perception of the value of a normative dichotomy (promise distinct from contract) or, alternatively, unity, may well inform our conclusions about the formation of

[1] *See* CHARLES FRIED, CONTRACT AS PROMISE: A THEORY OF CONTRACTUAL OBLIGATION 7–27, 136–56 (1981); *see also* Seana Valentine Shiffrin, *The Divergence of Contract and Promise*, 120 HARV. L. REV. 708, 710–11 n.2 (2007) (perceiving flaws in Fried's analysis); Charles Fried, *The Convergence of Contract and Promise*, 120 HARV. L. REV. F. 1 (2007) (responding to Shiffrin).

[2] Indeed, an intermediate basis of obligation, such as promissory estoppel, may enhance the normative range.

obligations, specifically the contract obligation. We could reach one conclusion about formation if we identify contract with promise and another conclusion if we distinguish the two. There is, though, as the canonical cases surveyed in the last chapter demonstrate, a tension between promise and contract that resonates through the formation cases. Depending on your perspective, that tension may be the result of confusion (a misunderstanding of the relationship between promise and contract) or a crucial determinant of the normative object of the contract law. It is either a complication to be overcome or a device to be exploited.

The contract formation issues would be crucial to our discovering a normative foundation of contract: If we cannot find that the formation elements vindicate an asserted normative foundation, then we have either failed to discover that normative foundation, as a positive matter, or established that the formation elements undermine (or are at least in tension with) the asserted normative foundation. So we will have to see what sense theory can make of the offer and acceptance, mistake, and consideration rules, as well as the operation of those requisites within the doctrine, as discerned from the canon. If theory cannot explain or account for consideration, for example, such theory cannot be positive, and may also fail as a normative matter. We could conclude that contract should dispense with the consideration requirement, but then we would no longer be positing a theory of contract. Our theory, instead, might be of something like a "unified theory of civil obligation."[3] This chapter measures deontic and consequentialist theory against the formation elements of contract.

A. Offer and Acceptance: The Objective–Subjective Tension

Contract begins with agreement, no matter how substantial or insubstantial we understand the requirement to be. And the measure of agreement is the offer and acceptance. There must be coincidence, perhaps something less than a perfect "meeting of the minds" but there must be sufficient coincidence of intent. There is sufficient coincidence if the normative object of contract would be served by our discovering sufficient coincidence. So again, we may appreciate the measure of the doctrine by reference to our judgment about the normative purpose contract serves.

Professor Steven Burton, in his *Elements of Contract Interpretation*,[4] has provided a taxonomy of "theories of contract interpretation" that may also inform our appreciation of the object of the offer and acceptance requisite of contract formation. There are, Burton tells us, three approaches: literalist, subjectivist, and objectivist. The contours of each are accessible; it is their interrelation that presents the challenge. "Literalism requires

---

[3] Grant Gilmore, Death of Contract 98 (2d ed. 1995).

[4] Stephen J. Burton, Elements of Contract Interpretation (2009).

interpretation according to the literal meaning of the directly applicable words used in a contract, without taking into account their context."[5] *Literalism* is an extreme view and would find contract or no contract or discover the terms of a contract wholly irrespective of the parties' subjective or objective intent. *Subjectivism* would concern itself *only* with the parties' subjective state of mind and would not be considerate of either the literal meaning of the terms used by the parties or the objective meaning that reasonable third parties would attach to them: "In its strongest form, subjectivism is the theory that prefers to interpret a contract according to the shared meaning the parties attached to the contract's language."[6] The focus is on the parties' mental state, their actual intentions as revealed from manifestations of that intention. And, finally, *objectivism* relies on the fiction that words have an objective, true meaning: "Objectivism takes into account a limited context to find the conventional meanings of the parties' expressions as used in the context."[7] We could likely find exemplars of each approach in the cases and in all *Restatement of Contracts* provisions. The point here, though, is to discern whether the formation doctrine reveals a particular mix of the literal, subjective, and objective that constrains one rather than the other normative account of contract.

The challenge confronting students of contract, particularly those encountering contract for the first time, is to makes sense of the objective–subjective tension in the offer and acceptance requirement. Must there be actual intent? Or will inferred consent suffice? The offer and acceptance doctrine is built on the scaffolding of promise. At some point, communication between two actors will result in an agreement, and if that agreement is legally enforceable, we will conclude that the agreement is a contract.

When we find *bargain*, we have found *contract*, and whether there is a bargain depends upon whether there is *agreement*, "a manifestation of mutual assent." There is, then, not much normative distance between bargain and agreement, indeed, not much normative distance between agreement and contract. Whatever normative purpose the offer and acceptance requisites vindicate, we should expect that they would be indistinguishable from the normative purpose served by the consideration and promissory estoppel bases of promise enforcement. As we have seen, if the representation is (or becomes) a promise, contract may enforce it. The fundamental question, then, is: When is a representation a promise? The circular answer contract provides is that a representation is a promise when contract will enforce it. The interests the two requisites of contract (offer and acceptance and consideration or promissory estoppel) serve have the same object: to discern when some normative object would be vindicated by enforcing the representations between the parties.

---

[5] *Id.* at 17–18.

[6] *Id.* at 28.

[7] *Id.* at 21–22.

The question that vexes with regard to contract formation, offer and acceptance, is: Just what happens when an offer is extended and accepted? Does the contract law provide an answer or is the answer to be found in the normative background? Perhaps we can approach an answer by appreciating the contours of offer and acceptance in the doctrine and elaborate from there. That is, once we understand what it means for A to make an offer and for B to accept it, we can discern some normative explanation for what must be going on. We can appreciate the mechanics and then infer from those mechanics what the normative foundation must be. But the mere statement of that approach intimates the bootstrap nature of it: We may construe the contours and the incidents of the offer and acceptance mechanism in such a way that we compel one normative gloss rather than another. So long as we are aware of that danger, though, we may better, more objectively, approach the endeavor.

1. DEONTOLOGY

Professor Charles Fried's promise theory is at least a very good place to start. For Fried, the moral force of a promise comes from the promise itself, and is not dependent on the promisee's choice to enforce the promise.[8] An offer is a promise, a promise to perform in the manner consistent with the terms of the offer should the offeree accept the offer. More specifically, Fried concludes that an offer is a conditional promise. He tracks the development of the law of offer and acceptance to the same time, the nineteenth century, as the recognition of conditional promises: "[T]he concepts of conditional promises and of offer and acceptance are closely related in principle as well as in history."[9]

The premise of promise, so far as Fried is concerned, is that the enforceability of promises expands "human liberty by self-imposed obligation,"[10] which "also entails that a man be able to condition his promise on receiving a return from the promisee."[11] When the offeror A makes the offer to B, the offeree, A's offer is a conditional promise and B's acceptance is also a conditional promise. That construction supports familiar rules governing offer and acceptance, such as the revocability of offers prior to acceptance, the mirror image rule, and option contracts. Fried posits a circuitry metaphor:

> Consider the force of a promise to be an electric current. For the current to flow, the circuit must be completed. There are two switches, the promisor's and the promisee's. If the promisor has closed his switch he is in a situation of vulnerability: The circuit

[8] FRIED, *supra* note 1, at 41.

[9] *Id.* at 46.

[10] *Id.*

[11] *Id.*

> placing him under an obligation can be closed by an act of acceptance by the promisee. But should the promisor reopen his switch before the acceptance, the acceptance by itself is insufficient to complete the circuit.[12]

The metaphor is helpful insofar as it captures the interdependence of offer and acceptance, but it does nothing to describe a normative basis of that interdependence. The metaphor does, though, depict well the vulnerability of an offeror. Once the offer is made and until it is rejected or rescinded, the offeree has the unilateral power to impose contract on the offeror, subject, of course, to the terms of the offer. As Fried puts it, the offeror is "in [the offeree's] power."[13]

There is also support for Fried's conception of offer as conditional promise to be gleaned from the normative foundation of promissory estoppel, which, as we'll soon see,[14] is co-extensive with the normative basis of bargain, or consideration-based promise enforcement. Fried considers doctrine that uses promissory estoppel theory to, effectively, enforce a promise that has not been accepted. Section 45 of the *Second Restatement* establishes the paradigm:

> Option Contract Created by Part Performance of Tender
>
> (1) Where an offer invites an offeree to accept by rendering a performance and does not invite a promissory acceptance, an option contract is created when the offeree tenders or begins the invited performance or tenders a beginning of it.
> (2) The offeror's duty of performance under any option contract so created is conditional on completion or tender of the invited performance in accordance with the terms of the offer.[15]

The *Restatement* provision overcomes the problem that the consideration doctrine would otherwise cause: failure of an option contract for want of consideration. Just as the promissory estoppel doctrine generally operates as a surrogate for consideration, Section 45 relies on the same type of estoppel to enforce an option contract not supported by consideration. This, then, confirms for Fried the promissory nature of offers; it completes his equation of offers and promises. Offers are promises before as well as after they are accepted; the difference between them is mechanical. Prior to acceptance, an offer is a conditional promise; after acceptance, the promise is unconditional. The same normative principle that explains the enforceable promise (which for Fried, is premised on deontic conceptions of autonomy) also explains the promissory nature of the offer and

---

[12] *Id.* at 47.

[13] *Id.* at 49.

[14] *See infra* Chapter 4, Part C 2.

[15] Restatement (Second) of Contracts § 45 (1981).

acceptance. Whatever reason we have for enforcing promises, then, also provides the normative foundation of our contract law of offer and acceptance.

Professor Randy Barnett's consent theory is no less libertarian than Fried's, but construes the signal of autonomy differently. Fried relies on the Kantian "will theory." Barnett concludes that consent, or, the manifestation of intent, will do. So though Barnett's theory is deontic too, it is only similarly deontic, vindicating a different conception of autonomy. It is objective indicia of consent that are determinative for Barnett:

> In contract law, . . . an assent to alienate rights must be manifested in some manner by one party to the other to serve as a criterion of enforcement. Without a manifestation of assent that is accessible to all affected parties, that aspect of a system of entitlements that governs transfers of rights will fail to achieve its main function. At the time of the transaction, it will have failed to identify clearly and communicate to both parties (and to third parties) the rightful boundaries that must be respected. Without such communication, parties to a transaction (and third parties) cannot accurately ascertain what constitutes rightful conduct and what constitutes a commitment on which they can rely. Disputes that might otherwise have been avoided will occur, and the attendant uncertainties of the transfer process will discourage reliance.[16]

Barnett's theory would be more fundamental than contract theories dependent on "concepts of will, reliance, efficiency, fairness, or bargain."[17] We cannot understand contract unless we first understand "more fundamental issues, namely the nature and sources of individual entitlements and the means by which they come to be acquired."[18] Barnett is interested in determining when we can derive individual rights (contract rights) from an entitlement theory, a moral theory.

Consent, for Barnett, is a "moral prerequisite to contractual obligation."[19] But to support his theory of contract based on consent, he needs to develop a sense of consent that is consonant with his normative theory of entitlement. That leads him, inexorably, to an objective theory of consent. He acknowledges at the outset that "consent" would, "at first blush," seem to intimate a "will" theory of contract.[20] But will theory fails to account for myriad contracts cases in which courts are enforcing the objective rather than subjective will of the contracting parties.[21] In the final reckoning, we must adopt an objective

[16] Randy E. Barnett, *A Consent Theory of Contract*, 86 Colum. L. Rev. 269, 302 (1986).

[17] *Id.* at 293.

[18] *Id.* at 294.

[19] *Id.* at 297.

[20] *Id.* at 300. Barnett associates the "will theory" with Morris R. Cohen, David Hume, A.S. Burrows, P S. Atiyah, and Charles Fried. *Id.* at 272–74 nn.7–16.

[21] *Id.* at 274.

theory of contract because the limits of human social intercourse leave us no alternative but to do so.

Contract is animated by objective consent, then, because we cannot reliably determine subjective consent and we need to be able to determine consent in order for contract to do what contract needs to do to vouchsafe the system of entitlements Barnett deems crucial to human thriving. So Barnett does fashion a theory of contract that is not dependent on the will theory, which never did seem to explain contract very well. (It certainly is difficult to reconcile subjective will with an objective theory of contract formation.) But does Barnett's objective theory of consent explain contract well enough to make sense of extant contract doctrine? It does not.

Although Barnett's theory could work on a normative level—there is no *prima facie* reason why you *could not* argue for a construction of contract that would serve the libertarian principles he champions—the theory is problematic on a positive level. There are just too many contract doctrines and too many judicial constructions of contract doctrine that gainsay ostensible consent as Barnett formulates it for us to conclude that his consent theory tells us very much that is helpful. Consideration of the consequentialist perspective reveals the inadequacy of basing contract on purely ostensible agreement, Barnett's consent.[22]

2. CONSEQUENTIALISM

The agreement calculus has recently attracted the attention of scholars who have tried to rationalize the consumer form contracting context.[23] They have considered specifically the credit card "agreement," pursuant to which consumers often find themselves subject to terms they did not appreciate (and perhaps never had the opportunity to review) when they opened their credit card accounts.[24] The stakes may be quite high: To the extent that consumers take advantage of bankruptcy protection when it comes time to pay and they are unable to do so, ripples running through the economy on account of such bad debt may result in welfare loss.[25]

Consequentialist commentators who have considered agreement issues in the credit card context are in fact further pursuing Judge Frank Easterbrook's analyses in *ProCD v. Zeidenberg* and *Hill v. Gateway 2000, Inc.* The question Easterbrook's conclusion begs is whether, in fact, we *can* be confident that a conception of formal agreement in place of substantial agreement really increases welfare. If mere formal agreement does function in

---

[22] *See* Peter A. Alces, Un*intelligent Design in Contract*, 2008 U. ILL. L. REV. 505, 526–32 (2008).

[23] *See* BOILERPLATE: THE FOUNDATION OF MARKET CONTRACTS (Omri Ben-Shahar ed., 2007).

[24] *See, e.g.,* Peter A. Alces, *Guerilla Terms*, 56 EMORY L.J. 1511 (2007); Oren Bar-Gill, *Bundling and Consumer Misperception*, 73 U. CHI. L. REV. 33 (2006); Oren Bar-Gill, *Seduction By Plastic*, 98 NW. U. L. REV. 1373 (2004).

[25] *See* Oren Bar-Gill, *The Behavioral Economics of Consumer Contracts*, 92 MINN. L. REV. 749, 767, 780–82 (2008).

the way Easterbrook concludes that it does, then the consequentialist interpretation of agreement doctrine may be viable. But if formal agreement compromises welfare, then there may be room for a deontic conception that takes real agreement more seriously. In that case, the deontic conception would not be at odds with consequentialist premises.

Though there would not be disagreement among consequentialists about the appropriateness of deferring to mere formal agreement, ostensible consent, there could be disagreement over the efficacy of such deference. That is, in fact, how the lines have been drawn. In a recent colloquy, Professors Oren Bar-Gill and Richard Epstein marshal arguments on both sides of the question. Bar-Gill relies on behavioral economics, a branch of cognitive psychology, to argue that we need to do more empirical research before we can have any confidence that formal agreement results in welfare gains.[26] The basis of Easterbrook's conclusion in *ProCD* and *Hill*, recall, was that standard form contracting is efficient, and creates welfare by reducing transactions costs. Epstein disagrees with Bar-Gill, and concludes that we can rely on what is essentially an agency theory to overcome Bar-Gill's reservations.[27] It is worthwhile to consider their arguments seriatim.

Bar-Gill expresses concern that credit card issuers actually exploit the cognitive mistakes that consumers make in order to "seek rent" at the expense of those less sophisticated consumers: "[S]ellers might prefer not to correct consumer mistakes and might even invest in creating misperception. Arguably, manipulation of consumer perceptions, and even preferences, is a main purpose of advertising."[28] He argues that analysis of seller behavior confirms that sellers inculcate and exploit consumer misperception in the design of their products.[29] His argument from design, as it were, concludes that "[s]ince sellers will only alter the design of their products and prices in response to robust, systematic mistakes, observing such product and price adjustments is powerful evidence of persistent consumer mistakes."[30] Bar-Gill does not trust the market to overcome "individual irrationalities,"[31] and he is certainly correct not to. An article cited by Bar-Gill, but

[26] *See id.*

[27] *See* Richard A. Epstein, *The Neoclassical Economics of Consumer Contracts*, 92 MINN. L. REV. 803 (2008).

[28] Bar-Gill, *supra* note 25, at 761.

[29] "[S]ellers may design their products and pricing schemes in response to consumer misperception. Such product design is evidence that consumers make systematic mistakes (or, at least, that sellers believe that consumers are making systematic mistakes)." *Id.* at 761. For an earlier rendition of that analysis and conclusion, see Alces, *supra* note 24.

[30] Bar-Gill, *supra* note 25, at 766.

[31] *Id.* at 755, citing Amos Tversky & Daniel Kahneman, *Rational Choice and the Framing of Decision*, 59 J. BUS. (CONFERENCE PROCEEDINGS) S251, S275 (1986), *reprinted in* RATIONAL CHOICE: THE CONTRAST BETWEEN ECONOMICS AND PSYCHOLOGY 67, 91 (Rubin M. Hogarth & Melvin W. Reder eds., 1987).

which he does not consider in sufficient depth,[32] makes the point quite clearly that *at equilibrium* sellers will exploit mistakes made by less sophisticated, myopic buyers, in order to seek monopoly profits.[33] So although Bar-Gill does not take account of the economic theory that would support his argument most directly, he does make the important empirical point about consequentialist analysis that is pertinent to this book's investigation of a normative theory of contract doctrine.

Bar-Gill recognizes that there will be a range of sophistication levels among consumers, and that some will overestimate the value of a product while others will underestimate its value.[34] We may not assume that the biases will wash, that the average valuation will be the value-maximizing one: "[T]he existence of both overestimators and underestimators does not mean that the average estimate is unbiased; and neither does it mean that the average bias is sufficiently close to zero that it can be safely ignored. *It is an empirical question.*"[35]

Epstein responds to Bar-Gill by offering essentially a series of what might be "just so stories."[36] For each example that Bar-Gill offers of at least apparent card issuer overreaching, Epstein suggests an alternative construction that identifies a market justification for the result Bar-Gill questions.[37] Maybe most provocative is Epstein's conclusion that people make fewer mistakes up to the age of fifty-three, when they make the fewest, and then the number of mistakes increases again thereafter.[38] The fact that we can plot the mistakes on a curve[39] confirms, he argues, that people really do learn, and ultimately make fewer mistakes (apparently for a brief time). So we can take this evidence of learning to support "the conclusion that education on how loans work is often the best protection against various kinds of dangerous credit practices."[40] There seems to be a logical leap from the assertion that people learn over time to the conclusion that card issuer exploitation of consumer myopia is efficient. That is, there should be room for precisely the type of empirical evidence Bar-Gill seeks. Why would we assume, along with Epstein, that education is the *best* protection against sharp practices? Education is certainly some protection (which might explain why credit card issuers would change the rules in order

[32] Xavier Gabaix & David Laibson, *Shrouded Attributes, Consumer Myopia, and Information Suppression in Competitive Markets,* 121 Q.J. ECON. 505, 507–10 (2006). Bar-Gill cites the article, *supra* note 25, at 759 n.46. I consider the impact of Gabaix and Laibson's conclusions in greater depth in Alces, *supra* note 24, at 1523–47.

[33] *See* Alces, *supra* note 24, at 1524. This would also be responsive to Epstein, *supra* note 27.

[34] Bar-Gill, *supra* note 25, at 767.

[35] *Id.* (emphasis added).

[36] *See* S.J. Gould, *Sociobiology: The Art of Storytelling,* NEW SCIENTIST 80 (Nov. 16, 1978), 530–33.

[37] *See* Epstein, *supra* note 27, at 821–31.

[38] *See id.* at 812.

[39] *Id.* ("after controlling for income, education, creditworthiness, and other observable variables").

[40] *Id.*

to frustrate education[41]), but how can we be sure that it is the *most efficient* protection, particularly insofar as we may have some confidence that paternalism can, in fact, be efficient?

Professor Eyal Zamir has argued that paternalism and efficiency may be compatible, a view that Epstein does not consider in his response to Bar-Gill. The terms of Zamir's analysis, even reproduced succinctly, make clear the need for careful empirical inquiry to support arguments such as those offered by Epstein:

> In fact, standard economic analysis does not embrace a pure actual preferences criterion of well-being. Once an assumption of rationality is introduced into a preferences theory of well-being, it is no longer an actual preferences theory. Between a pure actual preferences theory of well-being and a pure ideal preferences theory there is a whole spectrum of compromised, complex theories. The more demanding the definition of rationality introduced into a theory, the closer it becomes to an ideal preferences theory. Arguably, economic analysis does not rest on the normative claim that rational preferences are a superior criterion for human well-being than actual ones. It merely rests on the empirical claim that people's actual preferences are rational. However, to the extent that standard economic analysis is built on the assumption that people are rational maximizers, its normative implications are the same as those of a rational preferences theory of well-being.
>
> ... Once the prevalence of systematic deviations from the rational-maximizer model is acknowledged, principled anti-paternalism is no longer a tenable position of economic analysis.
>
> ... Paternalism can certainly be efficient once it is realized that normative economics is in fact much closer to an ideal (rational) preferences theory.[42]

The criteria that Zamir explores in determining the efficiency of paternalism[43] resonate with the empirical inquiries Bar-Gill imagines would resolve his difference with Epstein. Bar-Gill concludes that his disagreement with Epstein is a matter of their differing conclusions with regard to regulation. Though they both share an anti-regulation (and, so, anti-paternalistic) bias, Bar-Gill concludes that "a market-by-market analysis of the

---

[41] *See* Alces, *supra* note 24, at 1527 ("Form drafters can use a kind of 'three-card Monty' game to assure maintenance of the pool of naive: Each time consumers discover a particularly egregious term, hide the risk-shifting card by reshuffling the deck or by sleight of hand."); *see also* RONALD J. MANN, CHARGING AHEAD: THE GROWTH AND REGULATION OF PAYMENT CARD MARKETS 132 (2006) ("It is typical for major issuers to amend their agreements in important respects with remarkable frequency.").

[42] Eyal Zamir, *The Efficiency of Paternalism*, 84 VA. L. REV. 229, 250–52, 254 (1998) (footnote omitted).

[43] *Id.* at 237–54 (considering second-order preferences, norm theory, and bounded rationality versus ideal (rational) preferences theory).

costs and benefits is desirable."[44] This is essentially the analysis Zamir would pursue to determine the scope of efficient paternalism.

Now we need not conclude that Epstein is wrong and Zamir and Bar-Gill right in order to demonstrate the (at least) incompleteness of a pure consequentialist theory of contract doctrine, at least insofar as agreement is concerned. All that we need acknowledge is that central concepts, such as the criteria of agreement, lend themselves to the type of empirical inquiry that Zamir and Bar-Gill suggest. It is difficult to make sense of agreement, as a matter of extant doctrine, by certainly denying the pertinence of such empirical inquiry. There is sufficient imprecision, or flexibility, in the doctrine such as it is to support either the strictest consequentialist conclusion (per Easterbrook and Epstein), or the more empirical perspective (Bar-Gill and Zamir), or even a deontic view that takes autonomy seriously by requiring more of "bargain" than what would satisfy the broader conception of "agreement" that "contains no implication that legal consequences are or are not produced."[45] The nature of doctrine so revealed discloses as well the limitations of the prevailing normative dichotomy.

B. Mistake

This part of the chapter considers the fact pattern in which contracts are infirm because the parties' understanding at the formation stage was inaccurate. If one or both parties' understanding is incorrect with regard to circumstances as they exist at the time of contracting, the apposite avoidance doctrine is mistake. If the parties' understanding turns out to be inconsistent with events as they evolve, the apposite avoidance doctrine is impracticability or frustration. There is substantial affinity between the analyses that support the temporally distinct doctrines; indeed, it may all come down to risk allocation, which is, after all, what contract is about.

In the sections that follow, this chapter will focus on mistake. The doctrines that operate when circumstances evolve in ways the parties did not expect, *i.e.,* impossibility, impracticability, or frustration doctrine, are treated in Chapters Five, "Contract Performance Doctrine," and Six, "Theory of Contract Performance." Once again, we will see that though we can tell a story of the doctrine in either deontic or consequential terms, there is no reason to believe that the doctrine is necessarily explicable *only* in the terms of one or the other normative theories. Indeed, the power of the doctrine is in its normative agnosticism, or at least flexibility.

---

[44] Bar-Gill, *supra* note 25, at 753–54.

[45] *See* RESTATEMENT (SECOND) OF CONTRACTS § 3 cmt. a (1981).

I. DEONTOLOGY

The deontic perspective does not have to assume the consistently rational actor; people make mistakes and sometimes when they do they can avoid the contract liability that was the product of the mistake. The doctrine is pertinent when reality at the time of contracting does not mirror parties' understanding of it. As Professor Fried recognizes, contracting parties never anticipate all of the contingencies surrounding their bargain. They capture as much of reality as it is rational to capture, make all of the assumptions that it is rational to make without crossing every conceivable *t* and dotting every conceivable *i*.[46] Reality may fail to mirror the parties' understanding of it in myriad and unpredictable ways. If you buy a particular car with the expectation that it will provide certain social benefits, you may be mistaken, but such a mistake is of no interest to contract. (It would, of course, be an altogether different matter if the seller represented that the car would have a certain towing capacity it in fact did not have.) At most, we could describe the buyer disappointed because the car did not provide the hoped-for social advantages as the victim of his own unilateral mistake. The law will not unwind a contract on account of unilateral mistake unless the nonmistaken party was either a cause of the mistake or knew that the mistaken party was operating under an inaccurate impression and did not bring that misunderstanding to the attention of the mistaken party.[47] Fried explains why we treat unilateral mistake the way we do:

> The contract is enforced in these cases of unilateral mistake in spite of this lack of agreement and, therefore, on other than promissory principles. The most likely principle acknowledges that one party . . . is being forced to bear a loss he had not knowingly assumed, but that the other party supposed that the risk of this loss had been allocated between them, and so that as between the two parties the one who had acted reasonably and in the ordinary course should not have his expectations disappointed. He should not be disappointed because (1) if a loss is inevitable and both parties are innocent, the careless man should not be able to cast that loss on the prudent, and (2) the chances that buyer's . . . reservations are an afterthought are too great to warrant systematic legal inquiry.[48]

Note Fried's acknowledgement that the promise principle does not provide the means to order the parties' rights; the extent of enforcement is fixed by other (apparently tort) principles. The first of the two principles Fried offers may be based on fairness or

---

[46] FRIED, *supra* note 1, at 59 ("The language of mistake suggests that certainty is the paradigm, but in fact contracts are largely a deliberate attempt to deal with uncertainty.").

[47] RESTATEMENT (SECOND) OF CONTRACTS § 153 (1981).

[48] FRIED, *supra* note 1, at 62.

a consequentialist interest in encouraging contracting parties' exercise of due care.[49] *Fairness*, of course, seems to rest on deontic premises, but Fried does not suggest the source or substance of the fairness principles at work here; he just tells us that the promise principle is not operative. Indeed, he concludes that "[t]he futile attempt to bring these cases under the promise principle only plays into the hands of those who see nonpromissory principles of fairness at work throughout the law of contract."[50] So considerations of fairness invoke tort principles, and tort invokes consequentialism.

In the case in which both parties are mistaken, though, cases of so-called mutual mistake, contract will relieve the parties of their undertakings, even if one of the parties does not want to walk away from the deal. That is why we need a body of doctrine that would distinguish unilateral from mutual mistake. *Sherwood v. Walker* and *Wood v. Boynton* describe the parameters within which the distinction will be drawn, and we may understand those cases as occupying the poles of a continuum.

At (or toward) the one pole is *Sherwood*, in which the court concludes that the difference between a barren cow and a fertile cow is a matter of the character of the subject matter of the contract. *Boynton* would occupy the space at or toward the opposite pole on that continuum; the parties there were deemed by the court to be, at most, in *disagreement* but not *mistaken* as to the potential value of the contract subject matter. So in *Boynton* the court did not find mutual mistake. Putting the two cases together we are left with what looks like a "rule" to the effect that a mistake about character is the basis of contract avoidance but a mistake about value is not. That is, of course, a false dichotomy, but it provides the means for a court to do some justice, to take into account contextual factors that the doctrine may but does not necessarily implicate.

Fried's construction of the mistake law, though, does not guide application of the doctrine. He acknowledges that his promise principle is impotent in this setting and he does not describe a deontic calculus that would determine the doctrine's application. There is none. Though we could justify a result by reference to conceptions of individual autonomy, between two autonomous actors the contest is a zero sum game. Whatever we do to assure one party that she will not be prejudiced by the mistake imposes the burden of the mistake on the other party. And in the mutual mistake context, both parties are innocent. The law cannot even leave well enough alone and vindicate a deontologically desirable result because leaving well enough alone will let the party in receipt of the contract benefits retain them without consideration of that party's relative desert, assuming, as we must, that both parties are innocent. Recall, if one party is innocent and the other is not, we have unilateral rather than mutual mistake and we will impose the loss on the party in the best position to have avoided the misunderstanding, arguably a consequentialist conclusion. Now this is not to say that a court could not invoke deontic principles, perhaps based on

---

[49] *Id.* at 62–63.

[50] *Id.* at 63.

community interests;[51] but it is to say that the doctrine does not constrain the inquiry in deontic terms.

2. CONSEQUENTIALISM

In a particularly thoughtful article, Professors Eric Rasmusen and Ian Ayres consider "Mutual and Unilateral Mistake in Contract Law"[52] from the consequentialist perspective. Their analysis leads them to certain conclusions about the doctrine, and it will be worthwhile to take those conclusions into account. First, though, it is helpful to take some account of their method and the fragility of that method insofar as the normativity of the governing doctrine is concerned. It is necessary to spend some time on the exposition of their thesis and argument in order to appraise its contribution to normative contract theory.

The authors begin by putting the mistake cases and doctrine in context. *Mistake* is akin to but not the same as *misunderstanding*, their characterization of the *Peerless* case, and *impracticability*, which concerns events subsequent to contract formation that were not within (or are alleged not to have been within) the parties' contemplation at the time of contracting. Rasmusen and Ayres distinguish misunderstanding from mistake in that, in the case of misunderstanding, "the court could not simply 'enforce the contract.'"[53] In any event, it is not clear how that difference would distinguish the doctrine's normative response to misunderstanding from its normative response to mistake. Rasmusen and Ayres do not cast much light on the operative consequences of the distinction, so far as consequentialism is concerned, when they conclude in the margin that "[a contract that is the product of misunderstanding] is void, rather than voidable. In mistake cases, on the other hand, the contract obligations are unambiguous, but they are premised on mistaken beliefs."[54] They may draw a line more boldly than the doctrine would suggest they should.

The two doctrines seem to be much closer than the authors acknowledge, and so we would expect that the doctrine would have to treat the two quite similarly, even identically, as a normative matter, unless and until a substantial normative reason is offered for their inconsistent treatment. In so-called misunderstanding cases, both parties are mistaken as to the understanding of their counterparty, and we could not say with any certainty that the understanding of one rather than the other was more plausible and so "less mistaken." So a comparative fault analysis could work in the misunderstanding context as well as it would work in the prototypical mistake context. Now the authors could be saying that a "misunderstanding" rule applies where the parties are each at fault (or each faultless)

---

51 *See* Daniel Markovitz, *Contract and Collaboration*, 113 YALE L.J. 1417 (2004).

52 Eric Rasmusen & Ian Ayres, *Mutual and Unilateral Mistake in Contract Law*, 22 J. LEGAL STUD. 309 (1993).

53 *Id.* at 310 n.2.

54 *Id.*

in their misunderstanding, but they do not suggest that basis of distinction and it is not clear that doctrine would support it.

We may be cynical, too, about the possibility of there being any certain factual distinction between unilateral mistake, *not* a basis to excuse the mistaken party, and mutual mistake, a viable basis to excuse the party who would be prejudiced by the mistake. Indeed, at least one court has acknowledged that tension between the two rules can determine construction of the facts, but then falls back on a similarly insubstantial basis of distinction. The question in *Lenawee County Board of Health v. Messerly*[55] was whether the parties' error concerning the compliance of a septic system with governmental regulations rendered the sales contract unenforceable on account of mutual mistake or enforceable notwithstanding one party's incorrect valuation of the property.

The court describes the doctrine's distinction between mistakes concerning value (unilateral) and mistakes concerning "the substance [character?] of the consideration" (mutual) as "inexact and confusing."[56] Further, the court concludes that such a distinction "serves only as an impediment to a clear and helpful analysis for the equitable resolution of cases in which mistake is alleged and proven."[57] So the court turns to what was essentially a tort analysis, in order "to determine which blameless party should assume the loss resulting from the misapprehension they shared."[58] Because the purchaser had agreed to take the property as-is, the court concludes that the purchaser had assumed the risk of the property's deficiency. This case, then, was handled as an instance of unilateral mistake. The sellers knew what they were selling: real property that might or might not have deficiencies of which they were not aware, and which deficiencies could impair the market value of the property. Presumably, the sellers would have been able to demand a higher price if they had not sold the property as-is but had, instead, retained the risk that the property's value might be impaired by latent defects. The buyers alone were mistaken: They thought they were buying property with a septic system that would satisfy the local government's regulations. They assumed the risk (and paid, presumably, a lower price on account of that assumption of risk) that the property would have a latent defect impairing its market value. So the *Messerly* court could have used the unilateral—mutual dichotomy to arrive at the same place. Arguably, the court's equitable assumption of risk approach was more transparent.

The value of the case, though, for present purposes, is in the court's recognition that the unilateral—mutual dichotomy provides the means to label a conclusion[59] rather

---

[55] Lenawee County Bd. of Health v. Messerly, 331 N.W.2d 203 (Mich. 1982).

[56] *Id.* at 209.

[57] *Id.*

[58] *Id.* at 210.

[59] *See* Rasmusen & Ayres, *supra* note 52, at 312 (citing ROBERT COOTER & THOMAS ULEN, LAW & ECONOMICS 258 (1st ed. 1988)).

than a guide to analysis. The dichotomy ultimately must give way to something more substantial, or at least something more useful.

Rasmusen and Ayres too recognize the limitations of the doctrinal dichotomy, and, indeed, go further than to complain that it may mislead and get between a court and the right (that is "right" in consequentialist terms) result. They consider three potential rules in mistake cases. First, the law could conclude that mistake does not provide an excuse to the parties' contract performance obligations. Second, the law could find that mistake relieves one or the other party from the contract. Third, the law could relieve both parties from their obligations if a contract is the product of mistake on either side. We should, the authors conclude, develop and apply doctrine that will influence parties' incentives and avoid transactions that have negative gains from trade: "Efficiency-minded policymakers wish to encourage excuse for mistake if it increases the gains from trade and discourage it otherwise."[60]

The authors compare two states of the world: gains from mistaken trade are positive, and, the alternative, gains from mistaken trade are negative:

> If positive gains from mistaken trade:
>
> *No excuse*: "[S]eller will always disclose the high value, in order to charge a higher price, and the buyer will always refuse to disclose."[61]
>
> *Excuse for Mutual Mistake*: "[S]eller will disclose information to obtain a higher price[;]... buyer will refuse to disclose information of high value because when the mistake is unilateral he need not fear rescission."[62]
>
> *Excuse for Unilateral Mistake*: "Both... buyer and seller disclose the high value if they know it: the seller to obtain a higher price; the buyer, because the sale would be rescinded anyway if he failed to disclose."[63]
>
> If negative gains from mistaken trade:
>
> *No excuse*: "[B]uyer will not disclose to take advantage of private information[;]... [n]o trade occurs when the seller is informed that the value is high."[64]
>
> *Excuse for mutual mistake*: "[B]uyer refuses to disclose, in order to take advantage of private information[;]... informed seller refuses to trade."[65]
>
> *Excuse for unilateral mistake*: "[B]uyer is willing to disclose because any nondisclosure of high value will end in rescission[;]... the informed seller refuses to trade."[66]

[60] *Id.* at 314.

[61] *Id.* at 316.

[62] *Id.*

[63] *Id.* at 316–17.

[64] *Id.* at 317.

[65] *Id.*

[66] *Id.* at 320.

Recognize, first, that we do not know as either a general matter or with regard to specific contracts whether the gains from mistake are positive or negative.[67] The authors' treatment of *Sherwood* makes that clear:

> A fertile cow is different enough from a barren cow that a buyer willing to buy a barren cow at a low price might not be willing to buy a fertile cow at a high price. If both parties mistakenly believed the cow to be barren, the gains from trade were likely to be negative when the cow turned out to be fertile because the seller was well situated to sell both fertile and barren cows but the buyer would presumably have had higher costs of resale. Thus, voiding for mistake would avoid negative gains from trade.[68]

Rasmusen and Ayres are able to use their focus on gains from trade to reconcile *Sherwood* with *Boynton*: "Why the difference from [*Sherwood*]? In [*Boynton*], unlike [*Sherwood*], there is a much larger likelihood of gains from mistaken trade: the jeweler has more use for an uncut diamond."[69]

Of course, a court *could* use the distinction that the doctrine draws in order to reach the results Rasmusen and Ayres urge; indeed, that may be what the *Sherwood* and *Boynton* courts did, without realizing (or acknowledging) that they were doing so. In *Sherwood,* the court found mutual mistake and so voided the contract; in *Boynton,* the court found only unilateral mistake and did not void the contract.

> [T]he single legal rule that maximizes society's gains of trade can be either the no-excuse or the unilateral mistake rule, depending on the relative size of the gains of trade and the costs of rescission. The mutual mistake rule can never produce better results than the unilateral mistake rule because both produce the same surplus when the gains from mistaken trade are positive, and the mutual mistake rule is less efficient when gains from mistaken trade are negative.[70]

When a mutual mistake rule, that a contract is void only if both parties are mistaken, is effective, only the *uninformed* seller would trade; the *informed* seller would not. *Sherwood* applies the mutual mistake rule correctly to relieve the uninformed seller of its contract obligation because, in that case, Rasmusen and Ayres presume, there would be negative gains from the mistaken trade. Had the court applied a unilateral mistake rule (which, recall, for Rasmusen and Ayres means a void contract if either party were mistaken), the contract would also have been avoided. But if that were the rule (rather

---

[67] *Id.* at 314.

[68] *Id.* at 325.

[69] *Id.*

[70] *Id.* at 321.

than mutual mistake), the buyer would be "willing to disclose because any nondisclosure of high value will end in rescission"[71] anyway. So the buyer has no incentive *not* to disclose (so long as the seller's cost of rescission is lower than the cost of surrendering what the buyer would pay) and "[l]egal rules should encourage disclosure when nondisclosure would result in a transfer to someone [in *Sherwood*, by hypothesis, the buyer] who places less value on the good in question."[72]

So far, so good. Rasmusen and Ayres have demonstrated that, from the consequentialist perspective, the mistake doctrine should not require that both parties be mistaken in order to provide for rescission of a mistaken contract. Parties' incentives are better aligned if a mistake of either party may be grounds for excuse, rather than only when both parties are mistaken. But they then acknowledge that the doctrine may effect another consequentialist, albeit distributional, object.

> [A]lthough mutual mistake does not maximize total social surplus, it does maximize "consumer welfare" if the mistake is that the value is higher than expected. The law's facial preference for the mutual mistake rule might be understood as a preference for a rule that offers a more equitable distribution of the gains from trade – even if it means sacrificing the size of the total pie.[73]

So we would need to know the consequentialist object (or objects) before we could know whether the mutual mistake rule remains viable.

Rasmusen and Ayres also recognize that we must take into account the parties' relative cost of acquiring information in deciding which of the three alternatives provides the optimal result. If information costs are low, their unilateral mistake rule (a single mistaken party can rescind) maximizes surplus. They explain: "When information costs are low only the excuse rule of unilateral mistake deters sellers from acquiring information—because the seller is protected by the possibility of rescission."[74] So again, it is difficult to arrive at *the* correct rule, the rule that would *always* provide just the right consequences if we do not know were the parties start (their information costs) and if we do not agree on the consequences we want to realize.

The question of desired consequences arises also if we take into account, as Rasmusen and Ayres do, that there is productive information as well as merely redistributive information. Our mistake rule could be calibrated to assure the disclosure of information, even at some cost, if the information is "socially useful."[75] (Of course, you imagine we

[71] *Id.* at 320.

[72] *Id.* at 324.

[73] *Id.* at 322.

[74] *Id.* at 330–31.

[75] *Id.* at 332.

have to compare the costs of disclosing the information with the information's social utility, also a range of points on a continuum rather than a certain measure.)

Finally, notwithstanding their general conclusion that the mutual mistake rule is not desirable from a consequentialist, specifically welfare-enhancing, perspective, Rasmusen and Ayres acknowledge that *on the right facts*, that is, when the balance of information cost, gains from trade, and transactor incentives is just right, then the operation of the mutual mistake rule, perhaps in a case just like *Sherwood v. Walker*, is consistent with the consequentialist object:

> [In] *Sherwood v. Walker* [i]nformation acquisition was likely to be allocative rather than just redistributive since someone who discovered that Rose was fertile would breed her rather than put her to a less valuable use as meat. To encourage information acquisition, the legal rule should allow the buyer to profit from his information, even at the cost of negative gains from the trade itself. [This] justifies the court's decision. If Walker could somehow show that Sherwood bought the cow for meat, not for breeding, the contract should be voided because the trade was inefficient [the doctrinal mutual mistake rule]; otherwise it should be enforced, to reward Sherwood's good judgment.[76]

This treatment of the Rasmusen and Ayres analysis of mistake doctrine is designed to be illustrative of the considerations (and the relation between and among them) that must inform the normative consequentialist conclusion whether contract doctrine vindicates consequentialist premises. And, at least in this setting, which I assert is paradigmatic, the doctrine will not support the weight that a consequentialist construction would impose upon it. The doctrine might occasionally reach a particular and desired consequentialist conclusion, but if it does (or, for that matter, does not), that will be a matter more of serendipity than design. At least we may venture that that will often be the case, if what Rasmusen and Ayres do with mistake may be done with doctrine generally.

We will be able to confirm that conclusion, with regard to both deontology and consequentialism, when we consider two complementary bodies of contract doctrine: consideration and promissory estoppel.

C. The *Quid Pro Quo* Requirement

Obligation, in the legal sense, is desirable and can further important normative ends. Insofar as the instances and, so too, the *reasons* "promises should be enforced are too

[76] *Id.* at 335.

varied to be shoehorned into the confines of a single rationale,"[77] we should not be surprised if the doctrine, through the canonical cases, reflects a response to the range of normative reasons. One size will not fit all if we want our doctrine to be flexible enough to take account of normative differences. Now certainly the doctrine can respond by incorporating exceptions, for exceptional cases, but it can also respond by fixing normative parameters, a normative range in terms of a deontic—consequentialist continuum. This is what we see in the consideration cases. We see it too in the promissory estoppel cases, both in their recognition of an alternative basis to enforce a promise and in their express invocation of justice conceptions[78] to determine the extent of promise enforcement.

This part of the chapter reviews the contract exchange doctrine and demonstrates that the fit, such as it is, between the doctrine and normative theory is at best uneasy. The pertinent canonical cases describe the normative arch between the enforcement of promises supported by consideration and promises enforced on the alternative estoppel basis.

1. CONSIDERATION

Although positive accounts of contract recognize the pervasiveness of the consideration requirement, the normative significance (and, even, desirability) of the doctrine is less obvious. Both those proceeding from deontic premises and those proceeding from consequentialist premises have had trouble discerning firm ground in their perspective for the consideration doctrine to claim. It is not difficult to depict the nature of the problem as it has been appreciated by thoughtful commentators from both perspectives. This section will consider first the deontic quandary; the next section will depict the challenge from the consequentialists' vantage point.

a. Deontology

Charles Fried's Kantian explanation of contract relies on the normative affinity of contract and promise: Contract can mean no more and no less than what promise means to Immanuel Kant. Insofar as consideration can serve no purpose in promise—we bind ourselves by our word alone—consideration can at best be an unfortunate appendage, the reason for which has evolved away. So Fried does not so much explain consideration as a part of contract as try to explain why the doctrine persists notwithstanding the fact that it does no work; as far as we shall see Fried is concerned, consideration only confounds the operation and normative object of contract.

---

[77] E. ALLAN FARNSWORTH, CHANGING YOUR MIND: THE LAW OF REGRETTED DECISIONS 37 (1998).

[78] *See generally* Peter A. Alces, *On Discovering Doctrine: "Justice" in Contract Agreement*, 83 WASH. U. L.Q. 471, 512 (2005).

First he finds tension—a fatal inconsistency, really—between freedom of contract and bargain aspects of the consideration doctrine. We do not inquire into the adequacy (only the sufficiency) of consideration, and that vindicates the freedom of contract goal: We are all free to make bad deals, or at least deals that are objectively unattractive. But insofar as the contract must be a product of bargain, which is what consideration entails, we are only free to make that bad deal if it is the product of a substantial bargain: "Thus the classic conception seeks to affirm both exchange and freedom of contract. These two ideas turn out to be contradictory."[79] Indeed, Fried finds incoherence in the cases.

The promise of the uncle in *Hamer v. Sidway* is enforceable; it does not matter *why* the uncle made the promise, or what value he would receive on account of his promise. We do not inquire into his actual motives, whether there is any bargain in fact. In *Webb v. McGowin,*[80] the court enforces the promise although there is no bargain. Fried cites both of those cases[81] but could have cited others to make the point that consideration, at least as bargain, is of dubious substance in the contract law. *Bargain* as consideration may not mean what the colloquial sense of *bargain* would denote. He could have also cited *Allegheny College*[82] and *Wood v. Lucy, Lady Duff Gordon*[83] to assert the gossamer-like quality of bargain, and so consideration. Compare with those decisions a case like *Alaska Packers' Ass'n v. Domenico,*[84] in which there seemed to be a bargain, just not "new consideration." If we need to distinguish the cases in which there is consideration from those in which there is not, bargain cannot do the work for us.

> The bargain theory of consideration not only fails to explain why this pattern of decisions is just; it does not offer any consistent set of principles from which all of these decisions would flow. These cases particularly cannot be accounted for by the two guiding premises of the doctrine of consideration: (A) that only promises given as part of a bargain are enforceable; (B) that whether there is a bargain or not is a formal question only.
>
> . . .
>
> I conclude that the standard doctrine of consideration... does not pose a challenge to my conception of contract law as rooted in promise, for the simple reason that that doctrine is too internally inconsistent to offer an alternative at all.[85]

---

[79] FRIED, *supra* note 1, at 29.

[80] Webb v. McGowin, 168 So. 196 (Ala. Ct. App. 1935) (finding enforceable though past consideration on basis of moral obligation).

[81] *See* FRIED, *supra* note 1, at 30, 32, 141.

[82] Allegheny Coll. v. Nat'l Chautauqua County Bank, 159 N.E. 173 (N.Y. 1927).

[83] Wood v. Lucy, Lady Duff Gordon, 118 N.E. 1082 (N.Y. 1918).

[84] Alaska Packers' Ass'n v. Domenico, 117 F. 99 (9th Cir. 1902).

[85] *See* FRIED, *supra* note 1, at 33, 35.

Well, if coherence were the standard for the *existence* of legal doctrine, there might be a good deal less legal doctrine in existence. Nonetheless, Fried's point is well taken: We are hard pressed to defend the doctrine if we try to formulate consideration—on the head of a pin, as it were—and can reduce it to nothing more fundamental than bargain; the colloquial sense of bargain does not seem to fit with legal conclusions construing the term. But before the passage in which Fried gives up on consideration, because consideration is bargain and the cases do not seem to vindicate a bargain requirement, he acknowledges that we can make sense of what seem to be inconsistent decisions based on their "intuitive appeal."[86]

The challenge confronting legal doctrine, and certainly the challenge confronting the consideration doctrine in contract, is to determine results consistent with such an intuitive appeal. Now that is not to say that we should always rely on our intuitions; it is just to acknowledge the attractive force of them. A result (and so a rule that determines that result) that "feels" right will have more power, and more resilience. Fried describes the failure of consideration as a failure of candor: "The movement in the law rather suggests that we may have in the not too distant future a more candid set of principles to determine which promises should be enforceable in terms of the fairness of each type."[87]

P. S. Atiyah's essay, "Consideration: A Restatement," too finds the fit between statements of consideration doctrine and the cases applying that doctrine curious, to say the least. If consideration is conceived in terms of benefit or detriment, that conception fails to explain the cases:

> When a court refuses to enforce a promise despite actual benefit or detriment on the ground that there is no benefit or detriment "in the eye of the law," it is merely asserting that there are other reasons for refusing to enforce the promise. A restatement of the law must make it its business to try to find out what those other reasons are. Equally, when a court does enforce a promise despite the absence of factual benefit or detriment, on the ground that there is a benefit or detriment, "in the eye of the law," the court is plainly enforcing the promise for some other reasons. Again a search for these other reasons must be a necessary part of a restatement of the law.[88]

Atiyah reaches essentially the same conclusion with regard to a bargain theory of consideration. After examining courts' construction of the bargain requirement, Atiyah finds, essentially, that there is no requirement there. Bargain is not so much a test for the presence of consideration as it is a means to state the conclusion that there *is* consideration. His conception of bargain is the colloquial one, contemplating some type of

[86] *Id.* at 34.

[87] *Id.* at 39.

[88] P.S. Atiyah, *Consideration: A Restatement*, *in* Essays on Contract 179, 198–99 (1986).

actual exchange. Insofar as he could not find such an exchange in cases that had found sufficient bargain (*e.g.,* the past consideration cases[89]), he concludes that bargain too, like benefit and detriment, is a pretense.

Professor Stephen Smith, a thoughtful contracts and Atiyah scholar,[90] has described Atiyah's conclusion concerning consideration as "realistic" (we may infer in the best Llewellynesque sense): "The reality... is that [courts] manipulate the rule or the facts so that they can 'find' or 'invent' consideration—and vice versa. It is for this reason that Atiyah's theory is 'realist'; he asserts that the law in the books is different from the law in practice."[91] Smith recognizes that an exhaustive survey of the case law would turn up many cases that could confirm Atiyah's realist conclusion. He also recognizes that many cases could rely on common conceptions of benefit and detriment and bargain to find or not find consideration without doing violence to either the language or the doctrine. We should not be surprised that there is great coincidence between our ability to find a benefit, detriment, or bargain and our willingness to enforce an undertaking. The problem for Atiyah is that benefit, detriment, or bargain could be no more than indicia of the fairness of enforcing a promise; those determinants could not reveal all of the circumstances in which fairness would be served by enforcement.

Now not all courts at all times will be as uncomfortable with doctrine and orthodoxy as we sense Atiyah might be.[92] The problem, for Atiyah, is not that constructions of the consideration doctrine in terms of benefit, detriment, and bargain so much limit the fundamental fairness calculus as that with those tests we run the risk of *obscuring* the normative inquiry. Indeed, what impresses us about *Hamer,* and *Allegheny College*, and *Wood* (and, I would suggest, what makes those opinions canonical) is their execution of the normative calculus without being distracted by "limitations" the imprecision of language would seem to impose on the doctrine. *Mills* is canonical because it so strikingly ignores the normative calculus.

Atiyah acknowledges that we can explain many of the consideration cases by saying that the courts that find consideration are giving effect to the parties' "intent to create legal relations," an observation supported as well by review of the promissory estoppel

---

[89] *Id.* at 214–15.

[90] *See* Stephen A. Smith, Atiyah's Introduction to the Law of Contract (6th ed. 2005); Stephen A. Smith, Contract Theory (2004) [Smith, Theory].

[91] Smith, Theory, *supra* note 90, at 226.

[92] At one point, Atiyah equates orthodoxy with injustice. In the context of his treatment of the past consideration cases, Atiyah concludes that

> It will be apparent... that orthodoxy in this area has been stronger than elsewhere. There are no clear examples of actual decisions which cannot be reconciled with orthodox reasoning. It is therefore not surprising that the law here seems capable of producing greater injustice than elsewhere.

Atiyah, *supra* note 88, at 218.

cases.[93] But Atiyah remains skeptical even of consideration doctrine that would adopt those terms:

> Nobody can seriously propose that all promises should become enforceable; to abolish the doctrine of consideration, therefore, is simply to require the courts to begin all over again the task of deciding what promises are to be enforceable. They will, of course, have to use new technical justifications for this task, and the obvious one that lies to hand is the "intent to create legal relations." No doubt there is something to be said for beginning this task all over again, and for using a new technique for the purpose. Changes in social and commercial conditions, and changes in the moral values of the community, mean that the courts will not always find the same reasons for the enforcement of promises to be good today as their forbears did; equally, it is likely that they will often find good reasons for the enforcement of promises where their predecessors did not.[[94]] Moreover, I think there is less likelihood of the "intent to create legal relations" formula ossifying into a "doctrine"; though there is the converse danger that its application may create uncertainty as to what promises will be enforceable. But I question whether the "intent to create legal relations" formula will in the long run work any better than the rules of consideration.[95]

In fact, the problem Atiyah recognizes is the same problem that, according to Professor James Gordley, confronted English courts that struggled to appreciate the relationship between Aristotelian *causa*[96] and the nascent consideration doctrine developed by common law judges. Though *causa* could capture the *reasons* people make promises, it could not, indeed did not endeavor to, determine which promises the law should enforce. Perhaps as a result of that ultimately misguided effort to discover consideration in *causa*, the role and operation of the consideration doctrine was obscured for common law judges.

---

[93] *See, e.g.,* Daniel A. Farber & John H. Matheson, *Beyond Promissory Estoppel: Contract Law and the "Invisible Handshake,"* 52 U. CHI. L. REV. 903, 907 (1985) (discussing numerous instances when courts found consideration in order to satisfy the intent of the contracting parties).

[94] An example from the past century in which the court was willing to justify the enforcement of a promise when the promise may have not previously been enforced was Wood v. Lucy, Lady-Duff Gordon, 118 N.E. 214 (N.Y. 1918) (footnote added).

[95] ATIYAH, *supra* note 88, 241.

[96] JAMES GORDLEY, THE PHILOSOPHICAL ORIGINS OF MODERN CONTRACT DOCTRINE 49–57, 137–39 (2006). Gordley examines the historical conception of *causa* in Roman and medieval thought as traced back through Aristotle. The conception of *causa* concluded that an agreement can be binding between the parties only if both parties give consent for one of two permissible reasons—"liberality, or the receipt of something in return for what one gives." *Id.* at 49. Gordley also notes that Aristotle's conception of liberality "does not simply mean giving wealth away, but giving 'to the right people, the right amounts, and at the right time.'" *Id.* at 55.

> [C]onsideration meant that relief would be given in certain cases marked out by precedent such as breach of promises to exchange, and that in dubious cases relief would be limited by the ability and willingness of judges to draw far-fetched analogies to those. Consideration was a technique for limiting the action of assumpsit rather than a concept one can define.[97]

There could be *causa* in giving a gift, liberality, but no consideration. The purely gratuitous promise, though the product of a good reason to promise, would not be enforced.[98]

It is Gordley's observation about the vague nature of consideration, unmoored from any sense of Aristotelian *causa*, that is most pertinent to an appreciation of the consideration doctrine that emerges from the canonical cases: Consideration is a "technique" rather than a concept. It is a means to do something; it is not a thing in itself. Perhaps consideration provides the means to *reveal* a good reason for the law to enforce a promise; consideration is not, though, a good reason in itself. So if we find some symbiosis between *causa*, the reason to promise, and consideration, the reason to enforce a promise, then we get the better sense of the courts' method in canonical consideration cases such as *Hamer*, *Allegheny College*, and *Wood*. Consideration may reveal a normative calculus, and that calculus takes into account fairness, but it is premature to conclude that the best we can do is rely on fairness without appreciating that we may be able to unpack the concept of fairness in an even more fundamental sense.

Professor Randy Barnett posited "A Consent Theory of Contract."[99] His thesis, essentially, is that entitlements theory[100] based on individual rights defines "boundaries within which individuals may live, act, and pursue happiness free of the forcible interference of others."[101] His consent theory, then, contains "principles that describe how [individual] rights are initially acquired, how they are transferred from person to person, what the substance and limits of properly obtained rights are, and how interferences with these entitlements are to be rectified."[102] This entitlement theory "comports substantially" with the categories of private law, and contract, of course, concerns specifically "transfers of rights between rights holders."[103]

Barnett discovers a symbiosis between contract and entitlement theory, and then makes sense of contract (both as a positive and as a normative matter) by understanding contract in terms of entitlement theory. As a positive matter, there are gaps, but Barnett would

[97] *Id.* at 138.

[98] *Id.* at 139.

[99] Barnett, *supra* note 16.

[100] *Id.* at 291–92 nn. 93–97 (citing literature on legal entitlements).

[101] *Id.* at 291.

[102] *Id.* at 291–92 (citing ROBERT NOZICK, ANARCHY, STATE AND UTOPIA 150–53 (1974), in which Nozick discusses "a tripartite definition of justice consisting of justice in acquisition, transfer, and rectification").

[103] *Id.* at 292.

likely acknowledge these.[104] His argument is ultimately normative, in terms of the foundation contract *should* claim; he does not very certainly establish that extant contract in fact reflects his normative entitlements theory. He asserts, though, that his entitlement theory would be "more fundamental than the concepts of will, reliance, efficiency, fairness, or bargain."[105] It is, according to Barnett, entitlement theory that tells us how to order those less fundamental concerns.

Although a thorough critique of Barnett's approach is beyond the scope of this inquiry,[106] it is worthwhile to appreciate his treatment of consideration doctrine. He has little patience with consideration in any of its phases. According to consent theory, all that matters is ostensible consent, all that the law should be concerned with is such ostensible consent to an alienation of entitlement. A consideration requirement would burden that fundamental normative goal and result in the frustration of parties' expectations.

> A consent theory of contract... provides the missing theoretical foundation of formal contracts [those merely reciting consideration] and explains their proper place in a well-crafted law of contract. The voluntary use of a recognized formality by a promisor manifests to a promisee an intention to be legally bound in as unambiguous a manner as possible.... Formal contracts ought to be an "easy" case of contractual enforcement, but prevailing theories that require bargained-for consideration, induced reliance, or even economic "efficiency" would have a hard time explaining why. In a consent theory, by contrast, there need be no underlying bargain or demonstrable reliance for such a commitment to be properly enforced.[107]

---

[104] *See* Alces, *supra* note 22, at 526–32 (responding to Barnett).

[105] Barnett, *supra* note 16, at 293. Barnett relies on a number of different authors to support his presentation of the competing theories. In the section discussing his conception of will theory, he relies primarily upon FRIED, *supra* note 1; A. S. Burrows, *Contract, Tort and Restitution—A Satisfactory Division or Not?*, 99 LAW Q. REV. 217 (1983); and Morris R. Cohen, *The Basis of Contract*, 46 HARV. L. REV. 553 (1933). The discussion of reliance theories utilizes the work of P.S. ATIYAH, THE RISE AND FALL OF FREEDOM OF CONTRACT (1979); GRANT GILMORE, THE DEATH OF CONTRACT (1st ed. 1974); Jay M. Feinman, *Promissory Estoppel and Judicial Method*, 97 HARV. L. REV. 678 (1984); and Stanley D. Henderson, *Promissory Estoppel and Traditional Contract Doctrine*, 78 YALE L. J. 343 (1969). The discussion of efficiency draws on RICHARD A. POSNER, ECONOMIC ANALYSIS OF THE LAW (2d ed. 1977); RICHARD A. POSNER, THE ECONOMICS OF JUSTICE (1981); Ronald Coase, *The Problem of Social Cost*, 3 J.L. & ECON. 1 (1960); and Richard A. Posner & William M. Landes, *Legal Change, Judicial Behavior, and the Diversity Jurisdiction*, 9 J. LEGAL STUD. 367 (1980). Barnett focuses his discussion of substantive fairness theory on LUDWIG VON MISES, HUMAN ACTION (rev. ed. 1963); Cohen, *supra* note 105; Richard Epstein, *The Social Consequences of Common Law Rules*, 95 HARV. L. REV. 1717 (1982); and Richard Epstein, *Unconscionability, A Critical Reapprisal*, 18 J.L. & ECON. 293 (1975). Finally, his discussion of bargain theory relies upon A.W.B. SIMPSON, A HISTORY OF THE COMMON LAW OF CONTRACT 316 (1975); Melvin Aron Eisenberg, *The Principles of Consideration*, 67 Cornell L. Rev. 640, 640, 642 (1982); and Lon L.Fuller, *Consideration and Form*, 41 COLUM. L. REV. 799, 813 (1941).

[106] *See* Alces, *supra* note 22, at 526–32, for such a critique.

[107] Barnett, *supra* note 16, at 311–12 (footnote omitted).

Taking for the moment on faith Barnett's conclusion that his entitlement theory would make sense of portions of contract other normative theories could not, for present purposes, it is his conclusion about what consideration can indicate even in his consent theory that is noteworthy: Bargain may perform a "channeling function,"[108] indicating that the parties who strike a bargain have manifested an intent to transfer rights, have, at least arguably, *consented* to contract.

So Barnett's normative theory, premised on entitlement, effectively eviscerates much of what we may think of as a bargain or even benefit or detriment theory of consideration. Consideration matters more for what it intimates—an intent to transfer, consent—than for what it may be in substance. It is not bargain, or benefit, or detriment that matters; it is what each indicates about the parties' intent, their understanding. That perspective certainly makes good sense of cases such as *Hamer, Allegheny College*, and *Wood.* So again a deontic theory can make some sense of consideration in a manner familiar from the canon.

What emerges from the deontic perspectives considered here, then, is a view of a consideration that does not constrain. The consideration requirement *vindicated* by rights based theories is a requirement that facilitates the enforcement of contracts when it would be fair or just to do so. And, I would agree, that is just the conception of consideration in contract vindicated by the doctrine. Now that is not to say that there will not be cases that refuse to enforce a promise for want of nothing more than formal consideration,[109] but it is to suggest that such cases are inconsistent with the normative sense of the doctrine. Courts refusing to find consideration may not have taken due advantage of the nature of the doctrine, and so reach conclusions inconsistent with the normative object of contract revealed in the canonical cases, as least insofar as deontology is concerned.[110] We can confirm much of the same normative story of consideration when we consider the alternative perspective.

---

[108] *Id.* at 314 n.189 (observing that "the channeling function of formality 'has no place where men's activities are already divided into definite, clear-cut business categories. . . . It is for this reason that important transactions on the stock and produce markets can safely be carried on in the most 'informal' manner.'") (citing Fuller, *supra* note 105, at 806).

[109] *See, e.g.,* Harrington v. Taylor, 36 S.E.2d 227 (1945). In this case, a husband had been assaulting his wife, who took refuge in the house of a third person. The defendant-husband subsequently entered the house and continued assaulting the wife. The wife used an ax to knock her husband down and was about to kill him when the third person stopped the ax blow with her hand, badly mutilating it. The husband promised to pay the woman's damages; however, after a few small payments, the husband discontinued the compensation entirely. The North Carolina Supreme Court concludes that plaintiff failed to state a cause of action: "[H]owever much the defendant should be impelled by common gratitude to alleviate the plaintiff's misfortune, a humanitarian act of this kind, voluntarily performed, is not such consideration as would entitle her to recover at law." *Id.* at 227.

[110] This topic will be described at greater length during the discussion of the complementary promissory estoppel doctrine, *infra* Chapter 4 Part C 2.

b. Consequentialism

Few contract theorists have as consistently demonstrated a grasp of the normative calculus in both deontic and consequentialist terms as has Professor Michael Trebilcock. His work is always thoughtful, clear, and precise. His book, *The Limits of Freedom of Contract,*[111] considers the fundamental premises of contract and surveys the theories and theorists in order to take the normative measure of the doctrine. Chapter 8, "Consideration," endeavors to formulate the best argument for the doctrine. Trebilcock's analysis assumes the deontic and consequentialist justifications for contract generally;[112] his object is to identify the role consideration serves as a precondition for legal enforcement.

Just as, for deontologists, consideration can serve a channeling function, the requirement also similarly accommodates the parties' signaling so far as consequentialism is concerned. The fact that a promise is supported by consideration, is the product of a bargain (or sufficient bargain), is enough to signal the promisee that the promisor intends the promisee to rely on the promise differently, more certainly, than the promisee would rely on an expressed intention to act (or refrain from acting) that was not the product of bargain. A party who makes a promise not supported by consideration makes less of a representation (or a less valuable representation) and the promisee should take that into account when putting a value on that representation.

Trebilcock recognizes that a promisor may make an entirely gratuitous promise, say, to give her alma mater one million dollars, or the promisor may make a promise supported by consideration, say, to provide professional services in exchange for a one-million-dollar fee. The first, gratuitous promise could be subject to a range of conditions, such as the promisee's maintaining or achieving a particular standing in the academic or athletic community or offering a particular degree program. But the gratuitous promise may also contemplate conditions related to the promisor's financial condition. The promisor could promise to donate a certain sum over a term of years so long as the promisor's net worth remains in excess of ten million dollars. Were those or other conditions specified in terms that both parties could appreciate, then we could expect that the promisor would realize the true value of his promise[113] and the promisee would as well be able to more accurately value the promise and rely accordingly. The more certain the value of an asset, the more valuable that asset may be.

In the context of considering alternative damage measures, Trebilcock offers a construction of *Hamer* that demonstrates degrees of promise, in terms that may have some salience for our appreciating a consequentialist conception of the consideration doctrine:

> The relevance of demonstrated reliance by promisees on promises... creates many of the same problems of indeterminacy noted earlier in different contexts. For

[111] Michael J. Trebilcock, The Limits of Freedom of Contract (1993).

[112] *See id.*, chs. 1 and 4.

[113] *See* Richard A. Posner, Economic Analysis of the Law § 4.10 (7th ed. 2007) (Promisors can realize greater value if their gratuitous promises are enforceable.).

> example, suppose that an uncle promises his nephew $1000 as a Christmas present, with no explicit conditions attached, and the nephew buys a new suit for $500 on his credit card before Christmas Day. The gift does not materialize on Christmas Day and is in fact revoked. If the uncle really meant to be legally bound by his promise, as in *Hamer v. Sidway*, it would seem difficult to justify a remedy different from the expectation damages awarded for breach of an unrelied-upon promise under seal. To give the nephew full reliance damages puts a premium on precipitate action and penalizes more circumspect promisees who do not rely at all until the promise is fulfilled.[114] What constitutes "reasonable" reliance in this context is not clear. If, however, the promise was not intended to be legally binding, but was instead a "best efforts" promise or a "present intentions" commitment, then any reliance ought reasonably to be influenced by the probabilities of performance; and if performance does not materialize, the donee should have no cause for complaint.[115]

The extant consideration requirement, though, is too coarsely grained. There is either a bargain or there is not; the promise is either legally binding or it is not.[116] Whatever normative purpose the consideration requirement *could* serve will, it would seem, necessarily be frustrated by the doctrine's ostensible one-size-fits-all quality.

Now we might decide to limit *legal* enforcement to promises made in a commercial setting, in which the consequentialist could have more confidence that the transaction is welfare creating. Judicial resources are limited and in a world of such scarce resources it might make sense to rely on extra-judicial, perhaps purely reputational, inhibitions on promise breaking.[117] In an article cited by Trebilcock, Professor Andrew Kull makes the point that entirely gratuitous promises, those not the product of bargain or otherwise supported by some conception of consideration, may well involve economic, and efficiency, benefits that it would be worthwhile for the law to enforce.

> Much depends on the choice of a paradigm. [Judge Richard] Posner suggests that the promise typically denied enforcement by the general rule is one that is not worth enforcing, offering as a "good example of the rule and its economic logic... a case where a man promised to take a woman to dinner but later reneged." The example is ill chosen. Litigation of such a promise would be a freak occurrence, and the promise would properly be denied enforcement on other grounds: namely, that it was neither *intended nor understood* to create legal relations. If our paradigm,

---

[114] If we conclude, however, that such promisees *were* entitled to expectation damages, it is not clear that their circumspection would be warranted, or rational.

[115] TREBILCOCK, *supra* note 111, at 180.

[116] This is not to say that a court could not do a little justice by relying, for example, on promissory estoppel or adjusting its calculation of expectation damages.

[117] *See* Richard A. Posner, *Gratuitous Promises in Economics and Law*, 6 J. LEGAL STUD. 411, 415–17 (1977).

> instead, is a written promise to a friend or relative of a gift substantial enough to justify the cost of litigation, why should we suppose that the cost/benefit comparison is necessarily unfavorable to enforcement? A promise for an exchange of comparable magnitude might well yield a similar comparison. Perhaps enforcement of the bargain promise is also inefficient.[118]

The best argument we can make for consideration, then, is that the doctrine provides *a* means to signal the parties' intent, but, of course, we might well be able to discern that intent even in cases in which consideration is not in evidence. Trebilcock concludes that insofar as the parties have the power to decide whether a promise is legally enforceable, that is, by providing consideration to support the promise, "[n]othing justifies the conjecture that a gratuitous transfer produces less economic utility than otherwise comparable transactions in the bargain context."[119] So the best argument consequentialist theory can make on behalf of consideration remains the signaling argument.

That conclusion means that consequentialists' explanation for consideration, its role as indicator of the parties' intent, is entirely consistent with the deontic explanation. So consideration makes sense for consequentialists just when it makes sense for deontologists: if it confirms an intent to be bound in a particular way. That is not to say that, for either perspective, the consideration doctrine, whether construed in detriment, benefit, or bargain terms, is a particularly reliable indicator of the requisite intent; it may well not be. But the doctrine, in its several iterations, does channel the inquiry in ways that will vindicate values central to both the deontic and consequentialist perspectives. The doctrine is not *better* explained by reference to one rather than the other; the focus is on intent, and intent is no more important to one of the normative explanations of the doctrine than it is to the other.

Although promissory estoppel is treated further in Chapters Seven, "Contract Enforcement Doctrine," and Eight, "Theory of Contract Enforcement," it would be incomplete to consider the consideration doctrine wholly removed from its promissory estoppel complement at this juncture. The student of contract quickly appreciates that the substance of consideration is dependent on the complementary promissory estoppel doctrine, and the dependence is reciprocal. We cannot appreciate the normative scope of either doctrine in deontic or consequentialist terms without appreciating the scope and operation of the other.

2. PROMISSORY ESTOPPEL

The promissory estoppel doctrine provides the means to enforce *some* promises (and maybe even "not quite promises") that are not supported by consideration. The doctrine

---

[118] Andrew Kull, *Reconsidering Gratuitous Promises*, 21 J. LEGAL STUD. 39, 56–57 (1992) (footnotes omitted, emphasis added).

[119] TREBILCOCK, *supra* note 111, at 183.

does not make all promises without consideration enforceable. Plaintiff must establish that she relied in fact, that her reliance was reasonable, and that defendant should have foreseen that reasonable reliance.[120] Both deontology and consequentialism have to make room for promissory estoppel in terms of a consideration doctrine that, as we have seen, already serves the function of revealing intent and providing a sufficient basis to enforce a promise based on that revealed intent. To make sense of the coexistence of the consideration and promissory estoppel bases to enforce promises, we need to identify the subtle difference to which the promissory estoppel doctrine gives effect in terms that make normative sense. Both deontologists and consequentialists can make room for promissory estoppel, and it is worthwhile to appreciate the contours of their explanations by reference to the doctrine revealed by the canonical cases.

a. Deontology

P.S. Atiyah is a good place to start. He posits the prototypical promissory estoppel case, the case that tests the fit between the consideration and promissory estoppel doctrines:

> The promisor does not state any act which is to be performed by the promisee but the promisee does act in reliance on the promise in a way which was the natural and foreseeable result of the promise. This promise is said to be... enforceable to the limited extent recognized by promissory estoppel.[121]

Bargain, the fact of a *quid pro quo*, is the basis of the *distinction* between the enforcement of promises on consideration (contract) grounds and the enforcement of promises on promissory estoppel grounds. It is not immediately clear that bargain *qua* bargain provides a very good *reason* for the distinction. What does bargain add to the normative calculus? It surely must serve more than an evidentiary role; recovery on a promissory estoppel basis may be supported by very clear and unequivocal evidence of a promise and reliance thereon. Insofar as different damages may flow from application of the two alternative theories, a normative explanation for the difference can be tenable only if bargain has normative significance. That normative significance is the focus of Atiyah's inquiry:

> So long as it is believed that all contracts are bargains, there is some rational ground for requiring that the act to be performed by the promisee must be stated, if not actually requested, by the promisor; but once it is agreed that many promises are

[120] *See* RESTATEMENT (SECOND) OF CONTRACTS § 90 (1981).

[121] ATIYAH, *supra* note 88, 227 (This conception may not be so clearly prototypical: in *Red Owl* promisor did tell promisee exactly what to do; the question was whether there was a promise or not.).

> enforced though they are not bargains, it is hard to see what rational purpose is intended to be served by the insistence that the act must be stated.[122]

Now it is true that Atiyah's analysis of the fit between the bargain theory of consideration and promissory estoppel concerns particularly development of promissory estoppel as a doctrine of the English contract law. The focus of this book is the canon as it has developed, primarily, in American law. Though the question Atiyah addresses is "how can we make sense of bargain theory and the English promissory estoppel doctrine," a less robust "shield" rather than "sword" doctrine,[123] his inquiry pertains as well, perhaps even more profoundly, when we try to reconcile the normative bases of promissory estoppel and the consideration doctrine.

Atiyah concludes that consideration and promissory estoppel enforcement theories both vindicate the same opaque interest: justice. We enforce bargains because it is just to do so and we enforce promises not supported by consideration because it would be unjust not to do so. That is pretty much all we can take from Atiyah's comparison of the two doctrines.[124] That resolution to a focus on justice resonates too with the *Second Restatement's* invocation of justice to determine the appropriate damage award in promissory estoppel cases: "The remedy granted for breach may be limited as justice requires."[125] There is no substantial difference between saying that avoidance of injustice is the predicate of the cause of action and saying that the remedy available to plaintiff "may be limited as justice requires." That remedial "limitation" is in fact no limit at all, at least in comparison with the parallel consideration theory. Indeed, the essential identity of the two is confirmed by promissory estoppel cases in which the court awarded the successful plaintiff expectation damages[126] and the bargain cases in which the successful plaintiff received no more than reliance damages.[127]

Stephen Smith recognizes that making sense of promissory estoppel in relation to contract requires our first understanding the basis of promissory estoppel liability. That is, if we explain promissory estoppel as based on promissory theory, then promissory estoppel is just an adjunct of the contract law, which is essentially about promissory

---

[122] *Id.* at 230.

[123] SMITH, THEORY, *supra* note 90, at 240–43.

[124] Of particular note is Atiyah's construction and examination of Combe v. Combe, (1951) 2 K.B. 215. ATIYAH, *supra* note 88, at 231.

[125] RESTATEMENT (SECOND) OF CONTRACTS § 90 (1981).

[126] *See* E. ALLAN FARNSWORTH ON CONTRACTS § 12.1 (3d ed. 2004); FARNSWORTH, *supra* note 77, 110–14; *see, e.g.,* Ricketts v. Scothorn, 77 N.W. 365, 367 (Neb. 1898); Katz v. Danny Dare, Inc., 610 S.W.2d 121 (Mo. Ct. App. 1980); Crail v. Blakely, 505 P.2d 1027 (Cal. 1973).

[127] The essential identity of the two is confirmed by Fuller and Perdue's *Reliance Interest* article. Lon L. Fuller & William R. Perdue, Jr., *The Reliance Interest in Contract Damages: 1*, 46 YALE L.J. 52 (1936), and *The Reliance Interest in Contract Damages: 2*, 46 YALE L.J. 373 (1937). The article is in two parts, the first analyzing remedies for breach and the second surveying the case law.

obligation.[128] Alternatively, if we perceive promissory estoppel as vindicating primarily reliance, then promissory estoppel is not contractual.[129] Finally, if promissory estoppel is an amalgam of promise and reliance, "the purpose of estoppel is to enforce relied-upon promises."[130] Smith's taxonomy is useful. Indeed, one might even conclude that Smith describes not just alternative conceptions of promissory estoppel but alternative conceptions of all of contract as well. The fact is, the doctrine may not choose among the three alternatives of promise, reliance, or a promise—reliance amalgam in the case of either contract or promissory estoppel. The "bargain" concept, in the shapes it takes, may more clearly support an array of cases demonstrating reliance, or promise, or some combination of the two than it does provide a means to distinguish cases in which either reliance or promise is in evidence but the other is not. The more contract may be construed as not clearly based either on promise *or* reliance, the less we can have confidence in posited normative distinctions between liability based on contract or promissory estoppel.

Doctrine revealed in the canonical cases obscures the promise versus reliance bases of contract liability, and so undermines efforts to distinguish contract from promissory estoppel in normative terms. Indeed, though it is controversial,[131] we might conclude that protection of reliance seems to explain a good deal of what we are after when we enforce promises. And, of course, the very fact that we enforce promises *qua* promises, encourages reliance on promises and so enhances the normative argument for enforcing promises: The fact that promisees rely on promises is another good normative reason to enforce promises.

This view of the melding of contract and promissory estoppel has been endorsed by thoughtful studies in recent years. In addition to the Fuller and Perdue project,[132] Professor Grant Gilmore's book, *The Death of Contract,*[133] depicts contract law in large part subsumed by the same reliance principles that support promissory estoppel:

> We seem to be in the presence of the phenomenon which, in the history of comparative religion, is called syncretism—that is, according to Webster, "the reconciliation or union of conflicting beliefs." I have occasionally suggested to my students that a desirable reform in legal education would be to merge the first-year courses in Contracts and Torts into a single course which we could call Contorts. Perhaps the same suggestion would be a good one when the time comes for the third round of Restatements.

---

[128] Smith, Theory, *supra* note 90, at 234; *see also id.* at 56–78.

[129] *Id.* at 234.

[130] *Id.* at 235.

[131] *Id.* at 96. Smith rejects reliance based theories because they "are not grounded in a distinct and compelling moral foundation."

[132] Fuller & Perdue, *supra* note 127.

[133] Gilmore, *supra* note 3.

> ... This line, if it continues to be followed, may ultimately provide the doctrinal justification for the fusing of contract and tort in a unified theory of civil obligation. A remarkable passage in the Restatement (Second) § 90 explains how most "contract" cases, if not all of them, can be brought under § 90 so that resort to § 75 and consideration theory will rarely, if ever, be necessary.[134]

The commentary to Section 90 of the *Second Restatement* confirms the symbiosis, at least, of the promise and reliance bases of contract:

> It is fairly arguable that the enforcement of informal contracts in the action of assumpsit rested historically on justifiable reliance on a promise. Certainly reliance is one of the main bases for enforcement of the half-completed exchange, and the probability of reliance lends support to the enforcement of the executory exchange.[135]

The first comment to Section 75 of the *Second Restatement* also suggests the symbiosis of promise and reliance in both contract and promissory estoppel: "In modern times the enforcement of bargains is not limited to those partly completed, but is extended to the wholly executory exchange in which promise is exchanged for promise.... [T]he element of reliance, *if present at all*, is less tangible and direct than in the case of the half-completed exchange."[136] So, the comment continues, contract relies on bargain and, we might add, all that bargain may entail. But the relationship between reliance and bargain is at best opaque, and it is not difficult to appreciate how reliance could be a factor in discerning bargain.

Further support for the conclusion that there is symmetry if not perfect identity between bargain and promissory estoppel may be found in two papers published in the last few years of the twentieth century. In a 1985 article,[137] Professors Daniel Farber and John Matheson recognize that the traditional view divides promissory liability into two categories: bargained-for exchange and promissory estoppel. They survey the cases, and note the courts' merger of the two. Reliance has become a less important element of promissory estoppel and so a less certain way to distinguish the two bases of promissory liability: "With the decline of reliance, promissory estoppel is moving away from tort law. It has become a means of enforcing promises differing in doctrinal detail from traditional contract law but sharing a common goal."[138]

---

[134] *Id.* at 98.

[135] Restatement (Second) of Contracts § 90 cmt. a (1981).

[136] *Id.* § 75 cmt. a (1981) (emphasis added).

[137] Farber & Matheson, *supra* note 93.

[138] *Id.* at 945.

We could also say that the movement Farber and Matheson discern represents a movement toward common ground between the deontic and consequentialist normative perspectives. They would restate the basis of promissory liability in a revised Section 71 of the *Second Restatement*: "A promise is enforceable when made in furtherance of an economic activity."[139] That would not seem to exclude much, and would certainly capture, *in normatively neutral terms*, the common basis of the bargain and promissory estoppel categories of promissory liability. You might take issue with Farber and Matheson's reading of the cases, or conclude that they have not read enough of them,[140] but it is difficult to argue with their conclusion even if all you rely upon are the canonical cases that support both the consideration and promissory estoppel doctrines.

Professors Yorio and Thel reach a conclusion similar to Farber and Matheson's six years later.[141] Yorio and Thel read many of the same cases and conclude that reliance is just not a very important part of the promissory estoppel calculus. They go further, though, and construe the cases as supporting expectation recovery, either through benefit of the bargain substitutional relief or specific performance. Their argument begins with a recitation of a famous colloquy on the floor of the American Law Institute when the first iteration of Section 90 was being debated. Professor Samuel Williston was the Reporter for the *Restatement (First) of Contracts* and was asked by ALI member Frederic Coudert to resolve a hypothetical.

> Uncle, aware that Nephew is thinking about buying a car, promises to give Nephew $1,000. Nephew buys a car for $600. If Uncle reneges on his promise and Nephew sues, what does the Nephew recover, $1,000 or $600? Williston responded that Uncle would be liable for $1,000, the amount of his promise.[142]

Mr. Coudert disagreed with Williston, as did others in attendance.[143] Yorio and Thel conclude that the difference between the two damage measures is the difference in our way of thinking about the relationship between bargain-based contract liability and estoppel-based promissory liability: "Williston's insistence that the promise is either binding or not invites the response that the extent to which the promise should be enforced depends on the reason for judicial intervention. If the reason is to protect the promisee's reliance interest, the remedy should be limited to reliance damages measured by the cost of the

---

[139] *Id.* at 930.

[140] *See* Robert A. Hillman, *Questioning the "New Consensus" on Promissory Estoppel: An Empirical and Theoretical Study*, 98 COLUM. L. REV. 580, 586–88, 618 (1998) (concluding that although Farber and Matheson examined a large number of cases, they discuss only relatively few cases supporting their thesis, and criticizing fact that they base their conclusion only on amorphously defined "key cases").

[141] Edward Yorio & Steve Thel, *The Promissory Basis of Section 90*, 101 YALE L.J. 111, 166–67 (1991).

[142] *Id.* at 116 (citing *Proceedings at Fourth Annual Meeting*, 4 A.L.I. PROC. 95–96 (1926)).

[143] *Id.* at 116–18.

car. . . ."[144] So, succinctly, Williston and Coudert were not just disagreeing about the proper measure of damages in a promissory estoppel case; they were disagreeing about the normative basis of contract. We serve different normative principles if we vindicate expectation over reliance or reliance over expectation.

Yorio and Thel put that conclusion together with the Fuller and Perdue reliance interest thesis and conclude that insofar as bargain and estoppel-based promise enforcement theories share a common normative foundation, the two theories may, indeed should, support common damage measures *because* they share a common normative basis. The *reasons* why we enforce promises supported by consideration are no different from the *reasons* why we enforce promises by estoppel.

Their argument proceeds:

> Section 90 ensures that some of the functions of the bargain requirement are served in other ways. Among other things, the presence of a bargain helps to identify promises on which the promisor has seriously reflected. If she made the promise to get something in return, her promise was sufficiently well considered to justify legal enforcement. [145]

The fact that promissory estoppel serves "some of the functions of the bargain requirement" would justify the award of the same damages whether plaintiff prevailed on one theory or the other. Yorio and Thel prove their thesis by reviewing the promissory estoppel cases' award of damages: To the extent that courts enforcing promises on a promissory estoppel basis award expectation damages, the calculation that would generally follow enforcement of a promise on a bargain basis, the normative identity between bargain and estoppel-based promise enforcement is established. In other words, Yorio and Thel do for promissory estoppel what Fuller and Perdue did for consideration. According to Yorio and Thel, courts using promissory estoppel award expectation damages[146] and according to Fuller and Perdue courts using consideration theory award reliance damages.[147] The damage awards, then, establish the normative identity of the two promise enforcement theories. All that must distinguish them is the evidence requisite to application of each theory, but there is no reason to assume that evidentiary differences have normative significance.

The foregoing suggests that we cannot, or at least need not posit different normative bases of the two formation theories. Whether our perspective is deontic or consequentialist, we should expect that the same arguments from each will support both formation

[144] *Id.* at 118.

[145] *Id.* at 124 (footnote omitted).

[146] *Id.* at 129–51.

[147] Fuller & Perdue, *supra* note 127, at 417–20.

theories. Deontology will have to explain promissory estoppel in the same normative terms it uses to explain consideration theory, and consequentialists too will have to offer the same normative argument for both formation theories.

b. Consequentialism

Professor Robert Scott, a consequentialist commentator, has revisited *Hoffman v. Red Owl Stores, Inc.* in order to evaluate the decision's contribution to the promissory estoppel law and to comment, as well, on the fit among promises enforced as bargains (that is, on the consideration basis), promises enforced by the operation of promissory estoppel principles, and unenforceable "promises" arising in the course of negotiations preliminary to contract formation.[148] A consequentialist object would be served if courts were able to distinguish preliminary negotiations from the type of promises on which a promisee could rely, and then enforce by operation of promissory estoppel principles. So if courts obscure the distinction, effective preliminary negotiations may be undermined. For Scott, there needs to be a unitary conception of promise.

Scott's extended treatment of the *Hoffman* facts makes clear that he thinks both the trial court and the appellate court obscured the reality of the underlying transaction between Joseph Hoffmann[149] and representatives of Red Owl Stores. Succinctly, Scott concludes that, as between the two sides, Hoffman was not nearly so much an innocent victim of the representatives' guile as he was a victim of his own inattention to detail. Scott's recapitulation of the facts and careful exegesis of the trial record is interesting. Ultimately, though, it is quite beside the point. It does not matter what the trial court should have found as a matter of fact or how the appellate court should have construed the findings of fact. The doctrine of the case and, in turn, its canonical significance, is a product of the facts as found by the court. There may well have been good reason to construe the facts differently, but the law that emerges from *Hoffman* is the product of the facts recited. The *meaning* of *Hoffman* is not dependent on a true representation of the underlying facts; the *meaning* of the case depends only on the facts as found by the court. So Scott's historical reconstruction is interesting, but only as history.

For present purposes, though, there is a key portion of the Scott analysis that pertains to appreciation of the fit between the bargain and promissory estoppel bases of promise enforcement. Scott focuses on the appellate court's conclusion that Red Owl made a promise to Hoffman, a promise sufficient to support recovery on a promissory estoppel theory but insufficient to support a bargain consideration theory of recovery. He makes much of the point that, at the trial court, there was no specific finding that a promise *qua*

---

[148] Robert E. Scott, Hoffman v. Red Owl Stores *and the Myth of Precontractual Reliance*, 68 OHIO ST. L.J. 71 (2007).

[149] *Id.* at 85–90. During his extensive discussion of both the trial and appeal, Scott includes the transcript from the trial in which the court misspelled Hoffmann as *Hoffman*.

promise had been made. Instead, Scott reports that the court considered whether a mere *representation* "made by Red Owl officials that if Hoffman fulfilled certain conditions a deal for a franchise store would be concluded."[150] Now there may be a difference between A's *representation* that if B does X A will do Y and A's *promise* that if B does X A will do Y but the difference is not obvious. So I suggest Scott is splitting hairs to no effect in this part of his analysis and conclusion.

But no matter, the important point follows after Scott struggles with the nature of the promise characterization. The *Hoffman* court concludes, somewhat curiously, that the *promise* that is the focus of Section 90 of the *First Restatement* is not the same as the *promise* that is the product of a bargain, a consideration-based contract. Somehow promissory estoppel requires less of a promise. The court's explanation bears reproduction:

> If promissory estoppel were to be limited to only those situations where the promise giving rise to the cause of action must be so definite with respect to all details that a contract would result were the promise supported by consideration, then the defendants' instant promises to Hoffman would not meet this test. However, [Section 90] does not impose the requirement that the promise giving rise to the cause of action must be so comprehensive in scope as to meet the requirements of an offer that would ripen into a contract if accepted by the promisee....
>
> We deem it would be a mistake to regard an action grounded on promissory estoppel as the equivalent of a breach-of-contract action.[151]

The court cites a 1950 article by Dean Benjamin Boyer in support of its general conclusion that the promissory estoppel inquiry must remain "fluid."[152] The court does not cite specific language in the Boyer article that distinguishes among promises, but Boyer does reach such a conclusion: "[I]t is clear that [the promise which can support recovery on a promissory estoppel theory] stands midway between those promises which have been bought and paid for with a price and those which are purely gratuitous."[153] The article concludes, "[t]o promissory estoppel, then, is to be left the gap between the mere promise and the bargain. In this gap the doctrine can operate rationally, logically and usefully as a means of protecting justifiable reliance and avoiding injustice."[154] Boyer's effort is to find a role for promissory estoppel in a contract world. Why would we have an alternative basis of promise enforcement once we decide that consideration is requisite? Rather than appreciating the vagaries of consideration analysis, or at least the great

---

[150] *Id.* at 86.

[151] Hoffman v. Red Owl Stores 133 N.W.2d 267, 275 (Wis. 1965).

[152] *Id.* at 274 (citing Benjamin Boyer, *Promissory Estoppel: Requirements and Limitations of the Doctrine*, 98 U. PENN. L. REVIEW 459 (1950)).

[153] Boyer, *supra* note 152, at 497.

[154] *Id.* at 498.

breadth of circumstances that might support the conclusion that the promisor has received consideration, Boyer assumes that the consideration doctrine has a substance it may not have and so the promise supported by consideration somehow has more substance than the promise that Section 90 might enforce. In fact Boyer may not correctly understand what kind of promise is enforced on a consideration basis. His misunderstanding of such promises leads to his confusion about how the promissory estoppel promise is somehow different, less substantial.

We can, though, make sense of Boyer's (and *Hoffman*'s) confusion when we refer back to the Yorio and Thel contribution. Our conception of promissory estoppel and its fit with consideration based promise enforcement matured from Coudert's misimpression to a contemporary unitary conception of promise in line with Williston's understanding.[155] There is either a promise or there is not; there are not degrees of promising. Further, once we find a promise to be enforceable, on either promissory estoppel or consideration grounds, the measure of enforcement may be either an expectation or reliance (or even restitution[156]) measure whether the enforcement theory is promissory estoppel or consideration. Yorio and Thel confirm that the expectation measure operates in promissory estoppel cases and Fuller and Perdue had established, in the early part of the last century, that the reliance measure operates in consideration cases. That identity of enforcement measure intimates an identity of normative premises between the two bases of promise enforcement. Now it certainly may be true that there are some promises that contract will not enforce, even from the promissory estoppel perspective. But that is not because there is somehow less of a promise in normative terms; what is lacking is the certainty of the putative promisor's undertaking, and so perhaps "a reasonably certain basis for giving an appropriate remedy."[157]

Scott's recognition that there is only one sense of promise supports the argument here. The Boyer view is that there is a range of promises, some less enforceable than others and thus amenable to enforcement on promissory estoppel but not on consideration grounds. In criticizing the *Hoffman* court for its endorsement of the Boyer view, Scott confirms the unitary conception of promise that supports too the common normative basis of the alternative promise enforcement mechanisms. He cites the definition of "promise" in the *Second Restatement*[158] and notes that the definition does not distinguish between the promises consideration will enforce and those that promissory estoppel will enforce.

---

[155] Yorio & Thel, *supra* note 141, at 123–26.

[156] *See* FARNSWORTH, *supra* note 77, at 116–19.

[157] *See* UCC § 2-204(3) (2002). The language of UCC § 2-204(3) reflects the uncertainty in contract formation that is noted in Boyer's article.

[158] RESTATEMENT (SECOND) OF CONTRACTS § 2 (1) (1981). The Section provides in relevant part that: "(1) A promise is a manifestation of intention to act or refrain from acting in a specified way, so made as to justify a promisee in understanding that a commitment has been made."

> [T]he Restatement of Contracts has only one definition of a promise, and that definition applies equally to a promise that is the product of a bargained-for-exchange and a promise for which enforcement is sought on the grounds of induced reliance. The doctrine of indefiniteness holds that, for a representation to qualify as a promise, it must be sufficiently clear and definite that it justifies the promisee in believing that a commitment has been made. If the terms of a manifestation are uncertain or indefinite, then, by definition, it fails to qualify as a promise.[159]

Scott notes too that when the term "promise" is used in Section 90, the promissory estoppel provision, the term is defined by reference to the general definition of "promise" in Section 2.[160] There is, then, only one sense of promise, and that conception conveys the same normative sense wherever and whenever it operates in contract, including in the promissory estoppel setting.

That is not to say that all promises merit the same enforcement measure, but we cannot assume that different enforcement measures intimate different normative premises. Instead, we should understand that all promises proceed from the same normative foundation and that normative foundation may accommodate divergent enforcement measures depending upon considerations pertinent to that unitary normative premise, as well as perhaps other practical considerations (*i.e.,* computational).

What we see then, in the contract *quid pro quo* requirement, is concern with finding a reason to enforce a promise. Enforcement will serve the same normative purpose, whether the reason behind it is founded on consideration or estoppel principles. The story the canonical cases tell us, the story that emerges through the doctrine, is that, ultimately, the different enforcement theories reveal the same normative considerations. So if we can justify bargain on deontic or consequentialist grounds, we can also justify promissory estoppel on those same grounds. Further, there is nothing about bargain or promissory estoppel that is inconsistent with either deontic or consequentialist conceptions; the doctrine is agnostic, insofar as it is at least once removed from the normative object. It follows, then, that insofar as neither deontology nor consequentialism can make sense of consideration as a formal requirement but would enforce certain promises irrespective of that formality, the range of promises either normative perspective would enforce is not constrained by a distinction between promises enforced on a consideration rather than promissory estoppel basis. The good sense that Farber and Matheson and then Yorio and Thel discern in the enforcement of promises not supported by consideration is consistent with promises supported by consideration. And the doctrine, from *Allegheny College* to *Hoffman,* supports that normative consistency.

---

[159] Scott, *supra* note 148, at 90 (footnote omitted).

[160] *Id.* (citing RESTATEMENT (SECOND) OF CONTRACTS § 2 (1) (1981)).

5

CONTRACT PERFORMANCE DOCTRINE

THIS CHAPTER CONTINUES the project begun in Chapter Three, "Contract Formation Doctrine," the delineation of the contract canon, and here the focus is the group of cases that have contributed to that portion of the contract undertaking that may be included under the broad heading, *performance*. Again, the label is designed just to distinguish this part of the canon survey from the other two constituent parts proposed in this book, formation and enforcement, and not to suggest that another categorical label for other categorical purposes could not be as or more accurate. The labels are designed to be more functional than essential.

Just as Benjamin Cardozo determines much of our understanding of contract formation, his understanding of contract parties' performance responsibilities is a good place to begin the survey of performance doctrine through the canonical cases.

A. *Jacob & Youngs, Inc. v. Kent*[1]

The Cardozo opinion in *Jacob & Youngs, Inc, v. Kent* reaches an important, indeed canonical, conclusion largely unhindered by the actual facts of the case. *Jacob & Youngs* is about substantial performance or conditions, depending on how it is addressed in the contracts

[1] Jacob & Youngs, Inc. v. Kent, 129 N.E. 889 (N.Y. 1921).

casebook and course. Fundamentally, though, it is about what one contracting party can expect from the other, when close enough is good enough.

Perhaps not unlike other litigants whose cases have entered the canon, Kent tried to exploit a rigid construction of contract doctrine to avoid making the final payment to the contractor who built a country residence for him. The equities certainly did not lie with Kent, so Cardozo makes sure the law does not either. Although the contract called for the installation of Reading pipe, plaintiff contractor substituted an equivalent product, Cohoes pipe. The court acknowledges that "Reading pipe is distinguished from Cohoes pipe and other brands only by the name of the manufacturer stamped upon it at intervals of between six and seven feet."[2] Insofar as the pipe would be hidden within the walls of the structure, there could be no conscientious reason for Kent to insist that the Cohoes pipe be removed and replaced with Reading pipe. So Kent's argument was a transparent effort to steal, or so it seems to the court.

Now, if contract takes seriously the autonomy of the transactors, it would not question the parties' reasons for insisting upon particular aspects of performance. If the builder contracts to provide one kind of pipe, it would not be within the builder's discretion to provide another type, notwithstanding the substantial identity of the two products. After all, no one forced the builder to agree to provide Reading pipe. The builder could have agreed only to provide Reading pipe or its commercial equivalent, in which event the owner would have no grounds for objection. But "Reading pipe or its commercial equivalent" is not what Kent contracted for. And, as generations of law students have wondered, what more could Kent have done? Should he have included in the contract, after the reference to Reading pipe, something to the effect of "I really mean it"? It is unlikely that even that would have swayed Cardozo, who casts his analysis in terms of conditions.

Had Jacob & Youngs fulfilled the condition precedent to their receipt of payment on the building contract? Or, if they had not, did that failure to satisfy the condition effect a forfeiture?

> Some promises are so plainly independent that they can never by fair construction be conditions of one another. Others are so plainly dependent that they must always be conditions. Others, though dependent and thus conditions when there is a departure in point of substance, will be viewed as independent and collateral when the departure is insignificant. Considerations partly of justice and partly of presumable intention are to tell us whether this or that promise shall be placed in one class or another.[3]

---

[2] *Id.* at 890.

[3] *Id.* (citations omitted).

The independence and dependence of promises will, at least at the margins, be "plain." The significance of the consequences will determine whether promises are dependent or independent: If the consequence of a finding of dependence is a forfeiture, it is more likely that the conditions will be found independent. What determines the calculus?: "considerations partly of justice and partly of presumable intention." We may imagine further that "considerations of justice" (amorphous as they must be) will determine the "presumable intention." Intention, in turn, is to be inferred from justice:

> From the conclusion that promises may not be treated as dependent to the extent of their uttermost minutiae without a sacrifice of justice, the progress is a short one to the conclusion that they may not be so treated without a perversion of intention. Intention not otherwise revealed may be presumed to hold in contemplation the reasonable and probable.[4]

So certainly though Kent said Reading pipe what he meant was "Reading pipe only so long as insistence upon it would not cause the contractor hardship." The intention is to be determined by conceptions of justice; the terms of the contract, then, are to be determined by conceptions of justice. Whatever Kent may say in the event, it is his intention at the time of contracting that matters, and he never could have intended to visit a hardship on his counterparty. He just thought he wanted Reading pipe; he did not really want it. The just conclusion is also the conclusion most consistent with the parties' intention. Contract based on intention construed by reference to justice gives effect to the parties' true bargain.

Further, and consistently, contract will police the parties' bargain and performance for evidence of overreaching. Were there reason to conclude that Jacob & Youngs's breach was willful, the default intentional, with the object to take advantage of Kent, then the court would reach the opposite conclusion, but "[t]he evidence sustain[ed] a finding that the omission of the prescribed brand of pipe was neither fraudulent nor willful."[5] There is a range of mental dispositions between malignant and benign, and we may anticipate that contract will be sufficiently supple to match extent of enforcement with the innocence of the actors' state of mind along that continuum.[6] It is clear that Cardozo's *Jacob & Youngs* decision captures that dynamic in terms that resonate with the doctrine. For this,

---

[4] *Id* at 891.

[5] *Id.* at 890.

[6] Dissenting Judge McLaughlin noted that "[t]he plaintiff did not perform its contract. Its failure to do so was either intentional or due to gross neglect *which, under the uncontradicted facts, amounted to the same thing*[.]" *Id.* at 892 (McLaughlin, J., dissenting)(emphasis added). *See also* Ian Ayres & Gregory Klass, Insincere Promises 201–205 (2005) (discussing the relationship between liability and circumstances if breach is found); Symposium, *Fault in American Contract Law*, 107 Mich. L. Rev. 1341 (2009).

more than perhaps any other reason, the case is canonical, and has been recognized as such in the sources.

The *Restatement (First) of Contracts* (*First Restatement* or *Restatement*), in Section 275, endeavors to capture the *Jacob & Youngs* dynamic by offering a catalog:

> In determining the materiality of a failure to perform a promise the following circumstances are influential:
>
> (a) The extent to which the injured party will obtain the substantial benefit which he could have reasonably anticipated;
> (b) The extent to which the injured party may be adequately compensated in damages for lack of complete performance;
> (c) The extent to which the party failing to perform has already partly performed or made preparations for performance;
> (d) The greater or less hardship on the party failing to perform in terminating the contract;
> (e) The wilful, negligent or innocent behavior of the party failing to perform;
> (f) The greater or less certainty that the party failing to perform will perform the remainder of the contract.[7]

Cardozo's focus on the intent of the parties has been supplanted by a balance of the equities, if not all of the equities, then at least more than might be subsumed were the focus only on the parties' intent.

The *Restatement* formulation also takes account of the culpability of the breaching party. Though the effect of the breach may be no greater if the breach were intentional, "it does so far increase the demerit of the wrongdoer that the law is less inclined if a breach is wilful to require the injured party to perform."[8] There has been, of late, considerable scholarly focus on the culpability scale in the contract law and consideration of whether and how willfulness of breach should matter.[9] Indeed, it may not even be clear what is meant by "willful" as opposed to innocent breach.[10]

The *Restatement (Second) of Contracts* (*Second Restatement* or *Restatement*) continues the rule of *Jacob & Youngs* in Section 229: "Excuse of a Condition to Avoid Forfeiture," which provides that "[t]o the extent that the non-occurrence of a condition would cause disproportionate forfeiture, a court may excuse the non-occurrence of that condition

---

[7] RESTATEMENT (FIRST) OF CONTRACTS § 275 (1932). Note that illustration 6 to the section comes closest to the facts of *Jacob & Youngs*, though it is cast in terms of defendant's use of "defective materials." The materials used by the contractor in *Jacob & Youngs* were not defective.

[8] *Id.* § 275 cmt. a.

[9] *See* Symposium, *supra* note 6.

[10] Richard A. Posner, *Let Us Never Blame a Contract Breaker*, 107 MICH. L. REV. 1349, 1353 (2009) (questioning clear definition of "willful" breach).

unless its occurrence was a material part of the agreed exchange."[11] The comments recognize that the court may circumvent the effect of forfeiture by "interpreting" the contract language in such a way (against the party who would benefit from the forfeiture) so as to avoid an undesired result.[12] But if the terms of the contract do not accommodate such a construction—if the contract clearly calls for Reading pipe and admits of no leaven in the strict construction of that term—then Section 229 of the *Second Restatement* provides the means for the court to do some justice: "Under the present section a court may, *in appropriate circumstances*, excuse the non-occurrence of a condition solely on the basis of the forfeiture that would otherwise result."[13] The "appropriate circumstances" could well be the considerations of justice recited in Section 275 of the *First Restatement*, though that catalog is not reprised in the *Second Restatement*.

The focus of the *Second Restatement* formulation, at least in the commentary, seems to be on the proportionality of the forfeiture:

> In determining whether the forfeiture is "disproportionate," a court must weigh the extent of the forfeiture by the obligee against the importance to the obligor of the risk from which he sought to be protected and the degree to which that protection will be lost if the non-occurrence of the condition is excused to the extent required to prevent forfeiture. The character of the agreement may, as in the case of insurance agreements, affect the rigor with which the requirement is applied.[14]

The first illustration accompanying that commentary is taken from the facts of *Jacob & Youngs*, and the reporter offers a gloss on the Cardozo conclusion, without relying on construed intent, as the judge had:

> A court may conclude that the use of Reading rather than Cohoes pipe is so relatively unimportant to [the owner] that the forfeiture that would result from denying [the contractor] the entire balance would be disproportionate, and may allow recovery by [the contractor] subject to any claim for damages for [the contractor's] breach of his duty to use Reading pipe.[15]

The rule of Section 229 only applies, of course, where the failed condition was not "material."[16] "Materiality" is to be determined by reference to Section 241, which again

---

[11] RESTATEMENT (SECOND) OF CONTRACTS § 229 (1981).

[12] *Id.* § 229 cmt. a.

[13] *Id.* (emphasis added).

[14] *Id.* § 229 cmt. b.

[15] *Id.* § 229 cmt. b, illus. 1.

[16] *Id.* § 229 cmt. c. Comment c discusses the limitation on scope, stating that the rule only applies when "occurrence of the condition was not a material part of the agreed exchange."

incorporates *Jacob & Youngs* into the illustrations. The *Second Restatement* provision is based on Section 275 of the *First Restatement*. The *Second Restatement* iteration reveals the same equitable calculus as does the predecessor provision, but the terms are not precisely the same, and suggest (but only suggest) a departure from concern with intent:

> In determining whether a failure to render or to offer performance is material, the following circumstances are significant:
>
> (a) the extent to which the injured party will be deprived of the benefit which he reasonably expected;
> (b) the extent to which the injured party can be adequately compensated for the part of that benefit of which he will be deprived;
> (c) the extent to which the party failing to perform or to offer to perform will suffer forfeiture;
> (d) the likelihood that the party failing to perform or to offer to perform will cure his failure, taking account of all the circumstances including any reasonable assurance;
> (e) the extent to which the behavior of the party failing to perform or to offer to perform comports with standards of good faith and fair dealing.[17]

Subsection (e)'s reference to "good faith and fair dealing" comes close, one would have to think, to taking the state of mind, the intent, of the party urging forfeiture into account in the court's deciding whether the deficient performance of the counterparty would constitute a material breach. Comment a to Section 205 of the *Second Restatement* explains that "good faith . . . emphasizes faithfulness to an agreed common purpose and consistency with the justified expectations of the other party."[18] That language seems entirely consistent with Cardozo's observation in *Jacob & Youngs* to the effect that "[i]ntention not otherwise revealed may be presumed to hold in contemplation the reasonable and probable."[19] So the promisee's failure to make clear that Cohoes pipe just would not do was an unrevealed intention and neither reasonable nor probable, and so could not *in good faith* be asserted to accomplish a forfeiture after the fact.

Understood in terms of good faith, *Jacob & Youngs* makes sense too of a tension in Article 2 of the Uniform Commercial Code (UCC or the Code). The general contract performance standard is "strict compliance"[20] or "perfect tender."[21] Each contracting party is entitled to that for which she contracted, not something "just as good." The UCC

---

[17] *Id.* § 241.

[18] *Id.* § 205 cmt. a.

[19] Jacob & Youngs, Inc v. Kent, 129 N.E. 889, 891 (N.Y. 1921).

[20] *See* E. Allan Farnsworth, Farnsworth on Contracts § 8.12 (3d ed. 2004).

[21] *See* UCC§ 2-601 (2002).

incorporates that performance standard: "If the goods or the tender of delivery fail in any respect to conform to the contract, the buyer may (a) reject the whole; or (b) accept the whole; or (c) accept any commercial unit or units and reject the rest."[22] That standard applies in the case of single delivery contracts, that is, contracts in which the seller's performance is complete upon the delivery of a single shipment. The rule has not been without its critics,[23] but it has survived.

Section 2-612 of the Code provides an alternative performance standard, substantial performance, in the case of an installment contract, "one that requires or authorizes the delivery of goods in separate lots to be separately accepted."[24] The distinction in the uniform sales law, between single delivery and installment contracts, does not track the distinction in the common law, which sets off construction and some service contracts (subject to a substantial performance standard), from other contracts (subject to the general strict compliance standard).[25] The basis of the Code distinction might be the buyers' differing transactional objects: Ultimate consumers may have more of an interest in strict compliance than would intermediate distributors, and intermediate distributors would be more likely to buy multiple goods at one time, and in installments. But of course there is no reason why that would necessarily be the case. Perhaps there is no better explanation for the single delivery–perfect tender versus installment contract–substantial compliance tension than Karl Llewellyn's impatience with the perfect tender standard.[26] Section 2-612 may have been the principal drafter's effort to insinuate the substantial compliance standard into the commercial sales law, a modest incursion on the strict compliance standard that might otherwise operate to effect uncommercial results.

It is noteworthy, though, that the official comments to Section 2-612 include language that resonates with *Jacob & Youngs*:

> [A]n installment agreement may require accurate ["strict"] conformity in quality as a condition to the right to acceptance if the need for such conformity is made clear either by express provision or by the circumstances. In such a case the effect of the agreement is to define explicitly what amounts to substantial impairment of value impossible to cure. A clause requiring accurate compliance as a condition to the right to acceptance must, however, have some basis in reason, must avoid imposing

---

[22] *Id.*

[23] James J. White & Robert S. Summers, Uniform Commercial Code § 9-3 (6th ed. 2010) ("We are skeptical of the real importance of the perfect tender rule.").

[24] UCC§ 2-612 (2002).

[25] *See supra* note 20.

[26] *See* George L. Priest, *Breach and Remedy for the Tender of Nonconforming Goods Under the Uniform Commercial Code: An Economic Approach*, 91 Harv. L Rev. 960, 970–74 (1978) (describing Llewellyn's views and influence on the Code).

hardship by surprise and is subject to waiver or to displacement by practical construction.[27]

Judge Cardozo could have written that.[28]

Courts in England,[29] Canada,[30] and Australia[31] have followed the *Jacob & Youngs* approach and found that an insubstantial deficiency cannot be used to effect a forfeiture. So the concept seems well ingrained in the common law as the type of essentially equitable notion that contract just cannot do without. Indeed, it may be the type of irresistible force that the most formalistic doctrine could not overcome. For confirmation of that, we need only recognize that the UCC perfect tender rule, which could not be more certain and ostensibly inflexible in its formulation, is subject to the Code's cure[32] provision and good-faith[33] requirements. Perhaps at some point, rule utilitarianism *must* give way to act utilitarianism. As we shall see, there are other similar irresistible equitable forces that at least in part define contract. The next canonical case concerns another one of them, all the more striking because it would seem to unravel so much of what we understand contract to be.

B. *Williams v. Walker-Thomas Furniture Co.*[34]

The unconscionability doctrine in contract is at least a quarter of a millennium old.[35] So it is venerable. Its contemporary currency is owing perhaps primarily to Article 2 of the UCC, specifically Section 2-302:

[27] UCC§ 2-612 cmt. 4 (2002).

[28] *See* Karl N. Llewellyn, The common Law Tradition: Deciding Appeals 430–37 (1960) (admiring Cardozo's reasoning and technique in *McPherson v. Buick*).

[29] Reardon Smith Line Ltd. v. Yngvar Hansen Tangen, [1976] 1 W.L.R. 989, 998 (H.L.) (Failure to fulfill condition depends on "whether a particular item in a description constitutes a substantial ingredient in the 'identity' of the thing sold, and only if it does . . . treat it as a condition."); Hoenig v. Isaacs, [1952] 2 All E.R. 176 (C.A.) (Substantial compliance with contract requirements does not void contract, though plaintiff could recover cost of remedying substantial material defects.).

[30] Markland Assocs. v. Lohnes, [1973] 11 N.S.R.2d 181 (N.S. Sup. Ct.) (If there is substantial performance, recovery may be obtained for what has been done minus cost of making good defects and omissions.).

[31] Steele v. Tardiani (1946) 72 C.L.R. 386 (Austl.) (Contract divisible as to non-conforming work and plaintiff could recover for substantial performance.).

[32] UCC§ 2-508 (2002) (If buyer rejects goods pursuant to perfect tender rule, seller may cure defect by making conforming tender as long as it is still within agreed upon time and notice is given.).

[33] UCC§ 1-304 (2003) ("Every contract or duty within [the UCC] imposes an obligation of good faith in its performance and enforcement."). *See also* Neumiller Farms, Inc. v. Cornett, 368 So.2d 272 (Ala. 1979) (Buyer refused to accept seller's potato's because they were "unfit for 'chipping'"; court held that any rejection must be in good faith.).

[34] Williams v. Walker-Thomas Furniture Co., 350 F.2d 445 (D.C. Cir. 1965).

[35] *See, e.g.,* Earl of Chesterfield v. Janssen, (1751) 28 Eng. Rep 82 (Ch.).

> If the court as a matter of law finds the contract or any clause of the contract to have been unconscionable at the time it was made the court may refuse to enforce the contract, or it may enforce the remainder of the contract without the unconscionable clause, or it may so limit the application of any unconscionable clause as to avoid any unconscionable result.[36]

But what makes a contract or contract term unconscionable? The black letter of the Code provision offers no clarification. The comment cites cases that have found unconscionability,[37] but offers only one sentence that approaches the heart of the matter: "The principle is one of the prevention of oppression and unfair surprise and not of disturbance of allocation of risks because of superior bargaining power."[38] Now, of course, a party with superior bargaining power *may* have taken unconscientious advantage; but we cannot assume that is the case just because there is a disparity in the parties' relative bargaining power.

Williams v. Walker-Thomas Furniture Co. presents facts in which there may have been, according to the court, unconscionable conduct on the part of the party with superior bargaining power. The case was decided after the enactment of Section 2-302 but the contract in issue was executed by the parties prior to that enactment; so the court was left to apply a common law unconscionability conception, and used the Code formulation as its guide.[39] Judge Skelly Wright wrote the opinion for the District of Columbia Court of Appeals panel.

The opinion offers some, but not much, clarity with regard to the behavior the unconscionability doctrine is designed to police. The construction bears reproduction at length:

> Unconscionability has generally been recognized to include an absence of meaningful choice on the part of one of the parties together with contract terms which are unreasonably favorable to the other party. Whether a meaningful choice is present in a particular case can only be determined by consideration of all the circumstances surrounding the transaction. In many cases the meaningfulness of the choice is negated by a gross inequality of bargaining power. The manner in which the contract was entered is also relevant to this consideration. Did each party to the contract, considering his obvious education or lack of it, have a reasonable opportunity to understand the terms of the contract, or were the important terms hidden in a maze of fine print and minimized by deceptive sales practices? Ordinarily, one

---

[36] UCC§ 2-302 (2002).

[37] *Id.* § 2-302 cmt. 1.

[38] *Id.*

[39] Williams v. Walker-Thomas Furniture Co., 350 F.2d at 449.

> who signs an agreement without full knowledge of its terms might be held to assume the risk that he has entered a one-sided bargain. But when a party of little bargaining power, and hence little real choice, signs a commercially unreasonable contract with little or no knowledge of its terms, it is hardly likely that his consent, or even an objective manifestation of his consent, was ever given to all the terms. In such a case the usual rule that the terms of the agreement are not to be questioned should be abandoned and the court should consider whether the terms of the contract are so unfair that enforcement should be withheld.[40]

You get the distinct sense that unconscionability, like pornography, is difficult to define, but you know it when you see it.[41] In fact, it might not be difficult to discover unconscionability in the terms of the *Williams* opinion in a broad cross-section of consumer agreements: "when a party of little bargaining power, and hence little real choice, signs a commercially unreasonable contract with little or no knowledge of its terms." The focus, then, would be on the reasonableness of the terms of the *agreement*, which is likely a form contract. But that might prove too much, and unravel a good deal of what we accept as contract.

The contract in issue in *Williams* included a so-called cross-collateral provision, designed to encumber the consumer's assets with collateral interests the consumer would not have understood to be effective. The contract provided, essentially, that the seller retained a security interest in all goods purchased by the consumer-buyer from the seller until full payment had been made for all of the merchandise: "[T]he debt incurred at the time of purchase of each item was secured by the right to repossess all the items previously purchased by the same purchaser, and each new item purchased automatically became subject to a security interest arising out of the previous dealings."[42] So when the buyer defaulted on the payment for the last item purchased, she could lose all of the items previously purchased. Now such a provision would, certainly if understood by the buyer, assure that the buyer's attention remained focused on paying the seller. It is one thing to miss a payment and lose your new television; it is wholly another to miss that payment and lose your living room furniture, your kitchen appliances, *and* that new television.

Certainly, at first impression, that use of a cross-collateral clause would suggest overreaching, might even be unfairly surprising, in the unconscionability sense. But is the problem with the clause the likelihood that it might cause unfair surprise? Probably not; the problem would seem more to lie with the fact that the seller retained extraordinary—perhaps even *unreasonable*—leverage against the buyer. Judge Wright cannot decide the

---

[40] *Id.* at 449–50 (footnotes omitted).

[41] In Justice Stewart's concurring opinion in *Jacobellis v. State of Ohio*, 378 U.S. 184, 197 (1964), declining to define pornography, he famously wrote, "I know it when I see it."

[42] Williams v. Walker-Thomas Furniture Co., 350 F.2d at 447.

unreasonableness issue as a matter of law, so the case is remanded to the lower court "for further proceedings."[43]

It is not difficult to be critical of the vagueness of the unconscionability doctrine, and that is because the doctrine has to be vague in order to accomplish its object: providing the courts means to police agreements notwithstanding settled contract doctrine that denies courts the authority to appraise the *adequacy* of consideration. You may make a bad deal and the contract law will not come to your rescue. Unconscionability emerged as an equitable principle to limit the damages available to an overreaching contracting party.[44] It matters to the contract *law* largely because of the merger of law and equity. Insofar as law and equity are no longer separate, unconscionability has gained significance, and Karl Llewellyn brought it into focus in Article 2 of the UCC largely to insulate sales contracts from the creative manipulation of doctrine courts had pursued in order to do a little equity.

Unless you understood Llewellyn's object (the method to his madness), you might find little to commend and much to condemn in such an anti-doctrine. That certainly describes the perspective of Professor Arthur Leff, whose important article in the *Pennsylvania Law Review* revealed "The Emperor's New Clause."[45] Leff's article is, ultimately, wrong—he fails to understand what Llewellyn was up to and as a consequence pursues a critical analysis of the UCC's unconscionability provision that misses the forest for the trees. Essentially, Leff concludes that there is no there, there:[46] The provision lacks a "reality referent" insofar as it provides no guidance to either the parties to a transaction before the fact or the courts after the fact.[47]

To appreciate the operation of the unconscionability rule, you have to understand the equitable tug of the doctrine: One party is asking the court to use the contract mechanism to undermine the bigger object of contract. Leff is not troubled by the work unconscionability would do; he is troubled by its clandestine means.[48] Leff's argument is not difficult to follow and asserts that Section 2-302 and the unconscionability conception itself really offer no certain guidance. How is a court to know that a contract or a contract

---

[43] *Id.* at 450.

[44] *See* RESTATEMENT (SECOND) OF CONTRACTS § 208 cmt. b (1981) (In describing the historical standards of unconscionability, "[t]raditionally, a bargain was said to be unconscionable in an action at law if it was 'such as no man in his senses and not under delusion would make on the one hand, and as no honest and fair man would accept on the other' damages were then limited to those to which the aggrieved party was 'equitably' entitled.") (citations omitted).

[45] Arthur Allen Leff, *Unconscionability and the Code—The Emperor's New Clause*, 115 U. PA. L. REV. 485 (1967).

[46] GERTRUDE STEIN, EVERYBODY'S AUTOBIOGRAPHY 289 (Cooper Square Pu. 1971). The author famously wrote, "[T]he trouble with Oakland is that when you get there, there isn't any there there."

[47] Leff, *supra* note 45, at 558 ("[T]he academic community is generally friendly to the drafting effort, [sic] a single provision in a massive Code may get by even if it has, really, no reality referent, and all of its explanatory material ranges between the irrelevant and the misleading.").

[48] *Id.* at 527.

term is unconscionable? How is a court to know whether it is following precedent? Because Leff cannot find the certainty he expects a statutory provision to provide, he concludes that the section is at best a covert tool, and, borrowing the words of Karl Llewellyn, "covert tools are never reliable tools."[49] Leff, though, does not understand. He measures unconscionability as one would any statutory provision, and so mistakes Article 2 for just another statute and unconscionability for just another contract doctrine.

Section 2-302 tries to accomplish what legislation generally does not try to accomplish, perhaps because it cannot. Two analogies cooperate to explain the work unconscionability is supposed to do and describe how it is supposed to do it. First, the nuclear waste dump analogy: We may want to rely to some extent on nuclear power to provide a portion of our energy needs, but we do not want to live with, or even very near, the waste that results from the generation of nuclear energy. A reasonable fear is that nuclear waste will contaminate everything to which it is exposed. So you want the waste segregated in order to protect everything else. Think of unconscionability as the nuclear waste dump of contract. Llewellyn did: "In the past such [deal] policing has been accomplished by adverse construction of language, by manipulation of the rules of offer and acceptance or by determinations that the clause is contrary to public policy or to the dominant purpose of the contract."[50] He could as well have listed a number of other aspects of contract that courts could corrupt in order to police the parties' bargain. But the point is made clearly enough anyway: In order to protect the integrity of the Code, all of the cases that would otherwise encourage courts to corrupt the sales law (and contract common law too) would be relegated to the unconscionability waste dump. Courts would not have to explain why: Leff was right about that. Moreover, courts could not really explain the *why* very well—all they would have to do is label the contract or term "unconscionable"; enough said. Llewellyn recognized that by their so doing, courts could effectively insulate the rest of contract doctrine from the existential threat.

The second analogy may at first seem even more curious: unconscionability as self-administered morphine. Health care providers want to spare their patients the great physical pain illness or injury may entail. Morphine provides effective relief from pain, but there is a risk of developing dependency and so a natural reluctance to give patients all the morphine they request. It may also be upsetting to have patients ask for the medication. Curiously, but also very fortunately, health care providers discovered that if they put patients in control of the administration of the pain reliever, the patients would actually use less of the drug to control their pain. Giving patients the ability to respond themselves very directly to the pain has the effect of limiting the actual administration of the narcotic. So too with unconscionability: Think of unconscionability as the drug and the courts as the patient.

---

[49] LLEWELLYN, *supra* note 28, at 365 (quoting Llewellyn, Book Review, 52 HARV. L. REV. 700, 703 (1939)).

[50] UCC§ 2-302 cmt. 1 (2002).

The unconscionability doctrine puts courts in control of an important deal-policing mechanism. Section 2-302 provides that unconscionability is to be determined by the court as a matter of law (lest too-sympathetic jurors gain control of the drug).[51] In fact, perhaps as a consequence of the doctrine's direct incorporation into the law, courts are provided some guidance (granted, per Leff, not much) as to what should provide sufficient bases to upset the bargain. It may be that *because* the doctrine is so readily available that courts are reluctant to use it. Review of the case law confirms that courts do not very often find that a contract or term is unconscionable; the doctrine that could undermine other doctrine is seldom utilized.

M. P. Ellinghaus wrote a response in the *Yale Law Journal* to the Leff article. In a footnote, near the very end of his response, Ellinghaus recounts Leff's ironic quotation from Llewellyn, to the effect that "Covert tools are never reliable tools." Ellinghaus continues: "It is, of course, quite clear that Llewellyn intended Section 2-302 to be a substitution of overtness for covertness. Professor Leff's irony is, of course, intentional."[52] Well, we may be sure that Ellinghaus's irony was intentional, at least.

Leff's "Emperor's New Clause" article does, though, provide courts invaluable guidance as they try to make sense of the unconscionability doctrine. He reasons that unconscionability could refer to two things: The contract could be procedurally unconscionable or substantively unconscionable. A court would need a coincidence of the two to invalidate a contract or term. So subordinate contracting parties may be tricked into making fair deals, and the contract would not be voidable. They could knowingly and intelligently agree to a bad deal, and the contract would not be voidable. But subordinate contracting parties could not be tricked into making a bad deal without the unconscionability doctrine's being available to void the contract. The courts seem to be quite comfortable following this approach.[53] More recently, decisions have appreciated the two unconscionability forms, procedural and substantive, as cooperating on related axes: the more procedural unconscionability in evidence, the less substantive unconscionability necessary to render the contract voidable. In the same way, the more substantive unconscionability in evidence, the less procedural unconscionability necessary to support the

---

[51] *Id.* § 2-302. Comment 3 explains that "[this] section is addressed to the court, and the decision is to be made by it. The commercial evidence referred to in subsection (2) is for the court's consideration, not the jury's. Only the agreement which results from the court's action on these matters is to be submitted to the general triers of the facts." *See also* RESTATEMENT (SECOND) OF CONTRACTS § 208 cmt. f (1981) ("A determination that a contract or term is unconscionable is made by the court in the light of all the material facts. Under Uniform Commercial Code § 2-302, the determination is made 'as a matter of law,' but the parties are to be afforded an opportunity to present evidence as to commercial setting, purpose and effect to aid the court in its determination. Incidental findings of fact are made by the court rather than by a jury, but are accorded the usual weight given to such findings of fact in appellate review. An appellate court will also consider whether proper standards were applied.").

[52] M. P. Ellinghaus, *In Defense of Unconscionability*, 78 YALE L.J. 757, 815 n.269 (1969).

[53] *See* WHITE & SUMMERS, *supra* n. 23, § 5–7 (discussing relation of procedural to substantive unconscionability).

voidability determination.[54] There are also cases that have based an unconscionability determination on procedural irregularities alone.[55]

The unconscionability doctrine is very much a part of contract; theorists who have tried to make sense of contract have recognized the need to account for the doctrine. Professor Charles Fried in his *Contract as Promise*[56] acknowledges that concepts such as duress and unconscionability could undermine his unitary theory of contract based on Kantian conceptions of autonomy: "I consider whether it is possible to admit the defenses of duress and unconscionability without giving away the heart of my position. . . . I must . . . show that these doctrines perform distinct functions that are not only compatible with the concept of contract as promise but even essential to it."[57] Professor Peter Benson sets out to explain contract in terms of a transfer of entitlement, and in the course of that presentation argues that the unconscionability doctrine conforms to his conception.[58] Fried and Benson are not the only commentators to note the centrality of the unconscionability calculus to contract and contract theory.[59] The point is that the doctrine is not ancillary to contract; it is a part of contract and we cannot explain contract in theoretical terms unless that explanation can account for the role of the unconscionability doctrine.

Williams v. Walker-Thomas is canonical because it has come to be the vehicle by which the scope of the unconscionability doctrine is depicted in the common materials. The doctrine has also been incorporated into the law of England, Canada, and Australia,

---

[54] *See* Armendariz v. Foundation Health Psychcare Services, Inc., 6 P.3d 669, 690 (Cal. 2000) ("[T]he more substantively oppressive the contract term, the less evidence of procedural unconscionability is required to come to the conclusion that the term is unenforceable, and vice versa (citations omitted)."); State v. Wolowitz, 96 A.D.2d 47, 68 (N.Y. App. Div. 1983) ("However, in general, it can be said that procedural and substantive unconscionability operate on a 'sliding scale'; the more questionable the meaningfulness of choice, the less imbalance in a contract's terms should be tolerated and vice versa (citations omitted)") .

[55] *See, e.g.,* Weaver v. Am. Oil Co., 276 N.E.2d 144 (Ind. 1971) (finding unconscionable terms because facts demonstrated lack of voluntary agreement); Johnson v. Mobil Oil Corp., 415 F. Supp. 264 (E.D. Mich. 1976) (term unconscionable because plaintiff's illiteracy showed lack of awareness of term); *see also* UCC§ 2A-108(2) (2002) (relying on procedural unconscionability alone in respect to consumer leases).

[56] CHARLES FRIED, CONTRACTS AS PROMISE: A THEORY OF CONTRACTUAL OBLIGATION (1981).

[57] *Id.* at 93.

[58] Peter Benson, *The Unity of Contract Law, in* THE THEORY OF CONTRACT LAW: NEW ESSAYS 184 (Peter Benson ed., 2001).

[59] *See, e.g.,* James Gordley, *Contract Law in the Aristotelian Tradition, in* THE THEORY OF CONTRACT LAW: NEW ESSAYS 316–17(Peter Benson ed., 2001) (discussing Fried and unconscionability).

both by statute[60] and to greater and lesser degrees by common law cases.[61] Closely related to the unconscionability doctrine are public policy bases to question the enforceability of promises that are only ostensibly the product of consent. The next canonical case provides a transition from unconscionability to those public policy concerns.

C. *Henningsen v. Bloomfield Motors, Inc.*[62]

In *Henningsen v. Bloomfield Motors, Inc.*, the New Jersey Supreme Court directly invokes conceptions of justice to determine the scope of the contract warranty liability of the manufacturer of an automobile to the consumer-buyer injured by the car's deficiency. Defendant tried to avoid warranty liability by relying upon a disclaimer of the implied warranty of merchantability. The disclaimer was part of the boilerplate of the standard form sales agreement designed by the Automobile Manufacturers Association (to which all major automobile manufacturers belonged). So a consumer buyer could not avoid the disclaimer by buying the same car from another dealer or even buying a similar car from another dealer network. There was, simply, no choice: To buy the car, you had to agree to the warranty disclaimer.

The court did not rely on the unconscionability doctrine; indeed, there is only one, incidental reference to the concept in the opinion.[63] The decision is very much in step with its time, the infancy (if not quite the dawn) of strict products liability law.[64] The

---

[60] *See* Unfair Contract Terms Act, 1977, c. 50, § 3 (Eng.) (Non-breaching party cannot claim to be entitled to recover from breaching party something "substantially different from that which was reasonably expected of him."); Unfair Terms in Consumer Contracts Regulations, 1999, S.I. 1999/2083, art. 5, ¶¶ 1–2 (Individual contract terms which are not individually negotiated are unfair if they cause "significant imbalance to the parties' rights and obligations."); The Unfair Contract Terms Act of 1977 effectively imposes the American version of substantive unconscionability, but without requiring procedural prong; actions for "procedural unconscionability" fall under criteria of duress or undue influence; *see, e.g.,* Pao On v. Lau Yiu, (1980) A.C. 614 (P.C.); *see also* Consumer Protection Act, S.O. 2002, c. 30, Sch. A, §§ 14–19 (2002) (unfair practices) and Trade Practices Act, 1974, §§ 51AA, 51AB, 51AC (Austl.) (incorporating Commercial Bank of Austl. v. Amadio (1983) 151 C.L.R. 447 (Austl.), into statute and expanding unconscionability to businesses); Contracts Review Act, 1980, § 9 (N.S.W.) (Court should consider whether there was inequality in bargaining power, provisions of contract were subject of negotiation, reasonably practical for party to reject or alter any provisions.).

[61] *See* Lloyds Bank Ltd. v. Bundy, (1974) [1975] Q.B. 326; Boustany v. Pigott, (1993) 69 P. & C.R. 298 (P.C.) (Ant. & Barb.) (Unconscionability is generally disfavored in UK courts.) Harry v. Kreutziger, [1978] 9 B.C.L.R. 166 (C.A.) (Buyer who was taking advantage of seller's lack of knowledge of true value of item sold; contract was void for unconscionability.); Commercial Bank of Austl. v. Amadio (If parties meet on unequal terms, and stronger party knows or should know of special disability and takes advantage of it, stronger party obtains a bargain which would be unconscionable to retain.).

[62] Henningsen v. Bloomfield Motors, Inc., 161 A.2d 69 (N.J. 1960).

[63] *Id.* at 86 (citing 1 ARTHUR L. CORBIN, CORBIN ON CONTRACTS § 128 at 188 (1950)).

[64] *See* William L. Prosser, *The Assault Upon the Citadel*, 69 YALE L.J. 1099 (1960); William L. Prosser, *The Fall of the Citadel (Strict Liability to the Consumer)*, 50 MINN. L. REV. 791 (1966); RESTATEMENT (SECOND) OF TORTS § 402A (1965).

courts were reexamining the relationship between transactional norms and contract doctrine premised on conceptions of consent. The fabric of doctrine developed in times when arm's-length deals were the norm would, to say the least, be strained once buyers were remote from their sellers and the subject matter of the contract was not as easily understood as would be a buggy whip.

The disclaimer upon which defendant sought to rely was buried in the boilerplate of the form contract plaintiff signed:

> The type used in the printed parts of the form became smaller in size, different in style, and less readable toward the bottom where the line for the purchaser's signature was placed. The smallest type on the page appears in the two paragraphs, one of two and one-quarter lines and the second of one and one-half lines, on which great stress is laid by the defense in the case. These two paragraphs [containing the merger or integration clause incorporating the terms on the front and back of the form] are the least legible and the most difficult to read in the instrument, but they are most important in the evaluation of the rights of the contesting parties. . . . De-emphasis seems the motive rather than emphasis.[65]

In fact, though most of the contract form was printed in twelve-point type, the two paragraphs to which the excerpt above refers are in six-point type. Then, on the back of the form, and also in fine print (somewhere between six- and twelve-point type), the warranty disclaimer and limited remedy provisions appear.

The court is not favorably impressed by the manufacturer's warranty, the terms of which the court describes as a "sad commentary"[66] upon the industry's marketing practices. Plaintiff suffered personal injuries, and though defendant apparently did not make the argument,[67] the terms of the warranty would have insulated the manufacturer from any liability for those personal injuries.

The court first considers the privity defense–defendant manufacturer was not the seller of the car; the retail dealer was the seller–and finds no good reason to conclude that whatever warranty protection the manufacturer provided would not run to plaintiff. The court relies on evolved transactional norms:

> [W]e hold that under modern marketing conditions, when a manufacturer puts a new automobile in the stream of trade and promotes its purchase by the public, an implied warranty that it is reasonably suitable for use as such accompanies it into

[65] *Henningsen*, 161 A.2d at 73.

[66] *Id.* at 78.

[67] *Id.* at 80.

> the hands of the ultimate purchaser. Absence of agency between the manufacturer and the dealer who makes the ultimate sale is immaterial.[68]

The court takes judicial notice of the fact that defendant manufacturer utilized various media to advertise its product, and that advertising effort had an impact on the contract between defendant and the particular plaintiff before the court.

The court acknowledges the general rule of contract, and the "basic tenet" of contract doctrine, that, absent fraud, the party who signs a contract is bound by its terms. But "modern commercial life" requires a less strict application of that rule. The court's perspective says a good deal about contract: "The history of the law shows that legal doctrines, as first expounded, often prove to be inadequate under the impact of later experience."[69] Now this is crucial, because it says something not just about particular doctrine—what the rule is—but also about the nature of contract doctrine (and arguably all legal doctrine). That is, for this court, a crucial aspect of contract doctrine itself is that it is organic and so not fixed, not static. Doctrine, at one level, will conform to the shape of its container and that container is the social context in which the doctrine operates. The court finds the source of that conclusion in principles of justice: "[T]he need for justice has stimulated the necessary qualifications or adjustments [of doctrine]."[70]

The proliferation of automobiles (and their concomitant potential to do great harm) and the standardization of automobile purchase contracts changed the contract calculus. Forms such as those relied upon by defendant in *Henningsen* were not substantially like the "traditional contract[,] . . . the result of free bargaining of parties who are brought together by the play of the market, and who meet each other on a footing of approximate economic equality."[71] The court's conception of the traditional contract, certainly idealized, presents a challenge to the accepted understanding of doctrine, both its nature and its dictates. For the *Henningsen* court, if contract once meant bargain, those who draft the agreements attending new car sales have missed something. So if bargain is no longer a necessary prerequisite of such contracts, then we can no longer enforce them as though they were the product of bargain. *Bargain* has normative significance. There is, to be sure, a contract between the buyer and seller of a new car, but the enforceability of its terms is necessarily limited by the bargain conception.

Insofar as the buyer of the new car in *Henningsen* could not, in any meaningful sense, negotiate the warranty provisions of the form sales contract, the seller would not be able to enforce those warranty terms. The court draws attention, as well, to the fact that even had the buyer been aware of the limitation of remedy provision, it is not at all clear that

---

[68] *Id.* at 84.

[69] *Id.*

[70] *Id.* (relying on the opinion of Cardozo, J. in MacPherson v. Buick Motor Co., 111 N.E. 1050, 1053 (N.Y. 1916)).

[71] *Id.* at 86.

even a sophisticated consumer would have appreciated what she was giving up by signing the form:

> In the context of this warranty, only the abandonment of all sense of justice would permit us to hold that, as a matter of law, the phrase "its obligation under this warranty being limited to making good at its factory any part or parts thereof" signifies to an ordinary reasonable person that he is relinquishing any personal injury claim that might flow from the use of a defective automobile.[72]

The court concludes that it could provide the appropriate check on the manufacturer's overreaching—"[t]he task of the judiciary is to administer the spirit as well as the letter of the law"[73]—and could provide that protection by invoking conceptions of public policy.

The court acknowledges that public policy resists definition: "A contract, or a particular provision therein, valid in one era may be wholly opposed to the public policy of another."[74] *Henningsen* was decided in turbulent times so far as the law governing sales of goods that cause personal injury was concerned. The so-called "Citadel" was under assault,[75] indeed, had started to crumble, and plaintiffs hurt by products found ways to overcome common law tort and contract impediments to recovery for personal injuries.[76]

Given the personal injury involved, and the apposite economic loss doctrine (limiting recovery in tort for breach of contract),[77] *Henningsen* addressed a unique challenge to contract in an innovative way. Indeed, it would be difficult to determine the contours and limits of the public policy. That becomes even more problematic insofar as the court seems to recognize a distinction between unconscionability and the public policy rational. Unconscionability is, after all, a product of public policy (as, we might imagine, is all of contract), and yet *Henningsen* seems to suggest that a party who could not make out an unconscionability case could still prevail by using a public policy argument. Or is it the other way around? For present purposes, though, *Henningsen* is canonical because it

[72] *Id.* at 93.

[73] *Id.* at 94.

[74] *Id.* at 95.

[75] *See* Prosser, *The Assault Upon the Citadel*, *supra* note 64.

[76] *See, e.g.*, RESTATEMENT (SECOND) OF TORTS § 402A (1965); Greenman v. Yuba Power Prods., Inc., 377 P.2d 897 (Cal. 1962).

[77] *See* W. PAGE KEETON ET AL, PROSSER & KEETON ON THE LAW OF TORTS § 92, at 655 (5th ed. 1984); Timothy L. Bertschy, *Negligent Performance of Service Contracts and the Economic Loss Doctrine*, 17 J. MARSHALL L. REV. 249 (1984); Jay M. Feinman, *The Jurisprudence of Classification*, 41 STAN. L. REV. 661 (1989).

is a crucial part of the story of contract. And it is a crucial part of the story because it concerns a typical contracting context.[78]

The approach of *Henningsen* has been codified in the provisions of Article 2 of the UCC. Section 2-719 provides, in pertinent part: "(3) Consequential damages may be limited or excluded unless the limitation or exclusion is unconscionable. *Limitation of consequential damages for injury to the person in the case of consumer goods is prima facie unconscionable* but limitation of damages where the loss is commercial is not."[79] Note that the Code provision does not rely on a separate public policy deal-policing mechanism but instead treats the issue as one concerning unconscionability. Also, under each of the alternative forms of Section 2-318, "Third Party Beneficiaries of Warranties Express or Implied," a seller's liability for personal injury extends to buyers "injured in person by breach of . . . warranty" and the operation of the section, whichever alternative the state adopts, may not be excluded or limited by the seller."[80] So although a seller need not make any warranty at all, if the seller does provide a warranty, the seller cannot limit its liability for breach of that warranty so far as personal injury is concerned. *Henningsen* was really just bringing the contract law into step with the developing tort law—specifically, that of strict products liability. The case was at that vague border between tort and contract and as such concerned the tension between the consensual and non-consensual liability law.[81]

The specific work done by *Henningsen* as a matter of common law contract has now largely been superseded by legislation, both in the United States[82] and other common law countries.[83] So the canonical strength of the case may be more in its depiction of the courts' ability to rely on broad public policy and justice[84] conceptions to rebalance the transactional dynamic. Still, the contract treatises continue to pay attention to *Henningsen,* and we would be missing something important about the nature of contract doctrine were we to consider the decision an aberration rather than canonical.

Although *Henningsen* concerns the limits on the power of one contracting party to assert its will on the other, and so discovers limits on bargaining power, performance obligations under a contract may also be upset by circumstances beyond the control of

[78] Note that *In re* Baby M, 537 A.2d 1227 (N.J. 1988), for example, may mean less to contract and not be canonical precisely because it does not concern, yet, a typical contracting context, and is more likely regulated by separate legislation.

[79] UCC§ 2-719 (2002) (emphasis added).

[80] *Id.* § 2-318.

[81] *See* Richard A. Epstein, *The Many Faces of Fault in Contract Law: Or How to do Economics Right, Without Really Trying,* 107 MICH. L. REV 1461 (2009); Prosser, *The Fall of the Citadel (Strict Liability to the Consumer), supra* note 64, at 800.

[82] *See* UCC§ 2-302 (2002).

[83] *See supra* note 60.

[84] *See* Peter A. Alces, *On Discovering Doctrine: "Justice" in Contract Agreement,* 83 WASH. U. L.Q. 471 (2005).

either contracting party. As we see, such circumstances may likewise impede the efforts of one party to enforce the performance obligation of the other.

D. *Taylor v. Caldwell*[85] and *Krell v. Henry*[86]

Section 2-615 of the UCC is able to capture two common law performance concepts with a single formulation:

> (a) Delay in delivery or non-delivery in whole or in part by a seller . . . is not a breach of his duty under a contract of sale if performance as agreed has been made impracticable by the occurrence of a contingency the nonoccurrence of which was a basic assumption on which the contract was made. . . .[87]

Although the language of the section refers specifically to performance of the seller's obligation, the comments make clear that the sense of the section applies as well in the case in which the buyer's expectations have been frustrated:

> [W]here the buyer's contract is in reasonable commercial understanding conditioned on a definite and specific venture or assumption as, for instance, a war procurement subcontract known to be based on a prime contract which is subject to termination, or a supply contract for a particular construction venture, the reason of the present section may well apply and entitle the buyer to the exemption.[88]

The *Second Restatement* formulations, based on UCC Section 2-615,[89] continue to bifurcate the analysis, providing one rule in the case of a party whose performance other than the payment of money has been rendered "impracticable," and another formulation of the rule when the purpose of a party whose only performance obligation is to pay money has been frustrated. The *Restatement* bifurcation is consistent with the distinguishable if not all that distinct treatment of the performance issue in the two pertinent canonical cases.

Taylor v. Caldwell is the canonical "impossibility" case. Plaintiff entered into a contract with defendant pursuant to which defendant would make available a music hall for plaintiff's presentation of concerts. After entering into the contract but prior to the dates set for performance, the music hall burned to the ground, making it impossible for defendant to supply the premises for plaintiff's use. The question before the court, then,

[85] Taylor v. Caldwell, (1863) 122 Eng. Rep. 309 (K.B.).

[86] Krell v. Henry, [1903] 2 K.B. 740 (U.K.).

[87] UCC§ 2-615 (2002).

[88] *Id.* § 2-615 cmt. 9.

[89] *See* Restatement (Second) of Contracts § 261 cmt. c (1981).

was whether plaintiff would be able to recover damages from defendant on account of defendant's failure (because of inability) to fulfill the performance obligation stipulated in the contract.

The court's opinion begins from the premise that the law is not so much concerned with the reasons why a party fails to perform: "[W]here there is a positive contract to do a thing, not in itself unlawful, the contractor must perform it or pay damages for not doing it, although, in consequence of unforeseen accident, the performance of his contract has become unexpectedly burdensome, or even impossible."[90] The court does not dally long with that fictional assumption:

> But this rule is only applicable when the contract is positive and absolute and not subject to any condition either express or implied; and there are authorities which ... establish the principle that where, from the nature of the contract, it appears that the parties must from the beginning have known that it could not be fulfilled unless, when the time for the fulfillment of the contract arrived, some particular specified thing continued to exist, so that when entering into the contract they must have contemplated such continued existence as the foundation of what was to be done, there, in the absence of any express or implied warranty that the thing shall exist, the contract is not to be construed as a positive contract, but as subject to an implied condition that the parties shall be excused in case, before breach, performance becomes impossible from the perishing of the thing without default of the contractor.[91]

The court bases its conclusion on the presumed intention of the parties. That is, for all intents and purposes, it is as if the parties had in fact agreed to what they would do if a fire destroyed the music hall and they had just forgotten to write it down. The court then presumes that the parties (would have) agreed to walk away from the contract and forsake any damage recovery. So if one of the parties comes to court and asks for damages for nonperformance, that party is asking the court to do violence to the parties' original "agreement": "There seems little doubt that this implication tends to further the great object of making the legal construction such as *to fulfil the intention* of those who enter into the contract, for, in the course of affairs, men, in making such contracts, in general, would, if it were brought to their minds, say that there should be such a condition."[92]

In *Krell v. Henry*, plaintiff entered into a lease contract with defendant to make available to defendant an apartment overlooking the procession route for the Coronation of King Edward VII of England. The contract nowhere mentioned the event, though the advertisements announcing the availability of the premises made clear that the windows

---

[90] *Taylor*, 122 Eng. Rep. at 312 (K.B.).

[91] *Id.*

[92] *Id.* (emphasis added).

would provide a view of the processions.[93] When the king became ill, the ceremonies were cancelled, and the lease of the premises was rendered worthless.

The question was whether the lessee of the apartment was excused from paying the rent reserved. The *Krell* court recognizes the affinity between the facts before it and the facts of the *Taylor* case. But the terms of the court's conclusion do not similarly embrace considerations of intent, real or presumed:

> I think that the Coronation procession was the foundation of this contract, and that the non-happening of it prevented the performance of the contract; and secondly, I think that the non-happening of the procession . . . was an event 'of such a character that it cannot reasonably be supposed to have been in the contemplation of the contracting parties when the contract was made, and that they are not to be held bound by general words which, though large enough to include, were not used with reference to the possibility of the particular contingency which afterwards happened.'[94]

Quite starkly, then, the two decisions rely on diametrically opposed conceptions of the role of intent in contract risk allocation. Even though *Krell* understands itself to be following *Taylor*,[95] the later decision eschews any reliance on intent and, indeed, reaches its result by finding the king's illness not to be within the contemplation of the parties, actual or inferred.

The two opinions are also distinguishable insofar as they concern two different sides, as it were, of the impracticability defense.[96] *Taylor* is the prototypical seller impracticability case: The seller seeks to avoid liability on the contract because destruction of the contract subject matter renders performance impossible. On the facts of *Taylor*, performance really was rendered *impossible* when the music hall was destroyed by fire. Even had the seller been able to defy the laws of physics and rebuild the structure by the time for performance, the rebuilt structure would still not have been the specific music hall for which the parties contracted. Of course, the music hall owner could have sought and secured substitute premises, making an allowance for any deficiency by way of compensatory money damages. That would certainly have made plaintiff whole. Plaintiff was, in fact,

---

[93] Krell v. Henry, [1903] 2 K.B. 740, 749–50.

[94] *Id.* at 751–52.

[95] *See id.* at 748 (Williams, L.J.); *Id.* at 755 (Stirling, L.J., and Romer, L.J.).

[96] The defense was actually, at the time, impossibility, but it grew into impracticability; the idea is that performance need not be actually *impossible*, impracticable is enough—and impracticable means something more than just impractical, which might mean no more than "more expensive." See Restatement (Second) of Contracts § 261 (1981) for a modern formulation of this theory.

only seeking reliance damages.[97] Certainly defendant, as the owner of the music hall, was in the better position to insure against[98] or take precautions to avoid the destructive fire. Imposing some loss—even just liability for plaintiff's reliance loss—on defendant may have created desirable incentives. Further, once the law imposed that risk on defendant, or on either party for that matter, it is more likely that the parties would allocate that risk in their contract. Moreover, so long as other contracting parties in the position of plaintiff and defendant in *Taylor* were aware of the decision and the impossibility doctrine, they could allocate the risk of a court's invoking it if they deemed it in their interest to do so. Once we make that assumption, it is not clear that we have to rely on an intent *fiction* at all to get a result consistent with the equitable balance struck by *Taylor*.

The point of that analysis is to make clear that *Taylor* really is based on fictional, non-existent intent: The court indulges the fiction in order to be able to assert some fidelity with the consensual basis of contract liability. From that perspective, the *Krell* court is more forthcoming. *Krell* concerns impossibility from the perspective of the buyer, what we have come to call *frustration*.[99] That denomination of what is essentially the same performance doctrine from the opposite perspective captures better, more accurately and candidly, what happens upon the occurrence of a contingency the non-occurrence of which was a basic assumption of the parties, to paraphrase the UCC formulation. The *Krell* court's focus on "the foundation" of the contract does not indulge an intent fiction to preserve the contract form. Circumstances have changed in a way that the court deems *not* to have been within the contemplation of the parties—and it most likely was not, only becoming salient after the fact.[100] What differs factually about the two cases, and *seems* to be a basis for meaningful distinction, is the fact that a buyer's performance

[97] *Taylor*, 122 Eng. Rep. at 310 (Plaintiff was seeking expenses for "printing advertisements of and in advertising the concerts, and also . . . sums expended and expenses incurred . . . in preparing for the concerts and otherwise in relation thereto.").

[98] *See* Catherine MacMillan, *Taylor v. Caldwell (1863)*, *in* Landmark Cases in the Law of Contract 167, 171–172, 179–180 (Charles Mitchell & Paul Mitchell eds. 2008) (Although music hall was difficult to insure against fire due to use of exposed ironwork, it was nevertheless fully insured at time of fire.); Robin Pearson, Insuring the Industrial Revolution : Fire Insurance in Great Britain, 1700–1850 (2004); *See also* Richard A. Posner & Andrew M. Rosenfield, *Impossibility and Related Doctrines in Contract Law: An Economic Analysis*, 6 J. Legal Stud. 83, 90–97 (1977) (discussing generally role insurance and self-insurance play in determining party best able to bear risk).

[99] *See, e.g.,* Joseph M. Perillo, Calamari and Perillo on Contracts § 13.12 (5th ed. 2003); Restatement (Second) of Contracts § 265 (1981); Wm. Beaudoin & Sons, Inc. v. County of Milwaukee, 217 N.W.2d 373, 377 (Wis. 1974) ("Where, after a contract is made, a party's principal purpose is substantially frustrated without his fault by the occurrence of an event the non-occurrence of which was a basic assumption on which the contract was made, his remaining duties to render performance are discharged. . . .").

[100] Consistent with the "salience bias" described in Shelley E. Taylor, *The Availability Bias in Social Perception and Interaction*, *in* Judgment Under Uncertainty: Heuristics and Biases 190, 192 (Daniel Kahneman et al. eds., 1982) (Because of "salience bias," people find distinctive stimuli more available and so rely on them disproportionately in making judgments.).

obligation is only to pay, and money is fungible. So it would *seem* to make less sense to consider the buyer's actual performance impracticable in any meaningful way. It is not that it has become impracticable for the buyer to perform, to pay; it is just that it makes less, and, maybe, no sense for the buyer to pay: Why lease a room with a view if there is nothing to view? On the right facts, we could also assume that the lessor could have just relet the premises when the Coronation procession was rescheduled, though Edward the VII's procession never did take place. Ultimately, *Krell* presents the same question as does *Taylor*, so far as the doctrine is concerned, and resolves it by reference to a different conception, making clear that the doctrine does not have one and only one basis.

Constructions based on presumed intent, the *Taylor* approach, are, of course, fiction, the validity of which may at least be compromised by the fact that one of the contracting parties is before the court gainsaying any such intention. Now that denial may be entirely strategic; a convenient *post hoc* recollection or failure to recall that serves that party's selfish interest may in fact contradict the parties' actual understanding before the fact. But tying the doctrine into intention preserves more of formal contract, with its focus on vindicating parties' intent rather than accommodating courts' adjustment of the equities based on considerations extraneous to intent. And what might those considerations be?

Well, so long as we (correctly) understand that contracting represents parties' allocation of risk for a price, a contract is evidence of that allocation. Although thoughtful parties may have meant to anticipate every contingency—and even believe that they have done so—we know that in the course of human events, the unforeseen and unforeseeable happens. It may be, though, that even such incomplete contracts (as all contracts are) represent the parties' intention to allocate the risks of loss not expressly contemplated by the terms of the contract on the party on whom that loss falls rather than shifting it, to any extent, to the other party. That is not an implausible inference to draw, and may be even more viable given the parties' ability to include a *force majeure* clause in their agreements, which can describe with or without some specificity the range of events that would excuse one or both parties' performance obligation.[101]

Taylor and *Krell* leave us with a calculus. Even though both cases do not pursue the same analysis, we can infer from their parallel treatment of impracticability from the two perspectives – seller (*Taylor*) and the buyer (*Krell*)– that the two cases concern something fundamental to the nature of contract. The cases are canonical and the doctrine which they support in distinguishable ways from distinguishable perspectives is very much a part of what we understand contract to be. So theory that cannot account for the cases as part of the broader story of contract cannot be viable theory. Also, theory which insists upon one rational for the two courts' analyses may be normative, but cannot be positive. We will consider in the next chapter whether such a theory could be interpretive, in any meaningful sense.

---

[101] *See* PERILLO, *supra* note 99, § 13.19.

Both cases have provided the basis for legislation beyond the UCC, and have been followed in common law jurisdictions.[102] The impracticability doctrine has also received considerable attention in the legal periodicals, particularly (though not exclusively[103]) from the consequentialist perspective.[104]

Although, at least formally, intent remains crucial to determination of the scope of contract, there are several contexts, in addition to impracticability, in which the court's *post hoc* construction of that intent effectively fixes the allocation of risk, and does so after the risk becomes more salient—indeed, sometime after the risk has materialized. The third-party beneficiary law provides another canonical example.

E. *Lawrence v. Fox*[105]

The facts of *Lawrence v. Fox* are quite simple, and, given that simplicity, the persistent tension in this area of contract may not be relieved by reference to much nuance in the facts of the canonical cases formulating the third-party beneficiary doctrine. A generic presentation of the prototypical context reveals all of the equities we need consider: A is indebted to B and obtains the promise of C to discharge A's debt to B at T2 in exchange for A's paying a sum equal to the amount of that debt to C at T1.

The court first confronts and resolves the consideration question: A had in fact given C consideration sufficient to support the undertaking of C to discharge A's debt to B.

---

[102] In America, *see* Lloyd v. Murphy, 153 P.2d 47 (Cal. 1944) (Contract not void for frustration of purpose if purpose was merely restricted but not prohibited altogether.); *See also* Karl Wendt Farm Equip. Co. v. Int'l Harvester Co., 931 F.2d 1112 (6th Cir. 1991) (Impracticality and unprofitableness do not constitute frustration.); Transatlantic Fin. Corp. v. United States, 363 F.2d 312 (D.C. Cir. 1966) (describing modern view of impossibility). In the United Kingdom, *see* Maritime Nat'l Fish Co. v. Ocean Trawlers, [1935] A.C. 524, 529 (P.C.) (*Krell* rule is "not one to be extended."); Denny, Mott & Dickson, Ltd. v. James B. Fraser & Co., [1944] A.C. 265 (H.L.) (following *Taylor*). In Canada, *see* Capital Quality Homes v. Colwyn Constr., [1975] 9 O.R.2d 617 (C.A.) (adopting the reasoning of Lord Radcliffe in Davis Contractors v. Fareham Urban Dist. Council, [1956] A.C. 696 (H.L.) (party incapable of performing because circumstances render performance radically different from what was in the contract.); Kerrigan v. Harrison, [1921] 62 S.C.R. 374 (Can.) (When right-of-way was destroyed by flood, seller did not have to repair or find alternate route.). In Australia, *see* Brisbane City Council v. Group Projects Proprietary (1979) 145 C.L.R. 143 (Austl.) (Developer was not bound by contract to develop land when land was taken by city for use as public school so that developer's purpose (economic gain) was frustrated.); Codelfa Constr. Proprietary v. State Rail Auth. (1982) 149 C.L.R. 337 (Austl.) (Injunction prevented work from being done at night, so plaintiff could not use three-shift twenty-four-hour workday; injunction made it impossible for plaintiff to finish on time.).

[103] *See* John D. Wladis, *Common Law and Uncommon Events: The Development of the Doctrine of Impossibility of Performance in English Contract Law*, 75 GEO. L.J. 1575 (1987).

[104] *See* Richard Bronaugh, Peter Barton, & Thomas Roberts, *Commercial Impossibility and Frustration of Purpose: A Critical Analysis*, 16 CAN. J.L. & JURIS. 129 (2003); Kevin M. Teeven, *Decline of Freedom of Contract since the Emergence of the Modern Business Corporation*, 37 ST. LOUIS U. L.J. 117 (1992); Nicholas R. Weiskopf, *Frustration of Contractual Purpose—Doctrine or Myth?*, 70 ST. JOHN'S L. REV. 239 (1996).

[105] Lawrence v. Fox, 20 N.Y. 268 (1859).

Certainly had the interest of C not intervened, A and B could have entered into a contract, supported by consideration, pursuant to which A would repay the sum to B the next day. The court recognizes the settled rule "that upon proof of a promise made to the debtor to pay the creditor, a promise to the creditor would be implied."[106] The only clarification the settled common law required was to the effect that the rule was not limited to the trust setting.[107]

The dissent relies on principles of privity to question the majority's conclusion. This was 1859 and privity meant a good deal more than it might today, after "The Fall of the Citadel."[108] The dissent too is impressed with the argument that A could have, at any time, countermanded the direction to C and B would have had no cause of action against C. So it may be that *Lawrence* marks, if not the beginning, then an important point in privity's deterioration. Indeed, the good sense of the opinion essentially challenges the contract–tort divide.[109]

Lawrence is quite easy; the more difficult cases are those that draw distinctions between different types of third-party beneficiaries and, particularly, the incidence of the intended versus incidental beneficiary status. The *Restatements* offer formulations that determine the contours of the divide. The *First Restatement* recognizes three categories: donee beneficiaries, creditor beneficiaries, and incidental beneficiaries.

> (1) Where performance of a promise in a contract will benefit a person other than the promisee, that person is . . .
>
> (a) a donee beneficiary if it appears from the terms of the promise in view of the accompanying circumstances that the purpose of the promisee in obtaining the promise of all or part of the performance thereof is to make a gift to the beneficiary or to confer upon him a right against the promisor to some performance neither due nor supposed or asserted to be due from the promisee to the beneficiary;
>
> (b) a creditor beneficiary if no purpose to make a gift appears from the terms of the promise in view of the accompanying circumstances and performance of the promise will satisfy an actual or supposed or asserted duty of the promisee to the beneficiary, or a right of the beneficiary against the promisee which has been barred by the Statute of Limitations or by a discharge in bankruptcy, or which is unenforceable because of the Statute of Frauds;

[106] *Id.* at 272.

[107] *Id.* at 274.

[108] *See* Prosser, *supra* note 64.

[109] *See* generally Roy Kreitner, *Fault at the Contract-Tort Interface*, 107 MICH. L. REV. 1533 (2009).

(c) an incidental beneficiary if neither the facts stated in Clause (a) nor those stated in Clause (b) exist.[110]

The *Second Restatement* departs from that formulation, and recognizes two rather than three classes of third party beneficiaries: intended and incidental.

(1) Unless otherwise agreed between promisor and promisee, a beneficiary of a promise is an intended beneficiary if recognition of a right to performance in the beneficiary is appropriate to effectuate the intention of the parties and either
   (a) the performance of the promise will satisfy an obligation of the promisee to pay money to the beneficiary; or
   (b) the circumstances indicate that the promisee intends to give the beneficiary the benefit of the promised performance.
(2) An incidental beneficiary is a beneficiary who is not an intended beneficiary.[111]

In the but-for-cause sense, virtually every contractual relation we can think of will affect those who are not party to the contract. In fact, insofar as A and B appreciate that their transaction will impact C in some way, it is not always clear where and when we could say that the intent to affect C arises. The linchpin of the *Second Restatement*'s distinction between intended and incidental beneficiaries is the intent of the parties. This is not the first time we could acknowledge the potential vagaries of such an intent calculus, which may not much constrain a court bent on doing equity after the fact.

A good deal turns on the distinction under the *Second Restatement*: "A promise in a contract creates a duty in the promisor to any intended beneficiary to perform the promise, and the intended beneficiary may enforce the duty."[112] The incidental beneficiary may not. Once again we see that the contract doctrine takes us only so far. It answers what seems to be the easier question—the intent of the parties determines to whom the duty flows—but does not tell us very much about how we might discern that intent. That, of course, is the rub. And the cases demonstrate that the results may be easier to rationalize after the fact than predicted by reference to legal certainties before the fact. Consider *Martinez v. Socoma Companies, Inc.*[113]

Plaintiffs in *Martinez* brought a class action, alleging that defendants failed to provide plaintiffs the job training and employment defendants were obligated to provide plaintiffs under the terms of defendants' contracts with the United States Government.

---

[110] Restatement (First) of Contracts § 133 (1932).

[111] Restatement (Second) of Contracts § 302 (1981).

[112] *Id.* § 304.

[113] Martinez v. Socoma Cos., 521 P.2d 841 (Cal. 1974).

The terms of the contracts contemplated that defendant would lease space in a building owned by the City of Los Angeles, invest five million dollars in the renovation and conversion of the facilities, and provide training and employment for East Los Angeles residents certified as disadvantaged by the government. Plaintiff class comprised more than two thousand residents of East Los Angeles, who were qualified for employment under the program but who did not receive jobs on account of defendants' alleged breach.

The question before the court was whether plaintiffs were intended or incidental beneficiaries. If plaintiffs were only incidental beneficiaries, their actions would not be viable. The lower court dismissed the action and the Supreme Court of California affirmed the dismissal. The Supreme Court concludes that there was insufficient basis to infer that the government intended to confer a direct right on plaintiffs just because the government intended them to "enjoy the benefits"[114] of the contracts. The object of the government was to benefit all of the citizenry at large. Plaintiffs would have benefited more directly than would have other citizens, but that would not be enough to support their being intended beneficiaries with the right to bring an action against defendants. Plaintiffs were incidental beneficiaries.

The dissent draws a distinction and still gives effect to considerations of intent. Although the dissent acknowledges that the government intended to benefit the communities generally in which the jobs were to be made available, "[i]t is incorrect to label one [the community] as an intended *direct* beneficiary and the other [the individuals] as merely *incidental*."[115] The dissent also points out something both curious and telling about the effort to discern intent: "The intent of the contracts themselves is expressed in their preambles. . . . By these provisions, the contracting parties clearly state as one of their purposes their intent to find jobs for the hard-core unemployed."[116]

What we may glean from the difference between the majority and dissent is the nature of the intent inquiry. It is not, as might seem appropriate, a mere inquiry into the parties' intent, granted, a tautology. Instead, it is a vehicle to enable courts to fix, not arbitrarily, a point at which the benefits of the contract will not be available by way of action to some potential parties in interest. This is not very different from the tort damages rule: "In every instance, before negligence can be predicated of a given act, *back of the act must be sought and found a duty* to the individual complaining, the observance of which would have averted or avoided the injury."[117] Or somewhat more famously, "The risk . . . to be perceived defines *the duty to be obeyed* and risk imports relation; it is risk to another

[114] *Id.* at 845.

[115] *Id.* at 851 (Burke, J., dissenting).

[116] *Id.*

[117] Palsgraf v. Long Island R. Co., 162 N.E. 99, 99–100 (N.Y. 1928) (emphasis added) (Cardozo here is quoting directly from West Virginia C. & P. R. Co. v. State, 96 Md. 652 (McSherry, C.J.).).

or to others within the range of apprehension."[118] As with the tort duty, so too with the contract duty. Replace "range of apprehension" with "intent to benefit," and you get the sense of the scope of third-party beneficiary liability in contract.

That merger of tort and contract is complete in the alternative formulations of Section 2-318 of the UCC, which determines the scope of warranty so far as third parties are concerned. Consider the alternative treatments of the so-called horizontal privity[119] issue. Alternative A provides that a seller's warranty extends to "any natural person who is in the family or household of his buyer or who is a guest in his home if it is reasonable to expect that such person may us, consume, or be affected by the goods and who is injured in person by breach of the warranty." This is the most restrictive alternative and extends warranty only to natural persons (*i.e.,* not corporations) who suffer personal rather than economic injury. Alternative B extends further, still only to natural persons, but now to all such persons "who may reasonably be expected to use, consume or be affected by the goods and who [are] injured in person." The limitation to personal injury remains, but the limitation to family or household members is gone. Alternative C, the final possibility, is expansive. The seller is liable for injuries to "any person," natural or not, "who may reasonably be expected to use, consume, or be affected by the goods," and the seller is liable for both personal injuries and economic injuries. The comments note the relationship between the warranty third-party beneficiary alternatives and the then developing products liability law.[120] So we may appreciate a symbiosis between the contract third-party beneficiary law and some tort principles. And that may be inevitable.

The common law jurisdictions generally follow the third-party beneficiary doctrine of *Lawrence v. Fox*,[121] with a notable exception: *Beswick v. Beswick*, a 1967 decision of the House of Lords. Peter Beswick, uncle of John Joseph Beswick, agreed to sell John Joseph his coal business. Part of the consideration for the sale was John Joseph's promise to pay Peter's wife an annuity in the event of Peter's death. John Joseph also agreed to assume Peter's liability to certain creditors. After Peter died, John Joseph made one payment to Peter's widow and then ceased making the annuity payment to her. The widow sought back payments and specific performance of the continuing obligation. The lower court found for the nephew and the House of Lords dismissed the widow's appeal.

The question was whether the widow, as a third-party beneficiary of the promise made to her deceased husband, could enforce that promise against the promisor-nephew.

---

[118] *Id.* at 100 (emphasis added).

[119] *See* 9–43 John E. Murray, Jr., Corbin on Contracts § 43.2 (Joseph M. Perillo ed., rev. ed. 2001) (describing horizontal privity and distinguishing it from vertical privity).

[120] UCC§ 2-318 (2002) cmt. 3 ("The third alternative goes further, following the trend of modern decisions as indicated by Restatement of Torts 2d § 402A . . . in extending the rule beyond injuries to the person [As amended in 1966].").

[121] *See* Trident Gen. Ins. Co. Ltd. v. McNiece Bros. Pty. Ltd. (2000) 165 C.L.R. 107 (Austl.); Dyck v. Manitoba Snowmobile Assn. Inc. (1982) 136 D.L.R. (3d) 11 (Can.).

The House of Lords relies on prior authority to find for the nephew and against the widow in her personal capacity.[122] The case was not a difficult one so far as the third-party beneficiary law of England was concerned: "[T]hird parties, of course, cannot themselves enforce a contract made for their benefit, but the person with whom the contract is made is entitled to enforce the contract."[123] Later cases follow the *Beswick* result.[124] But by a 1999 statute, the British law was brought into line with the other common law jurisdictions, and in familiar terms:

Right of third party to enforce contractual claim

(1) Subject to the provisions of this Act, a person who is not a party to a contract (a "third party") may in his own right enforce a term of the contract if–
    (a) the contract expressly provides that he may, or
    (b) subject to subsection (2), the term purports to confer a benefit on him.
(2) Subsection (1)(b) does not apply if on a proper construction of the contract it appears that the parties did not intend the term to be enforceable by the third party.[125]

Intent, again, inferred by the finder of fact, is determinative.

The next canonical case provides an interesting contrast in that it displays a markedly different attitude toward the parties' intent. So we may find out more about contract once we appreciate the limitations of the decision.

F. *Alaska Packers' Association v. Domenico*[126]

The story of the parties' transactional circumstances and actions in what came to be litigated as *Alaska Packers' Association v. Domenico* is, in fact, more complex than would appear from the court's rendition of the facts.[127] But for purposes of formulating the

---

122 Beswick Appellant v. Beswick Respondent [1968] A.C. 58, 63 (H.L.) (dismissing wife's claim against her nephew in her personal capacity). The House of Lords also deals with the widow's rights as executrix of her husband's estate. The court denies specific performance because, in her administrative capacity, the widow was required to attempt to accrue damages for the benefit of the estate. *Id* at 64–67.

123 *Id.* at 82 (citing Lord Hodson).

124 *See, e.g.,* Evans v. Sec'y of State for the Env't, Transport and the Regions Motor Insurers' Bureau, [2001] 2 C.M.L.R. 10 (U.K.) (C.A.) (following reasoning in *Beswick* by restricting ability to bring suit on trust to only administrator, not trustees); Woodar Inv. Dev. v. Wimpey Constr. (U.K.), [1980] 1 W.L.R. 277 (H.L.) (following *Beswick*); Neale v. Willis [1969] 19 P. & C.R. 836 (U.K.) (C.A.) (adhering to third party distinction in *Beswick*).

125 Contracts (Rights Of Third Parties) Act, 1999, c. 31 § 1 (Eng.).

126 Alaska Packers' Ass'n v. Domenico, 117 F. 99 (9th Cir. 1902).

127 Debora L. Threedy, A Fish Story: Alaska Packers' Association v. Domenico, 345–48 in Contracts Stories (Douglas G. Baird ed.) (2007) (noting influence of class and ethnicity on burgeoning

doctrine that emerges from this canonical case, the factual presentation of the court suffices, as of course it must. We may be skeptical that the court itself was insensitive to unreported but salient facts, but that skepticism cannot determine the doctrine that emerges.

The factual context presented in *Alaska Packers* is not complex. In this admiralty case before the United States Court of Appeals for the Ninth Circuit, the parties were twenty-one seamen who signed on to work the *Two Brothers* charter between San Francisco and Pyramid Harbor. The agreed compensation for each was to be sixty dollars. Their employers had invested about $150,000 in a salmon cannery in Pyramid Harbor. A few days after arriving at their destination and after they had begun work "fitting up" the cannery, the seamen stopped working and refused to resume unless their compensation were increased to one-hundred dollars per man. The employers would not have been able to hire replacement workers and so acceded to the seamen's demand, signing amended contracts to that effect.

At trial, plaintiffs (libelants, actually[128]) alleged in support of their claim for the increased compensation that the nets they had been given to do their work were defective, which, they argued, changed the deal in such a way that their claim for additional compensation was justified. The lower court found, as "a self-evident" fact, that because the employers had every reason to provide plaintiffs with serviceable materials, plaintiffs' allegation was certainly wrong. The appellate court found that the evidence was "sharply conflicting" and did not disturb the finding of the lower court. So as the case came to the Ninth Circuit, the seamen were thought to have tried to extort money from their employers.

The question before the court was simple, from the perspective of contract: Was the employer's promise to increase the seamen's compensation supported by sufficient consideration? No, it was not: "Consent to . . . [the seamen's] demand, under such circumstances, if given, was, in our opinion, without consideration, for the reason that it was based solely upon libelants' agreement to render the exact services, and none other, that they were already under contract to render."[129] The court does, then, comment on the transactional tension that supports its doctrinal conclusion. The evidence demonstrated that there was no "voluntary waiver"[130] on the part of the employer. There was coercion. The seamen tried to take "an unjustifiable advantage"[131] of the employer.

Of course, there would be no requirement for new consideration supporting the promise to pay increased wages if the parties' actions could be characterized as a novation, and,

---

Alaska salmon packing industry and observing cannery in question, Pyramid Harbor, consistently spent disproportionate amount on fishing equipment and conversely paid lowest wages to its fisherman of all Alaska packing companies).

[128] In admiralty cases, the party asserting a claim is a *libelant* rather than a plaintiff.

[129] *Alaska Packers*, 117 F. at 102.

[130] *Id.*

[131] *Id.*

given the formalities concerned, there would be nothing to constrain a court from concluding that the parties had attempted to modify an existing agreement without additional consideration rather than effect a novation. The same balance of equities that would justify a determination that there was no new consideration supporting the employer's "promise" to pay the seamen an increased wage—the employer was getting only what the seamen had contracted to give—would as well support the conclusion that there was not a novation:

> It is urged upon us by respondents that this was a new contract. New in what? Jungenfeld was bound by his contract to design and supervise this building. Under the new promise he was not to do any more or anything different. What benefit was to accrue to Wainwright? He was to receive the same service from Jungenfeld under the new, that Jungenfeld was bound to render under the original, contract.[132]

That conclusion is not surprising, given what the court finds the facts to be. What is noteworthy, though, is the court's appreciation of the essentially equitable calculus that supports the *pre-existing legal duty rule*. We appreciate a resonance with that calculus in the elaborations of what are really exceptions to the rule.

The *Restatements* include iterations of the pre-existing duty rule that are largely consistent with *Alaska Packers*. Section 76 of the *First Restatement* includes the rule of the case in a general sufficiency of consideration provision.

> Any consideration that is not a promise is sufficient. . ., except the following:
>
> (a) An act or forbearance required by a legal duty that is neither doubtful nor the subject of honest and reasonable dispute if the duty is owed either to the promisor or to the public, or, if imposed by the law of torts or crimes, is owed to any person[.][133]

That formulation is not adjusted much in the *Second Restatement*:

> Performance of a legal duty owed to a promisor which is neither doubtful nor the subject of honest dispute is not consideration; but a similar performance is consideration if it differs from what was required by the duty in a way which reflects more than the pretense of a bargain.[134]

---

[132] *Id.* at 103 (quoting Lingenfelder v. Brewing Co., 15 S.W. 844, 848 (Mo. 1891)).

[133] RESTATEMENT (FIRST) OF CONTRACTS § 76(a) (1932).

[134] RESTATEMENT (SECOND) OF CONTRACTS § 73 (1981).

The *Second Restatement* elaborates:

A promise modifying a duty under a contract not fully performed on either side is binding

(a) if the modification is fair and equitable in view of circumstances not anticipated by the parties when the contract was made; or
(b) to the extent provided by statute; or
(c) to the extent that justice requires enforcement in view of material change of position in reliance on the promise.[135]

The statute most notably within the provision's reference is Section 2-209 of the UCC.

That section, "Modification, Rescission, and Waiver," changes the common law pre-existing duty rule of *Alaska Packers* but stays within the rationale supporting the rule.[136] Under the Code provision, a modification of a contract need not be supported by consideration; the comments make clear that the modification will be enforceable so long as it is the product of agreement and was sought (and granted[137]) in "good faith,"[138] a defined term in the Code. Consideration has been supplanted by good faith because the only function of consideration in the modification context is to assure that the modification was the product of agreement, *i.e.,* "the bargain of the parties in fact."[139] So it would seem that Section 2-209 is really just a statutory iteration of the *Second Restatement*'s focus on whether the modification was "fair and equitable in view of circumstances not anticipated by the parties when the contract was made." Granted, the Code provision may go further in permitting modifications than would that *Restatement* formulation—*i.e.,* there may be a good-faith modification even if there has not been a change of circumstances not anticipated when the contract was made—but the distinction, if any, does not obscure the point: The work of consideration[140] is now done by "good faith" or conceptions of the "fair and equitable."

So *Alaska Packers* is, perhaps curiously, canonical only in part for what it says but even more for what it exposes in contract, and the *Restatement* and UCC formulations respond

---

[135] *Id.* § 89.

[136] UCC§ 2-209 (2002).

[137] Double-E Sportswear Corp. v. Girard Trust Bank, 488 F.2d 292 (3d Cir. 1973) (Party cannot feign agreement to amend terms of contract and then attempt to avoid contract by claiming there was not actual agreement.).

[138] UCC§ 1-201(b)(20) (2003).

[139] *Id.* § 1-201(b)(3).

[140] Lon L. Fuller, *Consideration and Form,* 41 Colum. L. Rev. 799 (1940). Section 89 of the *Second Restatement* cites and relies upon Fuller's article when allowing the modification of not fully performed contracts if the modification is fair and equitable, permissible by statute, or required in the interests of justice. Restatement (Second) of Contracts § 89 (1981).

to what the case exposed. The pre-existing duty rule of *Alaska Packers* has been reflected as well in other common law jurisdictions.[141]

The final canonical case considered in this chapter concerns a tension that is revealed in the course of the parties' performance and refines the role of inferred intent in fixing the performance obligation. The opinion of California Supreme Court Chief Justice Roger Traynor is canonical. Insofar as Justice Traynor's understanding of intent reveals something fundamental about contract, it is crucial to determination of contract performance doctrine generally.

G. *Pacific Gas & Electric Co. v. G. W. Thomas Drayage & Rigging Co.*[142]

In *Pacific Gas & Electric Co. v. G. W. Thomas Drayage & Rigging Co.,* the parties entered into the contract pursuant to which defendant would perform certain work on plaintiff's steam turbine. The contract between them provided that defendant would indemnify plaintiff "against all loss, damage, expense and liability resulting from . . . injury to property, arising out of or in any way connected with" defendant's performance of the contract.[143] During the course of the work, the cover of the turbine fell and damaged the turbine rotor. Plaintiff brought an action for the amount spent on repairs. Defendant responded that the indemnity obligation was intended by the parties to extend only to injury or damage to the property of third parties, not loss suffered by plaintiff in the course of the project.

The trial court identified the contract language as consistent with an intention to create only a third-party indemnification, but found it necessary to defer to what it considered the "plain language" of the agreement that would extend defendant's obligation to plaintiff as well. So as the trial court saw it, there was a clear conflict between the parties' actual intent and the language of their agreement. The trial court concluded that the conflict would be resolved in favor of the plain language and in derogation of the parties' intent.

Justice Traynor finds the trial court's conclusion untenable:

> The test of admissibility of extrinsic evidence to explain the meaning of a written instrument is not whether it appears to the court to be plain and unambiguous on

---

[141] *See* Musumeci v. Winadell Proprietary (1994) 34 N.S.W.L.R. 723 (Austl.) (Landlord who agreed to reduce rent because he rented to competitor of plaintiff in same location as plaintiff was bound, since additional leases that landlord could make constituted additional consideration.); Gilbert Steel Ltd. v. Univ. Constr., [1976] 12 O.R.2d 19 (Ont. C.A.) (New contract void for lack of consideration if buyer agreed to supplier's request for higher price for delivery of same quantity of same steel, citing changes in market price.); Stilk v. Myrick, (1809) 170 Eng. Rep. 1168 (in facts nearly identical to *Alaska Packers*: no consideration for captain's promise to pay crew more for continuing their contractual obligation at sea).

[142] Pac. Gas & Elec. Co. v. G.W. Thomas Drayage & Rigging Co., 442 P.2d 641 (Cal. 1968).

[143] *Id.* at 643.

> its face, but whether the offered evidence is relevant to prove a meaning to which the language of the instrument is reasonably susceptible. . . .
>
> A rule that would limit the determination of the meaning of a written instrument to its four-corners merely because it seems to the court to be clear and unambiguous, would either deny the relevance of the intention of the parties or presuppose a degree of verbal precision and stability our language has not attained.[144]

The tension, then, as revealed by Traynor, is between the parties' intent and the inaccurate (perhaps necessarily so) written presentation of that intent. The case favoring "plain meaning" is clear: Courts cannot read the minds of litigants, so the clear expression of their intent is the best evidence of what that intent actually is (or, at least, was). Admission of extrinsic evidence that contradicts the plain meaning of the contract terms (and the party resisting introduction of that evidence is necessarily asserting that the extrinsic evidence is contradictory) certainly undermines parties' reliance on an integrated writing to memorialize their allocation of risk. But denying admission of that evidence may elevate form over substance and vouchsafe a result that actually contradicts the parties' intent. The balance is not unique in the contract law; in fact, it describes a tension familiar from other canonical case contexts.

Traynor is well aware that his conclusion, and predisposition toward the admission of extrinsic evidence, is at odds with an alternative conception of contract. He knows what is at stake in his understanding of the extrinsic evidence rule: nothing less than the essential foundation of contract. Traynor acknowledges the alternative view that concludes contract *is* the words parties use to describe their deal; contract is not the intent that those words might reveal: "Under this view, contractual obligations flow, not from the intention of the parties but from the fact that they used certain magic words. Evidence of the parties' intention therefore becomes irrelevant."[145] The question *is* whether we care about intent or, instead, about the terms of the expression of that intent.

Traynor fashions a nice argument in favor of intent. Essentially, he concludes that focus on intent is more reliable than focus on the expression of intent because words do not have "absolute and constant referents."[146] Of course, there is no reason to believe that intent provides any more certainty. After all, the controversy that sparks litigation may require a construction of intent that the parties never had because the parties never foresaw the developments that have become salient only after the fact. Certainly the parties, in the normal course of events, did not foresee that the circumstances giving rise to the controversy would in fact materialize. If they had, they may well have chosen (perhaps

---

[144] *Id.* at 644 (citations omitted).

[145] *Id.* at 644 (citing Hotchkiss v. National City Bank of New York, 200 F. 287, 293 (S.D.N.Y. 1911)).

[146] *Id.*

likely would have chosen) to more certainly fill the gap in the contract that the court would otherwise be called upon to fill. So intent may be no more substantial (and no less elusive) than the objective meaning of language.

It is safe to say that Traynor's attitude toward extrinsic evidence is consistent with both Section 2-202 of the UCC and Sections 213 through 216 of the *Second Restatement*. The UCC extrinsic evidence rule really keeps out very little extrinsic evidence. That is, creative (or, at least, persistent) counsel should be able to get extrinsic evidence in through one or more of the crevices left open by Section 2-202. The highlighted language indicates such potential points of entry:

> Terms with respect to which the confirmatory memoranda of the parties *agree* or which are otherwise set forth in a writing *intended by the parties as a final expression* of their agreement *with respect to such terms* as are included therein may not be *contradicted* by evidence of any prior agreement or of a contemporaneous oral agreement but may be *explained or supplemented*
> (a) *by course of performance, course of dealing, or usage of trade* . . ., and
> (b) by evidence of *consistent additional terms* unless the court finds the writing to have been *intended* also as a *complete and exclusive statement* of the terms of the agreement.[147]

Consider the potential pressure points: First, the court may find that the writings of the parties do not *agree*, in which case Section 2-207, the battle of the forms provision, would be apposite and the court could perform the calculus required by that provision to determine the terms of the contract and may depart from the parties' expression of their individual intent (because there is no discernible mutual intent). Second, the court may determine that the writing presented to it was not *intended by the parties as a final expression* of their agreement, in which case the rule on the exclusion of extrinsic evidence is wholly inapposite and the proffered evidence of a prior or contemporaneous understanding would not be barred *ab initio*. Third, even if the writing is partially integrated, that is, constitutes the parties' understanding *only* with regard to certain but less than all of the terms of the contract, the court may consider extrinsic evidence not related to matters within the scope of that partial integration. Fourth, even with respect to terms that are integrated, intended by the parties as their final expression, the court may consider evidence that does not actually *contradict* the writing but instead *explains or supplements* the writing by reference to the Code's interpretive hierarchy.[148] Fifth, in the event the

[147] UCC§ 2-202 (2002) (emphasis added).

[148] UCC§ 1-303 (2003). The apposite comment explains the purpose of the section:

> The UCC rejects both the *lay-dictionary* and the *conveyancer's* reading of a commercial agreement. Instead, the meaning of the agreement of the parties is to be determined by the language used by them and by their action, read and interpreted in the light of commercial practices and other surrounding

court finds that the writing is not *intended* to be a complete integration, the court may consider *consistent additional terms*.

From that brief exegesis, it is clear that the court will have access to extrinsic evidence if for no other reason than to decide whether it should consider extrinsic evidence. That is precisely what Justice Traynor had in mind, too: "[R]ational interpretation requires at least preliminary consideration of all credible evidence offered to prove the intention of the parties."[149] Section 214 of the *Second Restatement* seems to contemplate the same use of extrinsic evidence, for purposes of determining whether a writing is integrated:

> Agreements and negotiations prior to or contemporaneous with the adoption of a writing are admissible in evidence to establish
> (a) that the writing is or is not an integrated agreement;
> (b) that the integrated agreement, if any, is completely or partially integrated;
> (c) the meaning of the writing, whether or not integrated;
> (d) illegality, fraud, duress, mistake, lack of consideration, or other invalidating cause;
> (e) ground for granting or denying rescission, reformation, specific performance, or other remedy.[150]

The extrinsic evidence rule, so formulated, seems porous. Subsection 214(c), in particular, supports that conclusion by admitting extrinsic evidence to show the meaning of the parties *whether or not* the writing is integrated.

The *First Restatement's* iteration of the rule is less indulgent of the admission of extrinsic evidence. Again, two provisions of that *Restatement* present the substance of its scope:

> § 237 Parol Evidence Rule; Effect of Integration on Prior or Contemporaneous Agreements
>
> Except as stated in §§ 240, 241 the integration of an agreement makes inoperative to add to or to vary the agreement all contemporaneous oral agreements relating to the same subject-matter; and also . . . all prior oral or written agreements relating thereto.[151]
>
> § 238 Extent to Which Agreements Prior to or Contemporaneous With Integration Are Admissible In Evidence

circumstances. The measure and background for interpretation are set by the commercial context, which may explain and supplement even the language of a formal or final writing.

[149] *Pac. Gas & Elec. Co.*, 442 P.2d at 645.

[150] Restatement (Second) of Contracts § 214 (1981).

[151] Restatement (First) of Contracts § 237 (1932).

Agreements prior to or contemporaneous with an integration are admissible in evidence

(a) to establish the meaning of the integration . . .;
(b) to prove facts rendering the agreement void or voidable for illegality, fraud, duress, mistake or insufficiency of consideration;
(c) to prove facts in a suit for rescission or reformation of the written agreement showing such mistake as affords grounds for the desired remedy;
(d) to prove facts in a suit for specific performance showing such mistake, oppression or unfairness as affords grounds for denying that remedy.[152]

Subsection 240(1), then, provides the court a means to consider extrinsic evidence notwithstanding the "rule":

(1) An oral agreement is not superseded or invalidated by a subsequent or contemporaneous integration, nor a written agreement by a subsequent integration relating to the same subject-matter, if the agreement is not inconsistent with the integrated contract, and
   (a) is made for a separate consideration, or
   (b) is such an agreement as might naturally be made as a separate agreement by parties situated as were the parties to the written contract.[153]

That *First Restatement* formulation captures the facts and analysis of *Mitchill v. Lath*,[154] which pursued an approach to extrinsic evidence that has been supplanted by the later cases and the *Second Restatement*.

In *Mitchill* (also referred to as "the ice-house case"), the parties agreed to the sale of a farm. Across the road from the farm was an unsightly ice-house the purchasers wanted removed. The seller-defendants orally agreed to remove the eyesore. In reliance on that representation, the purchaser agreed to go forward with the transaction. When the ice-house was not removed, the purchaser brought an action that the sellers defended by interposing the parol evidence rule: Insofar as the removal of the ice-house was incident to the sales transaction, that undertaking had to be memorialized in the integrated writing or was not enforceable. The court agrees, finding that the removal of the ice-house was so "closely related to"[155] the real estate purchase transaction that it could not be separately proved. The court concludes that the question would be "how closely bound"[156] to the principal contract the collateral agreement was. The ice-house removal undertaking

[152] *Id.* § 238.

[153] *Id.* § 240(1).

[154] Mitchill v. Lath, 160 N.E. 646 (N.Y. 1928).

[155] *Id.* at 647.

[156] *Id.*

was bound closely enough to preclude enforcement within or without the scope of the contract.[157] *Mitchill* too may be canonical, but much of its sense has been subsumed by *Pacific Gas & Electric*.

Given the nature of the extrinsic evidence inquiry, we can see the progress from the *Mitchill* to *Pacific Gas & Electric* rules and from the *First Restatement* to the *Second Restatement* formulations as a refinement of the same idea rather than as a sea change. The nature of the inquiry, fact-dependent and intent-centered, does not change; all that changes are the terms used to describe the scope and method of the inquiry. Indeed, there would seem to be something about the extrinsic evidence rule that defies a formulation that could certainly preempt inquiry into context, and, of course, it is that very inquiry into context that the extrinsic evidence rule is designed to circumscribe.

The parol or extrinsic evidence tension in contract is fundamental; it concerns the very foundations of agreement in what may well be a charged setting: One party has not lived up to her agreement and hides behind a formality to avoid the consequences. The rule is an ostensibly anti-fraud mechanism that could be used by a less-than-conscientious party to effectively perpetrate a fraud.

The rule has been codified in non-uniform legislation[158] and has received considerable attention in the law journals.[159] *Pacific Gas & Electric* is regularly included in the casebooks and is covered by the leading treatises. The case is also regularly cited by the courts. Granted, Justice Traynor's construction of the rule is narrow, but it is narrow in a way that any theory of contract must account for. Indeed, the fact that the formulation of the rule cannot preclude such a narrow construction says a great deal about contract doctrine, and the limits of normative theory that would formulate it.

The next chapter continues under the performance heading, but will begin an examination of the apposite normative theory of contract, specifically, how courts' and parties' reactions to different sources of stress with regard to performance shape contract normativity.

---

[157] It is noteworthy that New York Chief Judge Benjamin Cardozo concurred with Judge William S. Andrews's majority opinion in *Mitchill*. Judge Andrews dissented from Judge Cardozo's majority opinions in two other famous cases that were decided within a year of *Mitchill*—Palsgraf v. Long Island Rail Co., 162 N.E. 99, 102 (N.Y. 1928) and Allegheny Coll. v. Nat'l Chautauqua County Bank, 159 N.E. 173, 177 (N.Y. 1927).

[158] Cal. Civ. Code §§ 13, 1625, 1636 & 1647 (1872); Cal. Code Civ. Proc. §§ 1856 & 1858 (1872).

[159] Lawrence Cunningham, *Toward a Prudential and Credibility-Centered Parol Evidence Rule*, 68 U. Cin. L. Rev. 269 (2000); Margaret Kniffin, *A New Trend in Contract Interpretation: The Search for Reality As Opposed to Virtual Reality*, 74 Or. L. Rev. 643 (1995); Peter Linzer, *Symposium: A Tribute to Professor Joseph M. Perillo: The Comfort of Certainty: Plain Meaning and the Parol Evidence Rule*, 71 Fordham L. Rev. 799 (2002); Harry Prince, *Contract Interpretation in California: Plain Meaning, Parol Evidence and Use of the "Just Result" Principle*, 31 Loyola L.A. L. Rev. 557 (1998).

6

THEORY OF CONTRACT PERFORMANCE

PERHAPS THE FABRIC of contract is never so accurately revealed as when it is under stress. If the parties' expectations are realized, that is, if all goes as expected, there is less reason to rely on conceptions of contract's normative foundation in order to resolve controversy. There is no controversy. But if the deal breaks down, either because one party is in breach or acts unconscientiously, or just because the world in which the contract actually operates is not the world the parties anticipated, courts are called upon to get to the bottom of things, to determine the normative contours of contract's mission. This chapter will pursue the normative question in the context of five pressure points that impose such revelatory stress on contract: unconscionability, excuse, modification, third-party beneficiaries, and, more summarily, the parol evidence rule.

The first part of the chapter focuses on the primary deal-policing mechanism:[1] unconscionability. This device fixes the limits of contracting, and as such implicates a normative calculus. What may we use contract to do? And at what point has one of the parties tried to use contract to do too much? Unconscionability concerns the acceptable scope of contract at the time of deal formation; a contract conscionable at formation does not

[1] There are others: *e.g.*, fraud, duress, illegality, infancy.

thereafter become unconscionable.[2] We will see that the unconscionability doctrine accommodates, though does not prescribe, a normative calculus.

The second part of the chapter treats related performance, or rather, excuse from performance, doctrines, including impossibility, impracticability, and frustration. These doctrines are concerned with circumstances developing after formation but before performance.[3] Another excuse from performance, mutual mistake, is concerned with circumstances at the time of contract formation, and has been previously examined in Chapters Three, "Contract Formation Doctrine," and Four, "Theory of Contract Formation." It could, however, just as easily fit into the following performance discussion: Both mistake and the excuse doctrines limit the performance obligation and come to the rescue of a party whose interest would be prejudiced were the performance obligation contemplated by the contract enforced. We will see, once again, that the doctrine does not so much constrain as it accommodates.

The third section concerns modification, the parties' efforts to adjust the terms of their contract in light of changed circumstances, or at least *allegedly* changed circumstances. Here the normative inquiry is not all that distinct from our concern in the unconscionability setting: How do we draw the line between duress and a good-faith effort to account for an occurrence, the nonoccurrence of which was a basic assumption on which the contract was formed? To the extent that the inquiry here mirrors, or at least tracks, the parallel inquiries in the unconscionability, impracticability, and frustration contexts, we would expect to discern some normative consistency. The doctrine, if it has normative content, should accommodate, if not prescribe, a consistent normative calculus.

The fourth part of the chapter perhaps bears only an apparently tangential relationship to the subject matter of the first three parts of the chapter. This section considers the third-party beneficiary law, which, very much like the focus of the first three sections of the chapter, is about the scope of contractual undertaking. At the margins, courts are asked to determine the scope of the contracting parties' intent: Who would have standing to bring an action on the contract? The normative questions are similar to those considered with regard to performance generally and may lend themselves to similar observations about the perspective of the apposite doctrine. Finally, the chapter presents a brief colloquy concerning the fit between extrinsic evidence doctrine and normative theory of contract.

---

[2] Restatement (Second) of Contracts § 208 (1981) ("If a contract or term thereof is unconscionable *at the time the contract is made* a court may refuse to enforce the contract, or may enforce the remainder of the contract without the unconscionable term, or may so limit the application of any unconscionable term as to avoid any unconscionable result.") (emphasis added); *see also* UCC §2-302(1) (2002) ("[if] the court . . . finds . . . the contract or any clause of the contract to have been unconscionable *at the time it was made*. . . .") (emphasis added).

[3] Restatement (Second) of Contracts § 261 (1981); *accord* UCC § 2-615(a) (2002) ("the occurrence of a contingency the non-occurrence of which was a basic assumption on which the contract was made").

A. Unconscionability

This section focuses on unconscionability, the doctrine that provides the court a means to rebalance the parties' contract to take into account either party's overreaching at the time of contract formation. The role of unconscionability seems clearly normative: Its focus is on policing bad behavior, whatever we take that to mean. Unconscionability responds to intentional wrongdoing. Contract, so the story goes, is not fault-based: The chips are left to lie where they fall regardless of the fault (or even malfeasance) of the other party. But unconscionability is about fault: One party is denied the benefit of the hard bargain she has struck because of her overreaching. We, in effect, punish the overreaching party insofar as we deny her the benefit of her ill-gotten bargain.

Commentators who would come to terms with all of contract must come to terms with unconscionability. The doctrine seems to collide head-on with the fundamental nature of the consideration requirement. Recall, we are not concerned with *adequacy* of consideration; you can make a bad deal, even a very bad deal. All that we require is a bargain for that deal. Further, complementary doctrines from the tort law, specifically fraud and duress, and even complementary contracting principles, such as the requisites of agreement, seem to do the work that unconscionability would do. The court could avoid the harsh deal by relying on the tort law to overcome the ostensible contract result. Alternatively, confronted with an unconscientious contract, a court could refuse to enforce the subordinate party's undertaking by finding that there was in fact no bargain, no agreement.

The unconscionability doctrine is necessary because it goes where those complementary doctrines do not go. Only *if* there has been a bargain *not* obtained by misrepresentation does unconscionability have any work to do that is not otherwise done. The last chapter described the leading canonical case, *Williams*,[4] and suggested a gloss on the doctrine that makes sense: Unconscionability is something of a "dump" in which we can isolate hard cases to avoid making bad law and corrupting doctrine. Understanding *how* the doctrine operates does not fully explain why the doctrine exists, what normative goal it vindicates. For unconscionability to fit within a normative theory of contract, we must discover its normative content, if it has any.

The inquiry is again bifurcated: First, the deontic is considered through representative contributions and, then, the consequentialist perspective is contrasted, if there is basis for contrast. We will see, though, that there may be more coincidence here than in the case of other doctrinal hot spots.

[4] Williams v. Walker-Thomas Furn. Co., 350 F.2d 445 (D.C. Cir. 1965).

1. DEONTOLOGY

The promise theory of Charles Fried again provides a good place to start, because he recognizes that unconscionability necessarily entails a normative premise and he posits one in terms of Kantian autonomy principles. Fried treats unconscionability along with duress, but understands unconscionability to be "a vaguer notion, which concentrates rather on the imbalance, the substantive unfairness of the agreement itself."[5] In the case of duress, we might conclude that there is no agreement as such because volition, the crucial element of agreement, is missing. Although we may disagree on how much volition agreement requires, someone who would build contract on promise has to take volition very seriously. It is not clear that unconscionability is as distinguishable from duress as Fried suggests. Certainly we can identify the facts that typically support both defenses; it is less clear that the normative foundations of the two are significantly dissimilar. This will bear further analysis when we consider modification in section C, "Modification," of this chapter. For now, though, it would be premature to assume that the mechanisms considered in this chapter vindicate different normative calculi just because the doctrine assumes different formulations. Although factual predicates may differ, there may ultimately be normative affinity.

Fried finds unconscionability to be enigmatic:

> The decided cases do not invoke the doctrine of unconscionability in any systematic or even coherent way. Claims of substantive unfairness are mixed with suggestions of fraud, cognitive deficiency, and duress, so that it is not possible to discern a pattern in the factual situations in which this episodic dispensing power is exercised. Certain leading cases do, however, represent distinct tendencies in the law.[6]

Fried affords little attention to the procedural dimension of unconscionability, focusing instead on the substantive unfairness criterion. That may not be consistent with the direction the unconscionability law has taken, increasingly emphasizing procedural considerations: We may be willing to let you make a bad deal, but we will insist you make it with your eyes open. Indeed, focusing on the procedural dimension is a way to reconcile the unconscionability defense with the fact that *adequacy* of consideration does not matter. If all unconscionability were concerned with were how bad the deal was for the complaining party, unconscionability would amount to a repudiation of the rule that adequacy of consideration just does not matter, and that might then too undermine the bargain requirement.

---

[5] Charles Fried, Contract as Promise: A Theory of Contractual Obligation 92 (1981).

[6] *Id.* at 103.

Fried is troubled by the conception of unconscionability that emerges from *Williams* but agrees with the doctrine's operation in contexts such as that presented in *Henningsen*. In the *Williams* setting, to void the contract on the basis of unconscionability is to burden a single economic actor who meets a market need in underprivileged areas with the consequences of a greater social failure: "[T]he provision of a just social minimum should be society's general responsibility, not the responsibility of individual economic actors, except as they pay taxes to fund that minimum."[7] So we must conclude that, under Fried's promise theory, there can be no deal that is unconscionable on the basis of substantive unfairness unless the cause of the unfairness is one party's overreaching, rather than a social and economic context that accommodates overreaching. If a payday loan storefront charges clients 400 percent interest (annualized), and essentially makes its profit getting the clients hooked on the rollover of the loans, that is not unconscionable because the clients are victims of macroeconomic disequilibria, not the type of behavior Fried finds in the *Henningsen* context.

For Fried, antitrust considerations provide the basis to determine the correct result, as a matter of contract doctrine, on the *Henningsen* facts:

> It may be, for instance, that difficulties of entry, the small number of competitors, the concentration of producers versus the dispersal of consumers, allow the automobile manufacturers... by their cartel-like agreement to lower the cost of accidents to themselves at the expense of consumers and thus to enjoy a monopoly profit – that is, a profit greater than is necessary to enlist an optimum level of investment in automobile manufacturing. By refusing to enforce the no-warranty clause, we force automobile manufacturers to give up their monopoly profits to consumers, and the result will be greater economic efficiency – manufacturers will be moved to manufacture more or safer cars at the lower price.[8]

The measure of unconscionability, for Fried, is monopoly profits. We need to do the consequentialist math in order to be able to decide whether a particular contract is void on the basis of unconscionability.

Now the point here is not that the unconscionability calculus contemplated by Fried might well be more complex than the rather spare formulation of the doctrine would suggest. The object instead is to make clear the breadth of normative analysis the doctrine accommodates. In fact, Fried's perspective, proceeding from Kantian autonomy principles, merges, at least formally, with a consequentialist analysis. Yet a difference between the two remains: The consequentialist would be concerned only with applying the law to

[7] *Id.* at 106.

[8] *Id.* at 107.

realize the best (in this case, most efficient) results, but Fried would coincidentally discover in the monopolistic, inefficient behavior an affront to the promise principle. His analysis, at this point, becomes harder to follow:

> By their agreement (conspiracy in restraint of trade) the automobile manufacturers create and maintain monopoly conditions; the retailer and small contractor do nothing of the sort. The automobile manufacturers' kind of conspiracy can be proscribed by general rules beforehand. But there is no way to distinguish the advantage taken by the enterprising retailer or employer from that enjoyed by the inventor of the hula hoop except that they draw their profit from the poor—and that alone, I have argued, is not a reason to strike down their bargains as unconscionable.[9]

Leaving aside for the moment the fact that antitrust laws would seem to be competent on their own to police monopolistic behavior, without help from unconscionability doctrine, there is nothing about promise that is vindicated by Fried's analysis. His deontology may suggest that promise is undermined in the settings of inner-city appliance store instalment sales and automobile warranty limitations, but it does not provide the means to distinguish which promise is avoidable on unconscionability bases and which is not. Indeed, insofar as his analysis relies on an efficiency calculus, determining when an economic actor is able to impose monopoly pricing, Fried's deontology reduces to a quantitative inquiry. Now we might object that that goes beyond the terms of the doctrine, but I would argue that is beside the point. The doctrine accommodates just the type of analysis Fried contemplates, deontology with a *soupçon* of consequentialism.

Fried's discovery of the normative basis of unconscionability does not accomplish much, even if his discovery were real. How do we treat the range of cases between *Williams* and *Henningsen*? Are we to determine on a case-by-case basis whether the party asserting unconscionability is the victim of greater social and economic forces rather than the overreaching of its counterparty? Isn't it likely that there will often be coincidence of general and specific forces, such as the more sophisticated seller who takes advantage of the less sophisticated buyer by imposing terms on the buyer that the buyer does not understand? Recall that the consumer in *Williams* was victimized by what was essentially a cross-collateral clause; the allegation was not that the consumer was charged too much for the goods. How likely is it that the salesperson on the appliance store floor could even have explained the operation of the offensive provision to the consumer-buyer, much less have done so in terms that the consumer would understand?

An obvious basis of distinction within the contemplation of the doctrine is that the retailer who does take advantage of the ignorance of its buyer has done something other than drawn profit from the poor. So long as we appreciate the procedural aspect of

---

[9] *Id.*

unconscionability, the doctrine provides the means to police transactions that would take advantage of ignorance (even rational ignorance). The *Official Comment* to the Uniform Commercial Code (UCC or the Code) unconscionability provision explains that "[t]he principle is one of the prevention of oppression and unfair surprise and not of disturbance of allocation of risks because of superior bargaining power."[10] There is nothing, then, in the unconscionability provision that disturbs the "allocation of risk because of superior bargaining power," but there is much that provides the means to police the unconscientious behavior of the party who uses that superior bargaining power to exploit the ignorance of its subordinate counterparty.

It is not clear how Fried's construction of the unconscionability doctrine serves his promise principle. Insofar as the principle vindicates individual autonomy, wouldn't the unconscionability doctrine be most consistent with the promise principle if it too vindicated individual autonomy? To that end, we could read the doctrine not as disturbing the allocation of risk because of superior bargaining power but as precluding the use of that superior bargaining power to oppress subordinate parties. The problem in *Williams* was not that the retailer *had* superior bargaining power, it was that the retailer exploited the ignorance of the consumer, and undermined her autonomy, by including a cross-collateral provision in the security agreement.

At bottom, though, the distinction the promise principle draws seems to be more procedural (a matter of bargaining infirmity) than substantive (a bad deal). The point of not reviewing the adequacy of consideration is that we want actors to be free to make good deals and bad deals, at least insofar as we do not want to expend resources deciding whether the deal is good or bad. Valuations are idiosyncratic so far as contract is concerned; even if there is a ready market measure, we will enforce your actual intent to pay too much for something.

The drift of the unconscionability law seems to be in the direction of procedural concerns.[11] Though we will defend your right to make a bad deal, we want some assurance that you have made the deal knowingly, that your counterparty has not deceived you in some way (short of provable fraud?) into making the bad deal. But against that concern with the procedural branch of unconscionability is the law developing from Judge Frank Easterbrook's *ProCD v. Zeidenberg*[12] and *Hill v. Gateway 2000, Inc.*[13]

---

[10] UCC § 2-302 cmt. 1 (2002).

[11] *See, e.g., id.* § 2A-108.

[12] ProCD, Inc. v. Zeidenberg, 86 F.3d 1447, 1452 (7th Cir. 1996) ("A vendor, as master of the offer, may invite acceptance by conduct, and may propose limitations on the kind of conduct that constitutes acceptance. A buyer may accept by performing the acts the vendor proposes to treat as acceptance."); *see* discussion *supra* Chapter Three, "Contract Formation Doctrine."

[13] Hill v. Gateway 2000, Inc., 105 F.3d 1147, 1149 (7th Cir. 1997) ("Customers as a group are better off when vendors skip costly and ineffectual steps such as telephonic recitation, and use instead a simple approve-or-return device. Competent adults are bound by such documents, read or unread."); *see* discussion *supra* Chapter Three "Contract Formation Doctrine."

decisions: Whether you actually appreciate what you are ostensibly agreeing to might not matter that much. This is also redolent of Barnett's consent theory of contract.[14] Given the elastic, if not malleable nature of the unconscionability doctrine, it can expand or contract to fit evolving notions of contractual intent. That, too, is a feature of doctrine not unique to the unconscionability principle.

Professor Peter Benson formulates the tension well: "At stake... is the relation between contractual liberty on the one hand and contractual fairness on the other."[15] Benson makes sense of unconscionability by starting from the premise that contract, and so unconscionability too, is indifferent to distributional concerns. He sees unconscionability as a necessary adjunct to the contract formation rules.

> Because the principles of contract formation are on their face indifferent to distributive concerns, this fit [between unconscionability on the one hand and the principles of contract formation on the other] is possible only if the proposed conception of contractual fairness is also non-distributive in character. This, I argue, is in fact the case. Indeed,. . . unconscionability not only fits with but also definitively completes these principles by specifying a content that fully realizes the form of contract set out in offer and acceptance and partially fulfilled by consideration.[16]

Benson is normatively consistent: Because the formation rules are non-distributive and the unconscionability doctrine must be coherent *vis-à-vis* the formation rules, unconscionability too must not be distributive. He is only right though, if there is a unitary normative object of all contract doctrine, or, at least in the context he considers, a common unitary normative object of the formation and unconscionability rules.

At the outset, we should be skeptical: Why should it be necessary that all of contract doctrine respond to the same normative concerns in the same way? There is nothing fundamentally incongruous about one doctrine's policing of formal, procedural concerns and another doctrine's assurance of substantive fairness. A bifurcated focus might provide alternative means to respond to different manifestations of the type of behavior we want to police: We could have one body of rules—say, formation rules—concerned with revealing actual intent, and another body of rules—say, unconscionability—concerned with avoiding substantively unfair results. Or, in Aristotelian terms, we could have one body of doctrine concerned with corrective justice and another concerned with

---

[14] Randy E. Barnett, *A Consent Theory of Contract*, 86 COLUM. L. REV. 269, 307 (1986) ("It is not paradoxical to adhere to an 'objective' notion of consent that is based on just those ordinary words and deeds of persons that are commonly understood to reflect their subjective assent to be legally bound, notwithstanding that they may not have in fact meant to convey the commonly understood meaning."); *see* discussion *supra* Chapter Four "Theory of Contract Formation."

[15] Peter Benson, *The Unity of Contract Law, in* THE THEORY OF CONTRACT LAW: NEW ESSAYS 118, 184 (Peter Benson ed., 2001).

[16] *Id.*

distributive justice. All that we would need to justify that type of bifurcation would be the fact that both corrective and distributive concerns are elements of the conception of *fairness* we vindicate if we invoke our bargain sense. But Benson's object is to discover "The Unity of Contract Law." It is not clear why we need to insist upon that unity, why it is necessary or even worthwhile to impose it. His thoughtful discussion of unconscionability provides a particularly good context in which to engage this theoretical challenge.

Benson's analysis proceeds from his transfer theory of contract, which is dubious in its own right. As applied to unconscionability, it is downright specious. His discussion of unconscionability and particularly his explanation of its fit with his transfer theory is not a model of clarity; it is obtuse. Unconscionability, he concludes, is necessary to complete the transfer idea posited in his offer and acceptance discourse: "[U]nconscionability alone fits with the doctrines of contract formation because it alone can complete them consistently with their underlying conception of contract."[17] As did Fried, Benson makes sense of unconscionability by focusing on its substantive dimension. Unconscionability requires the exchange of equivalent values. When I give you my dollars in exchange for your watch, we are exchanging relatively equal values, or at least there must not be "a gross discrepancy between the comparative values."[18] Benson proceeds in two steps. First, contracting parties reasonably may be presumed to intend a transaction for equal value. Second, in the context of the exchange of commodities, market price is, for juridical purposes, a reasonable measure of equal value. Benson's focus must be on relative equality of value exchanged because his transfer theory requires it: "It is a measure of value that perfectly fulfills the *contractual* function of value as the aspect under which the parties can have the same thing at the same time,"[19] a requirement of the transfer theory. That equivalence may be waived by the party who receives even a grossly disproportionate lesser value. If I show that you *intended* to accept a grossly disproportionate value in exchange for what you have given me, then there is no unconscionability, and I may enforce the contract against you. That might constitute a gift, but a contract of gift and enforceable as a contract. You can choose, or *intend* to make a bad deal, or at least a deal in which you receive substantially less from me than I give to you.

It would seem, then, that though Benson's explanation of unconscionability focuses on substantive considerations, insofar as an intent to accept disproportionate valuation may dispose of the unconscionability objection, procedural concerns still pertain. How would we assure ourselves of the subordinate party's intent to enter into a gift contract if we do not take into account the subordinate party's understanding, *as impacted by representations and actions* of *the dominant party* in securing that ostensible expression of intent? If unconscionability is dependent upon a finding with regard to the subordinate party's intent, it is dependent on procedural considerations.

---

[17] *Id.* at 185.

[18] *Id.*

[19] *Id.* at 190.

Benson infers from unconscionability's preoccupation with relatively equal exchange that the doctrine is not distributive. So he arrives at the same place as does Fried. Still, given the way he parses the procedural and substantive elements, we could not conclude that they would reach the same conclusion on the same facts. Benson says nothing about the impact of greater societal and economic forces on the doctrine; Fried thinks that the fact that some subordinate parties were the victims of broader forces would except them from what might otherwise be the protections provided by the unconscionability doctrine.[20] For Fried, unconscionability could not be used to accomplish distributive ends. Benson concludes that the design of unconscionability is not to redress distributive imbalance, but he does suggest that, on the right facts—grossly disproportionate value and no intent to form a gift contract—a court could find unconscionability.

Whether transfer theory explains anything at all about contract, it is clear that Benson's explanation of unconscionability is not really dependent upon it. Others have discovered unconscionability at the intersection of bargaining impropriety and substantive unfairness without needing to rely on the transfer fiction.[21] Benson has not solved the problem of the fit between the consideration requirement, in which we do not care about inadequacy, and the unconscionability doctrine, in which we do care whether there is evidence of bargaining impropriety.

In fact, we should not expend the energy Benson and Fried do in their efforts to de-emphasize the procedural piece of the unconscionability calculus. Consideration does not care about adequacy. Unconscionability *only* cares about adequacy if there is evidence of bargaining impropriety. We should focus instead on the difficult question neither Fried nor Benson answers: How does the unconscionability doctrine co-exist with the agreement requirement? It would seem that an unconscionable contract would be one to which there has been no real agreement, only some form of apparent agreement, and that leads us back to *ProCD*[22] and *Hill*.[23] So when Benson concludes that "[u]nconscionability fills the space that is unoccupied by consideration," he is wrong. It fills a space that is already occupied by "agreement." It is not a doctrine with its own unique portfolio. It is a means to enable courts to vindicate conceptions of fairness, consideration, and agreement. So far as deontology is concerned, at least, it need be no more than that. But would the unconscionability doctrine have to be more, or something else, to accommodate a consequentialist theory of contract?

---

[20] *See* Freid, *supra* note 5, at 105–106.

[21] *See* Arthur Allen Leff, *Unconscionability and the Code—The Emperor's New Clause*, 115 U. PA. L. REV. 485 (1967); *see also* Williams v. Walker-Thomas Furn. Co., 350 F.2d 445, 449 ("Unconscionability has generally been recognized to include an absence of meaningful choice on the part of one of the parties together with contract terms which are unreasonably favorable to the other party.").

[22] ProCD, Inc. v. Zeidenberg, 86 F.3d 1447 (7th Cir. 1996), discussed *supra* Chapter Three "Contract Formation Doctrine."

[23] Hill v. Gateway 2000, Inc., 105 F.3d 1147 (7th Cir. 1997), discussed *supra* Chapter Three "Contract Formation Doctrine."

2. CONSEQUENTIALISM

Professor Russell Korobkin focuses on the operation of the unconscionability doctrine in the form contract context,[24] but his conclusions resonate more broadly.[25] Succinctly, Korobkin believes that efficient terms ought to be enforced and inefficient terms ought not to be unenforced on unconscionability grounds, and he criticizes decisions that have found unconscionability without a showing that the challenged term was necessarily inefficient.[26] Korobkin equates unconscionability with inefficiency and would leave that determination to common law courts.

He begins with an uncontroversial observation: The rationality of human agents is bounded and, therefore, we rely on heuristics that may mask the imperfect rationality of our choices.[27] Indeed, it is rational to rely on heuristics that will lead us to suboptimal choices when the cost of making optimal choices is prohibitive.[28] So form drafters may exploit that reliance on heuristics in order to impose low-quality nonsalient terms on buyers.[29] Although we may trust market forces to assure the efficiency of salient terms, "there is no reason to assume that non-salient terms will be efficient."[30] His object is to provide a screening device to assure that only efficient terms in standard forms will be enforceable.

The salient–nonsalient distinction will support a good deal of weight in Korobkin's argument. Salience is not just a matter of awareness: A term is not salient merely because consumers know it exists; the consumer must also appreciate its operation and the impact of its operation on him. A form drafter could not always make the nonsalient form term salient simply by taking steps (such as having the buyer initial the form clause) to bring the term to the buyer's attention. Salience is a matter of understanding.

From there, Korobkin concludes that the potential nonsalience of form terms accommodates a market in misinformation: "[F]ar from operating as an invisible hand that promotes efficiency, market forces combined with the presence of non-salient product attributes can perversely enforce a regime of inefficiency."[31] Both groups suffer from the

---

[24] *See* Russell Korobkin, *Bounded Rationality, Standard Form Contracts, and Unconscionability*, 70 U. CHI. L. REV. 1203 (2003).

[25] *See generally* Peter A. Alces, *Guerilla Terms*, 56 EMORY L.J. 1511 (2007). Portions of this section are drawn from that earlier article.

[26] Korobkin, *supra.* note 24, at 1279 ("[T]he courts' approach to substantive unconscionability analysis is not well-suited to separating terms that are detrimental to buyers as a class from those beneficial to buyers as a class.").

[27] *Id.* at 1290.

[28] *Id.* at 1292.

[29] Korobkin observes that "form terms are particularly likely to be non-salient because their usual content makes them unlikely to attract buyers' voluntary or involuntary attention." *Id.* at 1226.

[30] *Id.* at 1225. That is not to conclude, as Korobkin does not, that nonsalient terms will in fact be inefficient: It is just to say that the market cannot guarantee that nonsalient terms will be efficient.

[31] *Id.* at 1234. *See also id.* at 1235 ("Ironically, far from guaranteeing a market equilibrium of efficient terms, competition can guarantee an equilibrium of inefficient terms.").

inefficiency, so it is in the interest of both form drafters and consumers to assure that inefficient nonsalient terms not be enforced.[32] If buyers do not take account of terms that it would be in their interest to consider, form drafters cannot compete among themselves on the basis of that term.[33] The seller would have no incentive to offer a product attribute, including a contract term that the buyer will not take into account in making the purchase decision.

The seller may rely on advertising to overcome the problem of nonsalient terms that should be salient. But Korobkin is skeptical: "[I]f the buyers most likely to find an attribute salient in response to advertising are likely to be unprofitable customers on average, sellers might choose not to promote that attribute." [34] That may ignore the ability of advocacy groups to bring the effects of a form term to the attention of media outlets that sell such information to consumers. Korobkin offers another plausible explanation:

> Such marketing efforts will be costly, so sellers will have to balance the benefits of exploiting their competitive advantage against the cost of making the market responsive to it. Often, the value to a seller of making a term salient will be relatively small and the cost of changing the way a substantial number of buyers shop for the product enormous.[35]

A seller will not advertise if the costs of doing so outweigh the benefits. That is an explanation for monopoly pricing of add-ons.[36] Ultimately, then, Korobkin remains skeptical: "[I]n a complex world in which products have many attributes, it seems likely that a seller could fail to make certain attributes salient no matter how many resources it expends on advertising."[37]

That skepticism is well founded. Though, as Professors Xavier Gabaix and David Laibson demonstrate,[38] it is not at all clear that the cost of advertising explains as much as Korobkin thinks it might. Whether a particular nonsalient term is efficient depends on

---

[32] *See id.* at 1234 ("In a competitive market, [refusal by courts to enforce terms that reduce both buyer and seller welfare]... would also increase seller's welfare.").

[33] Korobkin identifies this with the "'lemons problem': [W]hen buyers cannot verify quality the market will produce lower-quality goods." *Id.* at 1235 (citing George A. Akerlof, *The Market for "Lemons": Quality Uncertainty and the Market Mechanism*, 84 Q. J. ECON. 488 (1970); Melvin Aron Eisenberg, *The Limits of Cognition and the Limits of Contract*, 47 STAN. L. REV. 211, 244 (1995)).

[34] *Id.* at 1242.

[35] *Id.* at 1242–43.

[36] *See* Alces *supra* note 25, at 1530 nn. 64–65 (2007); *see generally* Glenn Ellison & Sara Fisher Ellison, *Search, Obfuscation, and Price Elasticities on the Internet* (Nat'l Bureau of Econ. Research, Working Paper No. 10570, 2004).

[37] Korobkin, *supra* note 24, at 1243.

[38] Xavier Gabaix & David Laibson, *Shrouded Attributes, Consumer Myopia, and Information Suppression in Competitive Markets*, 121(2) Q. J. OF ECON. 505 (2006).

what the term is. A nonsalient term may be efficient if the value of the term to the buyer would exceed the cost to the seller of the seller's providing that term: "[A]ssume that each buyer is willing to pay $15 more for a high-quality warranty term than a low-quality warranty term, and that a high-quality warranty costs sellers $10 more to provide per customer. Thus, in this example, a high-quality warranty term is efficient."[39] However, if it would cost the seller seven dollars to make the warranty term salient and that term is worth only five dollars to the buyer, the seller will not offer the term *even to buyers for whom it is already salient*. Korobkin's argument about the inefficiency of a low-quality term explains why inefficient terms may be pervasive. The law, then, should provide the incentive the market fails to provide, and the unconscionability doctrine affords the law the means to do just that.[40] Korobkin concludes that the unconscionability doctrine should be read to police inefficient terms,[41] but the doctrine would have to be modified. Korobkin concludes that, so reconfigured, the unconscionability doctrine reveals "the source of contractual inefficiency and focuses judicial attention on the form terms most likely to be inefficient,"[42] nonsalient terms. Korobkin notes that "[j]udicial determinations of which contract terms are efficient and which terms are inefficient are subject to a high likelihood of error."[43]

To appreciate the deficiencies of Korobkin's construction of unconscionability, it is worthwhile to consider how a court would have to do the math. Recall Korobkin's hypothetical based on a high-quality term worth fifteen dollars to buyers that it costs the seller ten dollars to provide.[44] It does not seem to advance the inquiry much to posit the value of the "high-quality warranty" as fifteen dollars for each buyer. It is more likely that the value of the warranty to each buyer will differ.[45] It would not also follow that it is *impossible* to know *ex ante* whether the seller's inclusion of the low-quality rather than the high-quality term is inefficient in each case. Korobkin's conclusion rests on a judgment regarding what the average value to the average buyer would be of the high-quality term. But if we rely on efficiency in the aggregate it might be better for the efficiency determination to be made by a regulatory agency rather than by a court. We cannot posit a value to the buyer for purposes of the efficiency calculus without taking into account the efficiency of the transaction from the perspective of the individual buyer. Yet, if we are to find efficiency only in the aggregate sense, then it is not at all clear that a court should be doing the calculation on an *ad hoc* basis.

---

[39] Korobkin, *supra* note 24, at 1236.

[40] *Id.* at 1294–95.

[41] *Id.*

[42] *Id.* at 1290.

[43] *Id.* at 1285.

[44] *Id.* at 1209–12.

[45] The buyer's sophistication might determine the efficiency of a particular term for her.

Korobkin is not the only scholar who has tried to justify the unconscionability doctrine on consequentialist grounds. Professor Richard Epstein, in one of his earlier articles, also tries to make sense of the unconscionability doctrine from the consequentialist perspective.[46] He concludes that the doctrine polices primarily deficiencies in the bargaining process, that is, procedural unconscionability. Epstein recognizes that unconscionability covers the same ground as do fraud, duress, and undue influence,[47] and he recognizes too that contract needs to police those impediments to contract formation. But each of those essentially tort-based devices entails evidentiary challenges. That is, a defendant who would interpose fraud, duress, or unconscionability to avoid contract liability might not be able to satisfy the burden of demonstrating that in fact defendant's ostensible consent *was* the product of such overreaching rather than free will.

> There is. . . a cost created by putting this [evidentiary] burden upon the defendant [subordinate party]. Solely because he cannot meet the appropriate standard of proof, he may not be able to establish a contractual defense in a case where it in fact applies. If this last form of error results in substantial costs, then it should be appropriate to modify the rules of evidence in a manner that makes it easier for the defendant to establish fraud, duress or incompetence.[48]

If the defense "in fact applies" notwithstanding the subordinate party's inability to prove that it does, then were we to enforce the deal against the subordinate party, we would be undermining consequentialists' interest in actors' being able to reveal accurately their preferences. There would be too much consumption and thereby corruption of our pricing of goods and services.[49] So, Epstein concludes, "the unconscionability doctrine protects against fraud, duress and incompetence, without demanding specific proof of any of them."[50] This is, of course, the conception of unconscionability reflected in Ellinghaus's appreciation of Llewellyn's intent in crafting the UCC unconscionability provision.[51]

---

[46] Richard A. Epstein, *Unconscionability: A Critical Reappraisal*, 18 J. L. & ECON 293 (1975).

[47] *Id.* at 293.

[48] *Id.* at 301–02. This is akin to the argument in favor of replacing the "reliance" requirement in the pre-UCC express warranty law with a "part of the basis of the bargain" standard instead. *See* John E. Murray, *The Revision of Article 2: Romancing the Prism*, 35 WM & MARY L. REV. 1447, 1486–88 (1994). Many jurisdictions require clear and convincing evidence for proof of fraud. *See, e.g.,* Gaidon v. Gaurdian Life Ins. Co. of Am., 94 N.E.2d 598, 607 (N.Y. 1999); Economopoulos v. Kolaitis, 528 S.E.2d 714, 719 (Va. 2000); *see also* 37 AM. JUR. 2D *Fraud and Deceit* § 208 (2010).

[49] Alces, *supra* note 25, at 1528–29 (citing Gabaix & Laibson, *supra* note 38, at 517–518).

[50] Epstein, *supra* note 46 at 302.

[51] M. P. Ellinghaus, *In Defense of Unconscionability*, 78 YALE L.J. 757, 796 (1969); *see* discussion *supra* Chapter Five, "Contract Performance Doctrine."

But Epstein also recognizes the cost associated with short-circuiting other deal-policing mechanisms:

> It may well be that the relaxation of the standard of proof required to make out any defense will increase the number of instances where the undeserving defendant is able to defeat the plaintiff's legitimate contractual expectations. But if the costs thereby created are low, then the change in rules of proof is justified on the grounds that it reduces the total error in enforcement, even though all error is not thereby eliminated.[52]

Epstein is certainly correct that it would be efficient to reach the correct result, the result consistent with vindicating the parties' intent, so long as the costs of our doing so are low. It would make no sense to expend one-hundred dollars of proof to avoid a ninety-dollar loss. The problem is, of course, that we have not done and cannot do the math; we just do not know what the cost of the change in rules of proof will be, and we cannot know what that cost will be because the cost of calculating it would be too great to justify the exercise. All we can do, then, is guess; perhaps we can rely on a heuristic as far as it will take us, but ultimately we guess. If the best consequentialist argument for the unconscionability doctrine is that it *might* cost less, then that may not be a very good argument for the doctrine.

Although the deontologists considered above, for illustrative purposes, conclude that unconscionability is primarily about substantive overreaching, the deal that is just too good for the promisee, Korobkin and Epstein find the best sense of unconscionability in its focus on the bargaining process, on so-called "procedural unconscionability." That follows from Korobkin's and Epstein's conclusion that unconscionability solves problems of proof in cases of fraud, duress, and incompetence, and is also explained in Epstein's presentation of the limits of "substantive unconscionability."

Epstein considers and defends several common contract provisions that have been subject to attack on unconscionability grounds: what he terms "add-on" clauses, such as the cross-collateral provision in *Williams*; waiver-of-defense clauses, now invalidated by the Federal Trade Commission (FTC) Holder in Due Course Rule;[53] consequential damages exclusions;[54] due-on-sale clauses, which were a much bigger issue at the time

[52] Epstein, *supra* note 46, at 302 (emphasis added).

[53] 16 C.F.R. § 433 (2010) (requiring consumer credit contracts to include provision that any holder of contract is subject to all claims and defenses which debtor could assert against seller).

[54] *See* UCC § 2-719(3) (2002) ("Consequential damages may be limited or excluded unless the limitation or exclusion is unconscionable. Limitation of consequential damages for injury to the person in the case of consumer goods is prima facie unconscionable but limitation of damages where the loss is commercial is not.").

Epstein wrote his unconscionability article;[55] and termination-at-will clauses that would operate in favor of franchisors who want to escape a franchise agreement.[56] In each case, Epstein defends the provisions from unconscionability attack, explaining how the deal makes sense as a substantive matter. He concludes that "when the doctrine of unconscionability is used in its substantive dimension, be it in a commercial or consumer context, it serves only to undercut the private right of contract in a manner that is apt to do more social harm than good."[57]

Epstein's conclusion, then? Unconscionability works if it focuses on, and provides the means to redress, a deficiency in the contract formation process: "Either there must be proof of some defect in the process of contract formation (be it duress, fraud, or undue influence); or there must be, but only within narrow limits, some incompetence of the party against whom the agreement is to be enforced."[58] Given his focus, one might even say preoccupation, with freedom of contract, Epstein, and others[59] who would insulate contracts from substantive review infer real agreement, real understanding, from the indicia of consent. That is potentially problematic if the dominant party controls and can manipulate the contract's formation. If a consumer signing an installment sales contract containing a cross-collateral provision does not appreciate the ramifications of that provision, what real sense does it make to "defend the consumer's right to freedom of contract"? If issuers of credit cards can hide less-than-scrupulous terms in the fine print forms enclosed with (or even sent separately from) the periodic statement, does it advance the inquiry very much to rely on freedom of contract? Arguably it does not, so it may be that consideration of substantive inequity may intimate something about the bargaining process. We can, then, see why the procedural–substantive dichotomy is ultimately false. The two prongs may just be alternative means to get at the same thing: avoidance of

---

[55] *See* Epstein, *supra* note 46, at 311 ("[T]he due on sale clause allows a lender to call in the outstanding balance on the loan when the mortgagor sells his interest in the property. . . ."). When current interest rates are higher than the rate of the mortgage, a seller may try to assign the mortgage to a buyer. This would allow the buyer to finance less of the purchase price at the higher rate. A due-on-sale clause would police this, requiring the buyer to obtain a new loan at the higher rate. Lenders are unlikely to enforce a due on sale clause, however, if market interest rates are below the mortgage rate. Thus, due-on-sale clauses become an issue if lenders hold mortgages below present interest rates.

[56] *See, e.g.,* California Franchise Relations Act, CAL BUS. & PROF. CODE § 20020 (2009) ("No franchisor may terminate a franchise prior to the expiration of its term, except for good cause."); New Jersey Franchise Practices Act, N.J. STAT. ANN. § 56:10–1 to 15 (2010) (prohibiting termination or failure to renew franchise without good cause); Dr. Pepper Bottling Co. v. Frantz, 842 S.W.2d 37 (Ark. 1992) (affirming judgment against manufacturer for termination of distributorship without good cause); Globe Liquor Co. v. Four Roses Distillers Co., 281 A.2d 19 (Del. 1971) (upholding Deleware Franchise Security Law, DEL. CODE. ANN. tit. 6 § 2551, which protects franchisees from termination "on short notice without just cause").

[57] Epstein, *supra* note 46, at 315.

[58] *Id.*

[59] *See, e.g.,* Douglas G. Baird, *Boilerplate and Market Power: The Boilerplate Puzzle*, 104 MICH. L. REV., 933, 940, 950–52 (2006).

contracts that are not the product of real intent (rather than constructed consent). If that is accurate, then the doctrine can accommodate just the analysis we need to do; the doctrine does not constrain us in terms *either* of deontology *or* consequentialism; the doctrine provides a more useful heuristic than discrete and unitary normative theories can provide.

B. Impossibility, Impracticability, and Frustration

When, after contracting, circumstances render the performance of one of the contracting parties actually "impossible" as a matter of physics, *e.g.,* the concert hall is destroyed by fire prior to the performance date,[60] then we can determine the rights of the parties *inter se* if that impossibility actually precludes performance altogether. Performance has not just become more difficult or even more expensive; performance is no longer possible, given the limits of physics as we have so far figured out the physical world. You cannot provide a concert hall that no longer exists. Indeed, even if you could rebuild Lincoln Center, it would not be the same Lincoln Center the contracting parties had in mind when they entered into the contract. In a very real sense, then, there can be contracts the performance of which has become existentially impossible.

Contrast such impossibility with impracticability: The subject matter of the contract may still exist, but the cost to the party responsible for provision of that subject matter has increased "considerably," or "substantially," or "significantly," or, even, "incalculably." So long as we understand contract as the product of the parties' intent to allocate risk, at some point we may be able to conclude that their particular allocation assumed a certain background or range of risk such that were that assumption undermined their contract purpose too would be undermined. That is, at some point enforcement would confound rather than vindicate the parties' intent. Now that point may well be short of physical *impossibility*, but still sufficiently removed from the parties' contemplation to justify avoidance of any contract duty to perform in light of the changed circumstances. Of course, one of the parties, the beneficiary of the now much more expensive (and so valuable) performance, will urge enforcement of the contract notwithstanding the changed circumstances, but the court will need to consider the deal from the perspective of both the beneficiary and the victim of the altered state of affairs, and it must do so in order to discern the intent of the parties at the time of contracting, the function of contract writ large. Impracticability is qualitatively different from impossibility. The party who would successfully assert it has an easier standard to satisfy than actual impossibility would contemplate.

---

[60] Taylor v. Caldwell, (1863) 122 Eng. Rep. 309 (K.B.).

Frustration, though, is not qualitatively different from impracticability. What changes is our perspective. Frustration is the excuse the party to pay would invoke in order to avoid the payment obligation. Though it is, of course, never *impossible* or even particularly *impracticable* to pay, it may be pointless to do so. If events subsequent to contracting have rendered performance of the contract (by making payment) pointless or worse from the perspective of the party to pay, we would conclude that that party's contractual purpose has been frustrated. So frustration, then, is essentially the same thing as impracticability, but from the standpoint of the buyer of goods or services.

What ties the three doctrines together is allocation of risk, and that is true whether we proceed from deontic or consequentialist premises. If we use the terms of deontology, it has become perhaps "unfair" to require performance or payment from a party whose purpose in entering into the contract has been undermined on account of circumstances beyond that (or any party's) control. The predicate of the rule captures well the reason for the rule: If an event occurs "the non-occurrence of which was a basic assumption on which the contract was made," the party whose performance was premised upon that non-occurrence may avoid the contract. Now it is difficult to say, even to certainly identify, when a particular non-occurrence formed a basic assumption of the parties to a contract. So it makes sense, for both deontologists and consequentialists, to cast the rule in terms of risk: Who bore the risk that the intervening event would occur? And what might allocation of risk in terms of foreseeability have to tell us about operation of the three doctrines?

1. DEONTOLOGY

Fried concludes that "contracts generally are a device for allocating risks."[61] When impracticability or frustration is interposed to excuse one of the contracting parties from the deal, the law must determine whether *in fact* the risk that materialized was beyond the contemplation of the parties or whether we may infer that the risk was assumed by one of the parties. In the difficult cases, the risk was beyond the parties' contemplation, as evidenced by their failure to have allocated it in their contract. Indeed, if the risk had been within their contemplation, the court is constrained to leave the loss where it has fallen, that is, to not excuse the party who, the court concludes, falsely or at least inaccurately alleges that the risk had not been contemplated.

When a contingency arises that the parties did not foresee, it is necessarily the case that "[t]he court cannot enforce the will of the parties because there are no concordant wills."[62] The problem is precisely the same as if the parties have left open a delivery method, place, or date, or price, or risk of loss. A court called upon to decide whether one party to the

[61] FRIED, *supra* note 5, at 59.

[62] *Id.* at 60.

contract is excused on account of a contingency the nonoccurrence of which was a basic assumption of the parties is called upon to fill a gap, and Fried treats the issue in just that way.[63]

> [I]n contract law there is a vaguely marked boundary between interpreting what was agreed to and interpolating terms to which the parties in all probability would have agreed but did not. The further courts are from the boundary between interpretation and interpolation, the further they are from the moral basis of the promise principle and the more palpably are they imposing an agreement. . . . So as we move further from actual intention the standard of presumed intention tends to merge into the other substantive standards used to solve the problems caused by a failure in the agreement.[64]

Conceptions of contract based on Fried's promise principle cannot resolve the impracticability–frustration problem. So whatever contract does if such excuses are asserted, it does without the scope of deontic theory premised on promise. Deontology, then, at least a deontology based on Kantian promise principles as understood by Fried, cannot guide the resolution of excuse cases. "[N]orms of fairness and honesty," though, whatever they might mean in the particular case, may be a worthwhile source.[65] Fried generalizes that those norms will lead to the conclusion that the contracting parties will share the unforeseen losses:

> Does this mean that there is no room for the principle of sharing in the contractual domain, that its admission there would threaten to undermine the healthy compromise of autonomy and community implicit in liberal democracies? I think not. By engaging in a contractual relation A and B become no longer strangers to each other. They stand closer than those who are merely members of the same political community. Like the persons in my examples they are joined in a common enterprise, and therefore they have some obligation to share unexpected benefits and losses in the case of an accident in the course of that enterprise. Just as we do not say that C must come in to share those losses, so we do not say that A and B must share losses that are wholly outside the scope of their enterprise.[66]

---

[63] *Id.* (including mistake, impossibility, and frustration in the chapter on gaps in a contract).

[64] *Id.* at 60–61.

[65] *Id.* at 73.

[66] *Id.* at 72.

But is that all deontology can do for us in the excuse context? It may be that deontology could take us some distance further by making clear what we mean by "unforeseen losses."

Two articles published in 1969 consider at some length the Suez Canal cases, the impracticability and frustration decisions that followed the closing of that waterway in 1956.[67] The closure of the canal had upset the expectations of buyers, sellers, and carriers of goods that would have traveled to their destinations through the canal, and also presented an accessible and important context in which to appraise the excuse doctrine. Professor John Henry Schlegel considers the doctrine in historical context in order to make sense of its operation and vagaries in the more contemporary context. Professor Robert Birmingham pursues a similar method to support his application of economic theory to the doctrine. Both articles demonstrate the limits of the doctrine, and, notwithstanding Birmingham's economic analysis, we may conclude that both writers reveal a deontic focus. The pieces are complementary insofar as they reduce the doctrine to its elements, and reveal what (little) there is to constrain courts' analyses.

Schlegel cuts to the quick:

> To demand that any court determine when the obligation of a contract is changed without a guide or standard is to ask that court to pinpoint the instance when the difference in degree becomes the difference in kind. Such a task is too burdensome for any court, especially when it appears that there may only be differences in degree in the situation and no differences in kind. Faced with the task of determining whether the obligation has changed, all that a court can do is give answers and state results, as the Suez courts did; it cannot give meaningful reasons for the decisions.[68]

He confirms what the cynical among us may have thought all along (and in other contexts as well): Doctrine provides the cover for the conclusion rather than the means to discover the conclusion; it obscures rather than illuminates. He continues: "[T]he rules for the construction of contracts generally are of little help other than in rationalizing a result"; "the judge is essentially unaided in considering all the factors which it is assumed he should consider."[69] Schlegel suggests that the doctrine obscures something akin to a comparative fault analysis. The party who breaches and the party who would be excused on frustration grounds are distinguished from one another on the basis of fault

---

[67] Robert L. Birmingham, *A Second Look at the Suez Canal Cases: Excuse for Nonperformance of Contractual Obligations in the Light of Economic Theory*, 20 HASTINGS L.J. 1393 (1969); John Henry Schlegel, *Of Nuts, and Ships, and Sealing Wax, Suez, and Frustrating Things—The Doctrine of Impossibility of Performance*, 23 RUTGERS L. REV. 419 (1969).

[68] Schlegel, *supra* note 67, at 439 (footnote omitted).

[69] *Id.* at 439.

and wrongdoing. The party at fault has done wrong; the party not at fault is the victim of circumstances beyond her control. But, "[i]t should be noted... that the notion of wrong distinguishes the situation not in terms of something inherent in them but in terms of the psychological reaction to them."[70] From that, his conclusion follows that "breach is only frustration [and so excused] in such extraordinary situations as not to seem wrongful."[71] Keep in mind that Schlegel is trying to explain the basis of the decisions; he is not offering a method to determine the result in the next case.

Schlegel is skeptical that a contract really constitutes the type of risk allocation that could support conclusions about excuse based on inference from the fact of the parties' ostensible allocation of risk. Parties choose one contract form rather than another for no better reason than that the form they used was at hand. Further, for Schlegel, contract is about more than risk allocation: "[C]ontract law may serve other social ends, *e.g.,* the control of business practices or the curtailment of economically or socially undesirable side effects of contract."[72] We could consider Schlegel's other concerns in terms of risk, were we to abstract the risk idea a bit more, but it is clear that he appreciates contract as treating a good deal more than might be determined by a conventional risk analysis, that *risk* may be too large a category to do much helpful work in the excuse setting. I think his criticism of Corbin,[73] though perhaps insufficiently developed here, is consistent with the conclusion that contract does not resolve into neat cost–benefit bundles that then admit of formulaic analysis. Now the reason that contract contexts, and perhaps most prominently excuse, defy formulae may be that the problems they present are polycentric[74] or that they are subject to incommensurable justice perceptions.[75] Whatever the source of the moral confusion, deontology can sensitize us to the possibility that allocation of risk neither tells the whole story nor captures the calculus; "[h]ence, tort notions—wrong, bad faith—abound in contract law."[76]

Birmingham's contribution to the discussion, through a consideration of economic theory, is not as valuable an exercise in economic analysis as it is a confirmation of Schlegel's perspective: "Seemingly divergent holdings can be reconciled with. . . each other through assumptions concerning implicit allocation of risk by the contracting

[70] *Id.* at 441.

[71] *Id.* at 442.

[72] *Id.* at 445 n.125.

[73] *Id.* at 445, (criticizing 6 ARTHUR L. CORBIN, CORBIN ON CONTRACTS §§ 1330–33 (1964)).

[74] James A. Henderson, Jr. & Aaron D. Twerski, *Closing the American Products Liability Frontier: The Rejection of Liability Without Defect,* 66 N.Y.U. L. REV. 1263, 1305 (1991) (citing Lon L. Fuller, *The Forms and Limits of Adjudication,* 92 HARV L. REV. 353 (1978)).

[75] *See* Peter A. Alces, *On Discovering Doctrine: "Justice" in Contract Agreement,* 83 WASH. U. L.Q. 471 (2005); *see also* Schlegel, *supra* note 67, at 446 ("[N]o matter how the theory is stated the court is essentially finding the just and reasonable solution.").

[76] Schlegel, *supra* note 67, at 447.

parties.... [F]airness... is arguably the foundation of all relief[.]"[77] Birmingham too finds much about the excuse doctrines that resolves to a matter of judicial discretion:[78] "[T]he rules of law applied appear to be less guides for decision than rationalizations of outcomes determined on other [fairness?] grounds."[79] The author follows those generalizations with a truly intimidating general equilibrium model and matrices that suggest even if they do not certainly demonstrate the limits of an economic consequences calculus. His point is that the courts' conclusions with regard to excuse *do not* reflect the type of calculus he pursues; indeed, his approach would suggest that the doctrine is too unwieldy. If an excusing event intercedes, the deal the parties thought they had made is no longer available to them.[80] The allocation of risk (perhaps broadly construed) they had intended has been undermined, and in order to provide them what they sought, the court would have to rewrite their contract. Rather than protecting their freedom of contract by affirming their deal, the court would have to revise the terms of the deal in order to preserve it. That perspective would present a challenge for a positive account of the excuse doctrine in consequentialist terms.

2. CONSEQUENTIALISM

The apparent consensus is that positive economic analysis of law has failed.[81] Although normative economic analysis might still have some traction, microeconomics has been discredited as an explanation of just what legal doctrine, generally, and contract doctrine, in particular, have been up to for the last few hundred years or so. We are now free to appraise positive economic analyses of the contract law as rhetoric, an effort to vindicate a particularly narrow brand of consequentialism by explaining that we have been Benthamites with a penchant for welfare creation all along, so long as we construe "welfare" in terms of something like "utiles"[82] or some other antiseptic value well removed from human thriving, or at least from distributive concerns. Nonetheless, it is worthwhile to take account of early positive economic analysis of law in order to distinguish rhetorical flourish from normative theory.

---

[77] Birmingham, *supra* note 67, at 1395–96 (footnote omitted).

[78] *Id.* at 1397.

[79] *Id.* at 1404.

[80] *Id.* at 1398 ("As currently conceived, the frustration option does not explicitly permit a graduated response to differing equities. Since performance must be either required or excused there is generally no solution other than clear victory for one contestant.").

[81] *See, e.g.,* Eric A. Posner, *Economic Analysis of Contract Law After Three Decades: Success or Failure?* 112 YALE L.J. 829 (2003).

[82] RICHARD A. POSNER, OVERCOMING LAW 505 (1995).

Professor and later-Judge Richard Posner will certainly be remembered as one of the towering jurisprudential figures of our time. His magisterial *Economic Analysis of Law*[83] changed the way law is taught in United States law schools, as well as how consequentialism contributes to our understanding of the theoretical foundations of legal doctrine. For the better part of the second half of the twentieth century, it seemed that the law journals were dominated by those who were sure that consequentialist economic analysis explained everything and those who were just as certain that it explained, if not nothing, at least far less than its champions claimed. Although the dust has settled and we are able to appreciate the limits of economic theory, certainly so far as the rational choice fiction is concerned,[84] the early positive accounts reveal a good deal about the fit between consequentialist theory and contract doctrine. Even though such positive accounts were assertions about what in fact informs the courts' decisions, we may also make sense of them in normative terms, as an argument about *how courts should* apply the doctrine.

An article written by Judge Posner and Andrew Rosenfield over thirty years ago captures well the consequentialist explanation for the impossibility, impracticability, and frustration doctrines in contract.[85] The authors begin by noting "the tendency of courts and commentators alike to treat the field as too broad and diverse to be adequately understood within a single theoretical framework,"[86] and then propose just such a unitary framework. Impossibility, impracticability, and frustration all respond to the same challenge: deciding who should bear the loss resulting from the occurrence of an event that has rendered performance uneconomical for one of the contracting parties. Although all contracting parties assume risks when they assume contract liability, few contracting parties "intend" in any meaningful sense to assume all risk of any and all contingencies. Insofar as the foundation of contract is parties' intent, contract *should* respond to circumstances in which there has been a failure of risk allocation, if the risk exceeded the parties' contemplation. The impossibility, impracticability, and frustration doctrines provide the means for contract to respond. If any of the doctrines is operative, the contract is unenforceable, at least insofar as the unforeseen risk frustrated the parties' expectations.

At the outset, Posner and Rosenfield establish their consequentialist perspective: "[T]he law of contract has, in fact, been informed by efficiency considerations, even if judges and lawyers may have found it difficult to articulate the underlying economic premises of the law."[87] The idea that judges and lawyers are somehow unwitting economists is the necessary predicate of a positive economic analysis of the contract law.

[83] Richard A. Posner, Economic Analysis of Law (7th ed. 2007) (1972).

[84] *See, e.g.,* Cass R. Sunstein, *Behavioral Analysis of Law*, 64 U. Chi. L. Rev. 1175, 1175 (1997) (discussing limitations of rational choice models).

[85] Richard A. Posner & Andrew M. Rosenfield, *Impossibility and Related Doctrines in Contract Law: An Economic Analysis*, 6 J. Legal Stud. 83 (1977).

[86] *Id.* at 84.

[87] *Id.* at 89.

The conclusion has met resistance.[88] Nevertheless, as a rhetorical device, it provides the authors a means by which to distance themselves from the values underlying their conclusion, in a don't-shoot-the-messenger kind of way: "We are interested not in whether a contract law based on efficiency is ultimately a good law, but in whether the assumption that contract law has been shaped by a concern with economic efficiency is a fruitful one in explaining the doctrinal positions and typical case outcomes of that law."[89]

From that perspective, Posner and Rosenfield are able to distill the doctrine and the case law construing the doctrine down to a simple rule: Allow discharge "where the promisee is the superior risk bearer."[90] And the superior risk bearer is the more efficient risk bearer "in the particular circumstances of the transaction."[91] The focus will have to be on the idiosyncrasies of the particular transaction. Once it has been established that the risk had not, in fact, been fixed between the parties, the doctrine will assign the risk *post hoc* in order to realize the most efficient results, which amounts to encouraging the most efficient behavior in the future. If the risk were already allocated by the parties, expressly or implicitly, the court would not upset that allocation, and the doctrine would not require that the court do so. Posner and Rosenfield's framework is able to cast the inquiry in terms of contract interpretation: The court will infer that the parties, as rational economic actors, would have allocated the risk efficiently. The authors illustrate their analysis by the use of a hypothetical.

> A, a manufacturer of printing machinery, contracts with B, a commercial printer, to sell and install a printing machine on B's premises. As B is aware, the machine will be custom-designed for B's needs and once the machine has been completed its value to any other printer will be very small. After the machine is completed, but before installation, a fire destroys B's premises and puts B out of business, precluding B from accepting delivery of the machine. The machine has no salvage value and A accordingly sues for the full price. B defends on the ground that the fire, which the fire marshal has found occurred without negligence on B's part—indeed (the same point, in an economic sense), which could not have been prevented by B at any reasonable cost—should operate to discharge B from its obligations under the contract.[92]

This would be a case of frustration: B, the buyer, seeks discharge of its obligation to pay for a good that is now of no use to B. It would not be impossible or impracticable for B to perform; performance requires only the payment of money and the facts do not present

---

[88] Stephen A. Smith, Contract Theory 108–36 (2004).

[89] Posner & Rosenfield, *supra* note 85, at 89.

[90] *Id.* at 90.

[91] *Id.*

[92] *Id.* at 92.

(though they may imply) B's impaired financial condition. We can assume that B could pay, but by doing so would obtain only a piece of machinery worthless to itself (and, by assumption, no less worthless to anyone else). If B is discharged from its contract obligation to A, it is A who will have expended resources that it will not be able to recover. So as between A and B, who should suffer the loss? Posner and Rosenfield pursue what we might term a "forensic economic analysis" and conclude that B should be discharged, the loss to be imposed on A. They offer several reasons supporting that conclusion:

1. Though the fact that the fire occurred on B's premises would suggest that B was in the better position to have avoided the fire, the fire marshal's conclusion that the fire was in no way B's fault undermines the imposition of the risk on B on that account.
2. A was in a better position to determine the magnitude of the loss if the fire were to occur and so A was in the better position to insure against loss of the machine's utility on account of the fire. A would have better appreciated the salvage value of the machine at each stage of its manufacture.
3. Because A might have had prior experience with contingencies such as B's fire, A might have been in a better position to self-insure by charging each of its purchasers a premium to reflect the risk of such a casualty precluding the performance of their contracts. B, though, "is less likely to be able to do so: the magnitude of its potential liability to A in the event of a default may greatly exceed any amount it could hope to pass on to its customers in the form of higher prices."[93]

The point here is not that we can well imagine counterfactuals that would undermine Posner and Rosenfield's story; the point, instead, is that there is absolutely nothing about the facts they marshal that could not vary significantly from case to case. That becomes very clear when the authors acknowledge the potential significance of A's and B's capital structure: "This inclination [to discharge B] would be strengthened if it turned out that A was a publicly held, and B a closely held, corporation, for then the owners of A could eliminate the risk of the loss of the machine's value simply by combining their shares in A with shares of other companies in a suitably diversified portfolio."[94] But if we go that far, why not take into account the wealth of the owners of the closely-held corporation? Or perhaps we could develop a special rule for contracting parties that assume particular corporate forms.[95]

---

[93] *Id.* at 93.

[94] *Id.*

[95] *See, e.g.,* UCC § 2-509(3) (2002) (changing allocation of risk based on whether either party is a merchant).

Posner and Rosenfield's second hypothetical is designed to demonstrate that a broad excuse standard makes it difficult to predict the outcome of particular cases,[96] though it would seem that the first hypothetical also does just that. The second hypothetical is based on the Westinghouse litigation.[97]

> [L]et C be a large and diversified business concern engaged in both coal mining and the manufacture and sale of large coal-burning furnaces. C executes contracts for the sale of furnaces to D, E, F, etc., in which it also agrees to supply coal to them for a given period of time at a specified price. The price, however, is to vary with and in proportion to changes in the consumer price index.
>
> A few years later the price of coal unexpectedly quadruples and C repudiates the coal-supply agreements arguing that if forced to meet its commitments to supply coal at the price specified in its contracts it will be bankrupted. Each purchaser sues C seeking as damages the difference between the price of obtaining coal over the life of C's commitment and the contract price. C argues that the rise in the price of coal was unforeseeable and ought to operate to discharge it from its obligations.[98]

Posner and Rosenfield suggest that C might be able to avoid the contracts by establishing that the buyers rather than C were the superior risk bearers. They focus on the amount of coal C contracted to sell and the degree of C's exposure to coal price changes. But because C was in the better position at the outset to know its net asset position and its contractual commitments, C should not be excused but should bear the risk of the price increase, no matter how precipitous. Insofar as C could hedge its position in coal, C would be in the best position to bear the risk of even a dramatic price shift. Add to that ability to hedge the fact that the owners of C can maintain a diverse portfolio of common stocks (or just own stock of C's buyers) and Posner and Rosenfield are comfortable concluding that the risk of price increase should rest with C and C would not be entitled to discharge. The authors also note that C's buyers might, on the right facts, be able to manage the price risk the contracts present as effectively as could C. They are not, though, sufficiently impressed with that possibility to relieve C of what has become a burdensome contractual obligation. It would seem that once the reality of C's bankruptcy is taken into account, the factors implicated by the Posner and Rosenfield analysis may defy easy calculation.

Would we care that the employees of C and their families might well suffer out of proportion to any benefit C's buyers would realize from having a maybe five-cents-on-the-dollar claim in C's bankruptcy? The honest answer might be that we just do not

---

[96] Posner & Rosenfield, *supra* note 85, at 96.

[97] *Id.* at 94 (citing Paul L. Joskow, *Commercial Impossibility, the Uranium Market and the Westinghouse Case*, 6 J. Legal Stud. 119 (1977)).

[98] *Id.*

know. Would we need to compare the hardship suffered by those who depend on C with the hardship suffered by those who rely on C's buyers? To what extent could we translate that balance of concerns with rules that would guide decision in the next case? The authors recognize the dimensions of the problem their calculus would entail:

> But there is a question whether so microscopic an examination of the facts is an appropriate predicate for decision, in light of the administrative costs... of applying the impossibility doctrine on a highly particularistic case-by-case basis rather than on the basis of rules that decide all of the cases within a specific category in the same way—for example, a rule deciding all lease discharge cases either in the lessee's or in the lessor's favor.[99]

Once the rule becomes categorical, the parties would just price that into their contracts, would, for example, include either an impracticability–frustration premium or discount. That pricing alternative would not, of course, overcome the problem because the excuse doctrine could still operate notwithstanding the fixed price. If a strict categorical approach were to replace the current regime, the impracticability–frustration doctrine would have to be abrogated, at least in part. Insofar as the party trying to take advantage of categorical discharge would have to establish some of the premises of impracticability–frustration, it is not clear that the game would be worth the candle. There might be something just *too* fundamental about the excuse doctrines to preclude courts' taking advantage of them, on the right facts. We see this in the *force majeure* cases.[100] Nonetheless, Posner and Rosenfield do suggest several categories in which they assert it might be possible to develop certain risk allocation rules.[101] But, ultimately, they acknowledge that it would likely not be possible to preclude a thorough examination of the facts in the cases, and that, then, would reduce contract to tort: the search for the cheapest cost avoider.[102]

Now the point here is not that Posner and Rosenfield err; indeed, I suspect that they get the doctrine right and have quite successfully demonstrated how courts should go about redetermining the contractual allocation of risk after the fact, which is what the excuse doctrine contemplates. The occurrence of the contingency that has brought the parties before the court perhaps *should* have and even *could* have been foreseen by one of the parties. The fact is the contract did not sufficiently reflect the allocation of risk to

---

[99] *Id.* at 103.

[100] *See, e.g.,* Melford Olsen Honey, Inc. v. Adee, 452 F.3d 956, 962–64 (8th Cir. 2006); Harriscom Svenska, AB v. Harris Corp., 3 F.3d 576, 580 (2d Cir. 1993); Suburban Newspapers of Greater St. Louis, Inc. v. Kroger Co., 886 F.2d 1060, 1062 (8th Cir. 1989).

[101] Posner & Rosenfield, *supra* note 85, at 100–08 (*e.g.,* contracts for personal services, transportation contracts, and grazing contracts).

[102] Guido Calabresi, The Costs of Accidents 135 (Student Ed. 1970).

certainly conclude that one party rather than the other should be the victim of the risk's materializing. It is not surprising that courts deciding contracts controversies, like courts generally, take into account the consequences of their application of doctrine and, upon doing so might reach conclusions that would minimize hardship. (Even if that conclusion minimizes hardship at the expense of more certain application of the doctrine: Hard cases have always made bad law.)

Although Posner and Rosenfield may be more optimistic about courts' ability to do the math that would need to be done in the thoroughgoing manner that would accurately reflect the parties' relative ability to bear risk, the fact remains that their observations about the proper application of the doctrine say a great deal about the nature of the doctrine. Excuse, at least insofar as impracticability and frustration are concerned, does not categorize. Now that is not to say that courts may not appreciate similarities across transactional contexts; that, of course, is a premise of *stare decisis.* All that Posner and Rosenfield are doing when they categorize is refining the excuse rule to take into account the likely risk allocation consistencies among recurring fact patterns. Ultimately, we would expect, the doctrine's risk allocation premise should overcome the categorization when the facts of the particular case indicate that the category is inconsistent with the doctrine. Posner and Rosenfield's categories, then, are as helpful as presumptions might be generally in the law and no more so. The categories should not go beyond the doctrine because the categories are merely heuristic: They *suggest* evidence of the doctrine's appropriate application; they do not determine it.

The doctrine accommodates consequentialism right up to the point at which we can no longer do the math. That is, we can engage Posner and Rosenfield's economic analysis just so long as we can follow the ripples in the water from both discharge and no discharge. That is also the limit we place on the computation of consequential damages: At some point, loss is not compensable because it was beyond the contemplation of the parties or otherwise speculative.[103] There is nothing particularly controversial, from either the deontic or consequentialist perspective, about understanding contract in terms of allocation of risk and then fashioning an excuse rule as a default if the parties' allocation has turned out to be less than prescient. So when Posner and Rosenfield invoke economic theory to focus on risk allocation, both *ad* and *post hoc,* they are not expecting more of the doctrine than the doctrine can provide. Theirs is a helpful construction of doctrine that focuses inquiry in a way that those who had preceded them may not have appreciated. But they have not made a case for consequentialism that undermines deontology so long as we appreciate the tension between deontology and consequentialism that the doctrine modulates.

---

[103] *See* Hadley v. Baxendale, (1854) 156 Eng. Rep. 145 (Ex.); *see* discussion *infra* Chapter Eight, "Theory of Contract Enforcement."

Once you understand the risk allocation focus of the impracticability and frustration doctrines, the parallels with another doctrine central to contract performance become clear. Modification *may* be a response to an unanticipated shift of risk. Indeed, the same principles that might support operation of the impracticability–frustration doctrine might as well support modification of an executory contract in response to changed circumstances. If the risk has remained unchanged from the time the parties entered into the contract, there would be no grounds for impracticability–frustration or modification, without something more. The normative approaches to modification trace, then, a calculus essentially similar to that informing operation of excuse doctrine.

C. Modification

The common law pre-existing legal duty rule relies on the presence of consideration to validate the modification of an executory contract. Yet the consideration requirement is, to be charitable, brittle, and does not provide a reliable normative basis to distinguish those modifications we should enforce from those we should not. The problem is well described, at least from the consequentialist perspective, by Professor Jason Johnston:

> [I]f a change in circumstances makes performance of the original contract a losing proposition for one of the parties, then that party may breach rather than perform if unable to enter into a legally enforceable contract modification. Such breach may be inefficient, in the sense that an exchange of the entitlement between the two parties would be ex post efficient but does not occur. If modifications are legally enforced, however, then under asymmetric information a party may have an incentive to extort or hold up the other party for more than was originally promised by threatening to not perform unless the contract is modified. The risk that this threat may be credible—that the threatening party may really be facing a loss from performing the original contract—may induce the victim of the threat to agree to modify, even when the threat was an extortionate bluff.[104]

Contract has no interest in making it difficult for parties to adjust the terms of their agreement in response to a change in risk allocation arising after the time of initial contracting on account of factors beyond the control of the parties. Contract does, though, have every reason to police reallocation of risk in response to one party's taking advantage of the bilateral monopoly contract creates. Once A and B enter into a contract, each is the only person with whom the law permits the other to negotiate with regard to

---

[104] Jason Scott Johnston, *Default Rules/Mandatory Principles: A Game Theoretic Analysis of Good Faith and the Contract Modification Problem*, 3 S. CAL. INTERDISC. L.J. 335, 340–41 (1993).

the contract subject matter. If A becomes contractually obligated to B, B has the right to enforce that obligation either specifically or by seeking substitutional relief. So if A bargains with C over that same subject matter, B may bring an action, and that is true whether or not we recognize efficient breach. It will, though, cost B something to enforce its rights against A, so A's threat to withhold performance may be extortionate: It may be a means by which A exacts rent from B, in the form of a better deal than A first obtained from B. Now if B has alternative sources of the same performance, A's threat will be insubstantial; indeed, A would likely not make the threat. But it could happen that in just the circumstances in which A's threat would be credible, B would be most exposed to the risk of A's breach and the value of A's performance will have increased beyond the value of it reflected in the original contract between A and B. The fact that the goods A is contractually obligated to deliver to B have increased in value, perhaps in response to market conditions, may also be the very reason A threatens to withhold delivery until B agrees to pay more for them. It is difficult to see why any increase in the value of the contract subject matter should justify modification, at least in most cases involving the sales of goods. It is just about tautological that in fixed price contracts the risk of price increases is allocated to the seller and of price decreases to the buyer. The fact that the value has increased should not be reason to modify the contract price, at least insofar as the seller already owned the goods prior to the value increase.

In the event that the value of A's performance increases on account of some reason other than general market conditions (that is, the type of risk allocated by the contract), then it is less clear that B should be the sole beneficiary of that value increase, particularly if B's realization of that enhanced value would compromise profoundly A's financial condition. The prototypical case is illustrative: A agrees to dig a well for B and shortly after beginning the work discovers that *unforeseen* difficulties, *e.g.*, solid rock where A expected to find only loose dirt, would make it economically infeasible for A to perform. Perhaps A would need to obtain equipment A cannot afford to obtain in order to dig through the solid rock, so requiring A to obtain the equipment would force A to do something A is incapable of doing. Faced with that choice, B might well be willing to increase the contract price of A's performance so that A will be able to perform and B will still realize the benefit of an efficient exchange. Had A and B been aware of the solid rock at the time of contracting, they may still have reached an agreement, but at a higher price that would have assured an efficient exchange. So there is no reason for the doctrine to categorically preclude the *re*-contracting or modification that would assure efficient exchange. Indeed, the categorical prohibition of modification would frustrate a conception of contract in consequentialist terms.

The device that classical contract doctrine used to police modification was the so-called pre-existing legal duty rule, a blunt instrument indeed if the object is to distinguish modifications we would want, either as a deontic or consequentialist matter, from those we would not want to enforce. Insofar as the pre-existing legal duty rule relies on the consideration doctrine and consideration has no direct connection with either fairness or efficiency, it might be no more than serendipity if the presence or absence of consideration is coordinated with the enforcement or non-enforcement of fair and/or efficient modifications. For that matter, other modification enforcement devices, such as novation or statutory rules validating modifications without regard to the provision of new consideration, may be no better able to distinguish the modifications we would want to accommodate from the modifications we want to prevent.

The challenge, then, is to find in the doctrine the means to do the heavy lifting—the means to distinguish the good modification from extortionate overreaching—with a finely calibrated and sensitive device. It is a setting in which less, or saying less, can be more, a setting better suited for a standard than a rule.[105] The doctrine has largely abjured reliance on the consideration doctrine in favor of the good faith standard: Courts will enforce modifications that are the product of good faith. What that standard might mean depends upon the perspective we bring to it: deontic or consequentialist.

1. DEONTOLOGY

Professor Robert Hillman, in an article focusing particularly on the good faith calculus contemplated by the UCC sales contract modification regime,[106] considers the uneasy fit between good faith and the distinction the contract law needs to draw in terms of fairness considerations, a deontic inquiry. Hillman does not believe that the good-faith inquiry is sufficient to the task:

> [T]he absence of explicit language in section 2-209(1) prohibiting the enforcement of coerced modifications and the lack of additional guidance on the issue of which modifications should be enforced has resulted in a failure of the Code to deal effectively with the problem.... At least as they affect contract modification, broad provisions such as the requirement of good faith have had only limited value under the Code.[107]

Fundamentally, it is difficult to determine the salient facts that would (and should) inform the decision whether it would be fair or efficient to enforce a modification.[108] It is not immediately clear that modification facts are any less accessible than other facts that determine the operation of contract doctrine, but Hillman is certainly correct that "the

[105] Pierre J. Schlag, *Rules and Standards*, 33 UCLA L. Rev. 379, 385 (1985) ("By describing the distinction between permissible and impermissible conduct in evaluative terms, standards allow the addressees to make individualized judgments about the substantive offensiveness or nonoffensiveness of their own actual or contemplated conduct.").

[106] Robert A. Hillman, *Policing Contract Modifications under the UCC: Good Faith and the Doctrine of Economic Duress*, 64 Iowa L. Rev. 849 (1979).

[107] *Id.* at 851.

[108] *Id.* at 855.

facts presented by the promisee often suggest that the modification was the result of fair bargaining and negotiation, while the facts offered by the promisor often suggest that the modification was the result of overreaching."[109] That is the choice: fair bargaining and negotiation versus overreaching. Indeed, even were there agreement on the facts, it is not clear that the actual facts would determine the good-faith question: Whether I am overreaching may be to at least some extent a function of whether your circumstances, including your state of mind, are as I understand them to be. I cannot always be certain, at the time I seek the modification, about the impact of my modification request or demand on your circumstances, and you may have good reason not to be too forthcoming with your negotiating and financial leverage. Hillman discloses what may be an even more fundamental flaw in the good-faith standard: "It is uncertain whether the test of honesty in fact[[110]] is violated only if the promisee intentionally misleads or lies to the promisor, or whether knowingly using methods that do not conform to society's view of fairness is sufficient for a finding of dishonesty."[111] Hillman's test of the UCC modification standard is whether good faith provides much traction so far as "society's view of fairness" is concerned. It is difficult to know what that view might be, other than perhaps an emotional reaction to the facts disclosed. And he does not ground his critique in any particular deontology, any elaboration of the term "fair."

Fairness, then, would seem to serve a heuristic function for Hillman, policing unconscientious behavior that results in a modification there is good reason not to enforce. The Code's good-faith standards are impotent to reveal if there has been sufficient unfairness. His criticism is of the Code's formulation, not in the reduction of the modification inquiry to a matter of fairness, as opaque as that might be. In Hillman's statement of how the Code fails, we get the sense of what he understands the object of the fairness inquiry to be: "[I]t is fair to conclude that the Code approach to modification law has not aided the courts and has not been used effectively to expose promisee overreaching."[112]

Hillman discovers that the good-faith inquiry, though ill fit to expose overreaching, is powerful insofar as it accommodates an amorphous fairness inquiry:

> [T]he strength of the Code's obligation of good faith performance is also its weakness. If good faith is defined, it leads to confusion; if good faith is left undefined, it confers on the courts broad powers that can easily be abused.

---

[109] *Id.*

[110] UCC § 1-201(b)(20) (2003) ("'Good faith,' except as otherwise provided in Article 5, means honesty in fact and the observance of reasonable commercial standards of fair dealing.") (footnote added).

[111] Hillman, *supra* note 106, at 859 (citing King, *New Conceptualism of the Uniform Commercial Code: Ethics, Title and Good Faith Purchase*, 11 St. Louis U.L.J. 15, 25 (1966)).

[112] *Id.* at 875.

> Perhaps the concept of good faith takes on so many different meanings in different contexts because at base it is nothing more than a requirement of fairness – a definition so broad as to be virtually meaningless.[113]

Your immediate reaction is, "Of course." Good faith, and fairness, for that matter, are insubstantial. What we expect from doctrine, if it is to mean any more than "do the right thing," is some guidance as to how we might parse the facts to realize some value (deontology) or vindicate some object (consequentialism).

Hillman does not fill in the object of the Code's modification rule in deontic or consequentialist terms (though he may give us a hint with his reference to overreaching). He offers instead a useful elaboration of the economic duress gloss on the doctrine's treatment of modification:

> [I]n applying economic duress to the issue of good faith in contract modification, the task is to determine the proper application of the rough equivalency-of-exchange principle, whether there was an absence of free choice and whether improper means were employed by the promisee.. . . If the modification would cause an immaterial net loss in value of the contact to the promisor, a presumption should arise that the modification is not a product of duress and is enforceable. In contrast, if the net loss on the contract would be material, the presumption should be that the modification is unenforceable because it was a product of unlawful means and the promisor was without a viable alternative.[114]

Hillman formulates a new test to police modifications that relies on evidentiary presumptions and material breach conceptions. What matters for present purposes is the fact that his test would permit a promisee to overcome the presumption by demonstrating, *inter alia*, "that under the circumstances it was reasonable for the promisor to enter into the modification."[115] Arguably, trading good faith for reasonableness (or either of those alternatives for fairness) does not advance the ball much. Johnston's description of the tension brought us closer to the crux of the problem.[116]

---

[113] *Id.* at 877 (footnote omitted).

[114] *Id.* at 883.

[115] *Id.* at 889.

[116] Johnston, *supra* note 104.

2. CONSEQUENTIALISM

An article written by Professors Varouj Aivazian and Michael Trebilcock with Michael Penny begins its presentation of the modification issue in consequentialist terms by distinguishing static from dynamic efficiency considerations:

> Static efficiency considerations will generally require that contract modifications be enforced on the grounds that the immediate contracting parties perceive mutual gains from recontracting that cannot, at the time modification is proposed, be realized as fully by any alternative strategy. . . . [D]ynamic efficiency considerations focus on the long-run incentives for parties at large imparted by a set of legal rules. In the modification context, these dynamic efficiency considerations adopt an ex ante perspective, rather than ex post perspective implicit in the static efficiency considerations.[117]

That static–dynamic dichotomy would seem to resolve into the "hard-cases-make-bad-law" maxim. Although static considerations alone might tell us how to resolve this controversy between these two parties, dynamic considerations encourage us to take into account the consequences of our adopting a rule that reaches the right result *ex post* while creating incentives and opportunities for argument that might undermine broader policy goals. The same device or approach that could serve static concerns might frustrate dynamic concerns. So much depends on our perspective: Are we more interested in reducing the costs of a particular contract *post hoc*, and enforcing a modification if the facts in evidence do not intimate unconscientious (or inefficient) overreaching? Or, is it more important to adopt "rules that will reduce the long-run costs of contracting"? The authors emphasize dynamic, long-run concerns.[118] The object is a rule, or set of rules, that will minimize transaction costs.[119]

From the perspective of Aivazian, Penny, and Trebilcock, the modification context is much like the impossibility–frustration context, and they build on the economic analysis of Posner and Rosenfield: "The economic considerations bearing on permissible rearrangements by virtue of contract modifications, the doctrine of frustration, or the doctrine of mistake would seem to be similar."[120] Modification is *a* response to the same type of circumstances that would support operation of frustration or impracticability principles. Frustration or impracticability would permit the parties to walk away when post-contracting events have affected the allocation of risk in ways unforeseen by the

---

[117] Varouj A. Aivazian, Michael J. Trebilcock, & Michael Penny, *The Law of Contract Modifications: The Uncertain Quest for a Benchmark of Enforceability*, 22 OSGOODE HALL L. J. 173, 175 (1984).

[118] *Id.* at 175.

[119] *Id.* at 187.

[120] *Id.* at 195 (footnote omitted).

parties at the time of contracting. Modification may respond to the occurrence of such a contingency, the non-occurrence of which was a basic assumption upon which the parties originally contracted. So the same facts that would support the frustration or impracticability excuses would support the court's enforcing a modification.

In the application of their economic approach, Aivazian, Penny, and Trebilcock consider the canonical modification case: *Alaska Packers' Association v. Domenico*. They read the case as involving the "problem of opportunism": "Modifications entered into in these circumstances are not Pareto efficient forms of recontracting, but are at best zero-sum games. In addition, distributional or ethical objections may be raised to the redivision of the gains from trade as a result of opportunism by one party."[121] So there is, on the facts of *Alaska Packers*, a coincidence of deontic and consequentialist values. From either perspective, the modification should not be enforced; the attempted modification is purely strategic and represents an effort to vindicate neither deontic nor consequentialist objects. Deontic interests would be frustrated were the shipowners bound to the terms of an agreement to which they in no real way consented. Enforcement of the modification would effect only a transfer of welfare; it would not be welfare creating. Indeed, even were the modification enforced on a more pro-crew construction of the static facts of *Alaska Packers*, the dynamic impact of the decision would drive up transactions costs for subsequent contracting parties. They would have to build in an opportunism premium to reflect the risk that the original (and efficient) risk allocation could be undone by a modification. Further, the very risk that a modification could be enforced on the *Alaska Packers* facts would undermine the risk allocation certainty that effects efficient exchange, the subject of contract from the consequentialist perspective.

But what of the *Alaska Packers*-like case in which the crew seeks a modification of the contract on account of the occurrence of a contingency the non-occurrence of which was a basic assumption on which the contract was formed? What should we do if an oil spill significantly complicates the crew's work but the shipowners are willing to pay the crew a premium to encourage them to perform that additional work? That may be the case if the unforeseen complication also makes the contract opportunity a more valuable one for the shipowners because all shipowners may confront the new challenge but the ship already on site with a crew willing to accept a premium to do more arduous work could exploit its position to significant advantage. The law would want to provide the parties the means to modify their deal in order to capture greater value. The authors recognize the need for contract to respond:

> [W]here the superior initial risk bearer cannot be confidently identified, or where he can be but the risk in question is very remote, modifications may be Pareto efficient in that losses to both parties associated with the breach can be at least partially avoided

[121] *Id.* at 197–98.

and long-run incentives for efficient risk-bearing by future contracting parties in the class of situation in question may not be significantly distorted.[122]

At the time of contracting, neither the shipowner nor the crew would be the superior risk bearer so far as an oil spill is concerned (unless, perhaps, the ship were an oil tanker). Even if the circumstances would indicate that the ship owner were the superior risk bearer, the risk of, say, an offshore oil rig's exploding and severely complicating the voyage's object would be very remote and so the parties would not expend resources allocating that risk at the time of contracting.

The challenge for contract would be to distinguish cases in which the *Alaska Packers* rule (pure strategic modification) would work (risk and superior risk bearer readily identifiable) from cases in which either the fact of risk or the superior risk bearer would not be readily identifiable. Recognizing that there will be a range of cases between those two poles, Aivazian, Penny, and Trebilcock nevertheless try to develop categories that would guide application of the modification rules. This is redolent of the categories Posner and Rosenfield discover in the impracticability–frustration setting. In the modification context we should, for example, distinguish the risks assumed *ex ante* by large contractors from those assumed by small contractors.[123] If the modification is sought by one of the contracting parties merely as a result of that party's change of preference (irrespective of their relative sizes and bargaining positions), we might look to the agreement to pay additional consideration to identify those modifications that should be enforced: "[R]eceipt of fresh consideration for a modification is important as an assurance that initially efficiently assigned risks have not been subsequently inefficiently reassigned."[124] The authors recognize that such reliance on the *fact* of additional consideration is problematic; it would be the adequacy of the additional consideration that would be probative of the efficiency issue. It is, though, axiomatic that contract does not inquire into the adequacy of consideration. The authors cite maritime salvage cases as a setting in which courts will imply a reasonable compensation term in order "to avoid the exploitation of situational monopolies."[125]

The authors' conclusion does not hold out much hope for the development of a doctrinal construction that will be able to anticipate the correct modification calculus before the fact, and so in time to allow the contracting parties to fix the modification risk in their initial contract: "While it is obvious. . . that the presence or absence of

---

[122] *Id.* at 200.

[123] *Id.* at 201.

[124] *Id.* at 203.

[125] *Id.* (footnote omitted).

consideration may be relevant to a determination of whether a modification is efficient, no simple rule can capture all possible factual nuances."[126]

That conclusion maintains as well in the case of long-term supply contracts, in which the parties' relative abilities to anticipate risk may not be sufficiently certain to fix a rule. The authors consider a supplier of ice subject to climatic extremes: "Only where the winter in question was *quite out of the ordinary* so that the gains from recontracting were likely to outweigh the long-run costs of moral hazard problems associated with permitting recontracting in these circumstances, could one support the decision [to enforce the modification]."[127] Of course, what will constitute "quite out of the ordinary" will be a matter of degrees (perhaps quite literally) and would seem to defy certain calculation before the fact. The same would be true of a distinction based on whether the contract was "relational" in nature, recognizing that in such cases a particular modification may appear inefficient although it is supportive of a broader and efficient contractual relationship. Again, the authors acknowledge that "the distinction between discrete and relational contracts cannot be elevated into a sharp doctrinal divide. . . . Degrees of integration and interdependence in commercial relationships reflect enormous variations."[128]

The consequentialist construction of the modification law certainly adds something that deontic accounts do not: an ostensibly more accessible measure of fairness. But that does not mean that the consequentialists provide a superior normative account. The consequentialists ultimately offer no more convincing account of the doctrine because they can offer no more certain guide to the doctrine's application: The uncertainties of fairness are no less confounding than the uncertain efficiency calculus of consequentialism. What economic analysis does add, though, is the recognition that static efficiency considerations (like fairness considerations) will impact dynamic efficiency considerations. That is not much different from recognizing that a fairness determination at T1 will impact a fairness determination at T2, and be taken into account by contracting parties accordingly. The observation is not uniquely consequentialist; it is an observation about human nature.

The lesson we glean from the normative commentary on modification is that the doctrine cannot capture the object of the law, at least not very well. The doctrine provides the means for the parties to get before the court the facts that would be determinative from either a consequentialist or deontic perspective. Further, the fairness calculus of deontology cannot do much better than vagaries of good faith, and the quantitative comparisons consequentialism would require are inaccessible, at least in any form that could support dynamic or likely even static efficiency considerations. The best we can do is the categorization of recurring contexts that *might* indicate some consistency from

---

[126] *Id.* at 204.

[127] *Id.* at 205 (emphasis added).

[128] *Id.* at 206–07.

one case to the next, but even then the potential for determinative differences among particular instances within those recurring contexts is significant. The doctrine, then, could not honestly be read to vindicate deontic or consequentialist premises. The doctrine facilitates either deontology or consequentialism, and is so normatively vague that it can serve fairness or efficiency as the agent applying the doctrine chooses. That choice is more a product of the agent's predisposition as well as cognitive strengths and limitations than it is a function of the doctrine's normative claim.

This role of doctrine is confirmed too in the third-party beneficiary setting.

D. Third Parties

If the source and limit of contract liability is the intent of the contracting parties, and both deontologists and consequentialists should follow that premise with nodding assent (though perhaps to different degrees), then it is not surprising that the scope or reach of contract liability should also be measured by intent. If A and B enter into a contract and intend thereby to confer contract rights on C, there is no obvious reason why contract should not accommodate that arrangement. Doing so would, indeed, serve both deontic and consequentialist objects. Again, though, the challenge for doctrine would be to provide the means to determine when the intent of A and B would be served by extending contract benefits to C. Before we could conclude that the doctrine vindicates one normative perspective rather than the other we would need to determine whether the doctrine is amenable to construction in terms of *either* deontology *or* consequentialism.

The law of third-party beneficiaries may be canonical in the common law of the United States but it does not enjoy the same recognition in other common law countries.[129] This could intimate that third-party beneficiary doctrine does not flow necessarily from the normative premises of contract, were there certain normative premises of common law contract. Before we could reach reliable conclusions about the doctrine's fit with some normative conception of contract, we would have to discern a normative predisposition of the third-party beneficiary doctrine. If we cannot find that the third-party beneficiary doctrine reveals a particular normative perspective, then that might confirm something too about the normativity of contract more generally.

Accepting *Lawrence v. Fox*[130] as the canonical third-party beneficiary case, we can read the *Restatements'* treatment of the doctrine as elaboration. The two *Restatements* represent an evolving view of the fit between contract generally and third-party beneficiary

[129] A.J. Waters, *The Property in the Promise: A Study of the Third Party Beneficiary Rule*, 98 HARVARD L. REV. 1109 (1985); *cf.* Melvin V. Eisenberg, *Third-Party Beneficiaries*, 92 COLUM. L. REV. 1358, 1360–61 & n. 14 (1992) (discussing English rule).

[130] Lawrence v. Fox, 97 N.W.2d 719 (Mich. 1959).

principles specifically. Professor Melvin Eisenberg, in his comprehensive treatment of the third-party beneficiary law,[131] appreciates the fit among *Lawrence*, contract doctrine more generally, and the *First Restatement*:

> Despite the awkward nature of its nomenclature, Restatement First initiated the modern law of third-party beneficiaries by taking two critical steps. First, it pushed aside by brute force the doctrinal objections to enforcement by third-party beneficiaries. Second, it set the stage for movement away from a rule-based body of third-party-beneficiary law, comprised of a collection of specific categories, toward a body of law in which enforceability by third-party beneficiaries would be determined by a general principle. But what is that principle?[132]

If we can find the principle Eisenberg looks for and formulate it in normative terms, either deontic or consequentialist, then we will have gone some way toward identifying the normative basis of third-party beneficiary law and maybe of other aspects of contract doctrine similarly dependent on conceptions of intent.

1. DEONTOLOGY

In response to his frustration with the vagueness of *Lawrence v. Fox* and the confusion of the two *Restatement* iterations,[133] Eisenberg offers his own statement of the principle(s) that animate the third party beneficiary rule:

> A third-party beneficiary should have power to enforce a contract if, but only if:
>
> (1) allowing the beneficiary to enforce the contract is a necessary or important means of effectuating the contracting parties' performance objectives, as manifested in the contract read in the light of surrounding circumstances; or
> (2) allowing the beneficiary to enforce the contract is supported by reasons of policy or morality independent of contract law and would not conflict with the contracting parties' performance objectives.[134]

This formulation of the third-party beneficiary principle certainly seems to rely primarily on deontic premises. Insofar as the two alternative enforcement mechanisms *are* alternative, the third-party beneficiary will be able to enforce its rights so long as "reasons of... morality" would be satisfied and enforcement "would not conflict with the contracting

---

[131] Eisenberg, *supra* note 129.

[132] *Id.* at 1374.

[133] *Id.* at 1376–77, 1381–84.

[134] *Id.* at 1385.

parties' performance objectives." The reference to "the contracting parties' performance objectives" in both subsections could, but need not, contemplate the recognition of consequentialist concerns, but only so long as the parties' performance objectives could be described in consequentialist terms, such as efficiency or wealth creation. It would also be sufficient, though, that enforcement would "effectuate the contracting parties' performance objectives," which just as well seems to be a vindication of autonomy principles. The second subsection's reliance on morality (including, we may assume, Kantian autonomy interests) is appropriate so long as such reliance would not conflict with the parties' performance objectives. Keep in mind that under Eisenberg's first subsection, we need not consider reasons of policy or morality at all: Then it is sufficient that enforcement would serve the parties' performance objectives. Although reliance on the intent of the parties may seem empty (at least Eisenberg thinks so[135]), Eisenberg's statement of the third-party beneficiary principle does not advance the ball much (if any) further at all. The difference between the parties' *intent* and their *performance objectives* ultimately seems to be semantic, and nothing more.

Eisenberg does try to distinguish his test from the *Restatement* test but is not convincing:

> Unlike the intent-to-benefit test [of the Restatements], which turns on whether the contracting parties had an *other-regarding* intent to benefit the third party, the first branch of the third-party-beneficiary principle [and the pertinent part of the second branch, we assume] turns on whether allowing the third party to enforce the contract will further the *self-regarding* interests of the contracting parties.
>
> To put this differently, under the first branch of the third-party-beneficiary principle, the law of third-party beneficiaries is largely conceived as remedial, rather than substantive. The question addressed by the first branch of the principle is not whether the contract creates a "right" in the third party, but whether empowering the third party to enforce the contract is a necessary or important means of effectuating the contracting parties' performance objectives.[136]

Eisenberg's formulation of the distinction between his principle and the *Restatement* focus on intent is not clear. What, exactly, is the difference between whether the contracting parties *intend* to create third-party rights or whether the contracting parties' performance objectives, revealed, we must assume, from indicia of their intent, would be effected by enforcement of third-party rights? Insofar as the parties' performance objectives are a product of their intent, the line Eisenberg draws seems to be too fine, if it

---

[135] *Id.* at 1377, 1379.

[136] *Id.* at 1386 (emphasis added) (footnote omitted).

has any substance at all. And to the extent that there might be anything of substance to the distinction he posits it is certainly obscured when he elaborates:

> [A] court asked to determine a remedial problem would normally do well to ask what the parties would have provided if they had bargained under ideal conditions – that is, where foresight was perfect and negotiation and drafting were cost-free. The rules that the courts apply to fill in contracts should be both fair and efficient. Contracts negotiated under ideal conditions will be efficient, and enforcing the terms of such contracts will usually be regarded as fair. Thus, a remedial rule is fair and efficient if it corresponds to the terms that rational parties situated like the contracting parties would have reached when bargaining under ideal conditions.[137]

Now although that elaboration does little more than describe the sources courts might consult to discern (or construct) the parties' coincident intent (maybe a fiction to begin with), it does suggest a merger of the deontic and consequentialist in the contract performance context and supports the thesis of this book.

2. CONSEQUENTIALISM

The fact that there is substantial identity between the "parties' performance objectives" in the Eisenberg formulation and intent in the *Restatements* and third-party beneficiary case law is significant insofar as it confirms the doctrine: In order to determine the enforcement right of a third party, focus on the intent of the promisor and promisee. Eisenberg is certainly correct that his third-party beneficiary principle explains the cases; of course it does: It merely restates the doctrine. Further, then, for present purposes, Eisenberg's survey of the case law and recapitulation accommodates his ultimate distillation of the normative object of the third-party beneficiary law. His formulation resonates with the same type of risk allocation analysis that makes consequentialist sense of the impracticability–frustration and modification rules.

Eisenberg equates the normative objects of fairness and efficiency: "The rules that the courts apply to fill in contracts should be both fair and efficient. Contracts negotiated under ideal conditions will be efficient, and enforcing the terms of such contracts will usually be regarded as fair."[138] He captures a great deal in that conclusion, and goes a long way toward identifying the almost necessary coincidence of the normative objects of deontology and consequentialism. It is from here that Eisenberg reaches a conclusion about risk allocation in consequentialist contract bargain terms:

---

[137] *Id.* at 1386.

[138] *Id.*

> [A] remedial rule is fair and efficient if it corresponds to the terms that rational parties situated like the contracting parties would have reached when bargaining under ideal conditions. That determination, in turn, rests largely on whether the promisee will realize the objectives he bargained for if the suit is not allowed; whether the promisor's risk of liability will be extended if the suit is allowed; and, if that liability will be extended, whether the parties have implicitly bargained for that risk. To put the matter simply, the question is whether it is likely that the promisee would have made the contract on the price terms he accepted if the contract had explicitly stated that the third party would be allowed to bring suit, and whether the promisor would have made the contract on the price terms she accepted if the contract had explicitly stated that the third party would not be allowed to bring suit.[139]

So we decide whether a plaintiff is a third-party beneficiary with the right to enforce by determining whether the promisor and promisee have priced that exposure, that risk, into their contract: If circumstances support the conclusion that the promisor and promisee had in fact priced in that risk, then we may conclude that their performance objectives would be served by third-party enforcement. That determination is to be made while keeping in mind both static and dynamic efficiency concerns because once we determine that *this* third party can enforce, then *all future similarly situated* promisors and promisees will have that same right, or at least *all future similarly situated* promisors and promisees will have to price that possibility (even likelihood) into their contract. Of course, the doctrine will determine in that *future* case whether promisor and promisee are *similarly situated*. Obviously, this could be circular.

Professor Eisenberg's contribution to the third-party beneficiary is valuable, particularly for those concerned with the normative basis of the doctrine. His analysis makes clear that the doctrine is normatively equivocal: It can vindicate fairness or efficiency or even vindicate fairness *by* vindicating efficiency. His structure, then, insofar as it understands risk allocation in terms of both static and dynamic efficiency and, ultimately, in terms of fairness, confirms the doctrine's resistance to normative characterization in *either* deontic *or* consequentialist terms.

Finally, it is worthwhile to consider briefly the doctrine's treatment of extrinsic evidence, and what normative story emerges from that treatment.

E. The Parol Evidence Rule

In something of a requiem for the parol evidence rule,[140] Professors Alan Schwartz and Robert Scott focus on the nature of the firm to formulate such entities' particular interest

---

[139] *Id.* at 1386–87.

[140] Alan Schwartz & Robert E. Scott, *Contract Theory and the Limits of Contract Law*, 113 YALE L.J. 541 (2003).

in doctrine as a mechanism to assure the results that matter to them. Fundamentally, firms do not share the same concerns as individual contracting parties and so, per Schwartz and Scott, courts should not apply doctrine to firms in the same way that they would to individuals. There should be, then, contract doctrine for firms and contract doctrine for the rest of us. It is necessary to consider the bases of the dichotomy they favor in sufficient detail to support conclusions about the significance of Schwartz and Scott's thesis for the relationship among context, doctrine, and normative theory.

The parol evidence rule[141] can serve as well as frustrate the expectations and objectives of the contracting parties. Succinctly, if the parties to a transaction reduce their understanding to an integrated writing,[142] that writing[143] may not be contradicted by extrinsic evidence[144] prior to or contemporaneous with the writing. The rule enables the parties to preserve the terms of their agreement: Neither can go behind the writing to adjust the allocation of risks fixed by the writing. That works well enough to reduce transactions costs and thereby promote efficiency so long as neither party's justified expectations are undermined by the rule. But it could be the case that one party understood that something said to her by the other, prior to execution of the writing, would be enforceable. For example, during negotiations, seller tells buyer that seller will repair or replace any component of the primary good that fails within thirty days of the buyer's receipt of the good. Seller then presents the buyer with a writing to be signed which contains an integration clause and the writing says nothing about repair or replacement of defective

[141] The common law, the Uniform Commercial Code, and the RESTATEMENT (SECOND) OF CONTRACTS contain differing but essentially similar renditions of the parol evidence rule. *See, e.g.,* Shultz v. Delta-Rail Corp., 508 N.E.2d 1143, 1150 (Ill. App. Ct. 1987) ("An agreement reduced to writing must be presumed to speak the intention of the parties who signed it. The intention with which it was executed must be determined from the language used, and such an agreement is not to be changed by extrinsic evidence."); 67 Wall St. Co. v. Franklin Nat. Bank, 333 N.E.2d 184, 186 (N.Y. 1975) (recognizing that parol evidence rule in New York "requires the exclusion of evidence of conversations, negotiations and agreements made prior to or contemporaneous with the execution of a written lease which may tend to vary or contradict its terms. . ."); UCC § 2-202 (2002); RESTATEMENT (SECOND) OF CONTRACTS § 213 (1981).

[142] An integrated contract is defined as "[o]ne or more writings constituting a final expression of one or more terms of an agreement." BLACK'S LAW DICTIONARY 824 (8th ed. 2004). Note that the RESTATEMENT (SECOND) OF CONTRACTS expressly refers to an integrated agreement, RESTATEMENT (SECOND) OF CONTRACTS§ 213 (1981), while the UCC implicitly refers to it, using the following language: "a writing intended by the parties as a final expression of their agreement with respect to such terms as are included therein. . . ." UCC § 2-202 (2002).

[143] "Writing" is defined in UCC § 1-201(b)(43) (2003) as including "printing, typewriting or any other intentional reduction to tangible form." Article 1 also defines "record" as "information that is inscribed on a tangible medium or that is stored in an electronic or other medium and is retrievable in perceivable form." *Id.* § 1-201(b)(31).

[144] Because the rule extends to all extrinsic evidence, oral or written, it is strictly speaking not just a rule about "parol" evidence.

parts. When a crucial part fails, buyer requests repair or replacement and the seller refuses, citing the "as is"[145] language in the writing.

Some courts have not been favorably disposed toward ignoring extrinsic evidence that would reveal the parties' intent more accurately than would the purportedly integrated writing.[146] At the same time, though, the good sense of the rule would be compromised were a sophisticated buyer, who understood that the writing took away what the oral representation seemed to give her, able to undermine the parties' written agreement by introducing evidence she knew she had surrendered (for a price, certainly) the right to introduce. Similarly the equities would rarely seem to lie on the side of the party who gives with one hand (orally) and then tries to rely on what may be fine print to take that away with the other. Indeed, that might explain both impatience with the rule's operation and with the structure of the rule in its statutory and *Restatement* iterations. The exceptions to the rule are significant.[147]

To appreciate what Schwartz and Scott want us to understand about transactional categories with regard to the parol evidence rule, it is enough to consider the basic dynamic: The parties have signed an integrated agreement and one of them, after the fact, tries to avoid operation of the writing because the terms are no longer desirable.[148] That type of regret is endemic to contract;[149] it is what happens when the person at T1 is not the "same" person at T2.[150] But an integrated agreement's function, in primary part, is to fix risk,[151] and regret just happens if one party either miscalculated the risk, perhaps

[145] On the sufficiency of an "as is" provision as a disclaimer of implied warranties, *see* UCC § 2-316(3)(a) (2002).

[146] *See* Pacific Gas & Elec. Co. v. G. W. Thomas Drayage & Rigging Co., 442 P.2d 641, 646 (Cal. 1968) (When defendant's performance of contract with plaintiff to replace upper metal cover of steam engine resulted in damage to plaintiff's property, appellate court held that lower "court erroneously refused to consider extrinsic evidence offered to show that indemnity clause in contract was not intended to cover injuries to plaintiff's property."); Masterson v. Sine, 436 P.2d 561, 567 (Cal. 1968) (Trial court erroneously excluded evidence in bankruptcy proceeding that non-assignable option to repurchase home was intended to keep home in possession of family.).

[147] *See* E. ALLAN FARNSWORTH, FARNSWORTH ON CONTRACTS § 7.4 (3d ed. 2004).

[148] Keep in mind that it may well be true that the party trying to resist the terms of the writing and enforce the "integrated-out" prior or contemporaneous representation may well have understood at the time she signed the writing that she was signing away her right to do just what she is now trying to do.

[149] *See* E. ALLAN FARNSWORTH, CHANGING YOUR MIND: THE LAW OF REGRETTED DECISIONS 18–27 (1998).

[150] *See* Daniel A. Farber, *Economic Efficiency and The Ex Ante Perspective*, in THE JURISPRUDENTIAL FOUNDATIONS OF CORPORATE AND COMMERCIAL LAW 54, 71–73 (Jody S. Kraus & Steven D. Walt eds., 2000).

[151] *See* J.F. McKinney & Assocs., Ltd. v. Gen. Elec. Inv. Corp., 183 F.3d 619, 622 (7th Cir. 1999) (Allowing jury to read an incomplete promise into a communication would "undermine the utility of contract as a risk-allocation device. . . ."); Hemenway v. Peabody Coal Co., 159 F.3d 255, 258 (7th Cir. 1998) ("Contracts allocate risks, and judicial decisions changing those allocations after the fact. . . make the institution of contract less useful *ex ante*.").

because of some cognitive bias,[152] or calculated it correctly but the event with a one-in-a-hundred chance materialized.

From the perspective of Schwartz and Scott, the parol evidence rule should mean different things when transactional contexts differ:

> A perennial question in contract law is why the state should enforce a contract against the wishes of a party to it. We exclude answers to this question that take the following form: The state should enforce a party's contractual promises the better to permit persons to enlist other persons in their projects, and thus to increase the sphere of autonomy within which persons can operate; or the state should enforce promises to reinforce the morality of keeping them. These answers are ruled out here because the business firms that make commercial contracts are *artificial* persons whose autonomy the state need not respect on moral grounds, and whose morality is ordinarily required by positive law. The relevant question for a normative theory of commercial contract law is just when, if ever, the goal of welfare maximization requires legal enforcement of the contracts that business entities make.[153]

Schwartz and Scott conclude that firms would prefer application of the parol evidence rule that results in courts' getting "things right on average."[154] Insofar as firms are repeat players and, even more important, those who own firms can have diverse portfolios of firm ownership,[155] getting it right "on average" will do quite well because "a firm's preference at contract time is to have courts make interpretations on the minimum evidentiary base unless it would be costless to widen the base. But it is not costless."[156] So long as firms *are*

---

[152] *See generally* Christine Jolls, Cass R. Sunstein & Richard Thaler, *A Behavioral Approach to Law and Economics,* 50 STAN. L. REV. 1471 (1998).

[153] Schwartz & Scott, *supra* note 140, at 556 (emphasis in original) (citation omitted).

[154] *Id.* at 556 (citation omitted).

[155] Professor Nathan Oman developed the analogy to a stock portfolio:

> A firm's contracts. . . become analogous to a diversified stock portfolio. The investor in such a stock portfolio should be risk-neutral as to any particular stock, since diversification allows one to balance declining stocks with advancing stocks. The only thing that matters is the aggregate performance of the portfolio. Similarly, if our sole goal is to maximize the value of a firm, we should be indifferent to the "performance" of any particular contract under a hyper-formalist interpretation regime. So long as "winning" interpretations are as frequent as "losing" interpretations, the risk of judicial "mistakes" is diversified away and the firm realizes the full benefits of the cheaper resolution of contractual disputes.

Nathan B. Oman, *Corporations and Autonomy Theory of Contract: A Critique of the New* Lex Mercatoria, 83 DENV.U. L. REV. 101, 132 (2005) (citation omitted). Oman takes exception, at some length and convincingly, to Schwartz and Scott's simplification of a firm into a collection of contracts about which it is indifferent with regard to matters of interpretation from one individual contract to the next. He finds room for autonomy theory to operate where Schwartz and Scott do not. *Id.* at 109–14.

[156] Schwartz & Scott, *supra* note 140, at 576.

risk neutral, and because their owners are repeat players firms normally are risk neutral,[157] they would prefer that courts get it right on average because the cost of getting it right every time (assuming that is even calculable) will overwhelm the benefits to the firm and its owners of having gotten it right. The cost of courts' getting it wrong on occasion is less than the cost of trying to get it right all the time. And if all that is at stake is the value of one contract in your portfolio, the loss in one case attributable to the court's getting it wrong will likely be balanced by gain in the next, when the court is as likely to err in your favor. The key is risk neutrality, and repeat players who can spread risk over a portfolio are risk neutral in the way that matters for the application of the parol evidence rule.[158]

Ultimately, here it does not matter whether Schwartz and Scott are correct in their conclusion about firms' limited concern with courts' getting it right in a particular case.[159] It is enough that Schwartz and Scott have posited a not-implausible basis for categorization that could matter to both deontologists and consequentialists: If individuals' risk neutrality generally differs from that of firms, the application of doctrine can be sensitive to that difference. If their respective attitudes toward risk are not the same, even in part because of the nature of the firm, that may be reason to understand that doctrine such as the parol evidence rule or its application must be different for each in order to reach the same normative result. We should not be surprised if courts tailor their application of doctrine to take into account normative discontinuities. It may well be that only when a court hearing an action between individuals takes into account extensive extrinsic evidence that it is applying the same *normative* formula that it would be if it were to limit its consideration of extrinsic evidence in a case involving an unexceptional contract between large multinational corporations. Anomalously, the two cases would have to be treated differently in order to be treated similarly, in the normative sense. This may explain the form doctrine takes.[160]

Professor Daniel Markovits has simplified the Schwartz and Scott conclusion so far as delineating categories by reference to transactor type is concerned. Recall that Schwartz and Scott could deny the operation of autonomy principles because they reason that contracts made by firms are significantly different from contracts made by individuals: Markovits concludes that "Schwartz and Scott undermine every sense of the moral

---

[157] Concerning volatile markets, Schwartz and Scott recognize that "when performance of a particular contract is important to the survival of the firm, say, a contract with a major supplier—or when the contract is new and is expected to be widely used, the firm may be unwilling to risk a seriously adverse interpretation." *Id.* at 576. The authors note the "bet the ranch" quality of such contracts. *Id.* at 577. It would seem likely, though, that if the parties are asking a court to resolve the parol evidence issue, for at least one of the litigants the contract may be of the "bet the ranch" variety. Litigation is too expensive to pursue unless there is a significant amount at stake.

[158] *See id.* at 550–54.

[159] *See* Oman, *supra* note 155, at 131–32.

[160] Peter A. Alces, *The Moral Impossibility of Contract*, 48 WM. & MARY L. REV. 1647 (2007).

separateness or distinctness of the parties to the transactions that they analyze."[161] Schwartz and Scott have explained contract by explaining away the bilateralism that defines the contractual relationship: "Whereas contracts, intuitively understood, involve coordination among multiple parties, the transactions addressed by Schwartz and Scott's economic theory involve only *one*, and they are, therefore, not in the end agreements *at all*."[162] Because Markovits appreciates contract in terms of "collaboration," which necessarily contemplates coordination of the interests of separate entities, Schwartz and Scott have nothing interesting to say about the contract doctrine, so far as Markovits is concerned.

There are transactions between individuals, between an individual and an organization, and between organizations.[163] According to Schwartz and Scott, our theory is most needed to explain the third type of contract. That is because statutory law, such as consumer protection law, generally takes care of transactions between firms and individuals.[164] So Schwartz and Scott conclude that it is contracts between firms that form "the main subject of what is commonly called contract law—namely, the rules of Article 2 of the Uniform Commercial Code (UCC) and the provisions of the *Restatement (Second) of Contracts*."[165] And Markovits, for his part, begins from the proposition that "contracts among individuals, natural persons... represent the *core* of contract."[166] Now we cannot have two diametrically opposed contexts that are both, simultaneously, the core or key to understanding the theoretical basis of the same doctrine. But the disagreement between Schwartz and Scott and Markovits does make clear one thing: Both perspectives recognize the importance of discovering *the* prototypical transactional relationship. Neither perspective is much interested in explaining the types of contexts not deemed predominant. Schwartz and Scott focus on economic efficiency because that is all firms care about;[167] Markovits concentrates on transactions between individuals because that is

[161] Daniel Markovits, *Contract and Collaboration*, 113 YALE L.J. 1417, 1469 (2004).

[162] Daniel Markovits, *Making and Keeping Contracts*, 92 VA. L. REV. 1325, 1350 (2006) (citation omitted).

[163] Ethan J. Leib, *On Collaboration, Organizations, and Conciliation in the General Theory of Contract* 24 QUINNIPIAC L. REV. 1, 2N. 3 (2005), *citing* Markovits, *supra* note 161 at 1464 ("The typology, of course, has roots in MEIR DAN-COHEN, RIGHTS, PERSONS, AND ORGANIZATIONS: A LEGAL THEORY FOR BUREAUCRATIC SOCIETY 82–84 (1986) and is a quite standard way of classifying contracts now."); *see also* Schwartz & Scott, *supra* note 140, at 544 (There are "four transactional categories: (1) A firm sells to another firm, (2) an individual sells to another individual, (3) a firm sells to an individual, and (4) an individual sells to a firm.").

[164] Schwartz & Scott, *supra* note 140, at 544.

[165] *Id.*

[166] Markovits, *supra* note 161, at 1421(emphasis added).

[167] *Id.* at 1468 (suggesting that Schwartz & Scott, *supra* note 140, at 555–56, are contributing to the theory of the "firm" rather than to the contract literature).

where he discovers his "morality of contract."[168] Nonetheless, a theory of contract must account for all of contract.[169]

This leaves us at something of an impasse: The contestants each declare victory but only after agreeing to engage one another, in a manner of speaking, on separate battlefields. The result: We learn nothing, really, about what the unitary theory could be. Schwartz and Scott do confirm something about contracts between firms for us, namely, that firms care about wealth maximization. Markovits tells us something about the contracts that individuals form, namely, that they vindicate autonomy values. Nevertheless, we have not moved very far off the mark if the object is to discover something more fundamental. It is not the fault of Schwartz and Scott or Markovits if they have reduced contract to the lowest common denominators the deontic–consequentialist dichotomy provides. It may be that their perspectives (even if not conclusions) could be accurate so far as they go and that we can go no further.

[168] *Id.* at 1420.

[169] Leib, *supra* note 163, at 9 (2005) ("It is simply impossible to present a coherent general account of contract without attending to all... of contracts.").

7

CONTRACT ENFORCEMENT DOCTRINE

YOU COULD CONCLUDE that it is only when we determine the consequences of breaching a contract, that is, when we fix the damage measure, that we necessarily come to terms with the foundation of contract, what it is that contract accomplishes. We would have a much different conception of contract if breach resulted in criminal liability, a fine, or payment to the state, than we have based on the bilateral, private nature of the enforcement mechanism. That bilateralism undermines the normative consistency, or at least the symmetry, of the standard damage measures as applied because it is not clear that what is fair or efficient with regard to the non-breaching party is fair or efficient with regard to the breaching party.[1] But critique is the province of Chapter Eight, "Theory of Contract Enforcement." Here, the object is to discover the enforcement doctrine, and grasp the warp and weave of its fabric. The point is exposition and we need, for present purposes, agree to

---

[1] *See* Jules Coleman, *The Normative Basis of Economic Analysis: A Critical Review of Richard Posner's The Economics of Justice*, 34 STAN. L. REV. 1105 (1982); Richard Craswell, *Contract Remedies, Renegotiation, and the Theory of Efficient Breach*, 61 S. CAL. L. REV. 629 (1988); Nathan B. Oman, *Corporations and Autonomy Theory of Contract: A Critique of the New* Lex Mercatoria, 83 DENV. U. L. REV. 101 (2005); *see also* RICHARD A. POSNER, THE ECONOMICS OF JUSTICE (1981) (discussing relationship between concepts of economic efficiency and justice); Charles J. Goetz & Richard E. Scott, *Liquidated Damages, Penalties, and the Just Compensation Principle: Some Notes on an Enforcement Model and a Theory of Efficient Breach*, 77 COLUM. L. REV. 554 (1977) (Application of penalty doctrine may frequently deny non-breaching party adequate compensation or opportunity to insure against harm.).

nothing more than that the canonical cases considered here reveal the way doctrine drives the damages calculus. Again, we will see that what the doctrine does not determine is every bit as important as what it certainly does reveal.

The enforcement cases respond to particular conclusions about what relationship, or change in relationship, contract effects. That is, what exactly happens when I make a promise to you? Have I given you something the instant I make you a promise supported by consideration (or some alternative basis of promise enforcement)? Or, have I just undertaken to give you something sometime in the future if certain contingencies are satisfied? How might that distinction matter? Once we decide *when* I give you something, how do we know what it is I have given you and whether and how that something may be translated into the standard form of substitutional relief, *i.e.,* money damages? Does my (or your) state of mind, in terms of scienter, matter in deciding either what I have given you or what the consequences of my frustrating your expectations may be? That list of questions is not intended to be exhaustive, by any means; it is just suggestive of the richness of the enforcement inquiries. That richness reveals why there is so much at stake in coming to terms with the normative assertions of the enforcement doctrine. Incongruities in the doctrine's normative position may reveal as much about the doctrine, and the nature of the doctrine, as would normative consistency and symmetry.

The first canonical case challenges contract on several levels and presents a question we have confronted earlier in this book, but in another context, and thereby demonstrates the persistency of the normative inquiries at different doctrinal junctures: Judge Cardozo's analysis in *Jacob & Youngs, Inc. v. Kent*[2] resonates with the analysis of the Oklahoma Supreme Court in the first case.

A. *Peevyhouse v. Garland Coal & Mining Co.*[3]

The facts of *Peevyhouse* may have received more attention than those of any of the other cases in the contract canon[4] (perhaps with good reason). The facts are compelling. But so far as doctrine is concerned, all that matters is the court's statement of them. "The rest of the story" may be of interest to those who inquire at the edges of the doctrine, but canonical status would be determined by the law the case makes and that law can be no more than what the facts as found allow.

---

[2] Jacobs & Youngs, Inc. v. Kent, 129 N.E. 889 (N.Y. 1921); *see* discussion *supra* Chapter Five, "Contract Performance Doctrine."

[3] Peevyhouse v. Garland Coal & Mining Co., 382 P.2d 109 (Okla. 1963).

[4] Judith L. Maute, Peevyhouse v. Garland Coal & Mining Co. *Revisited: The Ballad of Willie and Lucille*, 89 Nw. U. L. Rev. 1341 (1995); The Ballad of Willie and Lucille: Disappointed Expectations of Contract Law and the Legal System (University of Oklahoma College of Law 2008) (documentary film).

The Peevyhouses entered into a coal mining lease with defendant Garland Coal & Mining Company that required the mining company to restore the land to its original appearance after the strip mining operation. When the work was completed, the cost of restoring the land to its pre-contract state would have been in the neighborhood of $25,000. The restoration, though, would increase the value of the land (from its unrestored state) by only "about $300."[5] Plaintiffs relied on a Minnesota case, *Groves v. John Wunder Co.*,[6] to support their argument that the damages to which they would be entitled was the amount required to restore the land to the condition to which defendant had undertaken to restore it. Defendant responded that the damages should not compensate plaintiffs for more than plaintiff had lost, the diminution in the value of the land resulting from defendant's failure to restore it.

Insofar as *Peevyhouse* was decided in 1962, the decision postdated the *First Contracts Restatement (First) of Contracts* (*First Restatement*), and the court cites Section 346 thereof. That section focuses on "economic waste" as the operative inquiry and provides, in pertinent part:

> (1) For a breach by one who has contracted to construct a specified product, the other party can get judgment for compensatory damages for all unavoidable harm that the builder had reason to foresee when the contract was made, less such part of the contract price as has not been paid and is still not payable, determined as follows:
> (a) For defective or unfinished construction he can get judgment for either
> (i) the reasonable cost of construction and completion in accordance with the contract, if this is possible *and does not involve unreasonable economic waste*; or
> (ii) the difference between the value that the product contracted for would have had and the value of the performance that had been received by the plaintiff, if construction and completion in accordance with the contract *would involve economic waste*.[7]

The *Peevyhouse* court cites that *Restatement* provision and relies on it although the contract in issue, a lease with subsequent incidental remedial work, was not strictly speaking a construction contract. The terms of the *First Restatement* provision concern specifically construction contracts, and thereby directly vindicate the *Jacob & Youngs* result. The contract in *Peevyhouse* did not concern construction as such but, according to the court, falls within the *Restatement* rule disfavoring economic waste.

---

[5] *Peevyhouse*, 382 P.2d at 112.

[6] Groves v. John Wunder Co., 286 N.W. 235 (Minn. 1939).

[7] RESTATEMENT (FIRST) OF CONTRACTS § 346 (1932) (emphasis added).

Ordering defendant to pay $25,000 to restore $300 worth of value would "involve unreasonable economic waste." The court notes the case's affinity with *Jacob & Youngs*: "The owner is entitled to the money which will permit him to complete, unless the cost of completion is grossly and unfairly out of proportion to the good to be attained. When that is true, the measure is the difference in value."[8]

The court also cites and relies upon an Oklahoma statute, which it acknowledges was applied more often in tort than contract cases, but which the court finds determinative:

> § 96 . . . Notwithstanding the provisions of this chapter, no person can recover a greater amount in damages for the breach of an obligation, than he would have gained by the full performance thereof on both sides. . . .
>
> § 97 . . . Damages must, in all cases, be reasonable, and where an obligation of any kind appears to create a right to unconscionable and grossly oppressive damages, contrary to substantial justice no more than reasonable damages can be recovered.[9]

The court also likens the damage claim made by plaintiffs to liquidated damages recoverable for breach of contract. Oklahoma statutory law invalidated contract clauses "which attempt to fix the amount of stipulated damages to be paid in case of a breach, except where it is impracticable or extremely difficult to determine the actual damages."[10] That rule would obtain "in spite of the agreement of the parties."[11] Excessive liquidated damages would be void as a penalty, and that rule continues in the statutory[12] and common law[13] of contract.

The problem that would result from the court's analysis, though, is obvious: How could someone *ever* enforce a contract the performance of which would result in an objective loss of value even if it also were to result in an idiosyncratic increase of value? The court responds to that concern too: "Where such result is in fact contemplated by the parties, and is a main or principal purpose of those contracting, it would seem that the measure of damages for breach would ordinarily be the cost of performance."[14] This, too, was a problem confronting Judge Cardozo in *Jacob & Youngs* and he responded similarly. A court will enforce the clear intent of the parties with regard to idiosyncratic value, but there will be a strong presumption against such a construction of the contract. The court retains considerable discretion, it would seem, to determine whether the contract contemplated recovery of idiosyncratic rather than objective value.

---

[8] *Peevyhouse,* 382 P.2d at 113 (citing Jacobs & Youngs, Inc. v. Kent, 129 N.E. 889, 892 (N.Y. 1921)).

[9] *Id.* (citing OKLA. STAT. ANN. tit. 23, § 96 (1961); OKLA. STAT. ANN. tit. 23, § 97 (1961)).

[10] *Id.*

[11] *Id.*

[12] UCC § 2-718 (2002).

[13] RESTATEMENT (SECOND) OF CONTRACTS § 348, cmt. c (1981).

[14] *Peevyhouse,* 382 P.2d at 114.

The dissent makes clear that defendant's state of mind may matter[15] (as had Judge Cardozo in *Jacobs & Young*). There was evidence to the effect that plaintiff would not have entered into the contract with defendant if defendant had not agreed to restore the land. Indeed, plaintiffs may have insisted upon a different royalty fee had they not been assured the land would be restored. There was no overreaching on the part of plaintiffs; defendant was the dominant contracting party. The dissent would have followed *Groves*. Defendant appreciated what it had undertaken and the dissent concludes that the breach was willful. The willfulness of the breach too justified the award of damages measured by cost of performance rather than diminution of value.

Peevyhouse and *Groves* often travel in tandem, in the casebooks at least.[16] *Peevyhouse* has attracted significant attention and even scorn.[17] The *Restatement (Second) of Contracts* (*Second Restatement*) offers a rule that takes the decision into account. Section 348 concerns "Alternatives to Loss in Value of Performance," and provides:

> (1) If a breach delays the use of property and the loss in value to the injured party is not proved with reasonable certainty, he may recover damages based on the rental value of the property or on interest on the value of the property.
> (2) If a breach results in defective or unfinished construction and the loss in value to the injured party is not proved with sufficient certainty, he may recover damages based on
>   (a) the diminution in the market price of the property caused by the breach, or
>   (b) the reasonable cost of completing performance or of remedying the defects if that cost is not clearly disproportionate to the probable loss in value to him.
> (3) If a breach is of a promise conditioned on a fortuitous event and it is uncertain whether the event would have occurred had there been no breach, the injured party may recover damages based on the value of the conditional right at the time of breach.[18]

---

[15] *Id.* at 114–16 (Irwin, J., dissenting) (noting that all conditions at time of contracting were reasonably foreseeable and defendants willfully breached their duties established in contract).

[16] *See, e.g.,* Randy E. Barnett, Contracts: Cases and Doctrine 929–40 (4th ed. 2008); E. Allan Farnsworth & William F. Young, Cases and Materials on Contracts 612–21 (3d ed. 1980); Robert S. Summers & Robert A. Hillman, Contract and Related Obligation: Theory, Doctrine, and Practice 209–20 (5th ed. 2006).

[17] *See* Curtis Bridgeman, *Corrective Justice in Contract Law: Is There a Case for Punitive Damages?* 56 Vand. L. Rev. 237, 264–68 (2003) (Rationale ultimately applied by Oklahoma Supreme Court in *Peevyhouse* could create perverse incentives for parties with greater contractual sophistication to take advantage of less sophisticated parties.); Christopher L. Eisgruber, *Teaching Law Through Contracts and Cardozo*, 44 St. Louis U. L.J. 1511, 1515 n.4 (2000) (In *Peevyhouse,* "the 'tortfeasor' (if there was one) actually benefited from the court's departure from contract principles!"); Richard S. Wirtz, *Cost of Performance or Difference in Value?*, 59 Case W. Res. L. Rev. 61 (2008) (discussing shortcomings of many remedial theories and criticizing failure in *Peevyhouse* to restore Peevyhouses to position they would have been in had contract been fully performed).

[18] Restatement (Second) of Contracts § 348 (1981).

Though subsection 348(2) pertains most directly to *Peevyhouse*, the entire section concerns the calculation of the expectation measure of damages and we should be able to find some symmetry in each subsection's iteration of the rule. That provision operates only if plaintiff, the non-breaching party, is not able to prove the loss in value to him *with sufficient certainty*. The disappointed promisee may recover damages measured *either* by the diminution in market price, an objective measure, *or* reasonable cost of repair. In the first instance, the option is the promisee's. Only if "the cost [of repair] is . . . clearly disproportionate to the probable loss in value to him" is the promisee limited to the diminution in market price measure, the *Peevyhouse* measure. The quibble with *Peevyhouse* has been with regard to the court's construction of the facts: Had the Peeveyhouses in fact *not* made clear the diminution in value to them? Did the contract specifically fix that value? And had defendant already contracted away the right to question the promisee's valuation?[19] Indeed, that was the same pressure point that was prominent in *Jacob & Youngs*: What could the owner have done to make any more clear his insistence on Reading pipe?

So the challenge, then, in deciding whether the promisee has the option of insisting upon cost of repair is twofold. First, has the promisee made clear that he was in fact contracting for the *cost* rather than the *value* of repair? Second, if the promisee has not established that loss in value with sufficient certainty, is the cost of repair "clearly disproportionate to the probable loss in value to the promisee?" If it is clearly disproportionate, then the promisee will not be entitled to the cost of repair measure *unless* he can demonstrate with sufficient certainty the loss in value to him. Either way, the promisee should be able to recover the cost of repair upon a sufficient showing of diminution of even idiosyncratic value.

Comment c to Section 348 elaborates. The comment explains that in the event the promisee is not able to prove the loss in value to him "with reasonable certainty," then his recovery of damages measured by cost of repair "[may] give[] him a recovery somewhat in excess of the loss in value to him, [and] it is better that he receive a *small windfall* than that he be undercompensated by being limited to the resulting diminution in the market price of his property."[20] If, however, damages measured by cost of repair would result in a large windfall, "[s]uch an award will not be made."[21] Still the comment recognizes that idiosyncratic value may be recovered, on the right facts:

> "If an award based on the cost to remedy the defects would clearly be excessive *and the injured party does not prove the actual loss in value to him*, damages will be based instead on the difference between the market price that the property would have

[19] *See* Bridgeman, *supra* note 17, at 237, 264–65; Maute, *supra* note 4, at 1358.

[20] Restatement (Second) of Contracts § 348 cmt. c (1981) (emphasis added).

[21] *Id.*

had without the defects and the market price of the property with the defects."[22] Illustration 4 to that comment is based on *Jacob & Youngs*, and the *Reporter's Note* also cites *Peevyhouse* as *cf.* authority for that same illustration.[23] Interestingly, *Groves v. Wunder*,[24] the foil to *Peevyhouse*,[25] is cited, also preceded by the *cf.* signal, in the *Reporter's Note* to illustration 3 to comment c. That illustration is consistent with the language in the comment to the effect that a "small windfall" is acceptable.[26]

Peevyhouse is challenging for the same reason that *Jacob & Youngs* is challenging: Both cases straddle the normative tension between autonomy, the promisee's right to what she contracted for, no matter how idiosyncratic her valuation of that object, and consequentialist objectives, specifically efficiency. In both cases, you have to know more about the facts than the reports provide to be certain that the courts' resolution of the tension was wrong. But what makes *Peevyhouse* (and *Jacob & Youngs*, for that matter) canonical (or, rather, what contributes to their being canonical) is the case's presentation of the tension, not the case's resolution of it. Not only is the tension persistent, but it is fundamental to the doctrine and its operation. It is not surprising, then, that both *Jacob & Youngs*, a case that may be construed in formation terms, and *Peevyhouse*, a damages case, both betray the same doctrinal characteristic. Ultimately, both cases are fact-sensitive, and we can best take issue with the courts' conclusions by taking issue with the courts' presentation of the facts.[27] But we cannot appraise the canonical value of the *Peevyhouse* decision by reference to which facts the court chooses to present; we must only consider how the court's presentation of the facts supports the doctrine. Disagreements about the facts are interesting, but they do not shed much light on the doctrine that emerges from the case, not really.

The *Hoffman v. Red Owl Stores* case was considered with regard to treatment of the promise element in Chapter Three, "Contract Formation Doctrine." (A presentation of the *Hoffman* facts will not be repeated here.) It is worthwhile to consider the damages aspects of the decision at this juncture, followed by presentation of the damages doctrine developed in another canonical promissory estoppel case.

---

[22] *Id.* (emphasis added).

[23] When the SECOND RESTATEMENT was completed, the twelfth edition of the BLUEBOOK was in effect. The description of the signal *cf.* in that edition of the BLUEBOOK states "[c]ited authority supports a proposition different from that in text but sufficiently analogous to lend support. Literally, '*cf.*' means 'compare'. . . ." THE BLUEBOOK: A UNIFORM SYSTEM OF CITATION R. 2.3(a) at 7 (Columbia Law Review Ass'n et al. eds., 12th ed. 1976).

[24] Groves v. John Wunder Co., 286 N.W. 235 (Minn. 1939).

[25] Peevyhouse v. Garland Coal & Mining Co., 382 P.2d 109, 111–12 (Okla. 1963) (citing, but not following, *Groves v. John Wunder Co.*).

[26] The "windfall" provided in the *Groves* case was $15,000.

[27] *See* Maute, *supra* note 4, at 1341.

B. *Hoffman v. Red Owl Stores*[28]

In *Hoffman v. Red Owl Stores,* the court concludes that Mrs. Hoffman, to whom defendant had made no direct representations, could nonetheless recover for losses she sustained as a result of the promises made to her husband. So Red Owl was liable for the loss suffered by Mrs. Hoffman, the sale of jointly held property at a loss in reliance on Red Owl's promise, even though Mrs. Hoffman was not the promisee. The court reasons that Red Owl's liability to Mrs. Hoffman was premised on foreseeability: "[I]f the promisor actually foresees, or has reason to foresee, action by a third person in reliance on the promise, it may be quite unjust to refuse to perform the promise."[29] That result is an expansion of the general contract conception of damage liability: Although a breaching party may be liable in contract to intended third-party beneficiaries, there would be no liability to merely incidental beneficiaries.[30] The court also awards the Hoffmans reliance damages, measured by the rental paid on a home into which they would have moved and the moving expenses actually incurred in reliance on Red Owl's representations.

The element of damages to which the court devotes most attention is the loss the Hoffmans allegedly incurred as a result of having sold the grocery store they had acquired to gain experience in the trade, in anticipation of acquiring the Red Owl store. The question presented was whether plaintiffs were entitled to the benefit of their "bargain" with Red Owl, an amount that would have compensated them for profits lost as a result of selling the store, or merely the "actual loss sustained measured by the difference between the sales price and the fair market value"[31] of the store. The court reasons that, in a promissory estoppel action, the successful plaintiff is not entitled to the benefit of the bargain or expectation measure, *i.e.,* the profit plaintiff would have realized but for the promisor's breach, but instead can recover only an amount that would compensate plaintiff for the detriment suffered as a result of plaintiff's change of position.

Hoffman relied on the *First Restatement's* formulation of the promissory estoppel doctrine and the *Second Restatement*, in turn, relied on *Hoffman*. Section 90 of the *Second Restatement* provides, in pertinent part, that

> (1) A promise which the promisor should reasonably expect to induce action or forbearance on the part of the promisee or a third person and which does induce such action or forbearance is binding if injustice can be avoided only by enforcement of the promise. The remedy granted for breach may be limited as justice requires.[32]

---

[28] Hoffman v. Red Owl Stores, 133 N.W.2d 267 (Wis. 1965).

[29] *Id.* at 275 (citing Corbin on Contracts, p. 187).

[30] *See* discussion *supra* Chapter Five, "Contract Performance Doctrine."

[31] *Hoffman,* 133 N.W.2d at 277.

[32] Restatement (Second) of Contracts § 90 (1981).

That reformulation resonates with the *Hoffman* analysis and gloss on the *First Restatement*. The damages awarded by the court are consistent with the *Second Restatement*'s reformulation. The *First Restatement* says nothing specifically about damages, reflecting Williston's idea that promissory estoppel provides merely an alternative means to enforce a contract rather than an alternative theory of promise enforcement.[33] *Hoffman* concludes that the damages awarded "should be only such as in the opinions of the court are necessary to prevent injustice."[34] That becomes "may be limited as justice requires" in the *Second Restatement*. But the comment to the *Second Restatement* formulation makes clear that recovery on the promissory estoppel basis is recovery in contract: "A promise binding under this section is a contract, and full-scale enforcement by normal remedies is often appropriate."[35]

Hoffman has been read as a case more about the enforceability of promises made in the course of preliminary negotiations than a case about the contours of the promissory estoppel doctrine.[36] It clearly does present, if not so thoroughly illuminate, the questions surrounding liability arising in the course of preliminary negotiations. There has also been a relatively recent and rich literature concerning the substance of the doctrine. Is reliance necessary at all?[37] Or is a "serious promise"[38] enough? Does the promissory estoppel doctrine matter all that much?[39] This is not the place to recount the contours of that dialog or to offer empirical conclusions about the doctrine's viability in the courts. For present purposes, identifying the contract canon, it suffices to note the vibrancy of the debate as evidence of the doctrine's vitality.

Promissory estoppel is clearly doctrine contract theorists need to explain. The idea that a promise may be enforced with or without some modicum of reliance and certainly *without* consideration helps us make sense of, or at least supports our positing, a normative basis of contract. Promissory estoppel, as an enforcement mechanism operating without the consideration formality, presents starkly the normative challenge: *Why* do

---

33 *See* Edward Yorio & Steve Thel, *The Promissory Basis of Section 90*, 101 YALE L. J. 111, 116–19 (1991) (recounting colloquy between Williston and Coudert regarding measure of liability).

34 *Hoffman*, 133 N.W.2d at 276.

35 RESTATEMENT (SECOND) OF CONTRACTS § 90 cmt. d (1981).

36 *See* Joel M. Ngugi, *Promissory Estoppel: The Life History of An Ideal Legal Transplant*, 41 U. RICH. L. REV. 425 (2007); Jean Fleming Powers, *Promissory Estoppel and Wagging the Dog*, 59 ARK. L. REV. 841 (2007); Kevin M. Teeven, *A History of Promissory Estoppel: Growth in the Face of Doctrinal Resistance*, 72 TENN. L. REV. 1111 (2005).

37 Juliet P. Kostritsky, *The Rise and Fall of Promissory Estoppel Or Is Promissory Estoppel Really as Unsuccessful As Scholars Say It Is: A New Look at the Data*, 37 WAKE FOREST L. REV. 531, 537 n.32 (2002).

38 Daniel A. Farber & John H. Matheson, *Beyond Promissory Estoppel: Contract Law and the "Invisible Handshake,"* 52 U. CHI. L. REV. 903 (1985).

39 Robert A. Hillman, *Instinct with an Obligation and the Normative Ambiguity of Rhetorical Power*, 56 OHIO ST. L. J. 775 (1995); Juliet P. Kostritsky, *Uncertainty, Reliance, Preliminary Negotiations and the Holdup Problem*, 61 SMU L. REV. 1377 (2008).

we enforce some promises but not others? The empirical conclusions of those who have tracked the cases, though, certainly matter.[40] But it may be at least premature to conclude that the doctrine does not matter, or matters less because the cases do not take sufficient advantage of it.[41] Insofar as the doctrine takes up so much space in the *Restatements* and the casebooks (and time in most first-year contracts courses), we can easily conclude that promissory estoppel, as described if not strictly applied in cases such as *Hoffman*, informs our understanding of what contract would be without it. There must be a gap to which the doctrine responds; promissory estoppel must accomplish something that contract could not accomplish without it. Promissory estoppel completes, or at least complements, contract.

C. *Ricketts v. Scothorn*[42]

Ricketts v. Scothorn is a reliance case, pure and simple. There was certainly a promise supporting plaintiff's reliance, but there can be no question that it was the actual reliance that, in the court's estimation, made the promise enforceable. John Ricketts, grandfather of Katie Scothorn, gave her a promissory note in order to induce Katie to leave her employment as a bookkeeper "and cease to work for a living."[43] When Ricketts gave Scothorn the note, in return for no consideration, he told her he was doing so, so that she would not need to work: "[N]one of my grandchildren work, and you don't have to."[44] Katie immediately quit her job and remained unemployed for over a year. Then, with the permission and assistance of her grandfather, the maker of the note, she went back to work. The court finds that Ricketts required no *quid pro quo* for the promise evidenced by the note he gave Scothorn. It was a gratuitous promise.

The court begins its analysis by adverting to the charitable subscription cases, which, the court concludes, were based on considerations of estoppel: "[T]he true reason is preclusion of the defendant, under the doctrine of estoppel, to deny the consideration."[45] Now had the grandfather *required* the granddaughter to surrender her employment in return for the note, there would have been sufficient consideration supporting the promissory obligation. But he never imposed such a requirement, so plaintiff could not rely on

---

[40] *See* Sidney W. DeLong, *The New Requirement of Enforcement Reliance in Commercial Promissory Estoppel: Section 90 as Catch-22*, 1997 Wis. L. Rev. 943 (1997); Robert A. Hillman, *Questioning the "New Consensus" on Promissory Estoppel: An Empirical and Theoretical Study*, 98 Colum. L. Rev. 580 (1998); Kostritsky, *supra* note 39.

[41] *See* DeLong, *supra* note 40; Hillman, *supra* note 40; Kostritsky, *supra* note 39.

[42] Ricketts v. Scothorn, 77 N.W. 365 (Neb. 1898).

[43] *Id.* at 366.

[44] *Id.*

[45] *Id.*

the consideration doctrine and could only recover, if at all, on the basis of the equitable doctrine of estoppel, which the court finds helpfully formulated in a treatise on equity:

> Equitable estoppel is the effect of the voluntary conduct of a party whereby he is absolutely precluded, both at law and in equity, from asserting rights which might, perhaps, have otherwise existed, either of property, of contract, or of remedy, as against another person who in good faith relied upon such conduct, and has been led thereby to change his position for the worse, and who on his part acquires some corresponding right, either of property, of contract, or of remedy.[46]

The grandfather intentionally influenced plaintiff's actions. So the bases for equitable estoppel were satisfied.

The *Second Restatement* cites *Ricketts*, preceded by the *cf.* signal, in support of illustration 4 to Section 90. That illustration is based on *Feinberg v. Pfeiffer*:[47] "A has been employed by B for 40 years. B promises to pay A a pension of $200 per month when A retires. A retires and forbears to work elsewhere for several years while B pays the pension. B's promise is binding."[48]

The difference between *Ricketts* and *Feinberg*, as distilled by that illustration and the comment's *cf.* citation to *Ricketts,* must be that plaintiff in *Ricketts* went back to work but plaintiff in *Feinberg* did not, perhaps could not. Certainly the duration of the period of unemployment could not fix the *existence* of the promissory estoppel right, though it could, quite conceivably, fix the measure of damages the right would vindicate. The *cf.* signal then is, at best, ambiguous. It does not seem, though, that it does anything to impair the significance of *Ricketts* so far as the doctrine or the canonical status of the case is concerned.

What is particularly noteworthy about *Ricketts* and *Feinberg* (and other promissory estoppel cases, for that matter) is the fit between estoppel and the consideration-based promise enforcement they reveal. It may not be entirely accurate to appreciate the promissory estoppel doctrine in isolation, as separate and apart from consideration, in the bargain sense. That is, we might best understand how the two alternative enforcement bases operate when we come to terms with their cooperation. The breadth of the promissory estoppel enforcement mechanism may expand or contract by reference to the court's or jurisdiction's consideration rules: It may be that the more relaxed the jurisdiction's consideration requirement, the less the court would need to find promissory estoppel. The converse may be true as well: The more stringent the consideration requirement, the more likely to find the premises of promissory estoppel the court may be. That would also

---

[46] *Id.* at 367 (citing 2 POMEROY'S EQUITY JURISPRUDENCE 804).

[47] Feinberg v. Pfeiffer, 322 S.W.2d 163 (Mo. App. 1959).

[48] RESTATEMENT (SECOND) OF CONTRACTS § 90 illus. 4 (1981).

impact the elements of each of those enforcement mechanisms: When the court *needs* promissory estoppel to do "justice," the court may relax the reliance requirement or find the requisite promise from a less certain factual predicate. Problem is, the forces that would impact courts' factual conclusions could be largely hidden. We might not know what motivated a particular court's factual conclusion and even were we to learn "the rest of the story" that would not impact the doctrine formulated. The promissory estoppel calculus is so fact-dependent that its parameters, and perhaps most particularly its parameters *vis-à-vis* bargain, are vague (and malleable). Conceptions of justice are no more fixed and certain (and, indeed even less fixed and certain) than the premises of unconscionability. A 1988 decision of an Australian court recognizes the unconscionability–estoppel parallel.

In *Walton Stores (Interstate) Ltd. v. Maher,*[49] Walton Stores negotiated with Maher, the owner of land, to lease the land. The transaction contemplated that Maher would demolish a building on the land and construct another in its place according to Walton Stores's specifications. Having been led by Walton Stores to believe that the draft lease was acceptable, Maher demolished the existing building and actually completed about 40 percent of the new structure before Walton Stores notified Maher that it did not intend to go forward with the deal. The court does not find a promise sufficient to support enforcement on a consideration basis. Instead, the court finds that defendant was estopped to deny that a contract existed.

The court notes the development of promissory estoppel theory in the United States, particularly in the *Second Restatement,* Section 90 form, and notes too, somewhat curiously, Judge Cardozo's opinion in *Allegheny College v. National Chautauqua County Bank*, which was *not* a promissory estoppel case, but did have something to say about the fit between consideration and estoppel bases of promise enforcement. In the *Walton Stores* court's account of that fit we get the sense of the consideration-promissory estoppel dynamic:

> [In the United States] promissory estoppel developed partly in response to the limiting effects of the adoption of the bargain theory of consideration which has not been expressly adopted in Australia or England. It may be doubted whether our conception of consideration is substantially broader than the bargain theory . . ., though we may be willing to imply consideration in situations where the bargain theory as implemented in the United States would deny the existence of consideration. *It is perhaps sufficient to say that in the United States, as in Australia, there is an obvious interrelationship between the doctrines of consideration and promissory estoppel,*

[49] Walton Stores (Interstate) Ltd. v. Maher (1988) 164 C.L.R. 387 (Austl.).

> *promissory estoppel tending to occupy ground left vacant due to the constraints affecting consideration.*[50]

The court then notes that the *Restatement* formulation seems, at first, to owe more to contract than the equitable doctrine of unconscionability, the basis of the Australian and English estoppel concepts. But the fact that the United States conception is premised on the promisee's reasonable expectation and the "impossibility of avoiding injustice by other means . . . makes it clear that the promise is enforced in circumstances where departure from it is unconscionable."[51] So *Walton Stores* demonstrates both the nature of the codependent relationship between bargain and promissory estoppel and the symbiosis between the estoppel theory of promise enforcement and unconscionability.

The *Walton Stores* court's summation of its inquiry reveals an appreciation of the unconscionability within promissory estoppel that makes more sense of *Hoffman* than some contemporary commentators may have been able to appreciate:

> The foregoing review of the doctrine of promissory estoppel indicates that the doctrine extends to the enforcement of voluntary promises on the footing that a departure from the basic assumptions underlying the transaction between the parties must be unconscionable. As failure to fulfil a promise does not of itself amount to unconscionable conduct, mere reliance on an executory promise to do something, resulting in the promisee changing his position or suffering detriment, does not bring promissory estoppel into play. Something more would be required. . . . [T]his may be found, if at all, in the creation or encouragement by the party estopped in the other party of an assumption that a contract will come into existence or a promise will be performed and that the other party relied on that assumption to his detriment to the knowledge of the first party.[52]

So construed, there would seem to be agreement among common law jurisdictions about the basis of promissory estoppel and the relationship between promissory estoppel and bargain theory. That agreement might not be expressly acknowledged in the *Restatements'* and particular courts' formulations of the doctrine, but in substance it might well be inevitable.

Although promissory estoppel provides an alternative means to enforce a promise, as well as an alternative measure of damages, contract has often been understood in terms of the expectation or benefit of the bargain damages measure: The contract action should put the non-breaching party in the same position she would have been in had the promisor

---

[50] *Id.* at 402 (emphasis added).

[51] *Id.*

[52] *Id.* at 406.

not breached; no better, no worse. Indeed, it may be the damage measure that defines contract. That is, so long as damages put you in the same position you would have been in but for the breach of promise, your recovery is *in contract*, rather than the product of some other doctrinal means to vindicate your rights. So we may, then, better appreciate contract and its doctrinal footprint by coming to terms with the relationship between the contract doctrine and the damages calculus.

The promissory estoppel cases, particularly those construing Section 90 of the *Second Restatement*, consider what "justice requires" in fixing damages, which may be less than expectation. The reliance measure, for example, is akin to the out-of-pocket damages of tort law. But restitution also provides a measure of recovery in contract actions, and the doctrine is, again, formulated by a canonical case.

D. *Britton v. Turner*[53]

Decided by a New Hampshire court in the early part of the 19th Century, *Britton v. Turner* concerns the breaching party's recovery, on a *quantum meruit* basis, for services performed prior to the breach. The tension is obvious: If the breaching party does recover, on any basis, he has received some of the benefit of his bargain without having kept his promise; if the breaching party does not recover anything at all, the non-breaching party receives a windfall, something for nothing. Either way, someone will receive something they may not *deserve,* if desert is fixed by contract.

In *Britton*, the plaintiff-breaching party agreed to work for one year in exchange for $120 and failed to work for the full time specified by the contract. The court reasons that plaintiff could not recover on the contract because plaintiff had not performed the contract. The court is struck by the injustice of such a rule. If plaintiff's failure to complete the contract, which might well result in but small damage to the promisee, were an absolute bar to plaintiff's recovery, plaintiff-promisor who all but completely performed might be worse off than the promisor who breached immediately after making the promise but before beginning performance at all. Further, the promisor who performed in part may well have provided the promisee a greater benefit. So insistence upon full performance before permitting the promisor any recovery could both impose an inequitable hardship on the breaching promisor and provide the promisee a wholly inequitable benefit: something, perhaps something quite valuable, for nothing.

The court's analysis anticipates Judge Cardozo's opinion in *Jacob & Youngs*:

> The party who contracts for labor merely, for a certain period, does so with full knowledge that he must, from the nature of the case, be accepting part performance

---

[53] Britton v. Turner, 6 N.H. 481 (1834).

> from day to day, if the other party commences the performance, and with knowledge also that the other may eventually fail of completing the entire term.
>
> If under such circumstances he actually receives a benefit from the labor performed, over and above the damage occasioned by the failure to complete, there is as much reason why he should pay the reasonable worth of what has thus been done for his benefit, as there is when he enters and occupies the house which has been built for him, but not according to the stipulations of the contract, and which he perhaps enters, not because he is satisfied with what has been done, but because circumstances compel him to accept it such as it is, that he should pay for the value of the house.[54]

Just as in *Jacob & Youngs*, you might wonder what the promisee would need to do in order to assure that the promisor who incompletely performs cannot saddle the promisee with the consequences of that incomplete performance. After all, the promisee in *Jacob & Youngs* did specify Reading pipe, and the promisee in *Britton* did stipulate employment for one full year. The question could be construed as one of insufficiently expressed intent. Certainly there would not be any contract reason one could not promise to perform in accordance with the strictest requirements of the contract. Judge Cardozo even suggests that had Kent's requirements been more certainly provided the law would not have excused Jacob & Youngs's failure to more perfectly perform. It is difficult to imagine how Kent's intent could have been more clearly expressed. Similarly, it is difficult to imagine what part of "work one year from some time in March 1931, to March 1832"[55] would have been unclear to plaintiff in *Britton*. The court suggests, as Judge Cardozo does in *Jacob & Youngs*, that the promisee could have protected itself from the imposition of any liability upon the promisor's breach:

> It is easy, if the parties so choose, to provide by an express agreement that nothing shall be earned, if the laborer leaves his employer without having performed the whole service contemplated, and then there can be no pretence for a recovery if he voluntarily deserts the service before the expiration of the time.[56]

The court then *seems* to alter course. Though the promisee would have no liability *on the contract* for what the promisor's performance provided the promisee, the promisee would be liable in *quantum meruit* for the "reasonable worth, or the amount of advantage he receives upon the whole transaction, . . . and, in estimating the value of the labor, the

---

[54] *Id.* at 489.

[55] *Id.* at 481.

[56] *Id.* at 493–94.

contract price for the service cannot be exceeded."[57] So the breaching promisee will recover, and that recovery will even be measured by the valuation of the promisee's work set by the contract, but the promisee's recovery will not be in contract. Although the promisee will not recover for partial performance of the contract, he will recover to the extent of any benefit realized by the promisee as a result of that partial performance. On the facts of *Britton*, the breaching promisor was entitled to $95, for nine and one-half months work pursuant to a contract that would have paid him $120 for a full year's work. It is difficult to take issue with the conclusion that the case does some violence to conceptions of consent in contract. The only intellectually honest conclusion is that there is some intent contract will not brook, perhaps no matter how clearly and certainly recited. That is the point at which contract ends and restitution, *quantum meruit*, begins.

The *Britton* court acknowledges that it is extending *quantum meruit* into a setting in which it had not yet found purchase. The prior cases, in which the promisee was aware of deficiencies in the promisor's performance but seemed to suffer them without objection,[58] could support the conclusion that the promisee had, by its acquiescence, in fact agreed to a modification of the strict performance requirements of the contract. The facts of *Britton*, though, would support no such inference of consent.

> It cannot be contended that the defendant consented to receive a part of the labor, and be accountable for such part; no contract to this effect can be implied. He had it not in his power to prevent this part execution, as in the case of building the house, bridge, &c. nor could he deliver back the labor done. If any contract is fastened upon him, it is put upon him against his consent. He made a contract for an entire year's work. He has never consented to receive and pay for any time less than a year. No such consent can be implied.[59]

Well, if there is no consent, there cannot be a contract, unless we are willing to acknowledge that consent does not fix the borders of contract. And we must be willing to do so.

Britton recognizes the limits of consent in contract, just as do many of the canonical cases, *Jacob & Youngs* included, that go beyond the parties' consent to fix the parties' contract liability. The promissory estoppel cases, too, rely on what may be an equitable

---

[57] *Id.* at 494.

[58] *See* Hayward v. Leonard, 24 Mass. 181 (1828) (Because defendant failed to object to minor deviations in materials and workmanship until house he had contracted for was completed, he could not then refuse it.); Jewell v. Schroeppel, 4 Cow. 564 (N.Y. Sup. Ct. 1825) (requiring defendant to pay plaintiff for labor and material when defendant allowed plaintiff to complete construction of mill outside of time required in original contract); Hayden v. Madison, 7 Me. 76 (1830) (Partial payment made to plaintiff before he had completed construction of road for township constituted waiver, and town was required to pay for as much of road as had been completed.).

[59] *Britton*, 6 N.H. at 481.

adjunct to contract to determine liability beyond that consensually assumed. *Quantum meruit*, like promissory estoppel, reveals much about contract by circumscribing its scope.

Section 357 of the *First Restatement* captures the *Britton* rule, but adds a flourish or two:

> (1) Where the defendant fails or refuses to perform his contract and is justified therein by the plaintiff's own breach of duty or non-performance of a condition, but the plaintiff has rendered a part performance under the contract that is a net benefit to the defendant, the plaintiff can get judgment . . . for the amount of such benefit in excess of the harm that he has caused to the defendant by his own breach, in no case exceeding a ratable proportion of the agreed compensation, if
> (a) the plaintiff's breach or non-performance is not wilful and deliberate; or
> (b) the defendant, with knowledge that the plaintiff's breach of duty or non-performance of condition has occurred or will thereafter occur, assents to the rendition of the part performance, or accepts the benefit of it, or retains property received although its return in specie is still not unreasonably difficult or injurious.[60]

Note that the *First Restatement's* formulation of the rule expressly invokes the scienter consideration to which Judge Cardozo alludes in *Jacob & Youngs*: Plaintiff's breach must not have been willful or deliberate. Even if it is not so clear what sense it makes to consider a breach willful or deliberate as opposed to, maybe, inadvertent, it is noteworthy that the equitable balance is captured in the rule. The formulation also finds something like consent on the part of defendant, the non-breaching party. The rule seems to infer consent to restitution liability from the fact that defendant assents to the part performance *"or accepts the benefit of it."* On the facts of a case like *Britton*, the non-breaching party has benefitted from the part performance, the performance rendered prior to plaintiff-breaching party's walking off the job. Indeed, defendant could not return that part performance, so it is difficult to find anything like real consent.

Given the premises of the *First Restatement* rule, it may not be so clear that it captures *Britton*. In *Britton*, the breaching party had certainly willfully breached—perhaps left the non-breaching party's employ because he had found a better job,[61] not an inadvertent action in any event—so maybe the breaching party would not be entitled to recovery under subsection (1)(a) of the *First Restatement* rule. Further, the non-breaching party in *Britton* did not assent to the part performance, though perhaps had no choice but to

---

[60] RESTATEMENT (FIRST) OF CONTRACTS § 357 (1932).

[61] *Britton*, 6 N.H. at 481 ("And it was contended by the defendant that the plaintiff had no good cause for not continuing in his employment.").

accept the benefit of it. Even then, that acceptance of the benefit was not "with knowledge that the plaintiff's breach of duty or non-performance of condition has occurred or will thereafter occur." Plaintiff's breach was a *fait accompli* by the time defendant had received the benefit of plaintiff's labor. Indeed, were defendant able to argue that he could not return the labor to plaintiff, an obvious physical impossibility, perhaps defendant would be able to resist restitution on that basis. So maybe *Britton* would have slipped through the *First Restatement* formulation.

Though no illustration to the *First Restatement* section clearly presents the *Britton* facts, illustration 4 comes closest:

> A contracts to work for B for one year, at a salary of $200 per month. After working six and a half months, A deliberately leaves B's service because he is offered a better job. Before the breach, B had paid A $1000 and had temporarily retained the last month's salary of $200 with A's consent. B gets an equally good workman at once at the same salary and suffers no injury. A can get judgment for $200–the salary due for the last month—because the salary was apportioned; but he has a right to nothing for his half month's service, even though B has no counterclaim for more than nominal damages.[62]

It matters, in the illustration, that "the salary was apportioned." Presumably, such apportionment could matter only because it was the parties who bargained to it. On the facts of *Britton*, there was no evidence or allegation of such an express apportionment. Plaintiff had contracted to work for one year for $120 and had only worked nine and one-half months. Note too that plaintiff in the illustration provided defendant the benefit of one half month's work, for which plaintiff would receive no compensation under the *First Restatement* rule.

Nonetheless, the third subsection of the *First Restatement* provision resonates with the *Britton* court's damages calculus:

> (3) The measure of the defendant's benefit from the plaintiff's part performance is the amount by which he has been enriched as a result of such performance unless the facts are those stated in Subsection (1)(b), in which case it is the price fixed by the contract for such part performance, or, if no price is so fixed, a ratable proportion of the total contract price.[63]

That subsection would operate *in the event* that the provision's premises have first been satisfied, inadvertent breach or defendant's retention of the benefit on terms that suggest

[62] Restatement (First) of Contracts § 357 illus. 4 (1932).

[63] *Id.* § 357.

defendant's actual or implicit assent to plaintiff's incomplete performance. So although that third subsection mirrors the *Britton* approach, it is not clear that it would operate on the facts of the canonical case itself.

Subection 374(1) of the *Second Restatement* continues much of the *First Restatement* iteration in its formulation of the *Britton* rule, but with noteworthy blurring of the edges.

> (1) Subject to the rule stated in Subsection (2), if a party justifiably refuses to perform on the ground that his remaining duties of performance have been discharged by the other party's breach, the party in breach is entitled to restitution for any benefit that he has conferred by way of part performance or reliance in excess of the loss that he has caused by his own breach.[64]

That changes the rule of the *First Restatement* by excluding any limitation premised on the breaching party's state of mind. Further, the breaching party's recovery is fixed by reference to the restitution measure but without any certain limitation to "a ratable proportion of the agreed compensation."

It would also seem that the *Second Restatement* formulation better tracks the *Britton* analysis and conclusion. That is, we can see that the *Second Restatement* would accommodate the *Britton* result though it is less clear that the *First Restatement* formulation would do so. Since *Britton* predated both *Restatements*, it is fair to say that the American Law Institute (ALI) came around to the doctrine described in that 1834 case, though it is not clear that the doctrine was altered essentially by the *First Restatement* in any event. Though it may be that the doctrine has been liberalized from the *First Restatement* to the *Second Restatement*,[65] the idea has remained the same: Contract, perhaps much as equity generally, abhors a forfeiture and strives to differing degrees to deny even innocent nonbreaching parties a windfall, unless, of course, the equitable balance shifts on account of the breaching party's "willfulness," whatever that might mean.[66]

The sense of the case has been confirmed in the statutory law. Section 2-718 of the Uniform Commercial Code (UCC or the Code) provides, in pertinent part, that

> (2) Where the seller justifiably withholds delivery of goods because of the buyer's breach, the buyer is entitled to restitution of any amount by which the sum of his payments exceeds
> (a) the amount to which the seller is entitled by virtue of terms liquidating the seller's damages . . ., or

---

[64] RESTATEMENT (SECOND) OF CONTRACTS § 374 (1981).

[65] E. ALLAN FARNSWORTH, FARNSWORTH ON CONTRACTS § 8.14, n.1 and sources cited therein (3d ed. 2004).

[66] *See* Richard A. Posner, *Let Us Never Blame a Contract Breaker*, 107 MICH L. REV. 1349, 1353 (2009).

(b) in the absence of such terms, twenty per cent of the value of the total performance for which the buyer is obligated under the contract or $500, whichever is smaller.

(3) The buyer's right to restitution under subsection (2) is subject to offset to the extent that the seller establishes

(a) a right to recover damages under the provisions of this Article . . ., and

(b) the amount or value of any benefits received by the buyer directly or indirectly by reason of the contract.[67]

The Code formulation, then, very directly ties the liquidated damages right to the restitution right: The buyer's right to restitution can be limited by the buyer's consent to the particular liquidated damages fixed in the contract, so long as the premises of such "consent" are established. It is subsection 2-718(1) that fixes the scope of the liquidated damages right, which is certainly more circumscribed than other rights about which the parties may contract. Though it is not immediately clear why,[68] the common law of contract as well as Article 2 of the UCC limit the right of the parties to incorporate a liquidated damages provision in their agreement. So long as there is no fraud or unconscionability, the parties are free to make a one-sided deal: You can contract to pay too much for something; the contract law includes no *adequacy* of consideration requirement, no general *reasonableness* requirement. But you can only agree to a liquidated damages clause to the extent that such a clause fixes the damages "at an amount that is reasonable in light of the anticipated or actual loss caused by the breach and the difficulties of proof of loss."[69]

The Code provision nicely ties together the liquidated damages limitation and the restitution right. The court that awards a breaching plaintiff restitution is doing no more than reaching the conclusion that denying plaintiff restitution would provide the non-breaching party the same type of inequitable windfall that enforcement of an unreasonable liquidated damages award would provide. The same is true of the substantial performance or condition analysis of *Jacob & Youngs*. There is equity underlying contract, as well as a concern with intentional overreaching that may be obscure in doctrinal statements that

---

[67] UCC § 2-718 (2002).

[68] *See* Robert A. Hillman, *The Limits of Behavioral Decision Theory in Legal Analysis: The Case of Liquidated Damages*, 85 CORNELL L. REV. 717 (2000); Jeffrey J. Rachlinski, *The "New" Law and Psychology: A Reply to Critics, Skeptics, and Cautious Supporters*, 85 CORNELL L. REV. 739 (2000).

[69] RESTATEMENT (SECOND) OF CONTRACTS § 356 (1981); *see also* UCC § 2-718(1) (2002) ("Damages for breach by either party may be liquidated in the agreement but only at an amount that is reasonable in the light of the anticipated or actual harm caused by the breach, the difficulties of proof of loss, and the inconvenience or nonfeasibility of otherwise obtaining an adequate remedy.").

emphasize contract's "strict liability" nature. Recent scholarship has just begun to come to terms with this aspect of the doctrine.[70]

Britton was concerned with striking a balance between the benefit received by the non-breaching party and the loss imposed on the breaching party. Contract liability is, perhaps curiously, bilateral,[71] that is, the loss suffered by the non-breaching party (the compensation) is deemed equal (by a type of legal fiat) to the damages the breaching party must pay. Whatever reasons we may have for awarding substitutional relief, it would be serendipitous in the extreme if contract fixed the normative costs and benefits so neatly. There is no reason to believe that what would compensate plaintiff would also incentivize (or disincentivize) the breaching party to breach. That is further complicated by the fact that we are not sure that the normative object of contract involves any imposition of liability premised on fault or blameworthiness. A culpability calculus is only ambiguously incorporated into contract, and that is nowhere more apparent than in the damages doctrine.

So, although *Britton* endeavors to assure that the breaching party would not be unduly punished for the breach and that the non-breaching party would not receive a windfall at the breaching party's expense (contract liability, after all, is supposed to be strict liability), other case law reinforces the *Britton* perspective. A duty to mitigate follows naturally from the *Britton* restitution limitation. The next case formulates that duty.

E. *Rockingham County v. Luten Bridge Co.*[72]

In *Rockingham County v. Luten Bridge Co.,* plaintiff was engaged to build a bridge for Rockingham County, North Carolina. Sometime between the initiation of the work on the bridge and its completion, the county notified Luten that it no longer needed the bridge. Luten could then have suspended work, saved whatever additional expense it would have incurred by completing the work, and recovered from Rockingham the profit it would have realized from completion of the project. In the event, Luten continued the work (and so kept the meter running) and brought an action against the county for the full contract price, including the costs that would have been saved had Luten discontinued work when first advised of Rockingham's change of mind.

There is some uncertainty in the opinion regarding the regularity of the contract formation process, but the doctrine of the case is dependent only on a stark presentation of the facts: The breaching party notifies the non-breaching party of the breaching party's

---

[70] *See* Symposium, *Fault in Contract Law*, 107 MICH. L. REV. 1341 (2009).

[71] *See* JULES COLEMAN, THE PRACTICE OF PRINCIPLE 13–24 (2001) (discussing bilateralism); Nathan B. Oman, *The Failure of Economic Interpretations of the Law of Contract Damages*, 64 WASH. & LEE L. REV. 829 (2007).

[72] Rockingham County v. Luten Bridge Co., 35 F.2d 301 (4th Cir. 1929).

intent to breach in time for the non-breaching party to limit its loss; but rather than mitigating damages, the non-breaching party continues its performance of the contract and thereby increases the loss it suffers. Should the breaching party be liable for that increased and avoidable loss? To find the breaching party liable would be to encourage inefficient behavior, *i.e.,* construction of a bridge to nowhere. The problem would not seem intractable, but for the complication that contract generally is understood as vindicating the expectation interest, and the non-breaching party had every expectation that it would be able to complete its performance and receive the agreed compensation therefor. To relieve the breaching party from some of that loss would be to import an idea redolent of the tort law, the last clear chance, to the contract context. And there is no obvious reason why a breaching party should have the right to adjust the non-breaching party's expectations.

Of course, there must be a duty to mitigate, else the law would be wasteful. What good reason, in either deontology or consequentialism, could there be for a rule that would encourage waste? None. The court states the rule in generic terms:

> If A enters into a binding contract to build a house for B, B, of course, has no right to rescind the contract without A's consent. But if, before the house is built, he decides that he does not want it, and notifies A to that effect, A has no right to proceed with the building and thus pile up damages. His remedy is to treat the contract as broken when he receives the notice, and sue for the recovery of such damages, as he may have sustained from the breach, including any profit which he would have realized upon performance, as well as any other losses which may have resulted to him.[73]

The non-breaching party is as well off after it mitigates as it would have been had there been no breach and the breaching party is spared expense that would in any event have inured to no one's benefit. The object of contract damages is, after all, to provide the non-breaching party the benefit of its bargain, no more.

The *First Restatement* captures the mitigation rule succinctly: "Damages are not recoverable for harm that the plaintiff should have foreseen and could have avoided by reasonable effort without undue risk, expense, and humiliation."[74] Indeed, that formulation seems to be even more indulgent of the rights of the breaching party than *Rockingham County* insofar as it requires the non-breaching party to assume *due* risk, expense, and humiliation.

The venerability of this mitigation idea is confirmed as well by the *Second Restatement*'s similarly succinct reformulation: "[D]amages are not recoverable for loss that the injured

---

[73] *Id.* at 307.

[74] RESTATEMENT (FIRST) OF CONTRACTS § 336(1) (1932).

party could have avoided without undue risk, burden or humiliation."[75] Illustration 1 to comment b invokes *Rockingham County*:

> A contracts to build a bridge for B for $100,000. B repudiates the contract shortly after A has begun work on the bridge, telling A that he no longer has need for it. A nevertheless spends an additional $10,000 in continuing to perform. A's damages for breach of contract do not include the $10,000.[76]

The case law in several common law jurisdictions supports the mitigation principle,[77] and the principle is also firmly established in the statutory law. For example, the damages sections of the UCC incorporate the mitigation principle. Section 2-715 provides that the disappointed buyer may recover consequential damages that could not have been avoided by cover (a replacement purchase).[78] Statutory law in Britain,[79] Canada,[80] and Australia[81] also confirms the rule.

The mitigation principle would seem to limit the exposure of breaching parties, but it would be an error to conclude that the doctrine is overindulgent of those who do not fulfill their obligations. Though non-breaching parties' duty to mitigate operates to avoid waste, and so will often benefit breaching parties who could have been victimized by such waste, contract's provision of consequential damages assures that the non-breaching party will realize the full benefit of her bargain, the expectation measure of damages. The next canonical case captures the delicate balance that pertains to consequential damage recovery.

---

[75] Restatement (Second) of Contracts § 350(1) (1981).

[76] *Id.* § 350 illus. 1.

[77] Australian: Burns v. M.A.N. Auto. (Austl.) Proprietary (1986) 161 C.L.R. 653, 659 ("[A] plaintiff's duty to mitigate his damage does not require him to do what is unreasonable. . . ."); British: Payzu, Ltd. v. Saunders, [1919] 2 K.B. 581 (C.A.) (Plaintiff refused to mitigate damages, thereby sustaining larger loss which as prudent and reasonable people plaintiff ought to have avoided.); Canadian: Finelli v. Dee, [1968] 1 O.R. 676 (Ont. C.A.) (Contractor who paved driveway after being told by owner that he wanted to cancel contract was not allowed to recover contract amount, since anticipatory breach was definite.).

[78] UCC § 2-715(2) (2002) ("Consequential damages resulting from the seller's breach include any loss resulting from general or particular requirements and needs of which the seller at the time of contracting had reason to know and which could not reasonably be prevented by cover or otherwise.").

[79] Sale of Goods Act, 1979, c. 54, §§ 50(3), 51(3) (Eng.) (requiring seller to attempt to sell unaccepted goods and buyers to attempt to cover if there is market for goods).

[80] Sale of Goods Act, C.C.S.M. c. S10, § 51(3) (Can.) ("Where there is an available market for the goods in question the measure of damages is prima facie to be ascertained by the difference between the contract price and the market or current price at the time or times when the goods ought to have been accepted, or, if no time was fixed for acceptance, then at the time of the refusal to accept.").

[81] Sale of Goods Act, 1895, § 50(3) (S. Austl.) ("Where there is an available market for the goods in question the measure of damages is *prima facie* to be ascertained by the difference between the contract price and the market or current price of the goods at the time or times when they ought to have been delivered, or, if no time was fixed, then at the time of the refusal to deliver.").

F. *Hadley v. Baxendale*[82]

Part of the charm, or at least the mystery, of *Hadley v. Baxendale* is in the report of the facts. It is just not clear who knew what and when. The resulting ambiguity has determined, and also muddled, the doctrine. Plaintiffs were millers, and so dependent in their business on the steam engine that worked the mill. The crank shaft of the engine broke and in order to obtain a new one, plaintiff had to ship its old shaft to the artisan who needed the original in order to fabricate properly the replacement. Defendants were common carriers who undertook the carriage of the broken shaft to the fabricators of the new shaft. The delivery was to take two days and in fact took seven. The delay resulted in loss of business to plaintiff. The facts of the case reported seem to indicate that the carrier was well aware of plaintiff's need for haste:

> The plaintiff's servant told the clerk that the mill was stopped, and that the shaft must be sent immediately; and in answer to the inquiry when the shaft would be taken, the answer was, that if it was sent up by twelve o'clock any day, it would be delivered at Greenwich on the following day . . .; at the same time the defendants' clerk was told that a special entry, if required, would be made to hasten its delivery.[83]

Baron Alderson's statement of the apposite rule bears reproduction in full:

> Where two parties have made a contract which one of them has broken, the damages which the other party ought to receive in respect of such breach of contract should be such as may fairly and reasonably be considered either arising naturally, i.e., according to the usual course of things, from such breach of contract itself, or such as may reasonably be supposed to have been in the contemplation of both parties, at the time they made the contract, as the probable result of the breach of it. Now, if the special circumstances under which the contract was actually made were communicated by the plaintiffs to the defendants, and thus known to both parties, the damages resulting from the breach of such a contract, which they would reasonably contemplate, would be the amount of injury which would ordinarily follow from a breach of contract under these circumstances so known and communicated. But, on the other hand, if these special circumstances were wholly unknown to the party breaking the contract, he, at the most, could only be supposed to have had in his contemplation the amount of injury which would arise generally, and in the great multitude of cases not affected by any special circumstances, from such a

[82] Hadley v. Baxendale, (1854) 156 Eng. Rep. 145 (Ex.).

[83] *Id.* at 147.

> breach of contract. For, had the special circumstances been known, the parties might have specially provided for the breach of contract by special terms as to the damages in that case; and of this advantage it would be very unjust to deprive them.[84]

From plaintiff's perspective, that statement of the rule would seem attractive, and encouraging. After all, if the report of the facts is accurate, plaintiff did bring the urgency of the situation to the attention of defendant, though perhaps it is less clear that plaintiff spelled out the actual consequences of delay.

Baron Alderson's opinion seems to establish two branches of the consequential damages rule: Plaintiff could recover those damages that (1) resulted as a natural consequence of the breach *and* (2) plaintiff brought to the attention of defendant. It would not be clear that the loss of profits would flow as a natural result of the broken shaft. Alderson notes that plaintiff may have had a back-up shaft, and so presumably was only in a hurry so that it would be restored to a more secure position sooner. Nonetheless, it would seem that plaintiff could have made its case based on the second branch of the rule: Plaintiff had, apparently, told defendants' clerk to make a special entry if necessary to hasten delivery. Still, though, that special entry would not have disclosed the reason for plaintiff's concern, the loss of profits resulting from the mill's shutdown.

The headnotes to the opinion do not track the statement of the facts in the opinion, and the discrepancy is significant given the consequential damages calculus that emerges: "[D]efendants' clerk, who attended at the office, *was told that the mill was stopped,* that the shaft must be delivered immediately, and that a special entry, if necessary, must be made to hasten its delivery[.]"[85] The court either rejects that evidence[86] or concludes that the evidence does not compel the conclusion that the consequences of late delivery had been made sufficiently salient to the carrier.[87] In either event, the doctrine would not be much affected.

The focus of the opinion seems ultimately to be on consent, either actual or inferred. If the circumstances surrounding the transaction would be sufficient to impute to the reasonable observer knowledge that defendant's breach would occasion particular loss,

---

[84] *Id.* at 151.

[85] *Id.* at 145 (emphasis added).

[86] *See* Victoria Laundry (Windsor) v. Newman Indus., (1949) 2 K.B. 528, 537 (finding it "reasonably plain" that *Hadley* court rejected evidence).

[87] Baron Alderson is at least skeptical:

> [I]n the present case . . . the only circumstances here communicated by the plaintiffs to the defendants at the time the contract was made, were, that the article to be carried was the broken shaft of a mill, and that the plaintiffs were the millers of that mill. But how do these circumstances shew reasonably that the profits of the mill must be stopped by an unreasonable delay in the delivery of the broken shaft by the carrier to the third person?

Hadley, 156 Eng, Rep. at 152.

that will be enough to impose liability on defendant for that loss. Alternatively, if plaintiff makes clear to defendant the consequences of defendant's breach, that too will suffice to support the inference of consent to the consequent liability. You can tell a story of contract based on consent and accommodate either prong of the *Hadley* test. Granted, such a construction might get a bit too close to the disfavored "tacit agreement test,"[88] but the difference between *Hadley* and its tacit agreement variation may be no more than the difference between actual and inferred consent. In any event, the tacit agreement test has not survived the progress of contract.

The *First Restatement* formulation of the *Hadley* rule is redolent of the tort law, in which foreseeability fixes the scope of the duty:

> In awarding damages, compensation is given for only those injuries that the defendant had reason to foresee as a probable result of his breach when the contract was made. If the injury is one that follows the breach in the usual course of events, there is sufficient reason for the defendant to foresee it; otherwise, it must be shown specifically that the defendant had reason to know the facts and to foresee the injury.[89]

The standard is objective: what the circumstances demonstrate the breaching party had reason to know. The *Restatement*'s approach to the foreseeability of consequential damages and so defendant's liability conjures to mind the familiar tort calculus. But the question of foreseeability may be a close one, or so the commentary and illustrations to the *First Restatement* iteration suggest.

Comment c recognizes that "[a] seller or carrier of goods usually has reason to know that the buyer or shipper either has made or will probably make a contract for the sale of the goods at a reasonable profit. Such circumstances are in the usual course of things."[90] So the seller or carrier may be liable for the loss of that reasonable profit as consequential damages. But the first illustration following the section captures the *Hadley* facts and the *Hadley* court's conclusion: "B is not bound to pay the lost profits, since he did not know or have reason to know that his delay in carrying the shaft would prevent A from making such profits."[91] The distinction drawn by the *Restatement* commentary and illustration is not implausible, but the two cases would seem closer than the stark conclusion would suggest.

---

[88] Farnsworth notes that, historically, "[s]ome courts suggested that one was not liable for consequential damages unless, when one made the contract, one had made a 'tacit agreement' to assume the risk of that liability." FARNSWORTH, *supra* note 65, at §12.14. Farnsworth goes on to point out, however, that the test "has been generally rejected as overly restrictive and doctrinally unsound, and it is explicitly condemned in the comments to the Uniform Commercial Code." *Id.*

[89] RESTATEMENT (FIRST) OF CONTRACTS § 330 (1932).

[90] *Id.* cmt. c (emphasis added).

[91] *Id.* illus.1.

The *Second Restatement* rule is also consistent with *Hadley*, and also relies on foreseeability, though with some refinements:

> (1) Damages are not recoverable for loss that the party in breach did not have reason to foresee as a probable result of the breach when the contract was made.
> (2) Loss may be foreseeable as a probable result of a breach when it follows from the breach
> (a) in the ordinary course of events, or
> (b) as a result of special circumstances, beyond the ordinary course of events, that the party in breach had reason to know.
> (3) A court may limit damages for foreseeable loss by excluding recovery for loss of profits, by allowing recovery only for loss incurred in reliance, or otherwise if it concludes that in the circumstances justice so requires in order to avoid disproportionate compensation.[92]

Again, the test is stated in objective terms: what the breaching party had reason to foresee. But the *Second Restatement* disassociates the foreseeability pertinent to consequential damage recovery from the proximate causation of the tort law: "[T]he requirement of foreseeability is a more severe limitation of liability than is the requirement of substantial or 'proximate' cause in the case of an action in tort or for breach of warranty."[93] The sense of that declaration is not immediately obvious, and the commentary offers no elaboration.[94]

Perhaps the most provocative statement in the *Second Restatement*'s consequential damage provision is that appearing in subsection (3). Justice may impose a limitation on recovery of consequential damages even though, apparently, but for such considerations of justice, those damages would have been recoverable, because, we may assume, they were sufficiently foreseeable. The *Restatement* commentary makes clear that this confers a discretionary power on the court, which would, it seems, undermine the principled basis of the *Hadley* rule. The commentary observes that courts would exercise that power anyway, but would do so under the guise of foreseeability considerations when, in fact, the limiting concept was a product of a justice determination. That gloss on the doctrine is very helpful. It makes clear what we assume about doctrine anyway: Courts may take advantage of its flexibility, the vagueness of its terms, in order to do a little justice

---

[92] RESTATEMENT (SECOND) OF CONTRACTS § 351 (1981).

[93] *Id.* cmt. a.

[94] There is also no elaboration in the reporter's (E. Allan Farnsworth's) treatise on contracts. *See* FARNSWORTH, *supra* note 65, at § 12.14.

when they feel so compelled. So subsection (3) is not surprising, except perhaps in its candor.

It is worthwhile, at this juncture, to note a more recent case that reveals this aspect of the doctrine with regard to the consequential damages calculus. The United States Court of Appeals for the Seventh Circuit decided *Evra Corp. v. Swiss Bank Corp.*,[95] in an opinion written by Judge Richard Posner. In payment of its ship charter obligation, Hyman-Michaels Co. caused its bank to wire funds, $27,000, through Swiss Bank and ultimately to the account of its charterer held at Banque de Paris. The wire transfer failed when the telex machine at Swiss Bank apparently ran out of paper; in any event, the payment order was not effected and Swiss Bank was at fault. As a result of the missed payment, the charter was terminated and Hyman-Michaels lost a valuable interest: The market charter rate had increased precipitously. The lower court awarded Hyman-Michaels $2.1 million in lost profits, consequential damages.

Judge Posner decides that *Hadley* provided the applicable Illinois consequential damages law and concludes that "Swiss Bank did not have enough information to infer that if it lost a $27,000 payment order it would face a liability in excess of $2 million."[96] He identifies the "animating principle" of *Hadley*: "[T]he costs of the untoward consequence of a course of dealings should be borne by that party who was able to avert the consequence at least cost and failed to do so."[97] Though Judge Posner apparently concludes that *Evra* presents more of a tort than a contracts issue, he relies on *Hadley*:

> In *Hadley* the untoward consequence was the shutting down of the mill. The carrier could have avoided it by delivering the engine shaft on time. But the mill owners, as the court noted, could have avoided it simply by having a spare shaft. Prudence required that they have a spare shaft anyway, since a replacement could not be obtained at once even if there was no undue delay in carting the broken shaft to and the replacement shaft from the manufacturer. The court refused to imply a duty on the part of the carrier to guarantee the mill owners against the consequences of their own lack of prudence, though of course if the parties had stipulated for such a guarantee the court would have enforced it. The notice requirement of *Hadley v. Baxendale* is designed to assure that such an improbable guarantee really is intended.[98]

Judge Posner apparently has a better handle on nineteenth-century miller's costs of doing business and better business practices than might many contemporary commentators, but, in any event, it is clear that his statement of the doctrine is normative rather than

---

[95] Evra Corp. v. Swiss Bank Corp., 673 F.2d 951 (7th Cir. 1982).

[96] *Id.* at 956.

[97] *Id.* at 957.

[98] *Id.*

positive: There is nothing of the "cheapest cost avoider" in Baron Alderson's opinion. (And, after all, Swiss Bank probably only had to make sure there was paper in its telex machine.) *Hadley* is about consent (though not *tacit* agreement), not about extra-contractual duties of care. Judge Posner's reading does suggest that courts should understand *Hadley* as requiring clear evidence of the breaching party's appreciation of the consequences of its default, but neither *Hadley's* terms nor *Restatement* iterations of the doctrine collapse contract into tort as Judge Posner does.

Indeed, confirmation that *Hadley* is supported by contract conceptions of consent rather than tort conceptions of relative fault might be found in the *Second Restatement's* distinction of *Hadley* foreseeability from proximate causation in tort; recall: "[T]he requirement of foreseeability is a more severe limitation of liability than is the requirement of substantial or 'proximate' cause in the case of an action in tort or for breach of warranty."[99] That language would seem to suggest that the *Hadley* foreseeability requirement is more restrictive than is the tort and warranty conception: It "is a more severe limitation of liability." It may be that the difference between *Hadley* foreseeability and tort proximate causation to which the *Restatement* commentary refers is in the consent requisite. The liability of defendant, the tortfeasor or defendant-seller, is not determined by that party's consent, but extends beyond the range of that to which defendant would agree. Plaintiff relying on *Hadley* is not constrained by what damages would be proximate; but he is constrained by defendant's consent, either actual or as may be inferred from the surrounding circumstances. The limitation is more "severe" only insofar as plaintiff may have more to prove. But defendant's liability may extend beyond what would be foreseeable, so long as the court can find consent, actual or inferred.

Judge Posner's equation of *Hadley* and the analogous, though not parallel, tort conception is unfortunate. He would be on surer ground if he appreciated the limitation provided on consequential recovery by subsection 351(3) of the *Second Restatement*. A court may limit a breaching party's liability for consequential damages if "in the circumstances justice so requires in order to avoid disproportionate compensation."[100] That would have provided a basis to limit Swiss Bank's liability to no more than an amount in line with the fee it was to receive for making the payment, certainly no more than the amount of the transfer, $27,000, which we may infer the bank could have understood its correspondent's client stood to lose if the bank failed to effect the $27,000 payment.[101] Even though that figure may be a more salient than accurate measure of plaintiff's loss,

---

[99] Restatement (Second) of Contracts § 351 cmt. a (1981). *See supra* text accompanying note 94.

[100] Restatement (Second) of Contracts § 351(3) (1981).

[101] It would not be too speculative to imagine that a failure to make a $27,000 payment would result in the loss of a right of equal value; and certainly the bank might have been in the better position than its customer to know the reliability of its system to effect large dollar amount transfers. So the bank could have refused to agree to make such transfers or could have expressly limited its liability for failing to do so once it accepted the payment order.

the *Restatement* subsection does give the court leeway to do justice as the circumstances dictate "to avoid disproportionate compensation."

The consequential damages rule, *Hadley* as well as its *Restatement* and statutory iterations, is perched awkwardly on the consent precipice of contract. The object of contract damages is to vindicate the parties' expectation, to provide an enforcement mechanism that will largely mimic the result that would have obtained had there been no need for the mechanism to operate. That, indeed, is why the normative commitment may be revealed in the damages calculus (and so why those positing a particular normative construction of contract often focus on the damages rules).[102] So although contract is premised on consent, as revealed by objective indicia, it is also concerned with limiting recovery in the event of breach so that the damage rules in fact accurately mimic the performance result. As one of the prefatory provisions of the UCC puts it,

> The remedies provided by [the Code] must be liberally administered to the end that the aggrieved party may be put in as good a position as if the other party had fully performed but neither consequential or special damages nor penal damages may be had except as specifically provided in [the Code] or by other rule of law.[103]

So though the Code does provide, at several junctures actually, for the recovery of consequential damages, such recovery is constrained by the admonition that the non-breaching party be put only "in as good a position as if the other party had fully performed." If the consequential damages calculation works properly, the injured party will not receive a windfall. She will be in no better position than she would have been in had her counterparty not breached. Consequential damages rules must strike that balance between avoidance of windfall and vindication of the expectation interest, and, appropriately, rely on conceptions of consent to do so.

Just as the parties' expectations (and so their expectation interest) are a function of the terms of their bargain, the bargain may formulate their expectation in case of breach. By and large, the default position in contract is that consequential damages are available, limited by the *Hadley* or *Hadley*-like reasonableness considerations: circumstances of which the breaching party should have been aware either generally or because plaintiff

---

[102] *See, e.g.,* Richard R.W. Brooks, *The Efficient Performance Hypothesis*, 116 YALE L.J. 568 (2006) (developing efficient performance hypothesis in which promisee can compel performance or collect lost profits when nonperformance is chosen by promisor); Oman, *supra* note 71 at 829 ("Economic accounts of the current doctrine governing contract damages have failed, but efficiency arguments remain key to any adequate theory of contract law."); Alan Schwartz & Robert E. Scott, *Market Damages, Efficient Contracting, and the Economic Waste Fallacy*, 108 COLUM. L. REV. 1610 (2008) (Market damages are most important consideration in damages calculus.).

[103] UCC § 1-305 (2003).

brought special circumstances to defendant's attention at the time of contracting. Article 2 of the UCC tracks that presumption in Section 2-715(2):

> (2) Consequential damages resulting from the seller's breach include
> (a) any loss resulting from general or particular requirements and needs of which the seller at the time of contracting had reason to know and which could not reasonably be prevented by cover or otherwise; and
> (b) injury to person or property proximately resulting from any breach of warranty.[104]

Note that the inferred consent basis of consequential damages pertains only in subsection (2)(a), "loss resulting from general or particular requirements and needs of which the seller at the time of contracting had reason to know"; it does not pertain to personal or economic injury to other property. Subsection (2)(b) fits with the parallel products liability rule.[105]

Article 2 of the UCC, like the common law of contract, provides a set of rules and principles to govern what is, or what is presumed to be, an essentially bilateral relationship. The seller in one transaction may be the buyer in the next, so repeat players (which most all of us are in contract) would be in favor of rules that prefer neither seller nor buyer across the range of transactions. That is particularly true insofar as freedom of contract principles accommodate the parties' adjusting risk allocation in ways that might reflect their relative bargaining positions. So long as the contract law fixes primarily default rules, rules that are subject to "agreement otherwise," the bilateral nature of the rules will effectuate the parties' agreement at relatively modest transactions cost. The parties to a contract within the scope of Article 2 are free to "contract-out-of" the consequential damages rule, by the limitation or exclusion of them: "Consequential damages may be limited or excluded unless the limitation or exclusion is unconscionable. Limitation of consequential damages for injury to the person in the case of consumer goods is prima facie unconscionable but limitation of damages where the loss is commercial is not."[106] Article 2's

[104] UCC § 2-715(2) (2002). Subsection (2)(b) seems to conjoin consequential damages foreseeability and the type of warranty breach proximate causation that is expressly denied by the comments to the RESTATEMENT provision. *See* RESTATEMENT (SECOND) OF CONTRACTS § 351 cmt. a (1981), *supra* text accompanying note 94. Other common law countries have enacted statutory forms of the *Hadley* consequential damages rule. Canada: Sale of Goods Act, C.C.S.M. c. S10, § 51(2) (Can.) ("The measure of damages is the estimated loss directly and naturally resulting, in the ordinary course of events, from the buyer's breach of contract."); Australia: Sale of Goods Act, 1895, § 50(2) (S. Austl.) (same).

[105] The RESTATEMENT OF PRODUCTS LIABILITY defines "harm to persons or property":

> For purposes of this *Restatement*, harm to persons or property includes economic loss if caused by harm to: (a) the plaintiff's person; or (b) the person of another when harm to the other interferes with an interest of the plaintiff protected by tort law; or (c) the plaintiff's property other than the defective product itself.

RESTATEMENT (THIRD) OF TORTS: PRODUCTS LIABILITY § 21 (1998).

[106] UCC § 2-719(3) (2002).

recognition that the parties, the sellers particularly, have the right to limit liability for consequential damages by the terms of the sales contract confirms that conceptions of consent rationalize the damage measure. It is because Article 2 is bilateral legislation, balancing the rights of buyer and seller, that the presumption is fixed by the common law *Hadley* rule: Consequential damages are available unless limited or excluded.

Article 4A of the UCC, governing wire transfers, is not bilateral legislation. The dominant transactor is the financial institution, like Swiss Bank, that facilitates the transfer of funds, typically in very great amounts, on behalf of customers for modest fees. The presumption in Article 4A is the diametric opposite of that in the Sales article: Section 4A-305(d) provides, in pertinent part, that in the event a receiving bank does not effect a payment order "damages, including consequential damages, are recoverable to the extent provided in an express written agreement of the . . . bank, but are not otherwise recoverable."[107] The comment refers directly to *Evra*:

> If *Evra* means that consequential damages can be imposed if the culpable bank has notice of particular circumstances giving rise to the damages, it does not provide an acceptable solution to the problem of bank liability for consequential damages.
>
> . . .
>
> An originator's bank might be willing to assume additional responsibilities and incur additional liability in exchange for a higher fee.[108]

This Article 4A rule, insofar as it is based, even in part, on the relatively small fee banks charge for wire transfers, is consistent with the *Second Restatement*'s conclusion that sometimes consequential damage liability must be constrained in the interest of "justice."[109]

Just as the *Hadley* provision and limitation of consequential damages in contract is consistent with our understanding contract as the means for parties to vindicate their intentions, measured objectively, the next canonical case provides what amounts to an alternative damage measure, but a measure that is nonetheless woven deeply into the fabric of the doctrine.

G. *Security Stove & Manufacturing Co. v. American Railway Express Co.*[110]

In *Security Stove & Manufacturing Co. v. American Railway Express Co.*, plaintiff manufactured a furnace with an innovative combination of oil and gas burner and wanted to display it at a trade show in Atlantic City, New Jersey. So plaintiff entered into a contract

---

[107] UCC § 4A-305(d) (2009).

[108] *Id.* § 4A-305(d) cmt. 2.

[109] *See* RESTATEMENT (SECOND) OF CONTRACTS § 351(3) (1981).

[110] Sec. Stove & Mfg. Co. v. Am. Ry. Express Co., 51 S.W.2d 572 (Mo. Ct. App. 1932).

with defendant to ship the furnace from Kansas City, Missouri, to New Jersey for that purpose. The furnace was shipped in parts, twenty-one numbered packages. When the furnace was set up in Atlantic City, plaintiff discovered that one of the parcels, the single most important one, had not arrived; it had been misdirected and could not reach Atlantic City before the close of the convention. The furnace could not be effectively displayed and, so, the expenses that plaintiff incurred in reliance on the complete and successful shipment were lost.

In fact, what plaintiff was seeking in the case was not much different from what the *Hadley* and *Evra* plaintiffs were seeking, though perhaps in different terms. It would seem that Security Stove could demonstrate *less* loss than could have either of plaintiffs in those two consequential damages cases. But a crucial difference is the *Security Stove* court's finding that defendant was well aware of plaintiff's particular circumstance and the loss plaintiff would suffer if defendant did not perform consistently with its contract obligations. Curiously, what also distinguished those earlier cases is the *Security Stove* court's conclusion that plaintiff had suffered neither loss of profits nor business advantage as a result of the breach. Even though plaintiff made the special circumstances known to defendant and defendant would therefore have been liable for consequential loss of profits, there *were* no lost profits.

Plaintiff did not seek recovery measured by lost profits over the value of the lost business opportunity. Instead, plaintiff sought recovery of the shipping expense, which, as it turned out, was wasted. Defendant objected that plaintiff was trying to recover something the contract law would not provide the means to recover:

> [P]laintiff "is endeavoring to achieve a return of the status quo in a suit based on a breach of contract. Instead of seeking to recover what he would have had, had the contract not been broken, plaintiff is trying to recover what he would have had, had there never been any contract of shipment"; that the expenses sued for would have been incurred in any event.[111]

The court is not convinced by defendant's argument.

> It is no doubt, the general rule that where there is a breach of contract the party suffering the loss can recover only that which he would have had, had the contract not been broken, and this is all the cases decided upon which defendant relies. . . . But this is merely a general statement of the rule and is not inconsistent with the holdings that, in some instances, the injured party may recover expenses incurred in

[111] *Id.* at 576.

> relying upon the contract, although such expenses would have been incurred had the contract not been breached.[112]

Although the court's award to plaintiff of the expenses was vindication of the reliance interest, the award is entirely consistent with an award of consequential damages. The court notes that defendant was aware of plaintiff's purpose and surely plaintiff had been denied the value of defendant's promise and undertaking.

Security Stove is the basis of illustration 3 to comment a of the *Second Restatement*, Section 352. The rule of that section is succinct: "Damages are not recoverable for loss beyond an amount that the evidence permits to be established with reasonable certainty."[113] The illustration presents facts that are only similar to *Security Stove*, but substantially so:

> A and B make a contract under which A is to construct a building of radical new design for B for $5,000,000. After A has spent $3,000,000 in reliance, B repudiates the contract and orders A off the site. If the evidence does not permit A's lost profits to be estimated with reasonable certainty, he can recover the $3,000,000 that he has spent in reliance. He must, however, then prove that amount with reasonable certainty.[114]

The apposite comment also includes an interesting observation, or suggestion, that intimates the presence of some pervasive and fundamental normative calculus:

> Doubts are generally resolved against the party in breach. A party who has, by his breach, forced the injured party to seek compensation in damages should not be allowed to profit from his breach where it is established that a significant loss has occurred. A court may take into account all the circumstances of the breach, *including willfulness*, in deciding whether to require a lesser degree of certainty, giving greater discretion to the trier of the facts.[115]

The fault basis of a good deal of contract liability has received much notice lately.[116] It is especially curious that the reference to "willfulness" is in the commentary rather than the black letter of the *Restatement*. In any event, the language may do no more than

---

[112] *Id.*

[113] RESTATEMENT (SECOND) OF CONTRACTS § 352 (1981).

[114] *Id.* § 352 illus. 3.

[115] *Id.* § 352 cmt. a (emphasis added).

[116] *See* Symposium, *supra* note 70, at 1341; Steven Shavell, *Is Breach of Contract Immoral?*, 56 EMORY L.J. 439 (2006) (View that it is wrong to breach contract is misleading.); Seana Valentine Shiffrin, *The Divergence of Contract and Promise*, 120 HARV. L. REV. 708 (2007) (Legal significance of promise and its breach do not correspond with moral significance of promise and its breach.).

recognize what is human nature anyway: Resolve doubt by reference to a culpability scale.[117] Even if not part of the explicit doctrine, consideration of culpability would be impossible to eradicate from the law generally, no less the contract law specifically.[118]

From the foregoing survey of the canonical enforcement cases, it is now worthwhile to turn to the alternative normative accounts. Does unitary normative theory rationalize the doctrine?

---

[117] *See* David Morris Phillips, *The Commercial Culpability Scale*, 92 YALE L.J. 228 (1982) (UCC reveals "culpability scale" to allocate loss, with "intentional principle" on most culpable pole on scale and "strict liability principle" at least culpable pole.).

[118] *See* U.S. Naval Inst. v. Charter Commc'n, Inc., 936 F.2d 692 (2d Cir. 1991) (resolving uncertainty against willfully breaching party).

8

THEORY OF CONTRACT ENFORCEMENT

A. The Limits of Liability

IT MAY BE that the contract remedies define the normative commitments (or lack thereof) of contract. That is, we know better what contract does, as a normative matter, if we know what recovery is available to the victim of a breach of contract. Certainly we may infer that this is what United States Supreme Court Justice Oliver Wendell Holmes thought and asserts in his well-worn (but often misunderstood[1]) maxim: "The duty to keep a contract at common law means a prediction that you must pay damages if you do not keep it, —and nothing else."[2] He equates contract with the damages available upon breach of a contract . . . "and nothing else."

[1] Kraus offers a helpful, and more likely correct, gloss. Jody S. Kraus, *The Correspondence of Contract and Promise* 109 COLUM. L. REV. 1603, 1640 (2010).

[2] Oliver Wendell Holmes, *Path of the Law*, 10 HARV. L. REV. 457, 462 (1897); *see also* OLIVER WENDELL HOLMES, THE COMMON LAW 263 (Mark DeWolfe Howe ed., 1963) (1881) ("The only universal consequence of a legally binding promise is, that the law makes the promisor pay damages if the promised event does not come to pass."). It is not clear that Holmes means that willful breach should be treated the same as unintentional breach in terms of damages. Nevertheless, some commentators have interpreted Holmes's statement as the precursor of the theory of efficient breach. *See, e.g.,* Larry A. DiMatteo, *A Theory of Efficient Penalty: Eliminating the Law of Liquidated Damages*, 38 AM. BUS. L.J. 633, 675 n.168 (2001); David J. Seipp, *125th Anniversary Essay: Holmes's Path*, 77 B.U. L. REV. 515, 529–30 (1997). *But see* Joseph M. Perillo, *Misreading Oliver Wendell Holmes on Efficient Breach and Tortious Interference*, 68 FORDHAM L. REV. 1085, 1087 (2000)

Even if the damages calculus is not all there is to contract, it is at least true that we understand a good deal about contract once we understand how the law responds to breach. That obtains through the three crucial (and normatively revealing) phases of the damages inquiry: the measure (and form) of damages, the calculation of consequential damages, and the mitigation of damages.

This first section of this chapter begins where much of the conversation regarding contract damages has begun for nearly a century: the delineation of contract damages into expectation, reliance, and restitution interests. Once we appreciate what that interest analysis can reveal (and cannot) about the doctrine we are able to reach conclusions about the doctrine's normativity. The second section will consider the fit between damages for breach of a bargain, a consideration-based promissory obligation, and damages for upsetting the reasonable expectations of a promisee on the basis of estoppel. That contrast too reveals a good deal about the normativity of the doctrine.

I. MEASURES AND FORMS OF CONTRACT DAMAGES

Insofar as the measure of damages for breach of contract is concerned, focus has been on the extent to which the damage calculi afford the non-breaching party the benefit of her bargain and just what that bargain is. Breach should not make plaintiff better off, but we need to establish the baseline in order to compare plaintiff's circumstances post-breach with what they would have been had there been no breach. The literature has placed the contestant theories in accessible relief: Deontologists generally consider how damages doctrine vindicates certain "interests" or values of the non-breaching party and consequentialists conclude that analysis of such matters confounds more than it clarifies.

a. Deontology

Although efforts to distinguish, in normative terms, among transactional contexts have proliferated, in the common law scholarship there may be no more prominent project than the seemingly magisterial *The Reliance Interest in Contract Damages*,[3] by Lon Fuller and his research assistant William Perdue.[4] The article posits and defends the conclusion that contract law in fact protects the reliance "interest"[5] and not the expectation interest.

("[I]n Holmes's view, the breach of a contract was as much an offense against the law – a legal wrong – as a tort, not the free choice that the misinterpreters of Holmes believe he advocated.").

[3] Lon L. Fuller & William R. Perdue, Jr., *The Reliance Interest in Contract Damages: 1*, 46 YALE L.J. 52 (1936), and *The Reliance Interest in Contract Damages: 2*, 46 YALE L.J. 373 (1937). The article is in two parts, the first analyzing remedies for breach and the second surveying relevant case law on the subject.

[4] Perdue was a third-year law student and Fuller's research assistant and acknowledged the modesty of his contribution to the article.

[5] *See* Richard Craswell, *Against Fuller and Perdue*, 67 U. CHI. L. REV. 99, 107 (2000) (on disutility of "interest" terminology); Peter A. Alces, *Regret and Contract "Science,"* 89 GEO. L.J. 143, 161–66 (2000) (responding to Craswell).

Fuller and Perdue's efforts rely on aretaic theory to argue that the "harm principle"[6] precludes recovery of expectation damages and so damages can and should only compensate disappointed parties for the reliance losses imposed on them by breaching parties.[7] That conclusion, and, indeed, the article itself, remains quite controversial.[8] But what matters for present purposes is the authors' approach, their delineation of context to determine operative damage measures:

> The objection that damages measured by the expectancy are too "conjectural" to be allowed can obviously have no application to a case where the subject matter of the contract has a market value and the plaintiff seeks only the difference between the contract price and the market value. The objection can arise only (1) where the contract relates to a subject matter of uncertain value, that is, having no "market"; or, (2) where the plaintiff seeks to recover [uncertain] business profits. . . .[9]

So Fuller and Perdue identify certainty issues as something of a key to determining the apposite damages doctrine. A breach giving rise to certain market value damages would more likely be compensable by reference to expectancy; a breach causing less certainly determinable loss would be compensable by reference to the more accessible reliance measure. We might not be sure how much defendant's breach kept plaintiff from realizing, but we can know more certainly how much plaintiff expended in reliance on defendant's performance.

Fuller and Perdue acknowledge that mere "administrative convenience" could explain the duality[10]; but that is not the explanation upon which they rely. Instead, they assert

---

[6] Texas A&M University philosophy professor Robert Garmong draws this phrase from the work of J.S. Mill but traces its roots back to John Locke. Robert Allen Garmong, J.S. Mill's Re-conceptualization of Liberty (Dec. 2002) (unpublished doctoral dissertation, University of Texas at Austin) (*available at* http://repositories.lib.utexas.edu/bitstream/handle/2152/593); *see also* James Gordley, *Morality and Contract: The Question of Paternalism*, 48 Wm. & Mary L Rev. 1733 (2007) (discussing concepts of "distributive justice" as considered by Aristotle, and, much later, Professor E. Allan Farnsworth).

[7] Fuller & Perdue, *supra* note 3, at 56.

[8] *See, e.g.,* sources cited *supra* note 5; Charles Fried, Contract as Promise: A Theory of Contractual Obligation (1981); Peter Benson, *The Expectation and Reliance Interests in Contract Theory: A Reply to Fuller and Perdue*, Issues in Legal Scholarship, Symposium: Fuller and Perdue (2001): Article 5, at 2–3, *available at* http://www.bepress.com/ils/iss1/art5; Richard Craswell, *How We Got This Way: Further Thoughts on Fuller and Perdue*, Issues in Legal Scholarship, Symposium: Fuller and Perdue (2001): Article 2, at 1, *available at* http://www.bepress.com/ils/iss1/art2; James Gordley, *A Perennial Misstep: From Cajetan to Fuller and Perdue to "Efficient Breach,"* Issues in Legal Scholarship, Symposium: Fuller and Perdue (2001): Article 4, at 2–3, *available at* http://www.bepress.com/ils/iss1/art4; Stephen A. Smith, *"The Reliance Interest in Contract Damages" and the Morality of Contract Law*, Issues in Legal Scholarship, Symposium: Fuller and Perdue (2001): Article 1, at 8, *available at* http://www.bepress.com/ils/iss1/art1.

[9] Fuller & Perdue, *supra* note 3, at 373–374.

[10] *Id.* at 374.

that other considerations are determinative, such as the "wilfulness" of the breach,[11] and courts' general unwillingness to allow plaintiffs to recover damages on account of the "internal structure of the plaintiff's business."[12] Fuller and Perdue discern a judicial effort to restrict the scope of liability, and an inclination on the part of courts to utilize conceptions such as certainty to do just that. They conclude that "uncertainty" covers a multitude of sins, as it were.

> Concealed in the objection of "uncertainty," then, are a number of judicial impulses: (1) a desire not to broaden unduly the liability of the defaulter by making "remote" injuries compensable[[13]]; (2) a desire not to impose on the defendant a liability felt to be disproportionate to the gains which he stood to make from the contract[[14]]; (3) a desire to restrict liability imposed on the "innocent" defaulter in comparison with that imposed on the "wilful" defaulter[[15]]; (4) a desire for an easily administered rule. Where the last impulse is the controlling one, the reliance interest is often employed as a surrogate for the expectation interest. Where, on the other hand, the first objection ("remoteness") predominates, the reliance interest represents a midway station between no liability and a complete liability for the expectancy. As we have already recalled, losses through reliance are not immune to the objection of "remoteness"; yet because they make a stronger appeal to judicial sympathy than a claim for lost profits, the objection of remoteness is applied less strictly to them.[16]

Fuller and Perdue proceed from those general conclusions about courts' propensities so far as damages are concerned to a survey of damage analyses and awards in recurring transactional contexts.[17]

Once we follow the Fuller and Perdue argument through its elaboration of damages rules in particular contexts, we see that the authors' conclusion is that the damages rules *change* from one context to the next in order to take into account normative considerations not revealed by the terms of the apposite doctrine. If the ostensible doctrine says that successful plaintiffs are entitled to expectation damages but the cases are denying plaintiffs such recovery in recurring contexts, then that statement of doctrine so construed would be out of step with the law in fact. That is, statements of doctrine

---

[11] *Id.* at 375, (citing Ralph S. Bauer, *The Degree of Moral Fault As Affecting Liability*, 81 U. PA. L. REV. 586, 592 (1933)).

[12] *Id.* at 375.

[13] *See, e.g.,* Hadley v. Baxendale, 156 Eng. Rep. 145 (Ex. 1854).

[14] For a contemporary example, *see* Evra Corp. v. Swiss Bank Corp., 673 F.2d 951 (7th Cir. 1982).

[15] *See, e.g.,* United States Naval Institute v. Charter Communications, Inc. 936 F.2d 692 (2d Cir. 1991) (resolving damage uncertainty against party that willfully breached).

[16] Fuller & Perdue, *supra* note 3, at 376–77 (footnote omitted; footnotes added).

[17] *Id.* at 377–401.

which are insensitive to transactional nuance are simply wrong, or at least insufficiently doctrinal.

Of course, more significant than the accuracy of Fuller and Perdue's case analyses within each of the categories is their demonstration that the courts engage damage calculi from perspectives dependent on transactional realities that are actually obscured by doctrinal formulations. The universe Fuller and Perdue describe is essentially dual: Cases either lend themselves to commercial market-like analysis or to analyses in which market objectives are overcome by other considerations. There may be, then, something normatively significant, even determinative, about the market versus non-market dichotomy. It is worthwhile to consider increasingly sophisticated treatments of that dichotomy, such as that offered by contemporary consequentialist analysis.

b. Consequentialism

The consequentialist response to the corrective justice perspective of Fuller and Perdue is perhaps best captured in Professor Richard Craswell's "Against Fuller and Perdue,"[18] a thoughtful appraisal of the earlier scholars' contribution to our understanding of the contract damages doctrine. To be fair, Craswell seems to be more troubled by the pedagogical uses to which Fuller and Perdue's work has been put than by the authors' claims. He acknowledges that Fuller clarified his object in a letter written to Karl Llewellyn some years after the "Reliance Interest" article appeared. In that letter, Fuller explains that "I consider the contribution made in my article on the reliance interest to lie, not in calling attention to the reliance interest itself, but in an analysis which breaks down the Contract-No-Contract dichotomy and substitutes *an ascending scale* of enforceability."[19] But Craswell remains troubled by Fuller and Perdue's claims, too. Succinctly, Craswell concludes that the categories Fuller and Perdue provide in terms of the expectation, reliance, and restitution "interests" do not do much to guide courts' award of damages or to make sense of what it is we believe the damages law vindicates. It is difficult, though, to formulate Craswell's argument so summarily without denying his points a good deal of their power. So it is both necessary and worthwhile to appreciate the contours of his thesis at greater length.

At the outset Craswell states his thesis: "Fuller and Perdue's classification is not very helpful in understanding contract remedies."[20] The "modern *use*" of Fuller and Perdue's categories has obscured much that is important about the contract damages rules.[21] In fact, though, Craswell argues that the categories Fuller and Perdue use are actually

[18] Craswell, *supra* note 5, at 99.

[19] *Id.* at 105 n.21.

[20] *Id.* at 100.

[21] *Id.* at 154(emphasis added).

misleading insofar as they suggest similarities and consistencies between damage awards when those similarities and differences are inconsequential at least and even misleading at their worst.[22]

The crux of Craswell's problem with the deontology of Fuller and Perdue's approach is that it is insufficiently fundamental. Even if the three categories – expectation, reliance, and restitution – did fix certainly determinate and certainly calculable damage measures that remained distinct from one another in the cases, we still would not know whether one interest rather than the others should be most prominent and given effect over the others. Further, the cases themselves do not seem to treat the interests as distinct or even distinguishable in any very helpful way. A court may award damages by reference to one interest rather than another without making clear why that interest rather than another was dominant in normative terms. For example, if a court confronts problems of proof with regard to the award of expectation damages, the court may respond by awarding plaintiff relief based only on reliance, the out-of-pocket costs incurred by plaintiff.[23] That vindication of one interest rather than another on account of evidentiary challenges does not, at least not necessarily, respond to a viable normative distinction. Further, the categories are underinclusive. Courts may, for example, award a non-breaching plaintiff more than the benefit of that plaintiff's bargain in order, perhaps, to impose greater loss on a willfully breaching party. Fuller and Perdue's categories do not take into account that extra-expectation recovery.[24]

Craswell is certainly correct that the Fuller and Perdue categories do not rationalize all of the contract damages rules, even in deontic terms. In the authors' defense, that may not have been their object. Fuller and Perdue try to rationalize contract damages in Aristotelian, corrective justice terms. They describe the considerations that would pertain to the *aretaic calculus*—the interest in balance—and conform those considerations to the extant damage measures identified by the doctrine. What emerges from their effort is a presentation that reveals the potential cooperation of values that might inform, or at least animate, the courts' damage calculus. Why choose one interest (or one label for an interest) rather than another in the particular case? Not so clear; but perhaps the value of Fuller and Perdue's project is in its revelation of the deontic values (filtered through aretaic theory) that we might conclude courts' damage awards vindicate. Even if courts do not get it right, at least not consistently, it may be that Fuller and Perdue have helped us appreciate courts' method, or how courts would describe that method, in deontic terms.

It is more worthwhile at this juncture to take account of Craswell's contribution to our understanding of the doctrine, and the fit of consequentialism with the doctrine.

[22] *Id.*

[23] *Id.* at 103–04.

[24] *Id.* at 139–49.

Craswell's particular problem with Fuller and Perdue's division of damages into "interests" is that the expectation, restitution, and reliance trichotomy is not particularly helpful, as a pedagogical matter: "[I]t is not a useful way of understanding what courts are actually doing."[25] We could even say that, in Craswell's estimation, the interest analysis is not a useful way of understanding what courts are doing with the damages *doctrine*. It does seem as though Craswell agrees with the sentiment of Fuller's letter to Llewellyn, which "suggests something closer to a continuous scale of remedies, rather than three discrete interests."[26] Apart from the fact that we might read Fuller and Perdue more charitably by concluding that the interests they describe are the constituents of the range of the continuum Craswell acknowledges, we *can* understand Craswell's sense of the consequentialist appreciation of the nature and operation of the damages doctrine in terms of such a continuum. The crucial portion of Craswell's argument relies on the flexibility of doctrine, even if the only object were consequentialist:

> [W]henever different amounts of damages would be optimal for each of the different incentives to be optimized, the measure that is optimal when *all* of the relevant incentives are considered will often be some hybrid or intermediate number. . . . Once this has been recognized, it is not too far-fetched to say that the measure of damages that is truly optimal—optimal, that is, when *all* of the relevant factors have been considered—could lie anywhere on the real number line.
>
> To lawyers who think of remedies as protecting discrete, identifiable "interests," the prospect of a continuum of remedies to choose from may seem odd. To economists who view remedies in instrumental terms, though, there is nothing at all odd about this. . . . Indeed, if the exact consequences one wants to produce vary from one use of these tools to another, this sort of tweaking will often be needed. From an instrumental perspective, the focus is entirely on the *effect* one wants to produce, not on the "interest" one wants to protect.[27]

We have no reason to take issue with the conclusion of Craswell and other economists[28] that welfare creation may best be served by a damage regime that can serve both static and dynamic efficiency concerns.[29] But that is not the pertinent point here. The terms of Craswell's critique of Fuller and Perdue make clear that Craswell believes that the damages doctrine does in fact accommodate the flexibility that consequentialism would

[25] *Id.* at 106.

[26] *Id.* at 105.

[27] *Id.* at 110 (emphasis added).

[28] *See id.* at 108 nn.31–32, 109 n.41.

[29] *Id.* at 107–11; *see* discussion of *static* and *dynamic* efficiency *supra* Chapter Six, "Theory of Contract Performance."

require. A substantial portion of his article is devoted to revealing that Fuller and Perdue's interest analysis fails to describe the extant case law, and so the doctrine.

Craswell surveys cases that award more than expectation damages,[30] cases that approximate expectation damages,[31] and cases that award less than expectation damages.[32] His point, and it is a very good one, is that we do not get any closer to understanding what number the court will come up with, even allowing that it comes up with the right number, by casting the court's analysis in terms of the Fuller and Perdue interests. Courts that award more than expectation will take into account the *mala fides* of the breaching party in order to do so, but Fuller and Perdue would have no "interest" to describe that award. Courts might also award damages that approximate expectation but do so by ordering specific performance, or by using the non-breaching party's out of pocket cost as the measure. Courts that award less than expectation may use reliance or restitution as the next best measure because plaintiff's damages would be too speculative to calculate and award full expectation damages, notably in promissory estoppel cases.

In place of the Fuller and Perdue trichotomy, Craswell offers one of his own: Divide the cases into those that award (1) more than expectation, (2) expectation, and (3) less than expectation damages. What we are left with, then, is the sense that the Fuller and Perdue and Craswell critiques are complementary, so far as our discovering a normative basis for contract damages is concerned. Where Fuller and Perdue rely on expectation, reliance, and restitution "interests" to describe the *ingredients* that would inform a court's award of damages, Craswell would recognize that three categories (more than expectation, expectation, and less than expectation) describe what courts are doing (or should be doing) when they award damages to serve consequentialist goals: static and dynamic efficiency, in the right balance.

But the problem that Craswell discovers with the Fuller and Perdue interest analysis may also undermine his own analysis. We can only find the correct damage award to serve static and dynamic efficiency interests if we know, first, what the consequences of a particular damage award will be as both a static and dynamic matter (though we can rarely if ever have that type of certainty), and we need to know what it is we want to maximize—there needs to be a consensus and that consensus may not be discoverable, if it even exists. The compromise that the court effects in order to determine the damage award will require a balance of often inaccessible constituents. If we can do the math we will; if we cannot, we may rely on Fuller and Perdue's interests.

[30] *Id.* at 138–43.

[31] *Id.* at 143–46.

[32] *Id.* at 146–54.

2. CONSEQUENTIAL DAMAGES

There seems to be agreement, of sorts, between deontology and consequentialism concerning consequential damages: The canonical case, *Hadley v. Baxendale*, is wrong. That is, both those who understand contract as vindicating autonomy and those who understand contract as serving instrumental ends, efficiency particularly, find the *Hadley* decision to be inconsistent with the normative foundation of contract. So from the perspective of this book, the consequential damages doctrine pretty clearly does not track normative theories of contract. It is, though, worthwhile to appreciate how *Hadley* fails both deontology and consequentialism.

a. Deontology

Once again starting with Charles Fried to help us come to terms with the Kantian deontology, we should not be surprised that the *Hadley* rule is problematic, as least initially. Fried favors the Holmesian construction of the consequential damages doctrine in *Globe Refining Co. v. Landa Cotton Oil Co.*: "Defendant is liable only for those risks he explicitly or tacitly agreed to assume."[33] Fried acknowledges that modern iterations of *Hadley* have rejected that *tacit-agreement test* in favor of a *reason-to-know standard.* Though Fried does not believe that the difference between the standards is great, he favors Holmes's tacit-agreement test, as well he should given the deference Fried's promise theory affords the parties' expressions of autonomy.

Fried cites an article written in 1932 by George Gardner on the "Principles of Contracts."[34] In that essay, Gardner recognizes the tort basis of the consequential damages doctrine, and all that remains to be resolved is the time at which the parties' foresight would be determinative:

> Since *Hadley v. Baxendale* the existence of this [foreseeability] limitation on contract liability has not been doubted; but that case did not raise or decide the question whether the range of the promisor's reasonable foresight should be measured as of the date of promise or the date of breach. . . . The violation or repudiation of a promise which has been paid for thus has the essential aspects of a tort, and liability should extend, *as in other tort cases*, at least to all consequences within the promisor's vision when the wrong occurs.[35]

---

[33] FRIED, *supra* note 8, at 139 n.25.

[34] *Id* at 137 n.8 (citing George Gardner, *An Inquiry into the Principles of the Law of Contracts*, 46 HARV. L. REV. 1 (1932)).

[35] George Gardner, *An Inquiry into the Principles of the Law of Contracts,* 46 HARV. L. REV. 1, 29–30 (1932) (emphasis added).

Finally, in terms that are prescient so far as the thesis of this book is concerned, Gardner concludes, "the commercial [read, 'contract'] law should be thought of as a coherent system whereby economic cooperation is sought to be reconciled with an individualistic philosophy of life."[36] Of course, the two are reconcilable, even complementary.

To the extent, then, that the consequential damages doctrine relies on tort principles, the autonomy vindicated by real agreement is undermined. Consequential damages doctrine, so construed, is an aberration, not unlike the consideration doctrine. So it is not difficult to conclude that deontology cannot, or at least has not, made normative sense of the doctrine that flows from *Hadley*.

b. Consequentialism

Consequential damages doctrine does not fair much better with consequentialism than it does with deontology. We can approach the doctrine from two consequentialist perspectives and appreciate the deficiencies that each perspective discovers in the doctrine. The work of Professors Richard Epstein[37] and Barry Adler[38] demonstrates the inadequacies of *Hadley* for those who discover in contract an instrumentalist object.

Epstein is not convinced that the presumptive expectation measure of contract damages generally serves efficiency interests. Epstein (as Craswell[39]) begins from the premise that the expectation measure will not always assure the right combination of incentives to provide that the damage award will serve both static and dynamic efficiency concerns.[40] For Epstein, the problem is not so difficult to solve: All the law needs to do is give effect to the parties' bargain. If the parties have agreed to a term, enforce it; if they have not anticipated the particular contingency that has occurred, then supply the resolution the parties would have bargained to had they been more prescient. Insofar as contracting parties who have included provisions in their agreement regarding consequential damages have limited recovery of them, the default rule should reflect that bargain model: "All in all, the optimal contracting strategy does not appear to call for the high consequential damages, subject to defense rules [*i.e.,* unforeseeability], that courts have tended to adopt.... [T]here is reason to expect these damages to be kept relatively limited, which is what the express contracts have typically provided."[41] Of course, Epstein's

---

[36] *Id.* at 42.

[37] Richard A. Epstein, *Beyond Foreseeability: Consequential Damages in the Law of Contract,* 18 J LEGAL STUD. 105 (1989).

[38] Barry E. Adler, *The Questionable Ascent of* Hadley v. Baxendale, 51 STAN. L. REV. 1547 (1999).

[39] Craswell, *supra* note 5, at 109.

[40] Epstein, *supra* note 37, at 112, 116.

[41] *Id.* at 118.

presumptive deference to the terms of actual contracts reflects a confidence in the efficiency of contracting that may be misplaced.[42] Nevertheless:

> With its sophisticated client base and the competitors snapping at its heels, the limitations on damages found in the Federal Express agreement cannot be attributed to some mysterious contract of adhesion; after all, why stop at disclaiming expectation damages if, as dictator, you could just knock out all liability by dictating contract terms? Instead, the terms limiting liability are best understood as a way to maximize joint benefits to the parties ex ante: they minimize the costs of administration and mitigation that otherwise arise with breach while insuring a certain high level of contract performance by the firm.[43]

This reflects an essentially Panglossian approach to contract: Extant contracting practices must reflect the efficient result, else why would they be extant?

Professor Barry Adler offers a sophisticated response that better accounts for the lack of fit between the doctrine and consequentialist premises. He begins with the obvious (but overlooked): Damages are stochastic, not certain. He puts the economic question: Would "a rational rule impose the burden of contracting for exceptional damages on those who wish to avoid the limitation"? The *Hadley* rule forces information insofar as the party who would suffer more than generically foreseeable damage as a result of her counterparty's breach will bring that to the attention of her counterparty at the time of contracting. That is the conclusion of those who read *Hadley* in terms of penalty-default theory,[44] which was a response to traditional, bargain model theory, essentially Epstein's theory. Adler's reaction to the penalty-default theory reading of *Hadley* undermines not just that particular construction of the consequential damages doctrine but both bargain and penalty default models of contract generally.

Commentators preceding Adler had failed to appreciate that a high-value contracting party is not just one who would suffer particularly high consequential damages in the event of breach but also a party who would be more likely to suffer damages in the event of breach. There is, so far as penalty-default analysis is concerned, no difference between the party whose consequential loss in the event of breach would be ten times the norm and the party who would be ten times more likely to suffer the normal

---

[42] *See* Peter A. Alces, *Guerilla Terms*, 56 Emory L.J. 1511, 1533 (2007); *see also supra* Chapter Four, "Theory of Contract Formation," notes 124–44 and accompanying text (discussing Professor Oren Bar-Gill's argument to this effect).

[43] Epstein, *supra* note 37, at 121.

[44] *See* Adler, *supra* note 38, at 1548 n.3.

consequential loss.[45] From there, it is not far to Adler's conclusion that simplistic constructions of the doctrine are impotent:

> A correct determination of whether or to what extent a pool on a penalty-default rule will form in equilibrium requires information about the extent of the subsidy a pool would provide for high-value types. A determination of this subsidy, in turn, depends on perhaps unobtainable information about the full range of each type's expected damages from breach. Thus, an accurate evaluation of a penalty-default rule's efficacy in the *Hadley* setting could be a heroic task. . . . A lawmaker asked to set a default rule might well lack information about the refinements parties would use to set prices and other contract terms.[46]

Finally, "a limited-liability default rule would not *necessarily* be superior to an expansive-liability default."[47] We just cannot know with anything approaching the certainty consequentialism would require whether a limited or expansive liability rule would be preferable, from a social welfare perspective. The information forcing construction of the *Hadley* rule would only be superior "under specified assumptions," and those assumptions would be mistaken in some circumstances.

At the risk of oversimplification, but for the sake of the generalization that might best pertain to the argument of this book, Adler establishes that neither the legislature[48] nor the court[49] can do the math that would need to be done in order to establish that the doctrine vindicates a consequentialist normativity. Now that is not to say that we *necessarily* could not do the math in the particular case, but it does confirm that the doctrine might, at best, accommodate the efficiency calculus without mandating it.

Though we may not find the certainty in either deontology or consequentialism that can make sense of *Hadley* or consequential damages doctrine more generally, at least as a matter of contract, we might expect that some general damages conceptions resonate with both deontic and consequentialist premises. After all, both normative perspectives would have interests that would be served by assuring that resources are put to the use that would realize the parties' object, whether that object be found in the sanctity of promise or the conservation of scarce resources. We may, then, expect that *both* normative commitments could explain the doctrine, which says as little about *unitary* normative theory as would a doctrine that can be construed in neither unitary deontic nor unitary consequentialist terms.

---

[45] *Id.* at 1562.

[46] *Id.* at 1552.

[47] *Id.* at 1558.

[48] *Id.* at 1566–67.

[49] *Id.* at 1566.

3. MITIGATION

The deontic argument in favor of mitigation, at least in Kantian terms, is apparently self-evident. The consequentialist argument, alternatively, flows naturally from the efficiency of avoiding waste. Elaborations of the two positions suggest what construction of the doctrine would necessarily entail those alternative normative conclusions.

a. Deontology

Charles Fried does not have a good deal to say about mitigation in his *Contract as Promise*, but what he says appreciates mitigation's fit among complementary aspects of contract doctrine.

> These doctrines of waiver, repudiation, and estoppel are a response to the significant power a contract gives the promisee over a promisor; a promise may call for sacrifices far in excess of what residual, background nonpromissory principles of fairness and decency require.... If the victim of a breach can protect himself from its consequences he must do so. He has a duty to mitigate damages.... The duty to mitigate does go further than waiver or estoppel in one sense, however: The contract right is diminished not because the rightholder acted inconsistently with it but because he failed to take some further action, further action that in fact benefits the contract-breaker by reducing his potential liability. This is a duty, a kind of altruistic duty, toward one's contractual partner, the more altruistic that it is directed to a partner in the wrong. But it is a duty without cost, since the victim of the breach is never worse off for having mitigated. Rather it is a duty that recognizes that contractual liabilities are onerous enough that they should not be needlessly exacerbated. And if the victim of a breach fails in his duty the only penalty he suffers is the proportional loss of his own remedial rights.[50]

In support of his conclusion that the non-breaching party has a duty to mitigate, Fried cites a case that found such a duty, but no authority that fixes the source of the duty.[51] So we must assume that it follows ineluctably from Kantian autonomy premises. Professor Seana Shiffrin offers elaboration.[52]

Shiffrin appreciates a morality of promising that is not reflected, or at best imperfectly reflected, in contract. Her point, for present purposes, is that a moral agent would be compelled by the law of contract to act immorally: "legal norms regulating ... promises diverge in substance from the moral norms that apply to them.... [T]he contents of the

---

[50] Charles Fried, Contract as Promise 131 (1981) (citation omitted).

[51] Oloffson v. Coomer, 296 N.E.2d 871 (1973).

[52] Seana Valentine Shiffrin, *The Divergence of Contract and Promise*, 120 Harv. L. Rev. 708 (2007).

legal obligations and the legal significance of their breach do not correspond to the moral obligations and the moral significance of their breach."[53] She finds support for that conclusion particularly in the mitigation doctrine: "When breach occurs, the legal doctrine of mitigation, unlike morality, places the burden on the promisee to make positive efforts to find alternative providers instead of presumptively locating that burden fully on the breaching promisor."[54]

Shiffrin starts with a conception of morality apparently developed over the course of her scholarship[55] and it would neither be possible nor necessary to offer a recapitulation of that work to focus attention on the aspects of her theory pertinent to the normativity of doctrine. Although you might be dubious of her claims concerning the substance of morality, what is pertinent here is her discovery that the mitigation doctrine specifically, and large swaths of contract more generally, are not amenable to conception in terms of her morality, a morality of promising that entails more than contract requires. But Shiffrin does not maintain that there must be perfect correspondence between the contract law and the morality of promising. She instead stakes out an intermediate position between the reflective (law must reflect morality) and separatist (law and morality as independent domains): "[B]ecause there are moral duties to obey the law, legal rules should be sensitive to the demands placed on moral agents so that law-abiding moral agents do not, as a regular matter, face substantial burdens on the development and expression of moral agency."[56] The intermediate position maintains that "law's contents must be structured to make room for moral agents."[57]

From there, then, Shiffrin concludes that

> As a general rule, morality does not impose such [mitigation] requirements on disappointed promisees. True, morality does not look sympathetically upon promisees who stay idle while easily avoidable damages accumulate. But this is a far cry from what contract expects of the promisee and what it fails to demand of the breaching promisor.[58]

Shiffrin's thesis would ultimately be problematic for the argument of this book. Although doctrine does not adopt a particular normative perspective, it does accommodate potentially divergent (both deontic and consequentialist) values. Shiffrin concludes that the mitigation doctrine is not just amoral but actually immoral. She must be wrong; and

[53] *Id.* at 709.

[54] *Id.* at 710.

[55] *See, e.g.,* Seana Valentine Shiffrin, *Speech, Death, and Double Effect*, 78 N.Y.U. L. Rev. 1135, 1181–84 (2003).

[56] Shiffrin, *supra* note 52, at 715.

[57] *Id.* at 717.

[58] *Id.* at 724.

fortunately for the argument here, she is. Indeed, the problems with her conclusion are revealed in her more complete statement of it:

> It may sometimes be permissible for the promisor to *ask* the promisee to shoulder this [mitigation] burden when the substitute is *much* easier for the promisee to obtain or when the promisor is ill-suited to select a replacement (as when the promisee's judgment is necessary for the replacement to serve the promisee adequately). Still, even in such cases, it would usually be unacceptable for the promisor to insist were the promisee to refuse.
>
> ....
>
> Sometimes it can be morally wrong for the promisee to refuse to mitigate, especially when the costs of refusal are very steep and disproportionate to the seriousness of what is promised. But whether it is morally wrong for the promisee to refuse may depend on a number of factors to which the law is insensitive, including the closeness of the relationship, the history of the relationship, the reason for breach, the reason the promisor wants to shift the burden, and how cumbersome mitigation activities would be.[59]

It would certainly help Shiffrin's argument if she were to explore the doctrine more fully and carefully than her summary conclusions suggest. Neither the *Restatement (Second) of Contracts* (*Second Restatement*) in Section 350[60] nor the Uniform Commercial Code (UCC or the Code)[61] formulations would seem necessarily to exclude *any* of the factors that she suggests would be probative of a moral duty to mitigate. Indeed, in litigated matters, it is quite likely that counsel for both sides would afford finders of fact the opportunity to weigh the very considerations Shiffrin deems pertinent to the moral calculus.

So to the extent that Shiffrin finds the doctrine inconsistent with her deontic premises—insofar as the doctrine contemplates any duty to mitigate at all—her conclusion supports my argument. And insofar as she fails to recognize that the doctrine actually *accommodates* the kind of moral calculus she believes the normativity of promising requires, her conclusion is assailable on grounds that too support the thesis here.

The fundamental problem with Shiffrin's theory and analysis is that she does not really begin with a theory of promising. She cites an unpublished manuscript on file with the

---

[59] *Id.* at 725.

[60] Restatement (Second) of Contracts § 350 (1981) ("[D]amages are not recoverable for loss that the injured party could have avoided without undue risk, burden, or humiliation.").

[61] *See* UCC § 2-715(2)(a) (2002).

Harvard Law Review,[62] but never develops a deontic theory of promising in her critique of contract's coordination (or lack thereof) with the morality of promising. Though it may be that she could develop (or has developed) a moral theory of promising that would be inconsistent with contract generally and contract enforcement doctrines specifically, it is not clear that she can support the conclusion that *any* deontic theory of promise would fail to correspond with the normativity of contract doctrine.

Professor Jody Kraus makes just that point, quite convincingly, in his response to Shiffrin.[63] Kraus builds on (or at least applies)[64] the personal sovereignty conception of individual autonomy developed by Joel Feinberg.[65]

> I argue that neither the personal sovereignty account, nor any other plausible theory of self-imposed moral responsibility, is consistent with the legal enforcement of all promises, including promises intended not to be legally enforceable. . . . Correspondence theories of contract therefore cannot proceed without first specifying how the theory of self-imposed moral responsibility determines the content of the remedial rights and duties recognized by promissory morality.[66]

Because Shiffrin does not identify the theory of promissory morality that she would contrast with the normativity of contract, her critique fails. Shiffrin, quite simply, does not account for the possibility that a theory of promissory morality could accommodate a promisor's wanting to distinguish those promises that would be legally enforceable from those subject to less formal sanctions for their breach: "But what if an individual wants to make a promise without incurring legal liability for the resulting promissory obligation?"[67] Any coherent moral theory considerate of (and certainly one based on) personal autonomy would have to account for that particular exercise of autonomy: "Whether or not a promissory obligation can be justifiably enforced, then, requires correspondence accounts to determine whether the promisor intended his promise not to be given legal effect."[68] That would entail factual inquiry into whether the promisor utilized the signals of legally enforceable promising. If he did not, then *legal* enforcement

---

[62] Shiffrin, *supra* note 52, at 714 n.7.

[63] Kraus, *supra* note 1, at 1608.

[64] It is important to appreciate that Kraus does not endeavor to defend a normative foundation for promissory morality; his object is to demonstrate that before we can reach a conclusion about the doctrine's correspondence with morality we would need a theory of promissory morality with which to compare the doctrine. Insofar as Kraus's application of personal sovereignty would not undermine correspondence theory he can conclude that Shiffrin has not established the dissonance she set out to establish.

[65] Kraus, *supra* note 1, at 1608 n.11; *see* 3 Joel Feinberg, The Moral Limits of the Criminal Law: Harm to Self 52 (1986).

[66] *Id.* at 1609–10.

[67] *Id.* at 1616.

[68] *Id.* at 1619.

of the morality-based promise would undermine the autonomy of the promisor, and might well frustrate consequentialist objects as well.[69]

Kraus further observes that deontic explanations of promissory obligation do not generally offer "an account of the nature or content of the remedial moral duty to which breach gives rise."[70] Relying on the personal sovereignty model, Kraus reasons that just as the promisor would determine the legal enforceability of her promise, the parties who create the obligations would determine the extent of the damages that would flow from breach of the promise. Here Kraus must make sense of the default contracts damages rules:

> Majoritarian default rules maximize the probability that the terms to which promisors are being held correspond with the ones they intended but failed to express or imply, and they save the majority of individuals the costs of specifying those terms, which respects their personal sovereignty by decreasing the barriers to creating promissory obligations. Thus, majoritarian default rules can be justified as a method of interpreting promises grounded on the personal sovereignty conception of autonomy.[71]

Kraus's reconciliation of promissory morality based on personal autonomy with contract remedies as default rules is not absolute insofar as the law imposes limits on liquidated damages and also recognizes limitations on alternative damage formulae that do not seem to be considerate of the parties' sovereignty.[72] His point is nonetheless well taken and has particular resonance with mitigation doctrine.

Kraus reproduces Shiffrin's conclusion regarding mitigation doctrine and its fit with deontic theory of contract. From the premises described above, his response to Shiffrin is what you would expect: "The mitigation doctrine is . . . justified as an ordinary majoritarian default rule that imputes terms into parties' promises that they likely did want, but failed to express, or would want had they considered it."[73] He may not have made a strong (or even the best) case for damages doctrine as providing penalty default terms, but he has responded to Shiffrin in a way that leaves little of her argument unrefuted.

Perhaps most provocative about Kraus's contribution is his conclusion, in the margin, that insofar as default rules are concerned, at least, the normative commitments of deontology and consequentialism merge: "[A]ny penalty default that turns out to be economically justified on the ground that it reduces informational barriers would also

---

[69] *See* Robert E. Scott, *Commercial Calamities:* Hoffman v. Red Owl Stores *and the Myth of Precontractual Reliance*, 68 Ohio St. L.J. 71 (2007).

[70] Kraus, *supra* note 1, at 1627–28.

[71] *Id.* at 1632.

[72] *See id.* at 1635 n.63.

[73] *Id.* at 1645.

enjoy the support of an autonomy-based moral theory."[74] Kraus's deontic view lines up[75] just about perfectly[76] with what consequentialism would provide: Contract rules should vindicate majoritarian conceptions because to do so is most *likely* to also vindicate individual autonomy. We should, then, expect that consequentialists would reach the same conclusion about the mitigation doctrine that Kraus reaches.

b. Consequentialism

In a 1983 article, Professors Charles Goetz and Robert Scott discover a general theory of contract proceeding from "the mitigation principle."[77] Succinctly, "the mitigation principle . . . requires each bargainer to extend efforts to discover, share, and act on relevant information so as to minimize the *joint* costs of providing performance or its equivalent."[78] Their thesis draws on the bargain and transactions costs models[79] to develop a revision of doctrine that would better serve consequentialist objectives. Essentially, they conclude that the transactors ought to be afforded "wide latitude" to structure their deals.[80] So Goetz and Scott are troubled by the imprecision of the mitigation doctrine as well as limitations on the parties' right to fix their liability by using liquidated damages provisions:

> One can therefore derive a broad principle of mitigation by predicting how contractors would agree to cooperate if charged explicitly with designing a policy to cope with readjustment contingencies. The resulting mitigation principle would require each contractor to extend whatever efforts in sharing information and undertaking subsequent adaptations that are necessary to minimize the *joint* costs of all readjustment contingencies.[81]

---

[74] *Id.* at 1631–32 n.55.

[75] *See id.* at 1633 ("Thus, a promissory morality that fails to hold promisors morally bound by majoritarian default terms unnecessarily increases the costs of promising, thereby violating the positive liberty of individuals to undertake moral obligations as they see fit."); *see also id.* at 1647 ("In fact, both deontic moral theorists and economic analysts have persuasively argued that contract law's enforcement doctrines can be explained and justified on the ground that they refuse to enforce the kinds of promises that most promisors would not intend to be legally enforceable.").

[76] *See id.* at 1637 ("[E]conomic analysts err when they disregard the additional costs parties incur by undertaking and then breaching moral obligations. . . . [N]onconformance imposes intrinsic (psychological) costs. . . ."). I am not sure this is sufficiently thought through to support the weight Kraus would impose on it.

[77] Charles J. Goetz & Robert E. Scott, *The Mitigation Principle: Toward a General Theory of Contractual Obligation,* 69 VA. L. REV. 967 (1983).

[78] *Id.* at 969.

[79] *Id.* at 968–69 n.5.

[80] *Id.* at 970.

[81] *Id.* at 973.

The Goetz–Scott model combines the bargain and information forcing paradigms from the economics literature.[82] From this perspective flows the conclusion that the doctrine should, first, anticipate the majoritarian rule and then also provide wide latitude to freedom of contract principles so that the parties are able to accommodate the contours of their deal on their own terms.

The authors helpfully explain the extant mitigation doctrine as a response to the "classic case of 'moral hazard.'"[83] Were the contract law not to impose some duty to mitigate, the non-breaching party would have no reason, no incentive to make the "cost-effective adaptations" that could reduce the cost of breach, a cost imposed on the breaching party with no obvious counter balancing benefit to the non-breaching party. Even though, upon breach, the parties could negotiate an efficient allocation of responsibilities to minimize the cost of the breach, at that point their negotiation would confront bilateral monopoly problems: The parties could negotiate but only with one another and that might well generate substantial negotiation costs.[84]

The extant doctrine also, it would seem, forces information disclosure, but perhaps imperfectly:

> Requiring an obligee to convey information to the obligor will reduce the potential distortion of the obligor's adjustment choices [to breach or not when performance costs increase]. Optimal adjustment may also require an obligor to convey information to the obligee. Even if an obligee is perfectly willing to adopt mitigating adjustments, he may not be able to assess the available options without such crucial information as the obligor's estimated probability of nonperformance. Little can be done to remedy "invincible ignorance," a situation in which no one has access to the information necessary to recognize a cost-effective adjustment. But when one party does have access to information necessary for the other's cost-effective adjustment, the communication of that information should be ensured.[85]

The great variety of contract types exacerbates the challenges to which the doctrine would need to apply: Contracts involving goods for which there is a vibrant market for substitute performances present different questions than do contracts involving a subject matter for which there is not an accessible market for substitutes. We might expect that the parties to those two types of contract, and the range between the extreme forms of each, would adopt dramatically different contract provisions with regard to mitigation

---

[82] Adler, *supra* note 38.

[83] Goetz & Scott, *supra* note 77, at 980.

[84] *See id.* at 982; *see also* Walgreen Co. v. Sara Creek Prop. Co., 966 F.2d 273, 276 (7th Cir. 1992) for a discussion of the topic by Judge Richard A. Posner.

[85] Goetz & Scott, *supra* note 77, at 981.

were it rational for them to afford the consequences of breach adequate consideration: "More specialized transacting environments simply require more varied and complex strategies to encourage optimal contractual behavior than do market environments."[86]

So it would seem that, in order for the doctrine to respond to the range of contracts—fixed between those arising in competitive markets at one pole and more specialized, relational[87] contracts at the other—it would need to take into account the transactional context in ways that mitigation is not well-calibrated to do. Goetz and Scott conclude that the doctrine has, in part, "softened" the categorical quality of common law rules to accommodate transactional dynamics in the mitigation context:

> Through the doctrine of substantial performance and related provisions, common law courts have crafted rules for certain classes of contracts incorporating both performance and readjustment responsibilities. These more responsive rules reduce a potential mitigator's incentive to demand a premium for his cooperation, but their additional complexity also increases the threat of evasion by a disgruntled obligor.[88]

This observation explains, for example, the UCC's reliance on the perfect tender standard[89] for single-delivery contracts and substantial performance[90] for installment contracts, if we infer that the single-delivery–installment distinction is resonant with a distinction between competitive market contracts, on the one hand, and specialized, relational contracts, on the other. That is not to say that single-delivery contracts are necessarily competitive market contracts and that installment sales are the product of specialized, relational contracts. There is no reason to believe that that dichotomy would hold. The point, instead, is that for the essentially similar reason the tension between more responsive (*i.e.,* flexible and variable) rules and more categorical (*i.e.,* specific and invariable) rules arises in specialized, relational contracts versus competitive market contracts, the same tension may arise in the single-delivery (buyer more likely ultimate consumer) versus installment sale (buyer more likely retailer) contracts. It does not, for present purposes, matter so much whether that posited distinction maintains empirically; what does matter is that the courts may *use* the doctrine to accommodate the tension.

---

[86] *Id.* at 986.

[87] *Id.* at 1002 ("Contracts are relational to the extent that parties are unable to reduce *performance* obligations to definitive terms, either because of uncertain future conditions or the inherent difficulty of adequately characterizing certain complex situations.").

[88] *Id.* at 1002 (footnote omitted).

[89] UCC § 2-601 (2002).

[90] *Id.* § 2-612.

We can see the courts doing just that in three of the canonical cases that straddle the damages–conditions divide. Recall that in *Jacob & Youngs, Inc. v. Kent*,[91] Judge Cardozo finds that the use of Reading pipe was *not* a condition to the contractor's right to payment from the owner. Similarly, in *Peevyhouse v. Garland Coal & Mining Co.*,[92] the court refuses to grant the cost-of-performance remedy, also akin to specific performance, because of the economic "waste" such an award would entail. Goetz and Scott conclude that "[s]uch a carefully conditioned right of specific performance not only restrains evasion but also selectively filters the potentially opportunistic cases where the obligor's cost of performance is substantially greater than the market value of performance."[93] The accompanying footnote elaborates that "[i]n a specialized context, the value of performance to an obligee may well exceed any objective market calculation."[94]

Goetz and Scott conclude that the glass is at least half full: "Although many mitigation rules demonstrate a sensitivity to the market variable [competitive versus specialized, relational], absence of an explicit acknowledgement of its role tends to impose excess uncertainty costs on contracting parties."[95] So it would seem that here the doctrine might indeed reveal consequentialist normative values. And given Kraus's observation that, in this mitigation context, at least, there might be substantial coincidence between the apposite deontic and consequentialist concerns,[96] we could as well conclude that the doctrine has normative integrity from either of the dominant normative perspectives. But there remains a complication. Although there may be such coincidence in a particular case, there may also be dissonance. If there is such dissonance, which, if either, perspective dominates, or should?

Whether a market is competitive or specialized is an empirical question. That is *potentially* no less intractable than the question of whether the obligor or obligee is acting in good faith with regard to the duty to mitigate. We can posit categories, as consequentialists have suggested in analogous contexts,[97] but such categories provide heuristics, ultimately no more certain than guesstimates of efficiency or whether the parties have acted in good faith. We will do the math, if we can (consequentialism); if we cannot, we will rely on conceptions of fairness (deontology). Doctrine does the best it can if it guides us to that result.

---

[91] 129 N.E. 889 (N.Y. 1921); *see* discussion *supra* Chapter Five, "Contract Performance Doctrine."

[92] 382 P.2d 109 (Okla. 1963); *see* discussion *supra* Chapter Six, "Theory of Contract Performance.".

[93] Goetz & Scott, *supra* note 77, at 1003–04.

[94] *Id.* at 1004 n. 97.

[95] *Id.* at 1024.

[96] Kraus, *supra* note 1.

[97] *See, e.g.*, Varouj A. Aivazian, Michael J. Trebilcock & Michael Penny, *The Law of Contract Modifications: The Uncertain Quest for a Benchmark of Enforceability*, 22 Osgoode Hall L.J. 173 (1984); Richard A. Posner & Andrew M. Rosenfield, *Impossibility and Related Doctrines in Contract Law: An Economic Analysis*, 6 J. Legal Stud. 83 (1977).

B. Estoppel-Based Liability

Although it is axiomatic, but subject to significant qualifications, that the successful plaintiff in a breach of contract action will receive the benefit of his bargain, plaintiff who prevails on a promissory estoppel theory is entitled to whatever damages justice requires, and expectation is not the presumptive measure. Indeed, it would seem that more usually damages awarded on a promissory estoppel basis would be measured by plaintiff's reliance, his out-of-pocket expenditures on the promise not fulfilled. So construed, the doctrine apparently recognizes a normative distinction between plaintiff's deserts depending upon the enforcement theory. A normative interpretation of the doctrine, then, should be able to account for the different remedial results.

1. DEONTOLOGY

Professor Thomas Scanlon has posited a comprehensive and largely non-consequentialist account of contract from contractualist premises.[98] His contractarianism is derived from Kant (so is consistent with the deontic perspective assumed here), and endeavors to discover rules to which people would agree. It is not so clear that Scanlon develops a unique deontology; instead, he elaborates an analytical perspective designed to reveal moral choices and conclusions.

In his contribution to a collection of essays on contract theory,[99] Scanlon treats, *inter alia*, the issue that Shiffrin and Kraus treat in the context of mitigation: the correspondence of promise and contract. Scanlon posits that both morality and law can distinguish promises for the breach of which only moral sanctions pertain from legally enforceable promises. He describes the law's enforcement of certain promises on the basis (and to the extent) of reliance rather than expectation (or "assurance" as he comes to describe it). First, the premises of *loss prevention (L)* and *fidelity (F)*, stated as moral principles:

> *Principle L*: If one has intentionally or negligently . . . led someone to expect that one is going to follow a certain course of action X, and one has reason to believe that that person will suffer significant loss as a result of this expectation if one does not follow X, then one must take reasonable steps to prevent that loss.[100]

Scanlon concludes that Principle L can be satisfied by defendant's compensating the party misled, and it would "be *sufficient* for A to compensate B for any loss suffered as a result

---

[98] Thomas M. Scanlon, *Promises and Contracts*, *in* THE THEORY OF CONTRACT LAW: NEW ESSAYS 86, 87 n.5 (Peter Benson ed., 2001).

[99] *Id.* at 86.

[100] *Id.* at 91.

of relying on" the expectation A created in B. A created an "expectation" in B; A did not make a "promise" to B. Had A made a promise to B then not fulfilled it, as a moral matter B would be entitled to receive from A potentially greater damages: the amount (or form)[101] necessary to make B "as well off as he or she would have been had the promise been kept."[102] That follows from alternative Principle F:

> If (1) in the absence of objectionable constraint, and with adequate understanding (or the ability to acquire such understanding) of his or her situation, A intentionally leads B to expect that A will do X unless B consents to A's not doing so; (2) A knows that B wants to be assured of this; (3) A acts with the aim of providing this assurance, and has good reason to believe that he or she has done so; (4) B knows that A has the beliefs and intentions just described; (5) A intends for B to know this, and knows that B does know it; and (6) B knows that A has this knowledge and intent; then, in the absence of special justification, A must do X unless B consents to X's not being done.[103]

Thus, Principle F distinguishes giving an assurance from merely creating an expectation (the province of Principle L).

Scanlon infers the morality of state enforcement of the rights those two principles vindicate by relying on contractualism: "The use of state power to enforce contracts, or to require compensation when they are breached, is morally permissible if a principle licensing this use is one that no one, suitably motivated, could reasonably reject."[104] Continuing from that normative commitment, he reasons that the argument for legal enforcement of Principle L proceeds in two stages. First, we must identify the reasons for having such a principle. Second, based on the good reasons for accepting such a principle, enforcement of Principle L (EL) could not reasonably be rejected. His first stage seems to depend on consequentialist reasoning: "our need to rely on others' representations about what they are going to do, and the reasons we have for wanting to avoid significant losses that can result when these representations prove false."[105] He explains that those are reasons supporting EL "because most of us would be more likely to have to bear such costs if we were denied legal recourse of the kind that EL would permit."[106] Now this is not necessarily and ultimately a consequentialist argument: We might have entirely deontic reasons for wanting to avoid the "costs" to which Scanlon refers. The cost to

---

[101] *E.g.,* specific performance.

[102] Scanlon, *supra* note 98, at 92.

[103] *Id.* at 95.

[104] *Id.* at 100.

[105] *Id.*at 101.

[106] *Id.*

promisors (or, rather, those who create expectations in others) would be the cost of constraining misleading behavior. Scanlon concludes that the cost of that constraint would be less than the cost of suffering from frustrated (but well-grounded) expectations. Scanlon has found an *amoral* basis supporting EL. That is not to say that we could not also discover a *moral* basis for EL; it just makes clear that EL is not *dependent* upon the identity of morality and law.

Scanlon then makes clear the application of EL to the canonical promissory estoppel case:

> Principle EL . . . would . . . support the decision in *Hoffman v. Red Owl Stores*, in which Red Owl was required to compensate Hoffman for losses resulting from actions that they knew he was taking in the expectation, which they knew to be unrealistic, that he was going to get a Red Owl franchise. Principle EL explains why compensation can be required in such cases without appealing to the idea of an "imputed contract." But it also explains why appeal to the idea of contract might seem appropriate: Even when they do not involve contracts, situations falling under EL are *like* breaches of contract in involving responsibility for the expectations one has led others to form about one's future conduct.[107]

Scanlon's construction of *Hoffman* responds directly to Professor Scott's concern that the case confounds the law governing precontractual negotiations.[108] But maybe the two perspectives are reconcilable. Scanlon assumes that Red Owl in fact had created certain expectations in Hoffman, and Scott assumes that those expectations could not be reasonably held without a promise. Now there might be good reasons (consequentialist or otherwise) for wanting to develop more certain premises for the imposition of legal liability on account of the creation of expectations. That is, we could favor law that would impose liability more certainly (and indicate just as certainly when such liability does not arise), but, as a normative matter, that does not mean that the consequences of less certain law should be visited upon those who reasonably hold certain expectations, unless, of course, there are good independent reasons for that result.

Although Scanlon concludes that Principle EL would support legal, reliance-based, remedies for breach of contract, he recognizes that it may not preempt the field. That is, there may be good normative reasons for a legal remedy that goes beyond the reliance measure. That would be the case with Principle EF:

> It is permissible legally to enforce remedies for breach of contract that go beyond compensation for reliance losses, provided that these remedies are not excessive and

[107] *Id.* at 102–03.

[108] Scott, *supra* note 69, at 71–72.

> that they apply only in cases in which the following conditions hold: (1) A, the party against whom the remedy is enforced, has, in the absence of objectionable constraint and with adequate understanding (or the ability to acquire such understanding) of his or her situation, intentionally led B to expect that A would do X unless B consented to A's not doing so; (2) A had reason to believe that B wanted to be assured of this; (3) A acted with the aim of providing this assurance, by indicating to B that he or she was undertaking a legal obligation to do X; (4) B indicated that he or she understood A to have undertaken such an obligation; (5) A and B knew, or could easily determine, what kind of remedy B would be legally entitled to if A breached this obligation; and (6) A failed to do X without being released from this obligation by B, and without special justification for doing so.[109]

Morality does not require Principle EF; but EF describes "what it is morally permissible for a legal system to do."[110] That means, though, that EF does not certainly determine whether the damages in any particular case should be measured by reference to reliance, restitution, or expectation. Although courts may, by EF, award expectation damages, they are not constrained to do so. Other "good policy reasons" may determine the appropriate measure of damages on particular facts.

For present purposes, discerning the deontic basis of recognizing different damage measures in the bargain versus promissory estoppel contexts, it is enough that Scanlon has mobilized contractualist analysis to establish the moral permissibility of the alternative damage measures based on whether the promisor has merely encouraged the promisee's expectations or has, instead, made an assurance to the promisee. The difference between the creation of expectations and assurance is a moral difference that Scanlon can formulate in normative, specifically deontic, contractualist terms. The distinction that Scanlon draws is not on the basis of consideration; it is, instead, on the basis of intention to make a legally binding commitment.[111]

Principle EF requires that a contractor know that different consequences may flow from an assurance than would flow from the mere creation of expectations. There is a value in assurance that contracting parties may – and could want to – exploit. The principle vindicates the promisor's right to project himself into the future and realize the value of assuming an obligation. This is, essentially, a Humean[112] idea. It supports the contractualist narrative insofar as it justifies the state's exercise of power: "What EF allows a state to do is to deprive [would-be contractors] of the opportunity to offer . . .

---

[109] Scanlon, *supra* note 98, at 105.

[110] *Id.* at 106.

[111] *Id.*

[112] *See* David Hume, A Treatise of Human Nature 334–35 (David Fate Norton & Mary J. Norton eds., 2000) (1740); *supra* Chapter One, "The Failure of Normative Contract Theory," discussion of Hume accompanying note 27.

assurances and then not fulfill them, even in the absence of special justification, without fear of legal intervention."[113] It is in that ability of reliance and expectation damages to increase the options (and so the power) of would-be contractors to order their affairs, to project themselves into the future, that Scanlon discovers the basis for legal enforcement of expectation damages beyond the reliance measure.

It is not clear, though, that Scanlon's paradigm fits the contract doctrine. Principle EF "requires . . . that both parties know or can find out what remedies for breach"[114] are available to the disappointed party. As an empirical matter, it would probably be unrealistic to maintain that contracting parties know with anything approaching certainty what damages will flow from breach. But even were we to assume Scanlon requires no more than that the parties know the potentially apposite measures of damages, there still remains a gap between what morality might require and what the doctrine would provide: "[P]arties to a contract may have reason to want to be able to choose what the[] remedies will be."[115] Indeed, Scanlon acknowledges that this begins to look like another contract, "a 'remedy contract' specifying what is to happen if A fails to fulfill th[e] primary agreement."[116] But he rejects that characterization. His reasons are somewhat opaque:

> First, if the remedy contract is just another contract then the question arises what is to be done in the event that it, in turn, is breached. (Specific performance seems to be presupposed.) Second, while a second contract could specify additional penalties that are to apply if the first contract is breached, it is not clear how such a contract could lower the remedy that would be appropriate in this event. To do this the parties would have to exercise some legal power other than merely making another contract.[117]

Neither of those objections to the second-contract characterization would seem to have much purchase with regard to the question whether a contractualist account of contract can make sense of the fact that the parties to a contract often *are not* able to fix with anything approaching certainty the contours of the remedy upon breach. It would seem that if the moral case for contract relies on assuring would-be contactors the power to exploit the ability to obligate themselves, then crucial, too, would be their ability to determine the terms of that second, remedial contract. But contract has never made good

---

[113] Scanlon, *supra* note 98, at 108.

[114] *Id.* at 107.

[115] *Id.*

[116] *Id.*

[117] *Id.*

sense of liquidated damages.[118] To the extent that Scanlon's rejection of the second contract is an effort to conform his conception of contract with the uncertain liquidated damages doctrine, he is not successful. Liquidated damages would seem to make the same moral case as first contracts; indeed, Principle EF can also rationalize the normative foundation supporting such terms.

Further, if liquidated damages provisions are given effect, then Scanlon cannot rationalize their normative basis. His explanation for not treating remedies as the subject matter of second contracts undermines any contract-based justification for enforcing such provisions. If the provisions are enforced, what is the moral basis for their enforcement? Scanlon cannot have it both ways. Now he *can* make a case for altering the normative incidents for a new conception of contract that would conform with his contractualist approach, but that does not make the case for a normative account of extant doctrine.

Ultimately, there may not be much difference, on the ground, between Scanlon's deontic contractualist approach and consequentialist approaches.[119] The parallels merit consideration.

2. CONSEQUENTIALISM

In a comprehensive treatment of the promissory estoppel doctrine from the consequentialist perspective, Professor Avery Katz considers the fit between the doctrine and preliminary negotiations.[120] He understands the promisory estoppel doctrine to operate as economic regulation: "[The doctrine] shape[s] the bargaining process by influencing the negotiator's incentives to make and to rely on preliminary communications."[121] He explains that "from the regulatory perspective, the direction of analysis is top-down rather than bottom-up. The central question is not which legal rule is consistent with the parties' expectations, but what expectations the parties should be encouraged to have in the first place."[122] So Katz's analysis assumes repeat players, and likely sophisticated repeat players.

At the outset, it is important to recognize that the promissory estoppel doctrine is not limited in its operation to determining if ostensibly preliminary negotiations will give

---

[118] *See* Kenneth W. Clarkson, Roger LeRoy Miller, & Timothy J. Muris, *Liquidated Damages v. Penalties: Sense or Nonsense?*, 1978 WIS. L. REV. 351 (1978); Jeffrey B. Coopersmith, *Refocusing Liquidated Damages Law for Real Estate Contracts: Returning to the Historical Roots of the Penalty Doctrine*, 39 EMORY L.J. 267 (1990); Larry A. DiMatteo, *A Theory of Efficient Penalty: Eliminating the Law of Liquidated Damages*, 38 AM. BUS. L.J. 633 (2001).

[119] Scanlon, *supra* note 98, at 107 n.24.

[120] Avery Katz, *When Should an Offer Stick? The Economics of Promissory Estoppel in Preliminary Negotiations*, 105 YALE L.J. 1249 (1996).

[121] *Id.* at 1250.

[122] *Id.* at 1253.

rise to contract liability. Indeed, particularly in transactions between less sophisticated parties, the doctrine may operate to provide the basis to enforce a promise not supported by consideration. In those cases there is no question that there has been a promise; that is assumed. In the transactions to which Katz devotes his attention, the question is whether, in fact, there has been a promise, the acceptance of which accommodates legal enforcement. The subsidiary question in both contexts (in which it is clear that there has been a promise and where it is not) focuses on the damages that would attend "breach." We might still conclude, though, that grouping the preliminary negotiations promissory estoppel cases with the cases that more certainly concern the enforceability of a promise not bargained for is category error. In any event, it would seem that there could be worthwhile parallels so far as the damage calculus is concerned.

Though Katz's analysis of preliminary negotiations is more focused than is the general promissory estoppel inquiry, it is worthwhile to consider his consequentialist construction. He reveals a good deal about the doctrine that would be pertinent beyond the limited settings in which his analysis would pertain most directly. And his conclusions are more nuanced than a too-simplistic consequentialist analysis might assume. Rather than concluding that the doctrine works best when it provides parties certainty as to when their preliminary discussions mature into promises,[123] Katz's argument really goes to the essence of the conclusion that there has been what the law should construe as a promise, and what the law should construe as a promise may be determined by considerations beyond the form of the oral or written communication.

Insofar as the premise of the promissory estoppel doctrine is the protection of reliance, what should matter, so far as the regulatory perspective is concerned, is the encouragement of efficient, that is to say, just enough, reliance. Though space limitations preclude a thorough reconstruction of Katz's calculus, we can benefit from even a summary presentation of his understanding of the pertinent variables. The object is to encourage reliance at the optimal time, and whether the doctrine vindicates that result "depends on the information and incentives provided . . . by the legal regime."[124]

> [B]ecause both the productive value of reliance and the level of uncertainty change over time, there exists in any given negotiation, and for any transaction-specific investment, a moment at which it is optimal to begin investing. We can identify this moment by comparing the incremental value of waiting to see what uncertainty will be resolved with the incremental cost of delaying an otherwise productive investment.[125]

---

[123] This is essentially Professor Scott's point in his discussion of *Hoffman*. *See* Scott, *supra* note 69, at 90–91.

[124] Katz, *supra* note 120, at 1270.

[125] *Id.* at 1268.

Timing, so the saying goes, is everything.[126]

The doctrine works so long as it encourages the right amount of reliance at the right time, and the doctrine does just that if it compels the conclusion that the offeror has (or has not) made an enforceable promise at the right (or wrong) time. But there is, once more, a math problem:

> In order for this method of regulation to work effectively, however, courts must be able to compare the potential costs and benefits of reliance after the fact, and they must be willing to associate this cost-benefit calculus with the Restatement (Second)'s standard of reasonableness. It is questionable whether actual judges and juries can perform this exercise in practice, except with the roughest approximation. Given the difficulty of the task and given the courts' traditional focus on convention maintenance,[[127]] they are more likely to identify the reasonableness standard with customary expectations than with efficiency.[128]

Katz's solution to the math problem is to make the correct answer more salient. He draws on the Calabresian *least–cost avoider*[129] device to identify the party on whom liability should be placed in order to encourage optimal reliance, and concludes that "[o]ther things being equal, the least-cost avoider is the party with the bargaining power *ex post*."[130]

> If she can capture the full productive benefits of reliance, which she can accomplish if she has all the bargaining power, she will have the appropriate incentive to weigh costs against benefits. This position will induce her to wait to make an offer until the very moment it is socially optimal to rely, leading to the desired outcome. If the offeror cannot capture the full benefits of reliance, on the other hand, she will weigh

---

[126] *See* Charles J. Goetz & Robert E. Scott, *Enforcing Promises: An Examination of the Basis of Contract*, 89 YALE L.J. 1261, 1267–70 (1980).

[127] Katz explains the concept of convention maintenance earlier in the article. Convention maintenance includes "activities such as describing and promulgating the prevailing conventions; protecting the reliance investments of those who operate according to them; providing newcomers with incentives to learn them; and assisting everyone in applying them in ambiguous and novel situations—all for the sake of averting misunderstandings." Katz, *supra* note 120, at 1250–51.

[128] *Id.* at 1271 (footnote omitted).

[129] *Id.* at 1273. The least-cost avoider test posits that the parties can better evaluate costs and benefits at the time they act than courts can after the fact, and that courts should place liability on the least-cost avoider—the party that is best able to make and act on a cost-benefit analysis. *Id.* at 1272–73. *See* Guido Calabresi & Jon T. Hirschoff, *Toward a Test for Strict Liability in Torts*, 81 YALE L.J. 1055, 1060–76 (1972).

[130] Katz, *supra* note 120, at 1273 (footnotes omitted).

> the wasted reliance too heavily from the social viewpoint, and her incentive will be to wait too long before making an offer.[131]

Sometimes it will be the offeror who has the bargaining power and sometimes it will be the offeree. So long as the party with superior bargaining power has the liability, that party "does not need any legal protection to be induced to rely optimally; his bargaining power provides adequate protection."[132] Katz, then, translates what could be an impenetrable calculus into something ostensibly more accessible. But has he afforded us a construction of the doctrine that is easier than doing the math, or just *potentially* easier math?

Katz acknowledges that in the event bargaining power is equally distributed between the parties (and recognize that this may be dynamic both in terms of time and with regard to particular transactional issues) "there may be no particular efficiency advantage" to a categorical rule. Further, his model depends on the accessibility of crucial determinants: risk aversion, opportunities for investment in transaction-specific assets, and the parties' ability to go forward with the transaction.[133] So in response to these potential complicating factors, Katz offers several refinements, but even these reveal further potential complications. It is useful to consider his refinements seriatim.

Katz concludes that if the parties differ in their costs of bearing risk, then the risk of wasted reliance should be imposed on the party who can bear the risk at less cost. He recognizes, though, that the party who can bear risk at the lowest cost may not be the party with the greatest bargaining power. In that event, "we face a trade-off among costs, the precise nature of which will depend on the distribution of bargaining power."[134] This will require some potentially complicated calculation in order for the doctrine to comport with the math.

It would be difficult to conclude that there is a single optimal time to rely on a promise or offer; while it might be efficient to rely at T1 with regard to some form of investment, it may be more efficient to rely at T2 and T3 for other investments. Katz recognizes the challenge this presents to his approach. Still, though, he concludes that "so long as the [one party] has the bargaining power and the legal rule makes her bear the costs of wasted reliance, she will have the correct incentives to choose the second-best outcome."[135]

---

[131] *Id.* at 1273.

[132] *Id.* at 1276.

[133] *Id.* at 1281.

[134] *Id.* at 1284.

[135] *Id.* at 1287.

Katz's model assumes that both parties have equally good information about the costs and benefits of reliance. But what if their information is asymmetric or imperfect? Here he once again invokes *Hoffman*:

> Since Red Owl stood to receive a fraction of the revenues from the business under their standard franchise contract, they benefitted substantially from the Hoffmans' early reliance. While the Hoffmans had some experience in running a grocery, they were new to franchising and knew less than the defendants did about the factors that would govern the decision whether to award a franchise. Red Owl certainly had better information about its own internal procedures and about the actual authority of its regional agent, who had made most of the specific representations that induced the Hoffmans to rely so heavily.[136]

Once the analysis is cast in those terms, we can appreciate the coincidence of consequentialist and deontic values. And we can see, too, how a court applying the deontic language of the doctrine could reach the efficient result. Generally, "[p]utting the cost of lost reliance on offerors is a way of providing them incentives to search for and discover . . . information [regarding the risk of revocation or withdrawal]."[137] Just as information asymmetries are pertinent to the least-cost avoider calculus, they are probative too of the normative calculus that is considerate of deontic values: "[W]e want to put the loss from wasted reliance on the person in the best position to anticipate getting the gains from it at the end of the game. . . . This will tend to be the party with the bargaining power, and it will also tend to be the party who is better informed."[138]

The bottom line for Katz, though perhaps too simplistically stated, is to put the risk of reliance on the dominant party. Though it may not be the case that the doctrine assures that result, it does seem that the doctrine accommodates that result. So Katz's approach demonstrates the limits of doctrine, in one sense, and the power of doctrine, in another. We might not be able to get (or process) the information we need to arrive at the best (in the sense of most efficient) rule, but the doctrine can urge us toward the second-best result. Neither deontology nor consequentialism may reasonably aspire to do more than that.

From the observations and premises established in this and the foregoing chapters, what remains is to make what sense we can of the normativity of contract doctrine. That is the focus of Chapter Nine, "Toward an Empirical Morality."

---

[136] *Id.* at 1289 (footnote omitted).

[137] *Id.* at 1290.

[138] *Id.* at 1291.

9

TOWARD AN EMPIRICAL MORALITY

APPRECIATION OF THE RELATIONSHIP between deontology and consequentialism in the exemplary contexts considered in the preceding chapters demonstrates that the dichotomy cannot explain, cannot theorize the contract law actually revealed in the operation of doctrine. At this juncture, then, it is necessary to investigate further that relationship. That inquiry, in turn, will support conclusions of moral psychology that bear on and inform an empirical morality that makes more sense of the deontic and consequentialist as dialectical constituents of a coherent theory of the contract law.

Recall that we start from the premise that *consequentialism* determines the morality of an act by reference to its consequences, and only by reference to its consequences. In legal theory, consequentialism most typically takes the form of utilitarianism or welfare economics. Perhaps the prototypical consequentialist theory conclusion concerns so-called "efficient breach."[1] That is the idea that A may breach her contract with B in order to enter a contract with C, where C values the subject matter of the contract more than does B. A may then (be required to) compensate B with some of the proceeds A receives from C and at the end of the day A will have more than she would have had had she

---

[1] The idea comes from Holmes:

> The only universal consequence of a legally binding promise is, that the law makes the promisor pay damages if the promised event does not come to pass. In every case it leaves him free from interference until the time for fulfilment has gone by, and therefore free to break his contract if he chooses.

OLIVER WENDELL HOLMES, THE COMMON LAW 236 (Mark DeWolfe Howe ed., 1963).

performed the contract with B; B will be in as good a position as if A had performed; and C, who values the subject matter more than either A or B, will have it. So long as we can be confident of the math, A, B, and C should all be pleased with that result, were we able to capture their idiosyncratic valuations so simply. Consequentialism, then, could not make sense of law that would undermine such a result. But consequentialism, in that stark form, actually assumes its conclusions within its premises: It tells us that *so long as* we care only about allocating value among A, B, and C in the Pareto superior (or even Kaldor–Hicks efficient) way, then legal doctrine that effects that result comports with that object.

Although efficient breach has remained controversial among the commentators,[2] there does not seem to be much controversy in the courts: It is difficult to find courts that have reached conclusions consistent with the efficient breach model.[3] So there must be something else that is lost in such an application of the consequentialist perspective. That "something else" may be deontic, some "value" not readily amenable to valuation. Commentators have suggested that if A makes a promise to B, A instantaneously gives something to B,[4] and that "something" is therefore instantaneously no longer A's to take back. *Promise*, then, necessarily invokes a deontic conception, a conception perhaps founded on the likes of individual autonomy.[5] What the incidents of such autonomy or alternative deontic conception might be is not determinable by reference to consequentialist premises.

> Methodologically, it is difficult to ascertain, quantify, and aggregate people's disinterested preferences, . . . for moral norms. Conceptually, a judgment regarding

---

[2] *See* James Gordley, *A Perennial Misstep: From Cajetan to Fuller and Perdue to "Efficient Breach,"* Issues in Legal Scholarship, Symposium: Fuller and Perdue (2001) Article 4 at 11–17, *available at* http://www.bepress.com/cgi/viewcontent.cgi?article=1003&context=ils (concluding that efficient breach theories misunderstand the effect of promising); Fred S. McChesney, *Tortious Interference with Contract versus "Efficient" Breach: Theory and Empirical Evidence*, 28 J. Legal Stud. 131 (1999) (considering the literature and concluding that tortious interference provides the first best solution).

[3] Daniel Friedmann, *The Efficient Breach Fallacy*, 18 J. Leg. Stud. 1, 24 (1989) ("The dangers of the theory of efficient breach have not been lost on judges, whose decisions are evidence of that theory's failure not only as a normative but as a descriptive matter."). Of course, any decision in which a court awards plaintiff full compensation and then leaves the breaching promisor free to make the better deal could be seen as an instance of a court's acting consistently with an "efficient breach" rationale. But Friedmann's point is simply that courts may, and in some settings do, award specific performance or impose liability on third parties (for tortious interference) in order to deprive the breaching promisor the benefit that would otherwise flow from an "efficient" breach. *See id.* at 18–23, and cases cited therein.

[4] *See* Gordley, *supra* note 2, at 11–12; *see also* Peter Benson, *Contract as a Transfer of Ownership*, 48 Wm. & Mary L. Rev. 1673 (2007) (Promise effects instantaneous transfer from promisor to promisee.); Andrew S. Gold, *A Property Theory of Contract*, 103 Nw. U. L. Rev. 1 2009 (conceptualizing contract in terms of just property acquisition).

[5] *See* Charles Fried, Contract as Promise: A Theory of Contractual Obligation (1981).

> the morality of the act or rule, based on all relevant factors, must not be confused with one such factor, namely the act or rule's effect on the well-being of the person making the judgment. There is a fundamental difference between normative judgments and individual preferences. Judgments are either right or wrong, while individuals have the final say on the content of their preferences. The soundness of a judgment depends on the validity of the arguments underlying it, not on the number of its supporters or the intensity of their support.[6]

It is not enough, then, to identify preferences; we must assess their normative basis: Why does the actor hold those beliefs? Does the *preference* reflect a correct or incorrect *judgment*? So, for example, commentators who rely on the property paradigm to criticize economic breach conceptions are countering the consequentialist conclusion on the basis of normative premises.

Consequentialists have a response to that: In determining the valuations the actors impose on the transaction subject matter, for purposes of deciding whether and when a breach is efficient, we would take into account "the realization of moral rights."[7] That response might not be available to methods of economic analysis relying solely on preference satisfaction,[8] because the satisfaction of actual preferences rather than normatively ideal preferences results only in the satisfaction of actual preferences, not the realization of greater good, the consequence consequentialism would vindicate. But, so the argument goes, it might be available in certain sophisticated commercial and corporate contexts in which the good is measured solely by wealth maximization.[9] To the extent, though, that cost-benefit analyses, such as those necessary to maximize wealth, impact individual welfare, *i.e.,* sacrificing A's job to provide employment for B and C, deontic choices could not be removed from a comprehensive normative analysis.[10] At some point in the calculus, ideal preferences matter and to the extent that those ideal preferences are deontologically constructed, we cannot abide consequentialist formulations that are

[6] *See* Eyal Zamir & Barak Medina, *Law, Morality, and Economics: Integrating Moral Constraints with Economic Analysis of Law*, 96 Calif. L. Rev. 323, 338 (citations omitted) and text accompanying nn.53–55. Zamir and Medina should be understood not as offering a critique of all consequential analyses, only of those that would measure human welfare solely by reference to revealed preferences.

[7] *Id.* at 341.

[8] *Id.*

[9] *See* Daniel A. Farber, *Economic Efficiency and The Ex Ante Perspective, in* The Jurisprudential Foundations of Corporate and Commercial Law 54 (Jody S. Kraus & Steven D. Walt eds., 2000); Alan Schwartz & Robert E. Scott, *Market Damages, Efficient Contracting, and the Economic Waste Fallacy*, 108 Colum. L. Rev. 1610 (2008).

[10] *See* Zamir & Medina, *supra* note 6, at 342.

inconsiderate of such deontic constraints.[11] Indeed, it may well be the case that actual preferences must be constrained in order to maximize ideal preferences.[12]

Insofar as consequentialism entails a cost-benefit analysis, it can only operate once we have established what the costs and benefits are. For example, although we can well understand that the creation of wealth is a benefit, it is only an instrumental benefit. Wealth is a means to an end—health, education, longer and more comfortable life—not an end in itself, save for those who really believe that she who dies with the most toys wins. So to the extent that we need deontology to fill in those normative blanks, to reveal to us what the good things are (as well as what they are not), consequentialism lacks the data necessary to make sense of its invocations. Even the most obvious indicia of benefit may be incomplete: It may be that human happiness does not correlate directly with wealth *qua* wealth; the correlation instead may be with relative wealth. Then if the object of human striving is happiness, consequentialism might value relative similarity of wealth as a benefit and great dissonance in wealth as a cost, notwithstanding the fact that a Kaldor–Hicks (or even a Pareto) move might increase the size of the pie. What matters, ultimately, is our characterization of benefit.

Further, to the extent that actual and ideal preferences may be inconsistent, a consequentialist perspective insensitive to such inconsistencies will not result in realization of the greatest good for the greatest number. If we are not able to calculate accurately the costs and benefits to be set off against one another, realization of the greatest good is concomitantly undermined.[13] And, finally, there is reason to question whether the simple deontology–consequentialism dichotomy works at all in the psychology of human agents. To appreciate how that would matter to the appraisal of theory, it is necessary to consider as well the nature of the deontic inquiry and its relationship to positive theories of morality.

A moderate, or threshold, deontology need not necessarily be isolated from consequentialist considerations.[14] It is not difficult to see both the consequentialist and the deontic merge in a simple variant of the trolley hypothetical:[15]

---

[11] On such issues see 1 LAW AND ECONOMICS 93, 106, 109, 115, 129 (Jules Coleman & Jeffery Lange eds., 1992).

[12] *See generally* MATTHEW D. ADLER & ERIC A. POSNER, NEW FOUNDATIONS OF COST-BENEFIT ANALYSIS (2006) (on vagaries of constituents of cost-benefit analyses); Eyal Zamir, *The Efficiency of Paternalism*, 84 VA. L. REV. 229 (1998) (on actual rather than rational preferences).

[13] Eric A. Posner, *Economic Analysis of Contract Law After Three Decades: Success or Failure?* 112 YALE L.J. 829, 832–55 (2003).

[14] *See* Zamir & Medina, *supra* note 6, at 343 (discussing "threshold deontology"); *see also* JOHN RAWLS, A THEORY OF JUSTICE 26 (Rev. ed. 1999) ("[D]eontological theories are defined as non-teleological ones, not as views that characterize the rightness of institutions and acts independently from their consequences. All ethical doctrines worth our attention take consequences into account in judging rightness.").

[15] The source of the generic trolley hypothetical is Philippa Foot, *The Problem of Abortion and the Doctrine of Double Effect*, 5 OXFORD REVIEW 5–15 (1967).

> You see a trolley barreling down the tracks and the motorman is slumped over the controls, unconscious. A short distance ahead of the runaway trolley is a group of five workers who are unable to get out of harm's way in time. You notice a switch within your easy reach that would divert the trolley onto a side track, where there is another, single worker, similarly trapped who would be killed were you to throw the switch and divert the trolley. Throwing the switch saves five lives at the cost of the one life. Should you throw the switch?

Research has demonstrated that more people would throw the switch (or, at least, say they would throw the switch) than would not.[16] Fewer, though, would throw a large person (we can assume that the thrower himself would not be large enough to divert the trolley) from an overpass into the path of the runaway trolley if that is what it took to divert the trolley and save the lives of the five workers trapped on the tracks.[17] It is not immediately obvious how either the deontic or consequentialist hairs would be split to support those apparently divergent conclusions. From the perspective of the consequentialist, saving five lives at the cost of one is desirable—all things, of course, being equal.

The calculus may change again once we adjust the facts: The runaway trolley approaches five workers who cannot escape; if you throw a switch, the trolley will be diverted onto another track where it will strike one person, your child. The consequentialist, the true consequentialist should have no greater utilitarian problem with this revised scenario. Saving five lives at the cost of one is still the better deal, still preserves the best consequences, so long as we measure the quality of consequences based on the quantity of lives saved. But even if you were convinced that you might throw the switch to save five strangers' lives by taking the life of one other stranger, can you be as certain that you would do the same if the life sacrificed were that of your child? Of course not. The existential squeamishness you feel, that we may imagine even the most committed utilitarian would feel, is the deontic tug, and is entirely consistent with evolutionary theory.

Now we could put that sense of parental duty in consequentialist terms: Once a parent is asked to sacrifice the life of her child to save five strangers the "cost" of making what seems to be the "easy" consequentialist choice is obscured. That is, the cost of killing your own child, even in order to save the children of five other people, *feels* greater than the benefit realized by saving the five innocent lives. Consider:

> [A] consequentialist may argue that a suggestion to kill one person in order to use her organs to save the lives of three other individuals is only seemingly desirable.

---

[16] *See* Marc D. Hauser, Moral Minds: How Nature Designed Our Universal Sense of Right and Wrong 112–31 (2006).

[17] *Id.*

> If the victim were to be selected from among hospitalized patients, such a practice would in the long run deter people from being hospitalized lest their organs be harvested against their will. Such a fear may have a very detrimental effect on the overall health of the population. Should physicians be allowed to choose the victim from the entire population, this may result in arbitrariness and cause general anxiety. Even if one could guarantee that the choice of the victim would be random and fair, such a scheme might dramatically reduce peoples' incentive to look after their own health. In fact, assuming that sick people may not be suitable organ donors, such a general scheme may even create an incentive for people to become moderately sick. Rather than prolonging people's lifespan and enhancing quality of life, such a general scheme may in fact cause more deaths.[18]

But our thought experiment can adjust for such consequences of the consequentialist perspective and still not be able to avoid the deontic tug. Even the parent of the most loathsome child would still feel a sense of duty for which the consequentialist could not completely account. So just as the deontologist must acknowledge some concern with outcomes and consequences, the consequentialist must acknowledge a role for deontic concerns that cannot be captured in mere maximization of the good, or at least the good construed in strictly quantitative terms. Once quality cooperates with quantity, deontology and consequentialism intersect: "[T]here is nothing incoherent in maintaining that (contrary to consequentialism) the goodness of outcomes is not *the only* factor, and that (contrary to absolutist deontology) constraints may be outweighed by enough good outcomes."[19] That may describe so-called "folk morality,"[20] or "moderate" deontology.[21]

The confluence, or at least overlap, of the deontic and consequentialist intimates the operation of morality at a more fundamental level than that captured by either of the two dominant perspectives. They may, in fact, be ramifications rather than constituents of the moral calculus, as least so far as concepts such as legal doctrine are concerned. Ultimately, we must understand legal normativity in terms of general human normativity. That is, it would do us no more good to understand legal doctrine as accomplishing results beyond human moral functioning than it would to appreciate music at frequencies perceptible only to other species. Sure, we might recognize that there are frequencies inaccessible to us and that those frequencies matter in some phenomenal world, but we cannot rely on them to order our affairs within the accessible spectrum.[22] There is more on this below.[23]

---

[18] *See* Zamir & Medina, *supra* note 6, at 333–34.

[19] *See id.* at 344–45 (emphasis added).

[20] *See* Kwame Anthony Appiah, Experiments in Ethics 76–77 (2008).

[21] *See* Zamir & Medina, *supra* note 6, at 326, 328, 336 n.42, 342–3, 345 n.85, 347, 349, 353 n.106, 382, 391.

[22] Appiah, *supra* note 20, at 22–23.

[23] Professor Jesse Prinz discusses appreciation for the impact of empirical science on moral philosophy. *See infra* text accompanying notes 98–104.

First, it is necessary to consider what might be more crucial to appreciating doctrine than either deontology *or* consequentialism alone: the *relationship* between them.

A. The Limits of the Deontic–Consequentialist Dichotomy

It would *seem* to be the case that deontology and consequentialism could not be a matter of degree *vis-a-vis* one another. That is, given the structure of each perspective, there would not be degrees of deontology and consequentialism, such that at some point more of one, say, the cost—consequence—in terms of human-well being could be so great that a deontic value could be compromised. The consequentialist would not be troubled by any compromise of a deontic duty if the result of such a compromise were a Pareto superior move.[24] Similarly, if breaking a promise undermines the promissee's autonomy and so compromises a deontic object by treating a human agent as a means rather than an end in himself,[25] then the strict Kantian would have you disclose to the enraged and armed husband the true location of his unfaithful spouse, or at least you could not lie about it.[26] But that is not how we work: We put even the most ostensibly inflexible moral imperatives into a calculus that is redolent of cost–benefit. There is abundant reason to conclude that our moral commitments, such as they are, are in fact context-dependent.[27]

All this is not to say that there is a fundamental affinity between deontology and consequentialism. (I take no position here on that question.) It is to recognize that there are, for all intents and purposes, no pure deontologists and perhaps no pure consequentialists; we all reach conclusions that strike a balance somewhere between those two, *i.e.,* our deontology ("because it is the right thing to do!") is qualified by consequentialism ("not at that cost"), and our consequentialism, in turn, by our deontology. We can acknowledge that there is a bit of deontology in consequentialism (*What* are the values we want to maximize?)[28] and maybe a bit of consequentialism in deontology (Is not more of a good—*e.g.,* autonomy—better than less of it?).

---

[24] *See generally* Louis Kaplow & Steven Shavell, *Fairness versus Welfare*, 114 HARV. L. REV. 961 (2001) (arguing that consequentialist welfare principles of legal theory should always take precedence over principles of fairness); Louis Kaplow & Steven Shavell, *Notions of Fairness Versus the Pareto Principle: On the Role of Logical Consistency*, 110 YALE L.J. 237 (2000) (applying Kaplow and Shavell's argument from *Fairness versus Welfare* more specifically to the Pareto Principle).

[25] FRIED, *supra* note 5, at 7–17.

[26] *See* HAUSER, *supra* note 16, at 15 (suggesting that a strict application of Kant's categorical imperative might force otherwise moral 1930s Germans to surrender to the Nazis any Jews that they might be hiding).

[27] *See* JOHN M. DORIS, LACK OF CHARACTER 39–51 (2002) (concluding that Stanley Milgram's shock and obedience experiments reveal subjects' situational morality).

[28] *See* Guido Calabresi & A. Douglas Melamed, *Property Rules, Liability Rules, and Inalienability: One View of the Cathedral*, 85 HARV. L. REV. 1089, 1090 (1982) (discussing law's necessary decision-making as to relative "entitlement" of parties).

In their recent paper, Professors Eyal Zamir and Barak Medina consider the fit, such as it is, between deontic and consequentialist concepts in legal–moral settings.[29] They formulate the two normative objects in the terms suggested above: deontology based on fundamental obligation and consequentialism based on cost–benefit analyses. The authors recognize the "moral repugnance" of much of consequentialism and survey five responses, in particular.[30] Their conclusion is that policy analyses should incorporate deontic constraints, even if just as part of a cost–benefit analysis.[31]

What emerges, then, is an empirical morality, a depiction of the normative sense that better captures what we do when we perform normative analyses. Zamir and Medina recognize that it is difficult to ascertain just what the fit between cost–benefit and deontic obligation may be: considerations such as "lexical priority,"[32] small versus large benefit comparison,[33] "chronologically remote benefits and costs,"[34] "probabilistic costs and benefits,"[35] and the promotion of good compared with the elimination of bad.[36] Indeed, given the uncertainties they identify in setting up the formula to begin with, it is not surprising that their solution is valuable more as an illustration of the intractable nature of moral disagreement than as a means to reduce incidences of it. Their object is to demonstrate how deontic constraints can and need to be incorporated into cost–benefit analyses. It is difficult to take the ostensible certainty of their math too seriously and, for present purposes, there is no reason to assume that we must.

What Zamir and Medina capture quite well is the deontic–consequentialist dynamic in the moral psychology of human agents *as a dialectic*. We can, after all, see the deontic and consequentialist perspectives as points on a normative continuum. The way that we would value (for lack of a better word) the deontic constraint on cost–benefit analysis gives us the sense that the strictness of the cost–benefit analysis is in fact moderated by consideration of deontic constraints. The deontic constraint is either more or less significant (afforded more or less weight in the calculus) given a variety of factors such as those Zamir and Medina identify. What matters is whether the deontic–consequentialist relationship is in fact interdependent, and interdependent in a way that would matter to the normativity of legal doctrine, even in an area of the law as discrete as contract. If doctrine is sensitive to the deontic–consequentialist dynamic so construed, then we

---

[29] *See* Zamir & Medina, *supra* note 6.

[30] *Id.* at 333–42.

[31] *Id.* at 342; *see also* John M. Doris & Alexandra Plakias, *How to Argue about Disagreement, in* 2 MORAL PSYCHOLOGY 303, 322–23 (Walter Sinnott-Amrstrong ed., 2008) (describing the deontic–consequentialist tension).

[32] Zamir & Medina, *supra* note 6, at 354.

[33] *Id.* at 354–55.

[34] *Id.* at 356.

[35] *Id.* at 356–57.

[36] *Id.* at 358–59.

may have reason to question normative theories that are insensitive to that dynamic. And if doctrine *must, of necessity* reflect that dynamic, then we can see how a proposed unitary normative theory that does not must fail.

B. Moral Psychology

In order to reach a conclusion about the normative proclivities of legal doctrine, it is worthwhile (perhaps indispensable) to begin with a better understanding of moral reasoning than the deontic–consequentialist dichotomy suggests. Indeed, if Zamir and Medina are right insofar as they conclude that normative analyses must appreciate a fit, a dynamic relationship between the deontic and the consequentialist, then the source of that relationship must be in human moral psychology. Legal doctrine is, after all, a way for humans to order normative relations. The only source for such legal morality would be the human normative sense, and there is no obvious argument in favor of basing legal morality on anything other than human morality, which is a product of our moral psychology. This is *not* to suggest that moral reasoning, strictly deontic or strictly consequentialist, is not a worthwhile intellectual exercise in its own right. The point here is that such reasoning fails to explain adequately a human artifact, contract doctrine, which is, I believe, a response to the psychology of human agents in the exchange context. My critique is of either unitary deontic or consequentialist moral theory as an interpretation of doctrine, not of moral theory as theory.

There is just now emerging a vibrant literature on moral psychology,[37] the basis of an empirical morality. Though it is misleading to formulate the effort in too simplistic terms, there are certain aspects of the scholarly dialogue that are particularly pertinent to the instant inquiry, specifically: What is (are) the basis(es) of human moral psychology and what are the consequences of our answering that question for conclusions concerning the normativity of legal doctrine? Ultimately, it seems to be the case that our moral judgments reflect some fundamental calculus, the contours of which are not accessible to us, at least not accessible to each of us in the same way. Two sources of analogy have been the focus of a good deal of the literature: language and emotions.

1. MORALITY AND LANGUAGE AND EMOTION

The architecture that supports the language–morality analogy is the work of Noam Chomsky and John Rawls. It is impossible to do justice to the work of either theorist in

[37] *See* Walter Sinnott-Armstrong, *Introduction* to 1 MORAL PSYCHOLOGY at xiii, xiii-xiv (Walter Sinnott-Armstrong ed., 2008) ("Since the 1990s . . . many philosophers have begun to mine cognitive psychology and brain science . . . for general philosophical lessons. . . . This new way of doing philosophy . . . is especially strong in ethics or moral philosophy.").

the truncated presentation of their ideas necessary to support the argument of this book. But it is possible to describe how their suggestions have invigorated the work of empirical moral theorists.

> Chomsky transformed the study of language and mind by arguing that all normal human beings are endowed with a genetic program for language acquisition. Chomsky drew attention to the fact that, prior to any formal instruction, once a child has mastered her native language, she is able to make a wide range of judgments about the properties and relations of expressions in the language, including whether any random sound sequence constitutes a grammatical sentence; whether a given expression is ambiguous; whether, given two arbitrary expressions, one is a paraphrase or entailment or rhyme of the other; and a large number of additional properties and relations. Chomsky argued that these behaviors would be inexplicable without presupposing the child's tacit knowledge of the grammar of her language. He reoriented theoretical linguistics toward the empirical investigation of the principles underlying this postulated knowledge, or *linguistic competence*; and, in so doing, helped revive aspects of the rationalist tradition of Descartes, Liebniz, and Kant.
>
> Rawls was one of the first philosophers to notice the potential implications of Chomsky's project for moral philosophy. In *A Theory of Justice*, he pointed to several structural similarities between the explicative or descriptive part of ethics and theoretical linguistics, and suggested that just as the latter studies aspects of linguistic competence, so the former should be directed toward investigating our *moral* competence, or what Rawls there called our sense of justice. Rawls thus signaled a displacement of the narrower, semantic concerns of early twentieth-century philosophers like Moore, Ayer, and Stevenson, and a return to an older conception of ethics, assumed by all the leading Enlightenment moralists, who placed at the forefront of theoretical inquiry the empirical study of the human mind, and its various faculties and sentiments.[38]

From such premises over the last several years philosophers, psychologists, and anthropologists (among others[39]) have considered the innateness of morality in terms of the language analogy. The question, succinctly put, is whether morality, like language,

[38] John M. Mikhail, *Rawls' Linguistic Analogy: A Study of the "Generative Grammar" Model of Moral Theory Described by John Rawls in* A THEORY OF JUSTICE 2-3 (May 2000) (Ph.D. Dissertation, Cornell University) (Georgetown Public Law Research Paper No. 766464), *available at* SSRN: http://ssrn.com/abstract=766464.

[39] Including law professors such as John Mikhail, and, more recently, see Paul H. Robinson, Robert Kurzban, & Owen D. Jones, *The Origins of Shared Intuitions of Justice*, 60 VAND. L. REV. 1633 (2007) (Robinson is a law professor, Jones is a professor of both law and biology, and Kurzban is a professor of psychology). These ideas were perhaps first developed in RICHARD ALEXANDER, THE BIOLOGY OF MORAL SYSTEMS (1987).

emanates from some innate core understanding, perhaps inaccessible (at least so far) to empirical study, that fixes the contours of our morality as well as the potential and limits of moral consensus. If the analogy works, if it is apt, then the study of morality may in important respects parallel the study of language. There is no one correct elaboration of the innate language sense—no one perfect language—but there are certainly language patterns that are more accessible and even some language patterns that seem nearly inevitable.[40]

Further, we can identify language centers in the brain, and from that identification reach conclusions about the relationships among language patterns.[41] Insofar as those neural loci reveal something about the fit between language and emotion they may, in turn, support generalization as well as specification regarding the common physical manifestations of emotion. It is, then, not too great an extension to discover the source of morality, or at least the source of our moral sense, in emotion. Several commentators have posited a resonance between emotion and morality. The work of Professors Jonathan Haidt and Richard Joyce bears particular mention.

Haidt's method is "experimental philosophy," a means of isolating aspects of moral reasoning or reaction. With several co-authors over the course of several projects,[42] he has posited a necessary relationship between five general intuitive modules and familiar normative precepts: "harm/care, fairness/reciprocity, in-group/loyalty, authority/respect, and purity/sanctity."[43] There are good theoretical and empirical reasons to believe that these precepts are the product of evolutionary adaptation, and reflect context-appropriate responses (so long as you understand appropriateness in terms of survival and reproduction) to the array of circumstances that we confront, and which our hunter-gatherer Paleolithic ancestors confronted on the savannah:

> Morality evolved and developed in order to coordinate and harmonize the interests (both self- and other-regarding) of humans living in mutually dependent communities. Such communities would need to regulate conflicts of interest, divisions of labor, and

---

[40] Examples would include profanity, STEVEN PINKER, THE STUFF OF THOUGHT 327–31 (2007), politeness through indirect language, *id.* at 380, and limited counting words in primitive societies, *id.* at 138–41.

[41] *See, e.g., id.* at 331–37 (describing the neural origins of profanity).

[42] *See, e.g.,* Jonathan Haidt & Fredrik Bjorklund, *Social Intuitionists Answer Six Questions About Moral Psychology, in* 2 MORAL PSYCHOLOGY 181 (Walter Sinnott-Armstrong ed., 2008); Jonathan Haidt & Fredrik Bjorklund, *Social Intuitionists Reason, in Conversation, in* 2 MORAL PSYCHOLOGY 241 (Walter Sinnott-Armstrong ed., 2008); Jonathan Haidt & Jesse Graham, *When Morality Opposes Justice: Conservatives Have Moral Intuitions that Liberals may not Recognize,* 20 SOC. JUST. RES. 98 (2007); Jonathan Haidt & Craig Joseph, *The Moral Mind: How Five Sets of Innate Intuitions Guide the Development of Many Culture-Specific Virtues, and Perhaps Even Modules, in* 3 THE INNATE MIND 367 (Peter Carruthers, Stephen Laurence, & Stephen P. Stich eds., 2005); Dacher Keltner & Jonathan Haidt, *Social Functions of Emotions, in* EMOTIONS: CURRENT ISSUES AND FUTURE DIRECTIONS 192 (Tracy J. Mayne & George A. Bonanno eds., 2001).

[43] Haidt & Joseph, *supra* note 42, at 381.

> hierarchy arrangements, and systems of moral norms would help make such cooperative projects beneficial. On the self-regarding side, morality evolved to shape character and specify worthwhile lives and ideals of behavior to which to strive. To understand the full story, we will need what we only have pieces of—namely, insights from evolutionary biology, animal ethology, developmental psychology, learning theory, psychiatry, cognitive neuroscience, and cultural anthropology. All these disciplines and research programs are essential to (and thus have a say in) the genealogy [of morals].[44]

It is, of course, the case that the challenges we confront today are not identical to those our Paleolithic forebears confronted; but the differences are not so essential that the emotional–moral reactions that have evolved from that time render us incompetent to function today. The environment does, though, present challenges:

> Even when an animal lives in the environment for which it is adapted, the actual domain never perfectly matches the proper domain; the module produces false positives and false negatives. For a species such as ours, which has experienced rapid environmental change, and which deliberately manipulates its physical and social environment for a variety of reasons, we can be quite certain that the actual domain diverges from the proper domain to a substantial degree: Our moral intuitions are sure to be engaged—or suppressed—in ways that do not contribute to each individual's Darwinian success.[45]

The contemporary story, then, of our emotional–moral reaction mechanisms must be appreciated as not categorically dissimilar from any of our more obviously physical propensities. We are built the way we are in large part because of the physical challenges that confronted our ancestors, and that applies to our emotional–moral predispositions as much as to our physical characteristics.[46] Natural selection works on behavioral predispositions as well as physical ones.

Two questions immediately arise: First, is morality innate? And, second, is an innate morality a morality at all? The next section addresses those questions.

---

[44] Owen Flanagan, Hagop Sarkissian, & David Wong, *Naturalizing Ethics*, *in* 1 MORAL PSYCHOLOGY 1, 10 (Walter Sinnott-Armstrong ed., 2008).

[45] Haidt & Joseph, *supra* note 42, at 381.

[46] The thesis and argument of this chapter depends only on the accuracy of the psychological model; it is not dependent on the model's etiology, which may be more controversial. *See* Brian Leiter & Michael Weisberg, *Why Evolutionary Biology is (So Far) Irrelevant to Legal* Regulation, 29 J. LAW & PHILOS. 31 (2010).

2. IS MORALITY MORAL?

If morality is something the existence and development of which is without our conscious control, then that would impose limitations on normative argument, and those limitations might well circumscribe legal doctrine (and law) in ways that would matter to an effort to formulate coherently the normativity of a body of legal doctrine. It may be that what we think of as the core of our moral sense is necessarily innate, hard-wired. This is not to suggest that any particular moral code is innate and strongly predisposed; it is to suggest that the way we approach moral dilemmas is a product of the nature of our human agency. Even if we conclude that morality is innate in that way, we need to come to terms with what that means. If morality is akin to, indeed not normatively different from, our visual and aural capacities, that might have some impact on our reaction to deontic and consequentialist legal theory.

Once we think of morality in more empirical terms, it becomes clear that its normativity wavers, at least a bit. If, upon your arrival home each evening, your very affectionate dog jumps into your lap and begins licking your face with great zeal, you are likely to construe this as the type of affection that only such a devoted companion can provide. Do you feel differently about the display, and about your dog, if you learn that what you take as enthusiastic affection is nothing more than the dog's fondness for your skin's saltiness and the relief of separation anxiety? That is, if what appears to be a selfless expression of affection is instead the selfish satisfaction of a flavor preference, some of the "magic" is gone. Similarly, if what explains ostensibly protective proclivities toward our offspring is nothing more than reproductive narcissism, we may *feel* differently about the parent–child bond.[47] That is not to suggest that the bond is any less inviolable; it is just to observe that, once explained in more empirical terms, our emotional reaction to the innate changes. At some point, what we think of as the defining essence of morality seems to evaporate. We are not moral because we have a choice if our moral choices are strongly predisposed.

Professor Richard Joyce has suggested the evolutionary basis of morality and has built from it a conception of the relationship between morality and emotion that resonates well with familiar moral reactions.[48] For morality, as we have come to conceive of it, to have evolutionary substance (if morality alone does have evolutionary substance, and is not just a free rider on some other trait), it must result in benefit to oneself, at least indirectly (one's genes directly). Joyce reasons that if what we call *morality* did not provide

---

[47] This does not mean, however, that helpful or altruistic behaviors motivated by evolutionary considerations are any less helpful or altruistic. *See* RICHARD JOYCE, THE EVOLUTION OF MORALITY 17 (2006) (noting that although husband's behavior in looking after his sick wife may be described as motivated by reproductive self-interest, he may still genuinely feel that he wants to alleviate her suffering for her sake).

[48] *See id.*

a survival–reproductive advantage, we would not be moral, because our moral forebears would not have survived to pass along the *moral* propensity.

> The hypothesis, then, is that natural selection opted for a special motivational mechanism for this realm: moral conscience. If you are thinking of an outcome in terms of something that you desire, you can always say to yourself "But maybe forgoing the satisfaction of that desire wouldn't be *that* terrible." If, however, you are thinking of the outcome as something that is *desirable*—as having the quality of *demanding* desire—then your scope for rationalizing a spur-of-the-moment devaluation narrows. When a person believes that an act of cooperation is *morally* required—that it *must* be performed whether he likes it or not—then the possibilities for further internal negotiation on the matter diminish. If a person believes an action to be required by an authority from which he cannot escape, if he believes that in not performing it he will not merely frustrate himself, but will become *reprehensible* and *deserving of disapprobation*—then he is more likely to perform the action.[49]

The fact that a judgment is a moral judgment, with the consequences flowing from that heightened normativity, better assures that action (or inaction) consonant with that judgment will be realized.[50] Designation of a decision or action in moral terms invokes greater social significance. Not only do third parties have additional means to describe the agent's decision or action, that agent reacts to the attendant judgment with a more profound sense of his own self-image. It is one thing to confront the conclusion of another that your work is just not very good; it is wholly another to confront the accusation that it is dishonest. The latter is a more profound condemnation, a moral condemnation.

Now from the foregoing we should not assume that moral reasoning is necessarily something we do before the fact in order to actually arrive at a *moral judgment*. It could be that "reasoning concerning why [an] action is morally wrong is a kind of *post hoc* construction."[51] We are concerned both with how we will be able to describe our actions to ourselves and others (as well as with how others will view our actions before we even get the chance to explain ourselves). So if you were building an organism that would *act* morally (and that is what you would do if you first connected morality and survival–reproductive success),

---

[49] *Id.* at 111. Joyce also notes Daniel Dennett's theory that moral principles serve as "conversation stoppers," providing an "a-rational termination" of what would otherwise be "a decision process that spirals fruitlessly to infinity." *Id.* at 111–12 (quoting DANIEL DENNETT, DARWIN'S DANGEROUS IDEA 506 (1995)).

[50] JOYCE, *supra* note 47, at 114 (noting that moral principles "increas[e] the likelihood that certain adaptive social behaviors will be performed").

[51] *Id.* at 116 (citing Jonathan Haidt, *The Emotional Dog and its Rational Tail: A Social Intuitionist Approach to Moral Judgment*, 108 PSYCHOL. REV. 814-834 (2001)); *see also* Haidt & Bjorklund, *supra* note 42, at 189–90 (discussing the "post hoc reasoning link").

you would build in a *sense* of morality that would be coextensive with a reputation for such adaptive behavior: "[H]ypothetically, a prudent person *would* choose to have a conscience,"[52] just as a successful hunter would "choose" to have good hand–eye coordination.

Connecting judgment with some more concrete, perhaps even physical, manifestation better assures conformity with moral dictates.[53] So is the symbiosis between morality and emotion designedly coincident? Are our emotional reactions, which have discernable neural and even physical manifestations, tied to our moral sense in such a way that those emotional reactions reflect and reinforce that sense? And, if they are, what would that tell us about the normativity of morality in terms that would make a difference to our conception of the normativity of legal doctrine? Is an invitation to reach a "just" result an admonition to do "what feels good" (or at least, "doesn't feel so bad")?

Consider the famous case of Phineas Gage who suffered a profound and, as it turns out, emotion-altering injury in 1848 when, as a result of an industrial accident, an iron bar one inch and a quarter in diameter was blown through his skull.[54] The rod entered below his left eye and exited through the top of his head, damaging his ventromedial prefrontal cortex and dramatically changing his personality: "Previously temperate, likable, and conscientious, after the accident Gage was crude, irresponsible, imprudent, and disrespectful of moral considerations."[55] That is, Gage went from being a person who exhibited estimable interpersonal—including moral—skills to being a person "disrespectful of moral considerations." Injury to an isolated portion of his brain impaired Gage's moral fitness. This episode has attracted much attention over the years in the neuroscience literature.[56] There are, now, many more examples of the organic bases of human emotion.[57] So far as normative theory might be concerned, though, the question remains whether certain identification of the physical manifestations of emotional reaction can tell us anything about the morality of morality. Theorists who posit a relationship between emotion and morality find the connection significant.

For example, consider once again the trolley case.[58] Recall that many of the subjects asked to compare the morality of (more impersonally) throwing a switch to sacrifice one

---

[52] JOYCE, *supra* note 47, at 120.

[53] Joyce points out that certain physical rewards, such as the orgasm, are already spoken-for and to usurp them might reduce the likelihood of perhaps more essential behaviors, such as reproduction. *Id.* at 114–15.

[54] This is a case considered by both JOYCE, *supra* note 47, at 124 and ANTONIO R. DAMASIO, DESCARTES' ERROR: EMOTION, REASON, AND THE HUMAN BRAIN 3-14 (1994).

[55] JOYCE, *supra* note 47, at 124.

[56] *Id.* at 125.

[57] *See, e.g.,* DAMASIO, *supra* note 54, at 52–81; Steven W. Anderson, Antoine Bechara, Hanna Damasio, Daniel Tranel & Antonio R. Damasio, *Impairment of Social and Moral Behavior Related to Early Damage in Human Prefrontal Cortex*, 2 NATURE NEUROSCIENCE 1032, 1032–37 (Nov. 1999); Jeffrey. L. Saver & A. Antonio. R. Damasio, *Preserved Access and Processing of Social Knowledge in a Patient with Acquired Sociopathy Due to Ventromedial Frontal Damage*, 29 NEUROPSYCHOLOGIA 1241, 1241–49 (1991).

[58] *See supra* text accompanying notes 15–18.

life to save five with the morality of throwing the large person over the bridge to spare five reached different conclusions.[59] From either the deontic or consequentialist perspective, the issue is whether sacrificing one innocent to save five innocents is moral; the deontologist will say *no* and the consequentialist would say *yes*. But then what explains the different results when the means of sacrifice change? Emotional reaction *may* explain the differing moral conclusions. Might our reasons for not throwing the large man onto the tracks reflect concerns about the inviolability of personal space?[60] Perhaps, but it would seem just as likely that, if we were questioned, after the fact, about our reasons for not sacrificing the one to save five (if saving the one required such direct physical intervention), we would offer a *post hoc* justification and we would adopt moral terms: "It would just be wrong to sacrifice an innocent life." Such *post hoc* rationalization may be our means of imposing a moral gloss on what is essentially amoral emotional reaction. Indeed, we would not need to look too hard to find an evolutionary source of the emotional reaction. It is likely that our more successful (in the evolutionary sense) forebears generally thought it as prudent, on a cost–benefit basis, to avoid physical confrontation ten thousand years ago as we do today. And that reaction—to generally avoid physical confrontation—if reinforced in terms of morality, becomes more salient. We can see how the reaction might be cast in emotional terms, and from there, the move to morality is not far.[61]

The foregoing rationalization may, admittedly, be no more than just that, a *post hoc* rationalization rather than an accurate explanation. In any event, it does seem to undermine some of the magic of morality, particularly if the magic is that certain *je ne sais quoi*. But just because we feel as though we are doing more than reacting in an evolutionarily predisposed way does not mean that we are. There is a dignity, even a majesty to moral characterization that suggests we are acting nobly, that we deserve praise (and that those who do not act so are acting immorally and deserve no such approbation). And there is a very tangible benefit to acting in a manner consistent with one's moral sense: It feels good. If you act immorally you feel bad; you despair, at least until you have worked out a rationalization that allows you to recast your immoral choice as moral (or, what may be just as well, amoral because it is beyond your control). Once you have rationalized, your critics—or those whom you could imagine to be your critics if they but knew—are themselves the immoral actors because they lack your moral insight. You begin to manifest the glow of the righteous, even better, the enhanced glow of the misunderstood

[59] *See* Marc D. Hauser, Liane Young & Fiery Cushman, *Reviving Rawls's Linguistic Analogy: Operative Principles and the Causal Structure of Moral Actions*, *in* 2 MORAL PSYCHOLOGY 107, 129–35 (Walter Sinnott-Armstrong ed., 2008).

[60] *See id.* at 131. There may well be, of course, any number of deontic or consequentialist "just so stories" that can rationalize the decision not to throw the large man onto the tracks. *See, e.g.*, Judith Jarvis Thomson, *The Trolley Problem*, 94 YALE L.J. 1395 (1985). The point here, though, is that we can identify a basis of distinction that does not need to rely on our ability to do either the deontic or consequentialist "math."

[61] Hauser, Young, & Cushman, *supra* note 59, at 117.

righteous. It remains, then, to consider how such an innate moral sense matters to the normativity of legal doctrine.

3. OF HUMAN AGENCY

If behavioral biology and evolutionary psychology have exposed morality in terms that deny some of the magic, then there would seem to be a crisis: There is nothing particularly moral (in the magical sense) about morality (in the empirical sense). What we have come to describe as moral beliefs and actions are just rationalizations of our emotional reactions that themselves are designed to facilitate our survival and reproductive success. That is, there is nothing inevitable about deontic duty and no consequentialist calculus that underwrites the morality of our beliefs and actions. There are just the beliefs and actions, and the labels we affix to them after the fact.

If our *object* in formulating legal doctrine is to determine which party or argument should prevail based on deontic or consequentialist criteria, then we can try to formulate the doctrine to realize either of those two objects. Alternatively, the doctrine could be cast in terms that are neutral so far as the dichotomy is concerned, and we can rely on context to tell us whether deontic or consequentialist considerations should predominate. But in either event—whether we draft in the normative perspective or simply draft the doctrine so as to accommodate one or the other in the circumstances—at some point we will have to ask (at least) two questions. First, what is the object of doctrine? Second, to what extent must the discovery and instantiation of that object respond to fundamental and persistent characteristics of human agency? The answers to those two questions are interrelated.

Consider the premises formulated by H. L. A. Hart, whose legal positivism has determined the course of much twentieth- and twenty-first-century analytical jurisprudence. He identified the "*minimum content* of Natural Law": "[U]niversally recognized principles of conduct which have a basis in elementary truths concerning human beings, their natural environment, and aims, may be considered the *minimum content* of Natural Law, in contrast with the more grandiose and more challengeable constructions which have often been proffered under that name."[62] Hart concludes that it is the particular way people are constituted, with survival as their aim,[63] physically vulnerable,[64] approximately equal,[65] limited in both their altruism and resources,[66] limited in understanding and

---

[62] H.L.A. Hart, The Concept of Law 193 (2d ed. 1994).

[63] *Id.*

[64] *Id.* at 194–95.

[65] *Id.* at 195.

[66] *Id.* at 196–97.

strength of will[67] that certainly determines the law–morality relation. Were any of those contingencies otherwise, law and morality as we know them would not be related as we may conceive them to be. Morality, then, may be appreciated as a necessary consequence of our fundamental human condition. Now this is not to say that morality is convention, based solely on social sources; it is instead to recognize that morality must be determined in the context of the human agency available to us. Morality, as we understand it, is a uniquely human thing.[68]

So we must attend to human agency to appreciate morality as well as to appreciate the fit between morality and human conventions, such as legal doctrine.

> [B]y understanding the descriptive level we will be in a stronger position to work out the prescriptive details. This is no more (or less) profound than saying that an understanding of human nature, how it evolved, and how it has changed over recent times provides a foundation for understanding our strengths and weaknesses and the kinds of prescriptive policies that may or may not rub up against our innate biases.[69]

We would expect that doctrine, a product of human agency and a normative projection of human agency, would best make sense if appreciated as a human artifact, necessarily subject to the endowments and limitations, such as they are, of human moral reasoning.

To take stock, then: If we understand morality in a more psychologically sophisticated way than the simple deontic–consequentialist dichotomy would accommodate, we may be in a better position to appreciate what legal doctrine must capture if it is to be normative in any meaningful sense, any sense meaningful to the human agent so constituted. The innateness of morality matters, so far as our appreciation of doctrine is concerned, because of what we may infer about doctrine as human artifact, as necessarily determined by the human moral capacity. And to understand that capacity better, it is worthwhile to understand both morality's source (behavioral biology and evolutionary psychology may reveal this) and its substance (moral anthropology and psychology reveal this). What remains is to determine whether there is some aspect of morality particularly (even uniquely) suited to the exchange relationship that is the subject of the contract law. There well may be.

---

[67] *Id.* at 197–200.

[68] *See* JOYCE, *supra* note 47, at 82–85; Hauser, Young, & Cushman, *supra* note 59, at 112–13. *But see* Jesse J. Prinz, *Resisting the Linguistic Analogy: A Commentary on Hauser, Young, and Cushman*, *in* 2 MORAL PSYCHOLOGY 157, 164 (Walter Sinnott-Armstrong ed., 2008) (emphasizing role of learning in formation of human moral sense).

[69] Hauser, Young, & Cushman, *supra* note 59, at 140.

4. EVEN AN EXCHANGE MODULE?

Morality must necessarily have a human object. That is, decisions and actions consistent with morality must instantiate some value that we have some reason to instantiate. The moral object may be modular: We could determine that, in the context governed by contract rules, morality would serve a different function than it might in the criminal law. If that were the case, we could discover a specific bargaining domain rather than understand an exchange morality as but a particular application of some domain general deontic logic. Such a discovery might further demonstrate the space between the deontic–consequentialist dichotomy and a more robust conception of the morality that determines, and animates, doctrine.

Professors Leda Cosmides and John Tooby have posited the existence of a domain-specific social contract module that would account for the very particular way in which we calculate the morality of exchange, specifically the type of exchange that is the subject of contract doctrine.[70] They conclude that "the human cognitive architecture reliably develop[s] *social contract algorithms*: a neurocomputational system whose design features are adaptively specialized for producing the specific kinds of inferences and goals necessary to create cooperative interactions that implement an evolutionarily stable strategy. . . ."[71] For present purposes, it is the proof of their conclusion that is particularly resonant. To the extent that Cosmides and Tooby reveal distinct normative reactions to recurring reciprocal exchange contexts, they may have isolated an exchange morality distinguishable from the morality that informs other forms of human interaction.[72] If that is so, then a normative dichotomy that rests on the difference between conceptions of good in itself (deontology) and good as a means to an end (consequentialism) may miss something. That is not to say that the deontology–consequentialism dichotomy is not, in fact, played out as a dialectic in an array of legal contexts. That certainly could be the case. But if it plays out *differently* in the exchange context than it does, say, in the criminal law context,[73] we will have discovered a way in which one size fits all deontology versus consequentialism under-predicts (and under-explains) contract doctrine.[74] It is worthwhile to describe, briefly, Cosmides and Tooby's methodology.

---

[70] Leda Cosmides & John Tooby, *Can a General Deontic Logic Capture the Facts of Human Moral Reasoning? How the Mind Interprets Social Exchange Rules and Detects Cheaters, in* 1 MORAL PSYCHOLOGY 53, 53 (Walter Sinnott-Armstrong ed., 2008).

[71] *Id.*

[72] *Id.* at 58 ("[S]ocial interaction in humans will be regulated by a number of different evolved specializations, each of which is functionally specialized for negotiating a particular domain of social life.").

[73] *Id.* at 78, 95–96.

[74] *Id.* at 58 ("If this picture is even remotely correct, then the project of creating a deontic logic that is both general yet empirically descriptive may be doomed.").

Their study relies on responses to Wason selection tasks.[75] Essentially, the idea is to try to discern context-determined differences in task performance. If performance in a domain-general administration of the task[76] differs significantly from performance once the context is clearly one involving reciprocal exchange, then we may posit, as Cosmides and Tooby have, that there is something about the cues of a reciprocal exchange context that intimates a social contract[77] domain: "Ecologically rational inference systems . . . gain their inferential power by taking advantage of relationships that are true (or at least statistically reliable) within a particular problem domain, and they solve specific problems that arise within that domain."[78] It is the structure of the interpersonal, and therefore legal, context that determines the operation of the algorithm.[79] The "situation detector" activates the "social contract algorithms" that "map onto the deep structure"[80] of an exchange-specific normativity, a specialized (or at least distinct) "morality" of exchange.[81]

Cosmides and Tooby also discover that emotional reactions specific to the exchange setting confirm a discrete social contract module.[82] Further, they confirm that the exchange module is sensitive to differences in type among social contract violations: "Accidental violations of social contracts will not fully engage the cheater detection subroutine; intentional violations will."[83] This is consistent with the law's not wholly successful resistance to efforts to treat willful and "innocent" breaches just the same.[84] Although we have come to understand that (as a matter of doctrine) contract liability is strict liability,[85] the cases[86] and *Restatement* formulations[87] recognize the difference

[75] *See id.* at 60 (Wason's selection task is a logic puzzle, and as used by Cosmides and Tooby "was designed to see whether people would spontaneously and accurately look for potential violations of a conditional rule, linguistically expressed as *If P then Q*.").

[76] Such as the coincidence of particular symptoms and a particular disease. *See id.* at 61.

[77] *See id.* at 72 ("A *social contract* expresses this intercontingency and can be expressed in the form of a conditional rule: 'If you accept a benefit from agent X, then you must satisfy X's requirement.'").

[78] *Id.* at 67.

[79] *Id.* at 72–73.

[80] *Id.* at 77.

[81] Note here the particular pertinence of a "cheater detection" system, *id.* at 99–100.

[82] *Id.* at 101.

[83] *Id.* at 102; *see also id.* at 104 ("We found that the moral character of the potential rule violator affects violation detection for social contracts but not precautionary rules.").

[84] *See generally* IAN AYRES & GREGORY KLASS, INSINCERE PROMISES: THE LAW OF MISREPRESENTED INTENT (2005); Steve Thel & Peter Siegelman, *Wilfulness vs. Expectation: A Promisor-Based Defense of Wilful Breach Doctrine*, 107 MICH. L. REV. 1517 (2009).

[85] Eric A. Posner, *Fault in Contract Law*, 107 MICH. L. REV. 1431 (2009); Richard A. Posner, *Let Us Never Blame a Contract Breaker*, 107 MICH. L. REV. 1349 (2009).

[86] *See* U. S. Naval Inst. v. Charter Commc'ns Inc. 936 F.2d 692 (2d Cir. 1991); Jacob & Youngs, Inc. v. Kent, 129 N.E. 889 (N.Y. 1921); Peevyhouse v. Garland Coal & Mining Co., 382 P.2d 109 (Okla. 1963).

[87] *See, e.g.*, RESTATEMENT (SECOND) OF CONTRACTS § 261 (1981) (considering fault of party invoking impracticability).

between being kicked and being tripped over. There is apparently something irresistible (because predisposed?) about "punishing" willful breach.[88]

Hauser, too, has posited a transactional distinction that makes a normative difference, so far as domain-specific deontic logic is concerned. Relying on the work of Professor Joshua Greene,[89] Hauser observes that "emotions come into play in situations of a more personal nature and favor more deontic judgments, while reason comes into play in situations of a more impersonal nature and favors more utilitarian judgments."[90] Greene's thesis is that there are two types of moral "reasoning," and the quotation marks are crucial. If we are confronted by a personal moral challenge, one that is salient to us in the way that such challenges would have been salient to our evolutionary forebears, we respond emotionally, and then rationalize;[91] we rely on our emotions as we would heuristics to be our guide.[92] Conversely, if we confront less personal, that is, impersonal, moral challenges, we respond more "cognitively," and reach consequentialist conclusions.[93] The degree of emotional response effectively determines whether our cognitive processes will be able to overcome our emotional reactions: "People exhibit more 'cognitive' activity when they give the consequentialist answer."[94] (This may amount to the suggestion that our evolutionarily predisposed emotions are a rough heuristic *designed* to yield consequentialist results.[95]) Greene's conclusions are supported by empirical evidence.[96] Perhaps most interesting (certainly most provocative) is Greene's conclusion that socio-economic status—manifest in education level, "westernization," and aging (in the sense of maturing)—increase the range of contexts in which we are consequentialists rather than deontologists.[97] A question remains, though, even if we accept Greene's conclusion that deontology operates in the emotional domain and consequentialism operates in the cognitive domain: What do we make of that divide in the case of indeterminate or

---

[88] This may explain, in part, the antipathy toward "efficient breach." *See generally* Friedmann, *supra* note 3; Lon.L. Fuller & William R. Perdue, Jr., *The Reliance Interest in Contract Damages: 1*, 46 Yale L.J. 52 (1936), and *The Reliance Interest in Contract Damages: 2*, 46 Yale L.J. 373 (1937).

[89] Joshua D. Greene, *The Secret Joke of Kant's Soul*, *in* 3 Moral Psychology 35 (Walter Sinnott-Armstrong ed., 2008).

[90] Hauser, Young, & Cushman, *supra* note 59, at 116.

[91] Greene, *supra* note 89, at 62–63.

[92] *Id.* at 43.

[93] *Id.* ("As Josef Stalin once said, 'A single death is a tragedy; a million deaths is a statistic.'").

[94] *Id.* at 46.

[95] *See id.* at 72:

> What turn-of-the-millennium science is telling us is that human moral judgment is not a pristine rational enterprise—that our moral judgments are driven by a hodgepodge of emotional dispositions, which themselves were shaped by a hodgepodge of evolutionary forces, both biological and cultural. Because of this, it is exceedingly unlikely that there is any rationally coherent normative moral theory that can accommodate our moral intuitions.

[96] *Id.* at 43–44.

[97] *Id.* at 56.

indeterminable consequences? That is, if we cannot "do the math," do we essentially rely on emotion to resolve the utilitarian calculus?

What is most pertinent here is not the certain conclusion that there *are* distinct moral modules, with or without neurological basis. What matters here is the *empirical* evidence that, for whatever reason, we approach normative contexts in ways that do not reflect the simplistic deontic–consequentialist dichotomy. The very fact that there are different, context-specific normative calculi or mechanisms that evolutionary psychologists and neurobiologists have to explain suggests that the familiar normative categories drawn in moral philosophy fail to theorize sufficiently a human institution like an area of legal doctrine.

We are now in the position to confront the crucial tension between descriptive and prescriptive ethics: If we can—indeed, if we must—recognize that within the human agent's moral sense the deontic–consequentialist dichotomy is a dialectic rather than opposed alternatives, and if we further appreciate that distinct normative contexts elicit distinct moral reactions, what does that description intimate about legal theory, such as a theory of contract, that would be prescriptive? The case needs to be made that understanding how our morality operates is crucial to understanding how we can use normative theory to make sense of legal doctrine. That is the focus of the final section of this chapter and book.

C. The Limits of Normativity: Only So Much Doctrine Can Do

One of the more controversial contemporary issues in moral psychology concerns the innateness of morality, specifically, the nature and source of our moralizing functions. The issue is not whether we are bound to certain moral calculi; the issue, instead, is the nature of the moral apparatus that accomplishes the calculus. Of course, the subject of this book—the possibility of normative contract theory—assumes that the doctrine in fact serves (or at least facilitates) a normative function. The issue is whether that function reduces (in fact, *can* reduce) to something like the deontology or consequentialism that informs the extant normative theories. It is worthwhile to consider what difference moral psychology can make to the efficacy of moral philosophy so far as the possibility of legal theory is concerned. The innateness dialog sheds light on that "possibility" question, and, once again, the nature of human agency is determinative.

Professor Jesse Prinz has recognized why the empirical nature of morality matters to moral philosophy.[98] Although the focus of his argument is on the existence (actually, the nonexistence) of a discrete morality module,[99] his conclusions about that aspect of

---

[98] *See generally* Jesse J. Prinz, *Is Morality Innate?*, *in* 1 MORAL PSYCHOLOGY 367 (Walter Sinnott-Armstrong ed., 2008).

[99] *Id.* at 387–91.

innateness pertain as well to the empirical morality–moral philosophy question generally. Prinz posits four specific psychological capacities that underlie morality: (1) nonmoral emotions,[100] (2) meta-emotions,[101] (3) perspective taking (theory of mind),[102] and (4) nonmoral preferences and behavioral dispositions.[103] Each of those four provides a means (or at least a context within which) to exploit the morality–emotion relationship to effect normative results. That is, once we appreciate *how* emotions contribute to the formation of what we have come to call morality, we are in a better position to promote some behaviors and discourage others. That, of course, is what legal doctrine endeavors to accomplish: "There are some social pressures that all human beings face. In living together, we need to devise rules of conduct, and we need to transmit those rules in ways that are readily internalized."[104] So, we may continue, we need to know the ways we can facilitate such internalization as well as the obstacles we would *necessarily* confront when we endeavor to effect such internalization in the case of distinctly *human* agents.

It should not be difficult to see how Prinz's analysis might be applied to help us make sense of a body of legal doctrine *in normative terms*. Legal doctrine, no less, perhaps, than any other human normative endeavor, is subject to the same forces that shape human emotion and moral reaction. Similarly, and no less pertinently, *constructions* and *applications* of doctrine are subject to those forces. It is not clear, though this is an area ripe for empirical study, that corporate conclusions (such as those accomplished by drafting committees, legislatures, and juries) are necessarily any less subject to such normative forces; the cynical might even conclude that history is rife with discouraging examples of "mob morality."[105] Indeed, insofar as what passes for moral reasoning might be no more than *post hoc* rationalization, we could not but expect that our legal doctrine, both in its formation and application, would deconstruct just as would our moral reasoning.

Ultimately, it may be that the question of what empirical morality can do to make legal doctrine more normatively coherent than the deontic–consequentialist dichotomy can is similar to (or at least not entirely dissimilar from) the tension between moral realism and empirical moral theory generally. The moral realist maintains that there are certain and discernible moral truths. To the extent that there is disagreement about moral matters,

[100] *Id.* at 404 (Nonmoral emotions are "behavioral norms from our innate stock of emotions" based on emotional conditioning.).

[101] *Id.* (Meta-emotions are emotions about emotions, for example, feeling sad for being angry.).

[102] *Id.*

[103] *Id.* at 405 (nonmoral preferences and behavioral dispositions are "innate social behaviors that lend themselves to moralization").

[104] *Id.*

[105] *See, e.g.,* Loving v. Virginia, 388 U.S. 1 (1967) (striking down Virginia statute preventing marriages between persons solely on the basis of race); Plessy v. Ferguson, 163 U.S. 537 (1896) (upholding doctrine of "separate but equal" allowing racial segregation throughout the country).

those disagreements could be overcome "in appropriate discursive conditions";[106] that is, we can educate our way out of moral disagreement to discover the essential moral truth upon which we would all, once enlightened, agree. There is, then, a moral truth; all is not relative. Now the inquiry pursued in this book does not depend one way or the other on there being a tenable moral realism; the value of the analogy is in the similarities between the (1) empirical morality versus moral realism tension, on the one hand, and (2) empirical morality versus deontic–consequentialist dichotomy, on the other. The debate has been between those who question moral realism on empirical grounds with regard to what would constitute moral truth, the debate framed by (1). The focus here is on (2) with regard to contract doctrine. If empiricism could—in the sense of "would be competent to"—reveal the failure of moral realism for human agents, then we would know more about the nature of morality, and more as well about our efforts to evaluate conduct on moral bases. The deontic–consequentialist dichotomy *assumes* that if we could only be certain of the correct deontic or consequentialist result—which we assume is *real*, actually exists as something other than a matter of convention or consensus—then we could make sense of an area of legal doctrine in either deontic or consequentialist terms. *Analogously*, if empirical morality reveals that something like a persistent (and imperfect) deontic–consequentialist dialectic rather than deontology *or* consequentialism alone can better explain contract doctrine, then we can be confident that theories insensitive to the fact and nature of that dialectic (and so insensitive as well to the empirical bases and limitations of each perspective) could not explain the doctrine which is *necessarily* a product of such a dialectic correctly understood.

That first tension—between empirical morality and moral realism—has received attention in the moral psychology literature, and we may learn something from the observations and conclusions that flow from that colloquy that would help us with the second tension that has been the focus of this book. If contract doctrine looks more like a deontic–consequentialist dialectic than a deontic *or* consequentialist model, then a theory of the doctrine that depends on the certainty and inviolability of that dichotomy necessarily fails. What is pertinent here, from the empirical morality–moral realism literature, is that it is very difficult to falsify claims of moral realism at all, and particularly difficult to do so without help from the empirical human sciences.[107] Indeed, what would it mean to say that there is or is not such a thing as moral realism if you could not account for the nature of human agency (and so therefore the necessary pertinence of the empirical human sciences) to falsify the claim? And in order for the claim that there is such a thing as moral realism to be meaningful, the claim must be falsifiable, else it is empty.

[106] Doris & Plakias, *supra* note 31, at 305–06.

[107] *Id.* at 327.

In that very same way, we can appreciate that in order to resolve the deontic–consequentialist tension we need a basis upon which we could falsify the claim that either but not both normative perspectives support the best interpretive (in the normative sense) theory of the doctrine. Certainly the object of legal doctrine must be human thriving, constrained by the nature (limits?) of human agency. Although we can imagine that we might care about, for instance, corrective justice for corrective justice's sake (perhaps as an intellectual exercise, like playing chess), it would be surprising to discover that an enterprise—the development of contract doctrine—designed to support human thriving would not necessarily reflect the human agent as revealed by the empirical sciences, including moral psychology and its constituents. So for the same reasons that moral realism inconsiderate of empirical morality would fail, a deontic–consequentialist dichotomy insensitive to the empirical human sciences would likely fail to explain, to interpret doctrine. And the object of interpretive theory is, after all, to interpret doctrine in normative terms, in order to provide the leverage that comprehensive theory might provide.

Appendix

One important indicator of the canonical status of the cases discussed in this book is their inclusion in contract casebooks. The following is a list of major casebooks published since 1950 that reference the canonical cases. Casebooks are included if they have had two or more editions published since 1950. All casebooks listed include the case as a principle case, unless otherwise indicated parenthetically.

Alaska Packers Association v. Domenico, 117 F. 99 (9th Cir. 1902)

Randy E. Barnett, Contracts: Cases and Doctrine 658 (4th ed. 2008).

Brian A. Blum & Amy C. Bushaw, Contracts: Cases, Discussion, and Problems 331 (2d ed. 2008) (discussed).

John P. Dawson et al., Contracts: Cases and Comment 601 (9th ed. 2008).

E. Allan Farnsworth et al., Contracts: Cases and materials 325 (7th ed. 2008).

Robert W. Hamilton et al., Cases and Materials on Contracts 280 (2d ed. 1992).

Friedrich Kessler et al., Contracts: Cases and Materials 652 (3d ed. 1986) (discussed briefly).

Charles L. Knapp et al., Problems in Contract Law: Cases and Materials 715 (6th ed. 2007).

Edward J. Murphy, Richard E. Speidel & Ian Ayres, Studies in Contract Law 84 (6th ed. 2003).

John Edward Murray, Jr., Contracts: Cases and Materials 243 (6th ed. 2006) (discussed).

Robert S. Summers & Robert A. Hillman, Contract and Related Obligation 627 (5th ed. 2006).

Allegheny College v. National Chautauqua County Bank of Jamestown, 159 N.E. 173 (N.Y. 1927)

Randy E. Barnett, Contracts: Cases and Doctrine 731 (4th ed. 2008).
Brian A. Blum & Amy C. Bushaw, Contracts: Cases, Discussion, and Problems 337–39 (2d ed. 2008) (discussed).
Thomas D. Crandall & Douglas J. Whaley, Cases, Problems, and Materials on Contracts 199 (5th ed. 2008).
John P. Dawson et al., Contracts: Cases and Comment 234 (9th ed. 2008).
E. Allan Farnsworth et al., Contracts: Cases and materials 93 (7th ed. 2008) (discussed).
Bruce W. Frier & James J. White, The Modern Law of Contracts 54 (2d ed. 2008) (discussed briefly).
Friedrich Kessler et al., Contracts: Cases and Materials 501 (3d ed. 1986).
Charles L. Knapp et al., Problems in Contract Law: Cases and Materials 235 (6th ed. 2007) (discussed).
Ian R. Macneil & Paul J. Gudel, Contracts: Exchange Transactions and Relations 573 n.14 (3d ed. 2001) (discussed).
J. Stirling Mortimer, Cases on the Law of Contracts 304 (vol. 1 1975).
Addison Mueller, Contract in Context 99 (2d ed. 1952).
Edward J. Murphy, Richard E. Speidel & Ian Ayres, Studies in Contract Law 134 (6th ed. 2003).
John Edward Murray, Jr., Contracts: Cases and Materials 256 (6th ed. 2006).
Harold Shepherd & Harry H. Wellington, Contracts and Contract Remedies 271 (4th ed. 1957).
Robert S. Summers & Robert A. Hillman, Contract and Related Obligation 59 (5th ed. 2006) (discussed).

Britton v. Turner, 6 N.H. 481 (1834)

Randy E. Barnett, Contracts: Cases and Doctrine 256 (4th ed. 2008).
Steven J. Burton, Principles of Contract Law 493 (3d ed. 2006).
Thomas D. Crandall & Douglas J. Whaley, Cases, Problems, and Materials on Contracts 368 (5th ed. 2008).
John P. Dawson et al., Contracts: Cases and Comment 117 (9th ed. 2008).
E. Allan Farnsworth et al., Contracts: Cases and materials 736 (7th ed. 2008).
Robert W. Hamilton et al., Cases and Materials on Contracts 151 (2d ed. 1992).
Friedrich Kessler et al., Contracts: Cases and Materials 1021 (3d ed. 1986).
Charles L. Knapp et al., Problems in Contract Law: Cases and Materials 817 (6th ed. 2007) (discussed briefly).

Ian R. Macneil & Paul J. Gudel, Contracts: Exchange Transactions and Relations 121 (3d ed. 2001).

William McGovern et al., Contracts and Sales: Contemporary Cases and Problems 500 (2d ed. 2002) (discussed).

Addison Mueller, Contract in Context 976 (2d ed. 1952).

Edward J. Murphy, Richard E. Speidel & Ian Ayres, Studies in Contract Law 795 (6th ed. 2003).

John Edward Murray, Jr., Contracts: Cases and Materials 687 (6th ed. 2006) (discussed).

Arthur Rosett, Contract Law and Its Application 349 (4th ed. 1988).

Harold Shepherd & Harry H. Wellington, Contracts and Contract Remedies 988 (4th ed. 1957).

Robert S. Summers & Robert A. Hillman, Contract and Related Obligation 132 (5th ed. 2006).

Carlill v. Carbolic Smoke Ball Co., [1893] 1 Q.B. 256 (U.K.)

Randy E. Barnett, Contracts: Cases and Doctrine 343 (4th ed. 2008).

Brian A. Blum & Amy C. Bushaw, Contracts: Cases, Discussion, and Problems 142 (2d ed. 2008).

John D. Calamari et al., Cases and Problems on Contracts 107 (5th ed. 2007).

John P. Dawson et al., Contracts: Cases and Comment 327 (9th ed. 2008).

E. Allan Farnsworth et al., Contracts: Cases and materials 157 (7th ed. 2008) (discussed).

Robert W. Hamilton et al., Cases and Materials on Contracts 535 (2d ed. 1992) (discussed).

Friedrich Kessler et al., Contracts: Cases and Materials 373 (3d ed. 1986).

William McGovern et al., Contracts and Sales: Contemporary Cases and Problems 51–52 (2d ed. 2002) (discussed).

Edward J. Murphy, Richard E. Speidel & Ian Ayres, Studies in Contract Law 296 (6th ed. 2003).

John Edward Murray, Jr., Contracts: Cases and Materials 135 (6th ed. 2006).

Harold Shepherd & Harry H. Wellington, Contracts and Contract Remedies 154 (4th ed. 1957).

Robert S. Summers & Robert A. Hillman, Contract and Related Obligation 463 (5th ed. 2006) (discussed).

Dickinson v. Dodds, [1876] 2 Ch.D. 463

Randy E. Barnett, Contracts: Cases and Doctrine 328 (4th ed. 2008).

Brian A. Blum & Amy C. Bushaw, Contracts: Cases, Discussion, and Problems 137 (2d ed. 2008).

Thomas D. Crandall & Douglas J. Whaley, Cases, Problems, and Materials on Contracts 68 (5th ed. 2008).

John P. Dawson et al., Contracts: Cases and Comment 352–53 (9th ed. 2008) (discussed).

E. Allan Farnsworth et al., Contracts: Cases and materials 171 (7th ed. 2008).

Bruce W. Frier & James J. White, The Modern Law of Contracts 122 (2d ed. 2008) (discussed briefly).

Lon L. Fuller & Melvin Aron Eisenberg, Basic Contract Law 291 (8th ed. 2006).

Robert W. Hamilton et al., Cases and Materials on Contracts 428 (2d ed. 1992).

Friedrich Kessler et al., Contracts: Cases and Materials 316 (3d ed. 1986).

Charles L. Knapp et al., Problems in Contract Law: Cases and Materials 49 (6th ed. 2007) (discussed).

William McGovern et al., Contracts and Sales: Contemporary Cases and Problems 57 (2d ed. 2002) (cited but not discussed).

Addison Mueller, Contract in Context 346 (2d ed. 1952).

Edward J. Murphy, Richard E. Speidel & Ian Ayres, Studies in Contract Law 360 (6th ed. 2003).

John Edward Murray, Jr., Contracts: Cases and Materials 105 (6th ed. 2006).

Harold Shepherd & Harry H. Wellington, Contracts and Contract Remedies 134 (4th ed. 1957) (cited but not discussed).

Robert S. Summers & Robert A. Hillman, Contract and Related Obligation 442–43 (5th ed. 2006) (discussed).

Hadley v. Baxendale, (1854) 156 Eng. Rep. 145 (Ex.)

Randy E. Barnett, Contracts: Cases and Doctrine 93 (4th ed. 2008).

Brian A. Blum & Amy C. Bushaw, Contracts: Cases, Discussion, and Problems 783 (2d ed. 2008).

Steven J. Burton, Principles of Contract Law 332 (3d ed. 2006).

John D. Calamari et al., Cases and Problems on Contracts 683 (5th ed. 2007).

Thomas D. Crandall & Douglas J. Whaley, Cases, Problems, and Materials on Contracts 283 (5th ed. 2008).

John P. Dawson et al., Contracts: Cases and Comment 75 (9th ed. 2008).

E. Allan Farnsworth et al., Contracts: Cases and materials 657 (7th ed. 2008).

Bruce W. Frier & James J. White, The Modern Law of Contracts 559 (2d ed. 2008).

Lon L. Fuller & Melvin Aron Eisenberg, Basic Contract Law 175 (8th ed. 2006).

Robert W. Hamilton et al., Cases and Materials on Contracts 53 (2d ed. 1992).

Friedrich Kessler et al., Contracts: Cases and Materials 106 (3d ed. 1986).

Charles L. Knapp et al., Problems in Contract Law: Cases and Materials 869 (6th ed. 2007).

Ian R. Macneil & Paul J. Gudel, Contracts: Exchange Transactions and Relations 153 (3d ed. 2001).

William McGovern et al., Contracts and Sales: Contemporary Cases and Problems 376 (2d ed. 2002).

Addison Mueller, Contract in Context 774 (2d ed. 1952).

Edward J. Murphy, Richard E. Speidel & Ian Ayres, Studies in Contract Law 206 (6th ed. 2003).

John Edward Murray, Jr., Contracts: Cases and Materials 632 (6th ed. 2006).

Arthur Rosett, Contract Law and Its Application 323 (4th ed. 1988).

Harold Shepherd & Harry H. Wellington, Contracts and Contract Remedies 844 (4th ed. 1957).

Robert S. Summers & Robert A. Hillman, Contract and Related Obligation 245 (5th ed. 2006).

Hamer v. Sidway, 27 N.E. 256 (N.Y. 1891)

Randy E. Barnett, Contracts: Cases and Doctrine 622 (4th ed. 2008).

Brian A. Blum & Amy C. Bushaw, Contracts: Cases, Discussion, and Problems 267 (2d ed. 2008).

Steven J. Burton, Principles of Contract Law 135 (3d ed. 2006).

John D. Calamari et al., Cases and Problems on Contracts 202 (5th ed. 2007).

Thomas D. Crandall & Douglas J. Whaley, Cases, Problems, and Materials on Contracts 139 (5th ed. 2008).

John P. Dawson et al., Contracts: Cases and Comment 195 (9th ed. 2008).

E. Allan Farnsworth et al., Contracts: Cases and materials 34 (7th ed. 2008).

Bruce W. Frier & James J. White, The Modern Law of Contracts 35 (2d ed. 2008).

Lon L. Fuller & Melvin Aron Eisenberg, Basic Contract Law 26 (8th ed. 2006).

Robert W. Hamilton et al., Cases and Materials on Contracts 179 (2d ed. 1992).

Friedrich Kessler et al., Contracts: Cases and Materials 483 (3d ed. 1986).

Charles L. Knapp et al., Problems in Contract Law: Cases and Materials 72 (6th ed. 2007).

Ian R. Macneil & Paul J. Gudel, Contracts: Exchange Transactions and Relations 560 (3d ed. 2001).

William McGovern et al., Contracts and Sales: Contemporary Cases and Problems 10 (2d ed. 2002).

Addison Mueller, Contract in Context 63 (2d ed. 1952).

Edward J. Murphy, Richard E. Speidel & Ian Ayres, Studies in Contract Law 40 (6th ed. 2003).

John Edward Murray, Jr., Contracts: Cases and Materials 190 (6th ed. 2006).

Harold Shepherd & Harry H. Wellington, Contracts and Contract Remedies 295 (4th ed. 1957) (cited but not discussed).

Robert S. Summers & Robert A. Hillman, Contract and Related Obligation 56 (5th ed. 2006).

Hawkins v. McGee, 146 A. 641 (N.H. 1929)

Randy E. Barnett, Contracts: Cases and Doctrine 63 (4th ed. 2008).

Brian A. Blum & Amy C. Bushaw, Contracts: Cases, Discussion, and Problems 809 (2d ed. 2008) (discussed).

Steven J. Burton, Principles of Contract Law 3 (3d ed. 2006).
John D. Calamari et al., Cases and Problems on Contracts 19 (5th ed. 2007).
Thomas D. Crandall & Douglas J. Whaley, Cases, Problems, and Materials on Contracts 241 (5th ed. 2008).
John P. Dawson et al., Contracts: Cases and Comment 2 (9th ed. 2008).
E. Allan Farnsworth et al., Contracts: Cases and materials 2 (7th ed. 2008).
Bruce W. Frier & James J. White, The Modern Law of Contracts 347 (2d ed. 2008) (discussed).
Lon L. Fuller & Melvin Aron Eisenberg, Basic Contract Law 114 (8th ed. 2006).
Robert W. Hamilton et al., Cases and Materials on Contracts 1 (2d ed. 1992).
Friedrich Kessler et al., Contracts: Cases and Materials 133 (3d ed. 1986) (discussed).
William McGovern et al., Contracts and Sales: Contemporary Cases and Problems 353 (2d ed. 2002) (discussed).
Edward J. Murphy, Richard E. Speidel & Ian Ayres, Studies in Contract Law 949 (6th ed. 2003) (cited but not discussed).
John Edward Murray, Jr., Contracts: Cases and Materials 48 (6th ed. 2006) (discussed).

Henningsen v. Bloomfield Motors, Inc., 161 A.2d 69 (N.J. 1960)

Randy E. Barnett, Contracts: Cases and Doctrine 451, 1027 (4th ed. 2008) (cited but not discussed).
John P. Dawson et al., Contracts: Cases and Comment 664 (9th ed. 2008).
E. Allan Farnsworth et al., Contracts: Cases and materials 445 (7th ed. 2008).
Friedrich Kessler et al., Contracts: Cases and Materials 1243 (3d ed. 1986).
Charles L. Knapp et al., Problems in Contract Law: Cases and Materials 588–89 (6th ed. 2007) (cited but not discussed).
Ian R. Macneil & Paul J. Gudel, Contracts: Exchange Transactions and Relations 494 (3d ed. 2001) (discussed).
Edward J. Murphy, Richard E. Speidel & Ian Ayres, Studies in Contract Law 728 (6th ed. 2003).
John Edward Murray, Jr., Contracts: Cases and Materials 443–44 (6th ed. 2006) (discussed).

Hoffman v. Red Owl Stores, Inc., 133 N.W.2d 267 (Wis. 1965)

Randy E. Barnett, Contracts: Cases and Doctrine 752 (4th ed. 2008).
Brian A. Blum & Amy C. Bushaw, Contracts: Cases, Discussion, and Problems 348 (2d ed. 2008) (discussed).
Thomas D. Crandall & Douglas J. Whaley, Cases, Problems, and Materials on Contracts 223 (5th ed. 2008).
John P. Dawson et al., Contracts: Cases and Comment 284 (9th ed. 2008).

E. ALLAN FARNSWORTH ET AL., CONTRACTS: CASES AND MATERIALS 230 (7th ed. 2008).

BRUCE W. FRIER & JAMES J. WHITE, THE MODERN LAW OF CONTRACTS 79 (2d ed. 2008) (discussed).

ROBERT W. HAMILTON ET AL., CASES AND MATERIALS ON CONTRACTS 581 (2d ed. 1992).

FRIEDRICH KESSLER ET AL., CONTRACTS: CASES AND MATERIALS 223 (3d ed. 1986).

CHARLES L. KNAPP ET AL., PROBLEMS IN CONTRACT LAW: CASES AND MATERIALS 134–35 (6th ed. 2007) (discussed).

IAN R. MACNEIL & PAUL J. GUDEL, CONTRACTS: EXCHANGE TRANSACTIONS AND RELATIONS 679 (3d ed. 2001).

WILLIAM MCGOVERN ET AL., CONTRACTS AND SALES: CONTEMPORARY CASES AND PROBLEMS 129 (2d ed. 2002).

EDWARD J. MURPHY, RICHARD E. SPEIDEL & IAN AYRES, STUDIES IN CONTRACT LAW 435 (6th ed. 2003).

JOHN EDWARD MURRAY, JR., CONTRACTS: CASES AND MATERIALS 270, 278 (6th ed. 2006) (discussed).

ARTHUR ROSETT, CONTRACT LAW AND ITS APPLICATION 486 (4th ed. 1988).

ROBERT S. SUMMERS & ROBERT A. HILLMAN, CONTRACT AND RELATED OBLIGATION 95 (5th ed. 2006).

Jacob & Youngs, Inc. v. Kent, 129 N.E. 889 (N.Y. 1921)

RANDY E. BARNETT, CONTRACTS: CASES AND DOCTRINE 883 (4th ed. 2008).

BRIAN A. BLUM & AMY C. BUSHAW, CONTRACTS: CASES, DISCUSSION, AND PROBLEMS 676 (2d ed. 2008).

STEVEN J. BURTON, PRINCIPLES OF CONTRACT LAW 498 (3d ed. 2006).

JOHN D. CALAMARI ET AL., CASES AND PROBLEMS ON CONTRACTS 491 (5th ed. 2007).

THOMAS D. CRANDALL & DOUGLAS J. WHALEY, CASES, PROBLEMS, AND MATERIALS ON CONTRACTS 736 (5th ed. 2008).

JOHN P. DAWSON ET AL., CONTRACTS: CASES AND COMMENT 817 (9th ed. 2008).

E. ALLAN FARNSWORTH ET AL., CONTRACTS: CASES AND MATERIALS 645, 724 (7th ed. 2008).

BRUCE W. FRIER & JAMES J. WHITE, THE MODERN LAW OF CONTRACTS 674 (2d ed. 2008).

LON L. FULLER & MELVIN ARON EISENBERG, BASIC CONTRACT LAW 611 (8th ed. 2006).

ROBERT W. HAMILTON ET AL., CASES AND MATERIALS ON CONTRACTS 16 (2d ed. 1992) (discussed).

FRIEDRICH KESSLER ET AL., CONTRACTS: CASES AND MATERIALS 1042 (3d ed. 1986).

CHARLES L. KNAPP ET AL., PROBLEMS IN CONTRACT LAW: CASES AND MATERIALS 806 (6th ed. 2007).

IAN R. MACNEIL & PAUL J. GUDEL, CONTRACTS: EXCHANGE TRANSACTIONS AND RELATIONS 1028 (3d ed. 2001).

WILLIAM MCGOVERN ET AL., CONTRACTS AND SALES: CONTEMPORARY CASES AND PROBLEMS 474 (2d ed. 2002).

J. STIRLING MORTIMER, CASES ON THE LAW OF CONTRACTS 25 (vol. 2 1975).

ADDISON MUELLER, CONTRACT IN CONTEXT 1025 (2d ed. 1952).

Edward J. Murphy, Richard E. Speidel & Ian Ayres, Studies in Contract Law 780 (6th ed. 2003).

John Edward Murray, Jr., Contracts: Cases and Materials 557 (6th ed. 2006).

Arthur Rosett, Contract Law and Its Application 989 (4th ed. 1988).

Harold Shepherd & Harry H. Wellington, Contracts and Contract Remedies 624 (4th ed. 1957).

Robert S. Summers & Robert A. Hillman, Contract and Related Obligation 763 (5th ed. 2006).

Krell v. Henry, [1903] 2 K.B. 740 (U.K.)

Randy E. Barnett, Contracts: Cases and Doctrine 1099 (4th ed. 2008).

Brian A. Blum & Amy C. Bushaw, Contracts: Cases, Discussion, and Problems 652 (2d ed. 2008) (discussed).

Steven J. Burton, Principles of Contract Law 555 (3d ed. 2006).

John D. Calamari et al., Cases and Problems on Contracts 657 (5th ed. 2007).

Thomas D. Crandall & Douglas J. Whaley, Cases, Problems, and Materials on Contracts 686 (5th ed. 2008).

John P. Dawson et al., Contracts: Cases and Comment 555 (9th ed. 2008).

E. Allan Farnsworth et al., Contracts: Cases and materials 854 (7th ed. 2008).

Bruce W. Frier & James J. White, The Modern Law of Contracts 631, 689 (2d ed. 2008) (discussed).

Lon L. Fuller & Melvin Aron Eisenberg, Basic Contract Law 534 (8th ed. 2006).

Robert W. Hamilton et al., Cases and Materials on Contracts 663 (2d ed. 1992) (discussed).

Friedrich Kessler et al., Contracts: Cases and Materials 926 (3d ed. 1986).

Charles L. Knapp et al., Problems in Contract Law: Cases and Materials 686 (6th ed. 2007) (discussed).

J. Stirling Mortimer, Cases on the Law of Contracts 253 (vol. 2 1975).

Addison Mueller, Contract in Context 447 (2d ed. 1952).

Edward J. Murphy, Richard E. Speidel & Ian Ayres, Studies in Contract Law 845 (6th ed. 2003).

John Edward Murray, Jr., Contracts: Cases and Materials 620, 623 (6th ed. 2006) (discussed).

Harold Shepherd & Harry H. Wellington, Contracts and Contract Remedies 698 (4th ed. 1957).

Robert S. Summers & Robert A. Hillman, Contract and Related Obligation 946 (5th ed. 2006).

Lawrence v. Fox, 20 N.Y. 268 (1859)

Randy E. Barnett, Contracts: Cases and Doctrine 573 (4th ed. 2008) (discussed).

Brian A. Blum & Amy C. Bushaw, Contracts: Cases, Discussion, and Problems 876–77 (2d ed. 2008) (discussed).

Steven J. Burton, Principles of Contract Law 605 (3d ed. 2006).

John D. Calamari et al., Cases and Problems on Contracts 790 (5th ed. 2007).

Thomas D. Crandall & Douglas J. Whaley, Cases, Problems, and Materials on Contracts 820 (5th ed. 2008).

John P. Dawson et al., Contracts: Cases and Comment 843 (9th ed. 2008).

E. Allan Farnsworth et al., Contracts: Cases and materials 883 (7th ed. 2008).

Bruce W. Frier & James J. White, The Modern Law of Contracts 708 (2d ed. 2008).

Lon L. Fuller & Melvin Aron Eisenberg, Basic Contract Law 544 (8th ed. 2006).

Friedrich Kessler et al., Contracts: Cases and Materials 1333 (3d ed. 1986).

Charles L. Knapp et al., Problems in Contract Law: Cases and Materials 742–44 (6th ed. 2007) (discussed).

Ian R. Macneil & Paul J. Gudel, Contracts: Exchange Transactions and Relations 372–73 (3d ed. 2001) (discussed).

J. Stirling Mortimer, Cases on the Law of Contracts 332 (vol. 1 1975).

Addison Mueller, Contract in Context 848 (2d ed. 1952).

John Edward Murray, Jr., Contracts: Cases and Materials 708 (6th ed. 2006).

Arthur Rosett, Contract Law and Its Application 656 (4th ed. 1988).

Harold Shepherd & Harry H. Wellington, Contracts and Contract Remedies 466 (4th ed. 1957).

Robert S. Summers & Robert A. Hillman, Contract and Related Obligation 986 (5th ed. 2006).

Lucy v. Zehmer, 84 S.E.2d 516 (Va. 1954)

Randy E. Barnett, Contracts: Cases and Doctrine 296 (4th ed. 2008).

Brian A. Blum & Amy C. Bushaw, Contracts: Cases, Discussion, and Problems 71 (2d ed. 2008).

Steven J. Burton, Principles of Contract Law 11 (3d ed. 2006).

John D. Calamari et al., Cases and Problems on Contracts 1 (5th ed. 2007).

Thomas D. Crandall & Douglas J. Whaley, Cases, Problems, and Materials on Contracts 1 (5th ed. 2008).

E. Allan Farnsworth et al., Contracts: Cases and materials 117 (7th ed. 2008).

Bruce W. Frier & James J. White, The Modern Law of Contracts 1 (2d ed. 2008).

Lon L. Fuller & Melvin Aron Eisenberg, Basic Contract Law 236 (8th ed. 2006).

Charles L. Knapp et al., Problems in Contract Law: Cases and Materials 32–33 (6th ed. 2007) (discussed).

Edward J. Murphy, Richard E. Speidel & Ian Ayres, Studies in Contract Law 233 (6th ed. 2003).

John Edward Murray, Jr., Contracts: Cases and Materials 44 (6th ed. 2006) (discussed).

Robert S. Summers & Robert A. Hillman, Contract and Related Obligation 385 (5th ed. 2006).

Mills v. Wyman, 20 Mass. (3 Pick.) 207 (1825)

Randy E. Barnett, Contracts: Cases and Doctrine 640 (4th ed. 2008).
Steven J. Burton, Principles of Contract Law 190 (3d ed. 2006).
Thomas D. Crandall & Douglas J. Whaley, Cases, Problems, and Materials on Contracts 176 (5th ed. 2008).
John P. Dawson et al., Contracts: Cases and Comment 211 (9th ed. 2008).
E. Allan Farnsworth et al., Contracts: Cases and materials 50 (7th ed. 2008).
Lon L. Fuller & Melvin Aron Eisenberg, Basic Contract Law 86 (8th ed. 2006).
Robert W. Hamilton et al., Cases and Materials on Contracts 314 (2d ed. 1992).
Friedrich Kessler et al., Contracts: Cases and Materials 523 (3d ed. 1986).
Charles L. Knapp et al., Problems in Contract Law: Cases and Materials 286 (6th ed. 2007).
Addison Mueller, Contract in Context 27 (2d ed. 1952).
Edward J. Murphy, Richard E. Speidel & Ian Ayres, Studies in Contract Law 114 (6th ed. 2003).
Arthur Rosett, Contract Law and Its Application 184 (4th ed. 1988).
Robert S. Summers & Robert A. Hillman, Contract and Related Obligation 144 (5th ed. 2006).

Pacific Gas & Electric Co. v. G.W. Thomas Drayage and Rigging Co., 442 P.2d 641 (Cal. 1968)

Randy E. Barnett, Contracts: Cases and Doctrine 494 (4th ed. 2008).
Brian A. Blum & Amy C. Bushaw, Contracts: Cases, Discussion, and Problems 544 (2d ed. 2008).
Steven J. Burton, Principles of Contract Law 386 (3d ed. 2006).
John D. Calamari et al., Cases and Problems on Contracts 347 (5th ed. 2007).
Thomas D. Crandall & Douglas J. Whaley, Cases, Problems, and Materials on Contracts 484 (5th ed. 2008).
John P. Dawson et al., Contracts: Cases and Comment 434 (9th ed. 2008).
E. Allan Farnsworth et al., Contracts: Cases and materials 382 (7th ed. 2008).
Bruce W. Frier & James J. White, The Modern Law of Contracts 288 (2d ed. 2008).
Lon L. Fuller & Melvin Aron Eisenberg, Basic Contract Law 397 (8th ed. 2006).
Robert W. Hamilton et al., Cases and Materials on Contracts 707 (2d ed. 1992) (discussed).
Charles L. Knapp et al., Problems in Contract Law: Cases and Materials 406–07 (6th ed. 2007) (discussed).
William McGovern et al., Contracts and Sales: Contemporary Cases and Problems 217 (2d ed. 2002) (discussed).
Edward J. Murphy, Richard E. Speidel & Ian Ayres, Studies in Contract Law 638 (6th ed. 2003).

Arthur Rosett, Contract Law and Its Application 271 (4th ed. 1988).

Robert S. Summers & Robert A. Hillman, Contract and Related Obligation 678 (5th ed. 2006).

Peevyhouse v. Garland Coal & Mining Co., 382 P.2d 109 (Okla. 1963)

Randy E. Barnett, Contracts: Cases and Doctrine 934 (4th ed. 2008).

Brian A. Blum & Amy C. Bushaw, Contracts: Cases, Discussion, and Problems 759–60 (2d ed. 2008) (discussed).

Steven J. Burton, Principles of Contract Law 315 (3d ed. 2006).

John D. Calamari et al., Cases and Problems on Contracts 716 (5th ed. 2007).

Thomas D. Crandall & Douglas J. Whaley, Cases, Problems, and Materials on Contracts 245 (5th ed. 2008).

John P. Dawson et al., Contracts: Cases and Comment 16–18 (9th ed. 2008) (discussed).

E. Allan Farnsworth et al., Contracts: Cases and materials 653 (7th ed. 2008).

Bruce W. Frier & James J. White, The Modern Law of Contracts 513 (2d ed. 2008).

Lon L. Fuller & Melvin Aron Eisenberg, Basic Contract Law 138 (8th ed. 2006).

Robert W. Hamilton et al., Cases and Materials on Contracts 7 (2d ed. 1992).

Friedrich Kessler et al., Contracts: Cases and Materials 1053 (3d ed. 1986).

Charles L. Knapp et al., Problems in Contract Law: Cases and Materials 867 (6th ed. 2007) (discussed).

Ian R. Macneil & Paul J. Gudel, Contracts: Exchange Transactions and Relations 132 (3d ed. 2001).

William McGovern et al., Contracts and Sales: Contemporary Cases and Problems 394 (2d ed. 2002) (discussed).

Edward J. Murphy, Richard E. Speidel & Ian Ayres, Studies in Contract Law 936 (6th ed. 2003).

John Edward Murray, Jr., Contracts: Cases and Materials 677 (6th ed. 2006) (discussed).

Robert S. Summers & Robert A. Hillman, Contract and Related Obligation 218 (5th ed. 2006).

ProCD, Inc. v. Zeidenberg, 86 F.3d 1447 (7th Cir. 1996)

Randy E. Barnett, Contracts: Cases and Doctrine 473 (4th ed. 2008).

Brian A. Blum & Amy C. Bushaw, Contracts: Cases, Discussion, and Problems 156 (2d ed. 2008).

Steven J. Burton, Principles of Contract Law 68 (3d ed. 2006).

John D. Calamari et al., Cases and Problems on Contracts 127 (5th ed. 2007).

Thomas D. Crandall & Douglas J. Whaley, Cases, Problems, and Materials on Contracts 33 (5th ed. 2008).

JOHN P. DAWSON ET AL., CONTRACTS: CASES AND COMMENT 458 (9th ed. 2008).

E. ALLAN FARNSWORTH ET AL., CONTRACTS: CASES AND MATERIALS 211 (7th ed. 2008).

BRUCE W. FRIER & JAMES J. WHITE, THE MODERN LAW OF CONTRACTS 208 (2d ed. 2008) (discussed).

LON L. FULLER & MELVIN ARON EISENBERG, BASIC CONTRACT LAW 431 (8th ed. 2006).

CHARLES L. KNAPP ET AL., PROBLEMS IN CONTRACT LAW: CASES AND MATERIALS 197, 200–02 (6th ed. 2007) (discussed).

WILLIAM MCGOVERN ET AL., CONTRACTS AND SALES: CONTEMPORARY CASES AND PROBLEMS 82 (2d ed. 2002).

EDWARD J. MURPHY, RICHARD E. SPEIDEL & IAN AYRES, STUDIES IN CONTRACT LAW 343 (6th ed. 2003) (discussed).

JOHN EDWARD MURRAY, JR., CONTRACTS: CASES AND MATERIALS 178–80 (6th ed. 2006) (discussed).

ROBERT S. SUMMERS & ROBERT A. HILLMAN, CONTRACT AND RELATED OBLIGATION 515 (5th ed. 2006) (discussed).

Raffles v. Wichelhaus, (1864) 159 Eng. Rep. 375 (Ex.)

RANDY E. BARNETT, CONTRACTS: CASES AND DOCTRINE 396 (4th ed. 2008).

BRIAN A. BLUM & AMY C. BUSHAW, CONTRACTS: CASES, DISCUSSION, AND PROBLEMS 613 (2d ed. 2008) (discussed).

JOHN D. CALAMARI ET AL., CASES AND PROBLEMS ON CONTRACTS 361 (5th ed. 2007).

THOMAS D. CRANDALL & DOUGLAS J. WHALEY, CASES, PROBLEMS, AND MATERIALS ON CONTRACTS 512 (5th ed. 2008).

JOHN P. DAWSON ET AL., CONTRACTS: CASES AND COMMENT 292 (9th ed. 2008).

E. ALLAN FARNSWORTH ET AL., CONTRACTS: CASES AND MATERIALS 422 (7th ed. 2008).

BRUCE W. FRIER & JAMES J. WHITE, THE MODERN LAW OF CONTRACTS 109 (2d ed. 2008) (discussed).

LON L. FULLER & MELVIN ARON EISENBERG, BASIC CONTRACT LAW 240 (8th ed. 2006).

FRIEDRICH KESSLER ET AL., CONTRACTS: CASES AND MATERIALS 869 (3d ed. 1986).

CHARLES L. KNAPP ET AL., PROBLEMS IN CONTRACT LAW: CASES AND MATERIALS 350–51 (6th ed. 2007) (discussed).

IAN R. MACNEIL & PAUL J. GUDEL, CONTRACTS: EXCHANGE TRANSACTIONS AND RELATIONS 647 (3d ed. 2001).

ADDISON MUELLER, CONTRACT IN CONTEXT 148 (2d ed. 1952).

EDWARD J. MURPHY, RICHARD E. SPEIDEL & IAN AYRES, STUDIES IN CONTRACT LAW 393 (6th ed. 2003).

JOHN EDWARD MURRAY, JR., CONTRACTS: CASES AND MATERIALS 409 (6th ed. 2006).

ARTHUR ROSETT, CONTRACT LAW AND ITS APPLICATION 145 (4th ed. 1988).

HAROLD SHEPHERD & HARRY H. WELLINGTON, CONTRACTS AND CONTRACT REMEDIES 215 (4th ed. 1957).

ROBERT S. SUMMERS & ROBERT A. HILLMAN, CONTRACT AND RELATED OBLIGATION 401 (5th ed. 2006).

Ricketts v. Scothorn, 77 N.W. 365 (Neb. 1898)

Randy E. Barnett, Contracts: Cases and Doctrine 723 (4th ed. 2008).
Brian A. Blum & Amy C. Bushaw, Contracts: Cases, Discussion, and Problems 332 (2d ed. 2008) (discussed).
John P. Dawson et al., Contracts: Cases and Comment 231 (9th ed. 2008).
E. Allan Farnsworth et al., Contracts: Cases and materials 89 (7th ed. 2008).
Bruce W. Frier & James J. White, The Modern Law of Contracts 61 (2d ed. 2008).
Robert W. Hamilton et al., Cases and Materials on Contracts 220 (2d ed. 1992) (discussed).
Friedrich Kessler et al., Contracts: Cases and Materials 491 (3d ed. 1986).
Charles L. Knapp et al., Problems in Contract Law: Cases and Materials 222 (6th ed. 2007) (discussed briefly).
Ian R. Macneil & Paul J. Gudel, Contracts: Exchange Transactions and Relations 565 (3d ed. 2001).
William McGovern et al., Contracts and Sales: Contemporary Cases and Problems 25 (2d ed. 2002).
J. Stirling Mortimer, Cases on the Law of Contracts 275 (vol. 1 1975).
Addison Mueller, Contract in Context 96 (2d ed. 1952).
Edward J. Murphy, Richard E. Speidel & Ian Ayres, Studies in Contract Law 130 (6th ed. 2003).
John Edward Murray, Jr., Contracts: Cases and Materials 261 (6th ed. 2006) (discussed).
Arthur Rosett, Contract Law and Its Application 230 (4th ed. 1988).
Harold Shepherd & Harry H. Wellington, Contracts and Contract Remedies 259 (4th ed. 1957).
Robert S. Summers & Robert A. Hillman, Contract and Related Obligation 85, 90 (5th ed. 2006) (discussed).

Rockingham County v. Luten Bridge Co., 35 F.2d 301 (4th Cir. 1929)

Randy E. Barnett, Contracts: Cases and Doctrine 131 (4th ed. 2008).
Brian A. Blum & Amy C. Bushaw, Contracts: Cases, Discussion, and Problems 794 (2d ed. 2008) (discussed).
John D. Calamari et al., Cases and Problems on Contracts 687 (5th ed. 2007).
Thomas D. Crandall & Douglas J. Whaley, Cases, Problems, and Materials on Contracts 297 (5th ed. 2008).
John P. Dawson et al., Contracts: Cases and Comment 60 (9th ed. 2008).
E. Allan Farnsworth et al., Contracts: Cases and materials 630 (7th ed. 2008).
Lon L. Fuller & Melvin Aron Eisenberg, Basic Contract Law 167 (8th ed. 2006).
Robert W. Hamilton et al., Cases and Materials on Contracts 16 (2d ed. 1992).
Friedrich Kessler et al., Contracts: Cases and Materials 1314–15 (3d ed. 1986) (discussed).

Charles L. Knapp et al., Problems in Contract Law: Cases and Materials 887 (6th ed. 2007).

J. Stirling Mortimer, Cases on the Law of Contracts 200 (vol. 2 1975).

Addison Mueller, Contract in Context 724 (2d ed. 1952).

Edward J. Murphy, Richard E. Speidel & Ian Ayres, Studies in Contract Law 904 (6th ed. 2003) (cited but not discussed).

John Edward Murray, Jr., Contracts: Cases and Materials 662 (6th ed. 2006) (discussed).

Arthur Rosett, Contract Law and Its Application 316 (4th ed. 1988).

Harold Shepherd & Harry H. Wellington, Contracts and Contract Remedies 895 (4th ed. 1957).

Security Stove and Manufacturing v. American Railway Express Co., 51 S.W.2d 572 (Mo. Ct. App. 1932)

Steven J. Burton, Principles of Contract Law 336 (3d ed. 2006).

John P. Dawson et al., Contracts: Cases and Comment 48–49 (9th ed. 2008) (discussed).

E. Allan Farnsworth et al., Contracts: Cases and materials 629 (7th ed. 2008) (discussed).

Bruce W. Frier & James J. White, The Modern Law of Contracts 596 (2d ed. 2008) (discussed).

Lon L. Fuller & Melvin Aron Eisenberg, Basic Contract Law 213 (8th ed. 2006).

Robert W. Hamilton et al., Cases and Materials on Contracts 75 (2d ed. 1992).

Friedrich Kessler et al., Contracts: Cases and Materials 1188 (3d ed. 1986).

Charles L. Knapp et al., Problems in Contract Law: Cases and Materials 974 (6th ed. 2007) (discussed briefly).

Ian R. Macneil & Paul J. Gudel, Contracts: Exchange Transactions and Relations 126 (3d ed. 2001).

John Edward Murray, Jr., Contracts: Cases and Materials 24 (6th ed. 2006) (discussed).

Harold Shepherd & Harry H. Wellington, Contracts and Contract Remedies 927 (4th ed. 1957).

Sherwood v. Walker, 33 N.W. 919 (Mich. 1887)

Randy E. Barnett, Contracts: Cases and Doctrine 1051 (4th ed. 2008).

Brian A. Blum & Amy C. Bushaw, Contracts: Cases, Discussion, and Problems 618 (2d ed. 2008) (discussed).

Steven J. Burton, Principles of Contract Law 233–35 (3d ed. 2006) (discussed).

Thomas D. Crandall & Douglas J. Whaley, Cases, Problems, and Materials on Contracts 515 (5th ed. 2008).

John P. Dawson et al., Contracts: Cases and Comment 490 (9th ed. 2008).

E. Allan Farnsworth et al., Contracts: Cases and materials 815 (7th ed. 2008) (discussed).

Lon L. Fuller & Melvin Aron Eisenberg, Basic Contract Law 489 (8th ed. 2006).

Robert W. Hamilton et al., Cases and Materials on Contracts 599 (2d ed. 1992).

Friedrich Kessler et al., Contracts: Cases and Materials 887 (3d ed. 1986).

Charles L. Knapp et al., Problems in Contract Law: Cases and Materials 667–72 (6th ed. 2007) (discussed).

Ian R. Macneil & Paul J. Gudel, Contracts: Exchange Transactions and Relations 1212 (3d ed. 2001) (discussed).

Edward J. Murphy, Richard E. Speidel & Ian Ayres, Studies in Contract Law 482 (6th ed. 2003).

John Edward Murray, Jr., Contracts: Cases and Materials 436–37 (6th ed. 2006) (discussed).

Harold Shepherd & Harry H. Wellington, Contracts and Contract Remedies 1039 (4th ed. 1957) (cited but not discussed).

Robert S. Summers & Robert A. Hillman, Contract and Related Obligation 881 (5th ed. 2006).

Taylor v. Caldwell, (1863) 122 Eng. Rep. 309 (K.B.)

Randy E. Barnett, Contracts: Cases and Doctrine 1087 (4th ed. 2008).

Brian A. Blum & Amy C. Bushaw, Contracts: Cases, Discussion, and Problems 645 (2d ed. 2008) (discussed).

Steven J. Burton, Principles of Contract Law 551 (3d ed. 2006).

John D. Calamari et al., Cases and Problems on Contracts 629 (5th ed. 2007).

Thomas D. Crandall & Douglas J. Whaley, Cases, Problems, and Materials on Contracts 665 (5th ed. 2008).

John P. Dawson et al., Contracts: Cases and Comment 529 (9th ed. 2008).

E. Allan Farnsworth et al., Contracts: Cases and materials 825 (7th ed. 2008).

Bruce W. Frier & James J. White, The Modern Law of Contracts 688 (2d ed. 2008) (discussed).

Lon L. Fuller & Melvin Aron Eisenberg, Basic Contract Law 510 (8th ed. 2006).

Robert W. Hamilton et al., Cases and Materials on Contracts 645 (2d ed. 1992) (discussed).

Friedrich Kessler et al., Contracts: Cases and Materials 920 (3d ed. 1986).

Charles L. Knapp et al., Problems in Contract Law: Cases and Materials 685–86 (6th ed. 2007) (discussed).

Ian R. Macneil & Paul J. Gudel, Contracts: Exchange Transactions and Relations 1188 (3d ed. 2001).

J. Stirling Mortimer, Cases on the Law of Contracts 229 (vol. 2 1975).

Edward J. Murphy, Richard E. Speidel & Ian Ayres, Studies in Contract Law 813 (6th ed. 2003).

John Edward Murray, Jr., Contracts: Cases and Materials 597 (6th ed. 2006).

Harold Shepherd & Harry H. Wellington, Contracts and Contract Remedies 675 (4th ed. 1957).

Robert S. Summers & Robert A. Hillman, Contract and Related Obligation 918 (5th ed. 2006).

Williams v. Walker-Thomas Furniture, 350 F.2d 445 (D.C. Cir. 1965)

Randy E. Barnett, Contracts: Cases and Doctrine 1025 (4th ed. 2008).

Brian A. Blum & Amy C. Bushaw, Contracts: Cases, Discussion, and Problems 464 (2d ed. 2008) (discussed).

Steven J. Burton, Principles of Contract Law 244 (3d ed. 2006).

John D. Calamari et al., Cases and Problems on Contracts 434 (5th ed. 2007).

Thomas D. Crandall & Douglas J. Whaley, Cases, Problems, and Materials on Contracts 642 (5th ed. 2008).

John P. Dawson et al., Contracts: Cases and Comment 693 (9th ed. 2008).

E. Allan Farnsworth et al., Contracts: Cases and materials 497 (7th ed. 2008).

Bruce W. Frier & James J. White, The Modern Law of Contracts 450 (2d ed. 2008).

Lon L. Fuller & Melvin Aron Eisenberg, Basic Contract Law 34 (8th ed. 2006).

Robert W. Hamilton et al., Cases and Materials on Contracts 775 (2d ed. 1992) (discussed).

Friedrich Kessler et al., Contracts: Cases and Materials 596 (3d ed. 1986).

Charles L. Knapp et al., Problems in Contract Law: Cases and Materials 586 (6th ed. 2007).

Ian R. Macneil & Paul J. Gudel, Contracts: Exchange Transactions and Relations 460 (3d ed. 2001).

William McGovern et al., Contracts and Sales: Contemporary Cases and Problems 298 (2d ed. 2002).

Edward J. Murphy, Richard E. Speidel & Ian Ayres, Studies in Contract Law 538 (6th ed. 2003).

John Edward Murray, Jr., Contracts: Cases and Materials 456 (6th ed. 2006).

Arthur Rosett, Contract Law and Its Application 124 (4th ed. 1988).

Wood v. Lucy, Lady Duff Gordon, 118 N.E. 214 (N.Y. 1917)

Randy E. Barnett, Contracts: Cases and Doctrine 434 (4th ed. 2008).

Brian A. Blum & Amy C. Bushaw, Contracts: Cases, Discussion, and Problems 316 (2d ed. 2008).

Steven J. Burton, Principles of Contract Law 153 (3d ed. 2006).

John D. Calamari et al., Cases and Problems on Contracts 263 (5th ed. 2007).

Thomas D. Crandall & Douglas J. Whaley, Cases, Problems, and Materials on Contracts 158 (5th ed. 2008).

John P. Dawson et al., Contracts: Cases and Comment 361 (9th ed. 2008).

E. Allan Farnsworth et al., Contracts: Cases and materials 83 (7th ed. 2008).

Bruce W. Frier & James J. White, The Modern Law of Contracts 52 (2d ed. 2008) (discussed).

Lon L. Fuller & Melvin Aron Eisenberg, Basic Contract Law 60 (8th ed. 2006).

Robert W. Hamilton et al., Cases and Materials on Contracts 252 (2d ed. 1992).

Friedrich Kessler et al., Contracts: Cases and Materials 451 (3d ed. 1986).

Charles L. Knapp et al., Problems in Contract Law: Cases and Materials 438 (6th ed. 2007).

Ian R. Macneil & Paul J. Gudel, Contracts: Exchange Transactions and Relations 824 (3d ed. 2001).

J. Stirling Mortimer, Cases on the Law of Contracts 239 (vol. 1 1975).

Addison Mueller, Contract in Context 150 (2d ed. 1952).

Edward J. Murphy, Richard E. Speidel & Ian Ayres, Studies in Contract Law 100 (6th ed. 2003).

John Edward Murray, Jr., Contracts: Cases and Materials 234 (6th ed. 2006) (discussed).

Arthur Rosett, Contract Law and Its Application 38 (4th ed. 1988).

Harold Shepherd & Harry H. Wellington, Contracts and Contract Remedies 47 (4th ed. 1957).

Robert S. Summers & Robert A. Hillman, Contract and Related Obligation 70 (5th ed. 2006).

Bibliography

Adler, B. E., *Questionable Ascent of* Hadley v. Baxendale, 51 Stan. L. Rev. 1547 (1999).

Adler, M.D. & Posner, E.A., *Implementing Cost-Benefit Analysis when Preferences Are Distorted*, in COST-BENEFIT ANALYSIS: LEGAL, ECONOMIC, AND PHILOSOPHICAL PERSPECTIVE (Adler & Posner eds., 2000).

ADLER, M.D. & POSNER, E.A., NEW FOUNDATIONS OF COST-BENEFIT ANALYSIS (2006).

Aivazian, V.A., Trebilcock, M.J., & Penny, M., *The Law of Contract Modifications: The Uncertain Quest for a Benchmark of Enforceability*, 22 Osgoode Hall L.J. 173 (1984).

ALCES, P. A. & SEE, H. F., THE COMMERCIAL LAW OF INTELLECTUAL PROPERTY (1994).

ALCES, P. A., *Regret and Contract "Science,"* 89 Geo L.J. 143 (2000).

ALCES, P. A., *Contract Reconceived*, 96 NW. U. L. Rev. 39 (2001).

ALCES, P. A., *On Discovering Doctrine: "Justice" in Contract Agreement*, 83 Wash. U. L. Q. 471 (2005).

ALCES, P. A., *Guerilla Terms*, 56 Emory L.J. 1511 (2007).

ALCES, P. A., *The Moral Impossibility of Contract*, 48 Wm. & Mary L. Rev. 1647 (2007).

ALCES, P. A., Un*intelligent Design in Contract*, 2008 U. Ill. L. Rev. 505.

ALCES, P. A. & BYRNE, C., *Is It Time for the Restatement of Contracts*, Fourth?, 11 Duq. Bus. L.J. 195 (2009).

Alexander, L., *Theory's a What Comes Natcherly* 37 San Diego L. Rev. 777 (2000).

ALEXANDER, R.D., THE BIOLOGY OF MORAL SYSTEMS (1987).

American Law Institute, Principles of the Law of Software Contracts, Overview (P.F.D., 2009).

ANDERSON, S. W., ANTOINE BECHARA, HANNA DAMASIO, DANIEL TRANEL & ANTONIO R. *DAMASIO, Impairment of Social and Moral Behavior Related to Early Damage in Human Prefrontal Cortex*, 2 Nature Neuroscience 1032 (Nov. 1999).

Appiah, K. A., EXPERIMENTS IN ETHICS (2008).

Atiyah, P.S., *Consideration: A Restatement*, in ESSAYS ON CONTRACT 179 (1986).

AYRES, I. & KLASS, G., INSINCERE PROMISES: THE LAW OF MISREPRESENTED INTENT (2005).

Baird, D.G., *Reconstructing Contracts: Hamer v. Sidway*, in CONTRACTS STORIES 160 (Douglas G. Baird ed., 2007).

Baird, D.G., *Boilerplate and Market Power: The Boilerplate Puzzle*, 104 Mich. L. Rev. 933 (2006).

The Ballad of Willie and Lucille: DISAPPOINTED EXPECTATIONS OF CONTRACT LAW AND THE LEGAL SYSTEM (University of Oklahoma College of Law 2008).

Bar-Gill, O. *Seduction By Plastic*, 98 NW. U. L. Rev. 1373 (2004).

Bar-Gill, O. *The Behavioral Economics of Consumer Contracts*, 92 Minn. L. Rev. 749 (2008).

Barnett, R.E., *A Consent Theory of Contract*, 86 Colum. L. Rev. 269 (1986).

Barnett, R.E., PERSPECTIVES ON CONTRACT LAW (1995).

Benson, P., *The Unity of Contract Law*, in THE THEORY OF CONTRACT LAW: NEW ESSAYS 184 (Peter Benson ed., 2001).

Benson, P., *The Expectation and Reliance Interests in Contract Theory: A Reply to Fuller and Perdue*, ISSUES IN LEGAL SCHOLARSHIP, Symposium: Fuller and Perdue (2001): Article 5, available at http://www.bepress.com/ils/iss1/art5.

Benson, P., *Contract as a Transfer of Ownership*, 48 Wm. &. Mary L. Rev. 1673 (2006).

Bertschy, T.L., *Negligent Performance of Service Contracts and the Economic Loss Doctrine*, 17 J. Marshall L. Rev. 249 (1984).

Birmingham, R.L., *A Second Look at the Suez Canal Cases: Excuse for Nonperformance of Contractual Obligations in the Light of Economic Theory*, 20 Hastings L.J. 1393 (1969).

BIX, B.H., A DICTIONARY OF LEGAL THEORY (2004).

Bix, B.H. *Contract Law Theory* (Minnesota Legal Studies Research Paper No. 06-12, 2006), available at http://ssrn.com/abstract=892783.

BLACK'S LAW DICTIONARY (8th ed. 2004).

BLOOM, H., THE WESTERN CANON (1994).

THE BLUEBOOK: A UNIFORM SYSTEM OF CITATION R. 2.3(a) at 7 (Columbia Law Review Ass'n et al. eds., 12th ed. 1976).

BOILERPLATE: THE FOUNDATION OF MARKET CONTRACTS (Omri Ben-Shahar ed., 2007).

Bridgeman, C., *Corrective Justice in Contract Law: Is There a Case for Punitive Damages?*, 56 Vand. L. Rev. 237 (2003).

Bridgeman, C., *Alleghany College Revisited: Cardozo, Consideration, and Formalism in Context*, 39 U.C. Davis L. Rev. 149 (2005).

Bronaugh, R., Barton, P. & Roberts, T., *Commercial Impossibility and Frustration of Purpose: A Critical Analysis*, 16 Can. J.L. & Juris. 129 (2003).

Brooks, R.W., *The Efficient Performance Hypothesis*, 116 Yale L.J. 568 (2006).

BURTON, S.J., ELEMENTS OF CONTRACT INTERPRETATION (2009).

CALABRESI, G., THE COSTS OF ACCIDENTS: A LEGAL AND ECONOMIC ANALYSIS (Student Ed. 1970).

Calabresi, G. & Hirschoff, J.T. *Toward a Test for Strict Liability in Torts*, 81 Yale L.J. 1055 (1972).

Calabresi, G. & Melamed, A.D. *Property Rules, Liability Rules, and Inalienability: One View of the Cathedral*, 85 Harv. L. Rev. 1089 (1982).

CAMBRIDGE DICTIONARY OF LEGAL PHILOSPHY (Robert Audi ed., 1999).

CHIRELSTEIN, M.A., CONCEPTS AND CASE ANALYSIS IN THE LAW OF CONTRACTS (6th ed. 2010).

Clarkson, K.W., Miller, R.L. & Muris, T.J., *Liquidated Damages v. Penalties: Sense or Nonsense?*, 1978 Wis. L. Rev. 351 (1978).

Coleman, J., *The Normative Basis of Economic Analysis: A Critical Review of Richard Posner's The Economics of Justice*, 34 Stan. L. Rev. 1105 (1982).

Coleman, J., The Practice of Principle (2001).

Coopersmith, J.B., *Refocusing Liquidated Damages Law for Real Estate Contracts: Returning to the Historical Roots of the Penalty Doctrine*, 39 Emory L.J. 267 (1990).

Cosmides, L. & Tooby, J., *Can a General Deontic Logic Capture the Facts of Human Moral Reasoning? How the Mind Interprets Social Exchange Rules and Detects Cheaters*, in 1 Moral Psychology 53 (Walter Sinnott-Armstrong ed., 2008).

Craswell, R., *Contract Remedies, Renegotiation, and the Theory of Efficient Breach*, 61 S. Cal. L. Rev. 629 (1988).

Craswell, R. & Schwartz, A., Foundations of Contract Law (1994).

Craswell, R., *Against Fuller and Perdue*, 67 U. Chi. L. Rev. 99 (2000).

Craswell, R., *How We Got This Way: Further Thoughts on Fuller and Perdue*, Issues in Legal Scholarship, Symposium: Fuller and Perdue (2001): Article 2, available at http://www.bepress.com/ils/iss1/art2.

Craswell, R., *In That Case, What is the Question? Economics and the Demands of Contract Theory*, 112 Yale L.J. 903 (2003).

Cunningham, L., *Toward a Prudential and Credibility-Centered Parole Evidence Rule*, 68 U. Cin. L. Rev. 269 (2000).

Damasio, A.R., Descartes' Error: Emotion, Reason, and the Human Brain (1994).

Dan-Cohen, M., Rights, Persons, and Organizations: A Legal Theory for Bureaucratic Society (1986).

DeLong, S.W., *The New Requirement of Enforcement Reliance in Commercial Promissory Estoppel: Section 90 as Catch -22*, 1997 Wis. L. Rev. 943 (1997).

DiMatteo, L.A., *A Theory of Efficient Penalty: Eliminating the Law of Liquidated Damages*, 38 Am. Bus. L.J. 633 (2001).

Doris, J.M., Lack of Character (2002).

Doris, J.M. & Plakias, A., *How to Argue about Disagreement*, in 2 Moral Psychology 303 (Walter Sinnott-Amrstrong ed., 2008).

Dworkin, R., Law's Empire (1986).

Eisenberg, M.A., *Third-Party Beneficiaries*, 92 Colum. L. Rev. 1358 (1992).

Eisenberg, M.A., *The Limits of Cognition and the Limits of Contract*, 47 Stan. L. Rev. 211 (1995).

Eisgruber, C., *Great Contracts Cases: Teaching Law Through Contracts and Cardozo*, 44 St. Louis Y, L.J. 1511 (2000).

Eisgruber, C., *Teaching Law Through Contracts and Cardozo*, 44 St. Louis U. L.J. 1511 (2000).

Ellinghaus, M.P., *In Defense of Unconscionability*, 78 Yale L.J. 757 (1969).

Ellison, G. & Ellison, S.F., *Search, Obfuscation, and Price Elasticities on the Internet* (Nat'l Bureau of Econ. Research, Working Paper No. 10570, 2004).

Epstein, R.A., *Unconscionability: A Critical Reappraisal*, 18 J.L. & Econ. 293 (1975).

Epstein, R.A., *Beyond Foreseeability: Consequential Damages in the Law of Contract*, 18 J. Legal Stud. 105 (1989).

Epstein, R.A., *ProCD, Inc. v. Zeidenberg: Do Doctrine and Function Mix*, in Contracts Stories 94 (Douglas Baird ed., 2007).

Epstein, R.A., *The Neoclassical Economics of Consumer Contracts*, 92 Minn. L. Rev. 803 (2008).

Epstein, R.A., *The Many Faces of Fault in Contract Law: Or How to do Economics Right, Without Really Trying*, 107 Mich. L. Rev. 1461 (2009).

Farber, D.A. & Matheson, J. H., *Beyond Promissory Estoppel: Contract Law and the "Invisible Handshake,"*, 52 U. Chi. L. Rev. 903 (1985).

Farber, D.A., *Economic Efficiency and The Ex Ante Perspective*, in THE JURISPRUDENTIAL FOUNDATIONS OF CORPORATE AND COMMERCIAL LAW 54 (Jody S. Kraus & Steven D. Walt eds., 2000).

FARNSWORTH, E.A., CHANGING YOUR MIND: THE LAW OF REGRETTED DECISIONS (1998).

FARNSWORTH, E.A., FARNSWORTH ON CONTRACTS (3d ed. 2004).

FEDERAL COURT STORIES (Vicki C. Jackson & Judith Resnik, eds., 2010).

Feinman, J.M. & Brill, S.R., *Is an Advertisement an Offer? Why it is and Why it Matters*, 58 Hastings L.J. 61 (2006).

Feldman, N.A., 24 COMPUTER SHOPPER 30 (Oct. 1, 2004), available at 2004 WLNR 22375352.

Flanagan, O., Sarkissian, H., & Wong, D., *Naturalizing Ethics*, in 1 MORAL PSYCHOLOGY 1 (Walter Sinnott-Armstrong ed., 2008).

Foot, P. *The Problem of Abortion and the Doctrine of Double Effect*, 5 Oxford Review 5 (1967).

FRANK, J., LAW AND THE MODERN MIND (1930).

Freedman, M., *Cardozo's Opinion in Lady Lucy's Case: "Formative Unconscionability," Impracticality, and Judicial Abuse*, 28 Pace L. Rev. 395 (2008).

Fried, C., CONTRACT AS PROMISE: A THEORY OF CONTRACTUAL OBLIGATION (1981).

Fried, C., *The Convergence of Contract and Promise*, 120 Harv. L. Rev. F. 1 (2007).

Friedmann, D., *The Efficient Breach Fallacy*, 18 J. Leg. Stud. 1 (1989).

Fuller, L.L. & Perdue, W., The *Reliance Interest in Contract Damages* (pt. 1), 46 Yale L.J. 52 (1936).

Fuller, L.L. & Perdue, W., The *Reliance Interest in Contract Damages* (pt. 2), 46 Yale L.J. 373 (1937).

Fuller, L.L., *Consideration and Form*, 41 Colum. L. Rev. 799 (1940).

Gabaix, X. & Laibson, D., *Shrouded Attributes, Consumer Myopia, and Information Suppression in Competitive Markets*, 121(2) Q. J. of Econ. 505 (2006).

Gardner, G., *An Inquiry into the Principles of the Law of Contracts*, 46 Harv. L. Rev. 1 (1932).

Garmong, R.A., *J.S. Mill's Re-conceptualization of Liberty* (December 2002) (unpublished doctoral dissertation, University of Texas at Austin) available at http://dspace.lib.utexas.edu/handle/2152/672.

GILMORE, G., DEATH OF CONTRACT (2d ed. 1995).

Goetz, C.J. & Scott, R.E., *Liquidated Damages, Penalties, and the Just Compensation Principle: Some Notes on an Enforcement Model and a Theory of Efficient Breach*, 77 Colum. L. Rev. 554 (1977).

Goetz, C.J. & Scott, R.E., *Enforcing Promises: An Examination of the Basis of Contract*, 89 Yale L.J. 1261 (1980).

Goetz, C.J. & Scott, R.E., *The Mitigation Principle: Toward a General Theory of Contractual Obligation*, 69 Va. L. Rev. 967 (1983).

Gold, A.S., *A Property Theory of Contract*, 103 Nw. U. L. Rev. 1 (2009).

Goldberg, V., *Desperately Seeking Consideration: The Unfortunate Impact of U.C.C. Section 2-306 on Contract Interpretation*, 68 Ohio St. L. J. 103 (2007).

Gordley, J., *Contract Law in the Aristotelian Tradition*, in THE THEORY OF CONTRACT LAW: NEW ESSAYS (Peter Benson ed., 2001).

Gordley, J., *A Perennial Misstep: From Cajetan to Fuller and Perdue to "Efficient Breach,"* ISSUES IN LEGAL SCHOLARSHIP, Symposium: Fuller and Perdue (2001): Article 4, available at http://www.bepress.com/ils/iss1/art4.

GORDLEY, J., THE PHILOSOPHICAL ORIGINS OF MODERN CONTRACT DOCTRINE (2006).

Gordley, J., *Morality and Contract: The Question of Paternalism*, 48 Wm. & Mary L. Rev. 1733 (2007).

Gould, S.J., *Sociobiology: The Art of Storytelling*, New Scientist 80 (Nov. 16, 1978), 530–33.

Greene, J.D., *The Secret Joke of Kant's Soul*, in 3 MORAL PSYCHOLOGY 35 (Walter Sinnott-Armstrong ed., 2008).

Haidt, J. & Joseph, C., *The Moral Mind: How Five Sets of Innate Intuitions Guide the Development of Many Culture-Specific Virtues, and Perhaps Even Modules*, in 3 THE INNATE MIND 367 (Peter Carruthers, Stephen Laurence, & Stephen P. Stich eds., 2005).

Haidt, J. & Graham, J., *When Morality Opposes Justice: Conservatives Have Moral Intuitions that Liberals may not Recognize*, 20 Soc. Just. Res. 98 (2007).

Haidt, J. & Bjorklund, F., *Social Intuitionists Answer Six Questions About Moral Psychology*, in 2 MORAL PSYCHOLOGY 181 (Walter Sinnott-Armstrong ed., 2008).

Haidt, J. & Bjorklund, F., *Social Intuitionists Reason, in Conversation*, in 2 MORAL PSYCHOLOGY 241 (Walter Sinnott-Armstrong ed., 2008).

HARRIS, S., THE END OF FAITH (2005).

HART, H.L.A. THE CONCEPT OF LAW 193 (2d ed. 1994).

HAUSER, M.D., Moral Minds: How Nature Designed Our Universal Sense of Right and Wrong (2006).

Hauser, M.D., Young, L., & Cushman, F., *Reviving Rawls's Linguistic Analogy: Operative Principles and the Causal Structure of Moral Actions*, in 2 MORAL PSYCHOLOGY 107 (Walter Sinnott-Armstrong ed., 2008).

Henderson, J.A. Jr. & Twerski, A.D., *Closing the American Products Liability Frontier: The Rejection of Liability Without Defect*, 66 N.Y.U. L. Rev. 1263 (1991).

Hillman, R.A., *Policing Contract Modifications under the UCC: Good Faith and the Doctrine of Economic Duress*, 64 Iowa L. Rev. 849 (1979).

Hillman, R.A., *Instinct with an Obligation and the Normative Ambiguity of Rhetorical Power*, 56 Ohio St. L.J. 755 (1995).

Hillman, R.A., *Questioning the "New Consensus" on Promissory Estoppel: An Empirical and Theoretical Study*, 98 Colum. L. Rev. 580 (1998).

Hillman, R.A., *The Limits of Behavioral Decision Theory in Legal Analysis: The Case of Liquidated Damages*, 85 Cornell L. Rev. 717 (2000).

Hillman, R.A., & Rachlinski, J.J., *Standard-Form Contracting in the Electronic Age*, 77 N.Y.U. L. Rev. 429 (2002).

HILLMAN, R.A., PRINCIPLES OF CONTRACT LAW (2d ed. 2009).

HOLMES, E.M., CORBIN ON CONTRACTS (Joseph M. Perillo ed., 3d ed. 1996).

Holmes, O.W., *Path of the Law*, 10 Harv. L. Rev. 457 (1897).

Holmes, O.W., *The Theory of Legal Interpretation*, 12 Harv. L. Rev. 417 (1899).

HOLMES, O.W., THE COMMON LAW (Mark DeWolfe Howe ed., 1963).

HUME, D., A TREATISE OF HUMAN NATURE (David Fate Norton & Mary J. Norton eds., 2000) (1740).

Johnston J.S., *Default Rules/Mandatory Principles: A Game Theoretic Analysis of Good Faith and the Contract Modification Problem*, 3 S. Cal. Interdisc. L.J. 335 (1993).

Jolls, C., Sunstein, C.R., & Thaler, R., *A Behavioral Approach to Law and Economics*, 50 Stan. L. Rev. 1471 (1998).

JOYCE, R., THE EVOLUTION OF MORALITY (2006).

Katz, A., *When Should an Offer Stick? The Economics of Promissory Estoppel in Preliminary Negotiations*, 105 Yale L.J. 1249 (1996).

Katz, L., *What We Do When We Do What We Do and Why We Do It*, 37 San Diego L. Rev. 753 (2000).

KEETON, W.P. ET AL., PROSSER & KEETON ON THE LAW OF TORTS (5th ed. 1984).

Kniffin, M., *A New Trend in Contract Interpretation: The Search for Reality As Opposed to Virtual Reality*, 74 Or. L. Rev. 643 (1995).

Konefsky, A.S., *How to Read, or at Least Not Misread, Cardozo in the Allegheny College Case*, 36 Buff. L. Rev. 645 (1988).

Kaplow, L. & Shavell, S., *Notions of Fairness Versus the Pareto Principle: On the Role of Logical Consistency*, 110 Yale L.J. 237 (2000).

Kaplow, L. & Shavell, S., *Fairness versus Welfare*, 114 Harv. L. Rev. 961 (2001).

Keltner, D. & Haidt, J., *Social Functions of Emotions*, in EMOTIONS: CURRENT ISSUES AND FUTURE DIRECTIONS (Tracy J. Mayne & George A. Bonanno eds., 2001).

Korobkin, R., *Bounded Rationality, Standard Form Contracts, and Unconscionability*, 70 U. Chi. L. Rev. 1203 (2003).

Kostritsky, J.P., *The Rise and Fall of Promissory Estoppel Or Is Promissory Estoppel Really as Unsuccessful As Scholars Say It Is: A New Look at the Data*, 37 Wake Forest L. Rev. 531 (2002).

Kostritsky, J.P., *Uncertainty, Reliance, Preliminary Negotiations and the Holdup Problem*, 61 SMU L. Rev. 1377 (2008).

Kraus, J.S., *Reconciling Autonomy and Efficiency in Contract Law: The Vertical Integration Strategy*, in 11 Phil. Issues 420 (2001).

Kraus, J.S., *The Correspondence of Contract and Promise* 109 Colum. L. Rev. 1601 (2001).

Kreitner, R., *Fault at the Contract-Tort Interface*, 107 Mich. L. Rev. 1533 (2009).

Kull, A., *Reconsidering Gratuitous Promises*, 21 J. Legal Stud. 39 (1992).

Leff, A.A., *Unconscionability and the Code–The Emperor's New Clause*, 115 U. Pa. L. Rev. 485 (1967).

Leib, E.J., *On Collaboration, Organizations, and Conciliation in the General Theory of Contract*, 24 Quinnipiac L. Rev. 1 (2005).

Leiter, B. & Weisberg, M., *Why Evolutionary Biology is (So Far) Irrelevant to Law* (U of Texas Law, Pub. Law Res. Paper No. October 89, 17, 2007), available at http://papers.ssrn.com/sol3/papers.cfm?abstract_id=892881.

Lessig, L., *The Law of the Horse: What Cyberlaw Might Teach*, 113 Harv. L. Rev. 501 (1999).

Linzer, P., *Symposium: A Tribute to Professor Joseph M. Perillo: The Comfort of Certainty: Plain Meaning and the Parole Evidence Rule*, 71 Fordham L. Rev. 799 (2002).

Llewellyn, K.N., *Across Sales on Horseback*, 52 Harv. L. Rev. 725 (1939).

LLEWELLYN, K.N. & HOEBEL, E.A., THE CHEYENNE WAY: CONFLICT AND CASE LAW IN PRIMITIVE JURISPRUDENCE (1941).

LLEWELLYN, K.N., THE COMMON LAW TRADITION: DECIDING APPEALS (1960).

MacMillan, C., *TAYLOR* v. *CALDWELL* (1863), in LANDMARK CASES IN THE LAW OF CONTRACT (Charles Mitchell and Paul Mitchell eds., 2008).

MANN, R.J., CHARGING AHEAD: THE GROWTH AND REGULATION OF PAYMENT CARD MARKETS (2006).

MARGOLIS, H., PATTERNS, THINKING, AND COGNITION: A THEORY OF JUDGMENT (1987).

Markovits, D., *Contract and Collaboration*, 113 Yale L.J. 1417 (2004).

Markovits, D., *Making and Keeping Contracts*, 92 Va. L. Rev. 1325 (2006).

Maute, J.L., Peevyhouse v. Garland Coal & Mining Co. *Revisited: The Ballad of Willie and Lucille*, 89 Nw. U. L. Rev. 1341 (1995).

McChesney, F.S., *Tortious Interference with Contract versus "Efficient" Breach: Theory and Empirical Evidence*, 28 J. Legal Stud. 131 (1999).

Mikhail, J.M., *Rawls' Linguistic Analogy: A Study of the "Generative Grammar" Model of Moral Theory Described by John Rawls in A Theory of Justice* (May 2000) (Ph.D. Dissertation, Cornell University) (Georgetown Public Law Research Paper No. 766464), available at SSRN: http://ssrn.com/abstract=766464.

MOORE, M.S., PLACING BLAME: A GENERAL THEORY OF THE CRIMINAL LAW (1997).

MURRAY, J.E. JR., CORBIN ON CONTRACTS (Joseph M. Perillo ed., rev. ed. 2001).

MURRAY, J.E. JR., MURRAY ON CONTRACTS (2001).

MURRAY, J.E. JR., CORBIN ON CONTRACTS (2009).

Murray, J.E. Jr., *The Revision of Article 2: Romancing the Prism*, 35 Wm. & Mary L. Rev. 1447 (1994).

Ngugi, J.M., *Promissory Estoppel: The Life History of An Ideal Legal Transplant*, 41 U. Rich. L. Rev. 425 (2007).

Oman, N.B., *Corporations and Autonomy Theory of Contract: A Critique of the New Lex Mercatoria*, 83 Denv. U. L. Rev. 101 (2005).

Oman, N.B., *The Failure of Economic Interpretations of the Law of Contract Damages*, 64 Wash. & Lee L. Rev. 829 (2007).

The Paper Chase (Thompson Films 1973).

PEARSON, R., INSURING THE INDUSTRIAL REVOLUTION: FIRE INSURANCE IN GREAT BRITAIN (2004).

Perillo, J.M., *Misreading Oliver Wendell Holmes on Efficient Breach and Tortious Interference*, 68 Fordham L. Rev. 1085 (2000).

PERILLO, J.M. & CALAMARI, J.D., CALAMARI AND PERILLO ON CONTRACTS (6th ed. 2009).

Phillips, D.M., *The Commercial Culpability Scale*, 92 Yale L.J. 228 (1982).

PINKER, S., THE STUFF OF THOUGHT (2007).

Posner, E.A., *Economic Analysis of Contract Law After Three Decades: Success or Failure?* 112 Yale L.J. 829 (2003).

Posner, E.A., *Fault in Contract Law* (U of Chicago Law & Econ., Olin Working Paper No. 3 March 96, 2008), available at SSRN: http://ssrn.com/abstract=1106399.

Posner, R.A., *Gratuitous Promises in Economics and Law*, 6 J. Legal Stud. 411 (1977).

Posner, R.A. & Rosenfield, A.M., *Impossibility and Related Doctrines in Contract Law: An Economic Analysis*, 6 J. Legal Stud. 83 (1977).

POSNER, R.A., OVERCOMING LAW (1995).

POSNER, R.A., THE ECONOMICS OF JUSTICE (1981).

POSNER, R.A., ECONOMIC ANALYSIS OF THE LAW (7th ed. 2007).

Posner, R.A., *Let Us Never Blame a Contract Breaker*, 107 Mich. L. Rev. 1349 (2009).

Powers, J.F., *Rethinking Moral Obligation as a Basis for Contract Recovery*, 54 Me. L. Rev. 1 (2002).

Powers, J.F., *Promissory Estoppel and Wagging the Dog*, 59 Ark. L. Rev. 841 (2007).

Priest, G.L., *Breach and Remedy for the Tender of Nonconforming Goods Under the Uniform Commercial Code: An Economic Approach*, 91 Harv. L. Rev. 960 (1978).

Prince, H., *Contract Interpretation in California: Plain Meaning, Parol Evidence and Use of the "Just Result" Principle*, 31 Loy. L.A. L. Rev. 557 (1998).

Prinz, J.J., *Is Morality Innate?*, in 1 MORAL PSYCHOLOGY 367 (Walter Sinnott-Armstrong ed., 2008).

Prinz, J.J., *Resisting the Linguistic Analogy: A Commentary on Hauser, Young, and Cushman*, in 2 MORAL PSYCHOLOGY 157 (Walter Sinnott-Armstrong ed., 2008).

Prosser, W.L., *The Assault Upon the Citadel*, 69 Yale L.J. 1099 (1960).

Prosser, W.L., *The Fall of the Citadel (Strict Liability to the Consumer)*, 50 Minn. L. Rev. 791 (1966).

Rachlinski, J.J., *The "New" Law and Psychology: A Reply to Critics, Skeptics, and Cautious Supporters*, 85 Cornell L. Rev. 739 (2000).

Rasmusen, E. & Ayres, I., *Mutual and Unilateral Mistake in Contract Law*, 22 J. Legal Stud. 309 (1993).

RAWLS, J., A THEORY OF JUSTICE (Rev. ed. 1999).

Robinson, P.H., Kurzban, R., & Jones, O.D., *The Origins of Shared Intuitions of Justice*, 60 Vand. L. Rev. 1633 (2007).

Saver, J.L. & Damasio, A.R., *Preserved Access and Processing of Social Knowledge in a Patient with Acquired Sociopathy Due to Ventromedial Frontal Damage*, 29 Neuropsychologia 1241 (1991).

Scanlon, T.M., *Promises and Contracts*, in THE THEORY OF CONTRACT LAW: NEW ESSAYS (Peter Benson ed., 2001).

Schlag, P.J., *Rules and Standards*, 33 UCLA L. Rev. 379 (1985).

Schlegel, J.H., *Of Nuts, and Ships, and Sealing Wax, Suez, and Frustrating Things—The Doctrine of Impossibility of Performance*, 23 Rutgers L. Rev. 419 (1969).

Schwartz, A. & Scott, R.E., *Contract Theory and the Limits of Contract Law*, 113 Yale L.J. 541 (2003).

Schwartz, A. & Scott, R.E., *Market Damages, Efficient Contracting, and the Economic Waste Fallacy*, 108 Colum. L. Rev. 1610 (2008).

Scott, H.S., *The Risk Fixers*, 91 Harv. L. Rev. 737 (1978).

Scott, R.E., *Commercial Calamities:* Hoffman v. Red Owl Stores *and the Myth of Precontractual Reliance*, 68 Ohio St. L.J. 71 (2007).

Seipp, D.J., *125th Anniversary Essay: Holmes's Path*, 77 B.U. L. Rev. 515 (1997).

Shavell, S., *Is Breach of Contract Immoral?*, 56 Emory L.J. 439 (2006).

Shiffrin, S.V., *Speech, Death, and Double Effect*, 78 N.Y.U. L. Rev. 1135 (2003).

Shiffrin, S.V., *The Divergence of Contract and Promise*, 120 Harv. L. Rev. 708 (2007).

Sinnott-Armstrong, W., Introduction to 1 MORAL PSYCHOLOGY at xiii, xiii-xiv (Walter Sinnott-Armstrong ed., 2008).

SMITH, S.A., CONTRACT THEORY (2004).

Smith, S.A. *Contracts for the Benefit of Third Parties: In Defense of the Third-Party Rule*, 17 Oxford J. Legal Stud. 643 (1997).

Smith, S.A., *"The Reliance Interest in Contract Damages" and the Morality of Contract Law*, ISSUES IN LEGAL SCHOLARSHIP, Symposium: Fuller and Perdue (2001): Article 1, available at http://www.bepress.com/ils/iss1/art1.

STANFORD ENCYCLOPEDIA OF PHILOSOPHY (2009), http://plato.stanford.edu/entries/identity-time/.

STEIN, G., EVERYBODY'S AUTOBIOGRAPHY (1937).

Stephens, C.A., *Escape From the Battle of the Forms: Keep It Simple, Stupid*, 11 Lewis & Clark L. Rev. 233 (2007).

Sterk, S., *The New York Court of Appeals: 150 Years of Leading Opinions*, 48 Syracuse L. Rev. 1391 (1998).

Sunstein, C.R., *Behavioral Analysis of Law*, 64 U. Chi. L. Rev. 1175, (1997).

Symposium, *Fault in American Contract Law*, 107 Mich. L. Rev. 1341 (2009).

Tat, P.K. & Schwepker, C.H. Jr., *An Empirical Investigation of the Relationships Between Rebate Redemption Motives: Understanding How Price Consciousness, Time and Effort, and Satisfaction Affect Consumer Rebate Redemption*, 6 J. Marketing Theory & Prac. 61 (Spring 1998).

Taylor, S.E., *The Availability Bias in Social Perception and Interaction*, in JUDGMENT UNDER UNCERTAINTY: HEURISTICS AND BIASES (Daniel Kahneman et al. eds., 1982).

Teeven, K.M., *Decline of Freedom of Contract since the Emergence of the Modern Business Corporation*, 37 St. Louis U. L.J. 117 (1992).

Teeven, K.M., *A Legal History of Binding Gratuitous Promises at Common Law: Justifiable Reliance and Moral Obligation*, 43 Duq. L. Rev. 11 (2004).

Teeven, K.M., *Origins and Scope of the American Moral Obligation Principle*, 46 Clev. St. L. Rev. 585 (1998).

Teeven, K.M., *A History of Promissory Estoppel: Growth in the Face of Doctrinal Resistance*, 72 Tenn. L. Rev. 1111 (2005).

Thel, S. & Siegelman, P., *Wilfulness vs. Expectation: A Promisor-Based Defense of Wilful Breach* 107 Mich. L. Rev. 1517 (2009).

Thomson, J.J., *The Trolley Problem*, 94 Yale L.J. 1395 (1985).

THREEDY, D.L., A FISH STORY: ALASKA PACKERS' ASSOCIATION v. DOMENICO in CONTRACTS STORIES (Douglas G. Baird ed.) (2007).

TREBILCOCK, M.J., THE LIMITS OF FREEDOM OF CONTRACT (1993).

Townsend, M., *Cardozo's Allegheny College Opinion: A Case Study of Law as Art*, 33 Hous. L. Rev. 1103 (1996).

THE TREASURY OF AUSTRALIA, THE AUSTRALIAM GUIDELINES FOR ELECTRONIC COMMERCE (2006), available at http://www.treasury.gov.au/documents/1083/PDF/australian_guidelines_for_electronic_commerce.pdf.

VONNEGUT, K., PALM SUNDAY (1981).

Waters, A.J., *The Property in the Promise: A Study of the Third Party Beneficiary Rule*, 98 Harv. L. Rev. 1109 (1985).

Watson, G., *In the Tribunal of Conscience: Mills v. Wyman Reconsidered*, 71 Tul. L. Rev. 1749 (1997).

Weiskopf, N.R., *Frustration of Contractual Purpose–Doctrine or Myth?*, 70 St. John's L. Rev. 239 (1996).

WHITE, J.J. & SUMMERS, R.S., UNIFORM COMMERCIAL CODE (6th ed. 2010).

WILLISTON, S. & LORD, R.A., A TREATISE ON THE LAW OF CONTRACTS (4th ed. 2009).

Wirtz, R.S., *Cost of Performance or Difference in Value?*, 59 Case W. Res. L. Rev. 61 (2008).

Wladis, J.D., *Common Law and Uncommon Events: The Development of the Doctrine of Impossibility of Performance in English Contract Law*, 75 GEO. L.J. 1575 (1987).

Yorio, E. & Thel, S., *The Promissory Basis of Section 90*, 101 Yale L.J. 111 (1991).

Zamir, E., *The Efficiency of Paternalism*, 84 Va. L. Rev. 229 (1998).

Zamir, E. & Medina, B., *Law, Morality, and Economics: Integrating Moral Constraints with Economic Analysis of Law*, 96 Calif. L. Rev. 323 (2008).

Index